TOUCHDOWN JESUS

FAITH AND FANDOM AT NOTRE DAME

Scott Eden

SIMON & SCHUSTER

New York   London   Toronto   Sydney

SIMON & SCHUSTER
Rockefeller Center
1230 Avenue of the Americas
New York, NY 10020

For information about special discounts for bulk purchases,
please contact Simon & Schuster Special Sales at
1-800-456-6798 or business@simonandschuster.com

Designed by Dana Sloan

Manufactured in the United States of America

10   9   8   7   6   5   4   3   2   1

Library of Congress Cataloging-in-Publication Data
Eden, Scott, date.
   Touchdown Jesus : faith and fandom at Notre Dame / Scott Eden.
      p.   cm.
   1. University of Notre Dame—Football.   2. Notre Dame Fighting
Irish (Football team).   3. Sports—Religious aspects.   I. Title.
GV958.N6E35   2005
796.332'63'0977289—dc22   2005051639

ISBN-13: 978-0-7432-8165-2
ISBN-10:   0-7432-8165-9

The author gratefully acknowledges permission from the following sources to reprint
material in their control: Andrews McMeel Publishing for an excerpt from *Monk's Re-
flections: A View from the Dome*. Written by Rev. Edward A. Malloy, C.S.C. © 2002
Andrews McMeel Publishing. Used by permission. All rights reserved: 325–26; Atria
Books for an excerpt from *The Fighting Spirit: A Championship Season at Notre
Dame* by Lou Holtz with John Heisler. Copyright © 1989 by Lou Holtz and John
Heisler. Reprinted with permission of Atria Books, an imprint of Simon & Schuster

Page 350 constitutes an extension of the copyright page.

For Carleen and Philip Eden

Contents

Longing on a large scale is what makes history.

—DON DELILLO

And thrice they cried like thunder
On Our Lady of the Victories
The Mother of the Master of the Masterers of the world.

—G. K. CHESTERTON, "THE ARENA"

TOUCHDOWN JESUS

1

Game Day

A congregation of about fifty people stood in a semicircle, three and four people deep, trying to pay attention to an elderly priest murmuring important words. Draped in a white alb, a white stole around his neck, he was celebrating a Mass, and he worked off a card table unfolded in front of him. A chalice stood on the table, and he faced the tailgate of an SUV.

It might have been difficult for the parishioners to hear the priest with any clarity, given their immediate surroundings—a parking lot mostly full, boys chucking a football, men and women clustered in groups with beers inside beer cozies inside their hands, the "Victory March" playing from someone's car stereo, shouts and whoops from those of undergraduate age milling about nearby. Smoke rose from portable Weber charcoal grills and portable Coleman propane grills— the air like some kind of briquette incense. The members of this congregation could in no way be distinguished from those of the secular tailgates. Everyone wore T-shirts of green and blue and yellow-gold, bearing leprechauns and interlocking *N's* and *D's* and the words *Fighting Irish*. Less than two hundred yards to the northeast rose the dish of Notre Dame Stadium. It blocked from view the spire of the Basilica of the Sacred Heart, the Mother Church of the Congregation of Holy Cross, the religious community that had founded the university. Had the priests of Notre Dame known about the site of this particular Mass—"It's an inappropriate place at an inappropriate time," one of them said later—they would not have given their approval.

A Notre Dame alumnus of the 1970s, now a Notre Dame employee, witnessed the scene while working his way through the lots on his way to a somewhat less ritualized tailgate. Thirty years in and around the university, and he'd never seen anything like it. He did a double take;

1

at first he couldn't quite believe what he caught sight of. Too concisely did it seem to establish the milieu, here at a place where religion and sport are so famously entwined. He likened the gathering to a hedge Mass, those Reformation-era services conducted in the fields of Ireland by priests whose churches had been torched by the English.

The parishioners had likely arrived on campus from somewhere far afield—from eastern Pennsylvania or northern Ohio or western New York or northern New Jersey, regions traditionally dense with Notre Dame fans. Doubtless the communion hosts had come from the local parish, as had the priest, who was probably a fan like the rest of them, and the local parish may very well have organized the trip, probably in a rented bus or two, the universal method for gathering all the Irish fans in a particular community and hauling them to campus. They had reached their pilgrimage destination, and they were sealing the deal with a sacrament—the hosts consecrated on the grounds of Notre Dame, or close to them anyway, on pavement and within eyeshot.

Unperturbed by the commotion around him, the priest at the tailgate read from the Gospel according to Luke. He might have read from the Sunday missal, he might have read from the Saturday, and if the latter, he said, "But the one who hears and does not act is like a man who built a house on the ground without foundation. When the river burst against it, immediately it fell, and great was the ruin of that house."

This was the home opener, the biggest home game of the year, versus the University of Michigan, September 11, 2004. Despite the date, the weather made the day jovial—a few high cirrus clouds at the corners of the earth like hair on an old man's head, still summertime, leaves green, people in T-shirts, coeds in tank tops, everyone in sunglasses, eighty-four degrees in northern Indiana. Around the campus and in the parking lots and on the peripheral streets of South Bend, somewhere near a hundred thousand people were gathering for a game that, to many of them, carried far more significance than what the scoreboard would eventually tell of the day's sport. One hundred thousand people, despite the fact that the stadium holds 80,700, leaving the surplus to witness the game on a drive-in-size screen at the Joyce Center basketball arena, or inside the bars around town.

They had been amassing in South Bend for days. From Interstate 80-90, the automotive pilgrimage gridlocked at the exit tolls, cars and buses and recreational vehicles bearing plates from all over. Green signs on the tollway announced the mileage remaining to Notre Dame. After the tollbooths, as the cars descended the exit ramp, a view suddenly emerged: above woods in the middle distance rose the spire of Sacred Heart and the golden dome of the Main Building. The ramp aims its outflow traffic directly at this picture, and if you're sitting in your front seat, your windshield frames the vantage in concise perspective. It could be a poster sold at the university bookstore—so much so that one wonders if the interstate's surveyors had received instructions to lay down the ramp with this view in mind. The day was bright and the sun exploded off the dome. You almost had to avert your eyes.

The hoi polloi came by auto, but all through Friday and into the night you could look up into the sky and see the lights on the wings of the private jets—Citations, Leers, Gulfstreams, Challengers, Boeing Businesses, eighty and ninety and a hundred of them—in descent toward the South Bend Regional Airport. They were carrying the most moneyed of fans, the whales, known in the development office as "Friends of the University."

ND Harvey, a different kind of friend of the university, presided over something close to chaos. On an Internet message board for Notre Dame fans, I had seen a post: "Stop over and have a 'Cold one' before, during and after we (ND) beat Michigan on Sat. afternoon. . . . . . Keep the faith, IRISH fans." Beer cans were handed off to anyone with empty hands, beer cans were lateraled through the air. There was hooting and hollering and there were rude renditions of "Hail to the Victors," the Michigan fight song, in which the choir replaced "victors valiant" in the lyric with "fornicators" and "conqu'ring heroes" with "masturbators" and sometimes vice versa. There were teenagers in green wigs, and young men with gold earrings, and middle-aged men festooned in strands of green and gold Notre Dame–themed Mardi Gras beads. They all stood in front of a rented fifty-seat motor coach, the first bus in a long train of buses parked outside the front gate of the Joyce Athletic and Convocation Center, the twin-cupped basketball arena and hockey rink, directly across the street from the football stadium.

A good spot, a coveted spot, but ND Harvey knew what he was

doing. Once a year for the last twenty-seven years he has led a group of around forty Notre Dame fans ranging in age from eighteen to eighty-three, all male, on a bus trip originating in South Philadelphia and terminating on this very slice of campus. Everyone spoke in clipped, round-voweled Philadelphia accents. Five or six beer coolers sat on the curb near the bus. The tailgate had the air of a neighborhood social club, of a weekly poker game held in someone's basement. It was as if a beer joint had emptied out, its clientele beamed all at once to northern Indiana—which, as it happens, is pretty close to the truth. The bus driver, a retired fire captain with the nickname Mean Joe Green, said the party had commenced at around six thirty Wednesday evening at a place called Dean's Bar, on Twenty-ninth and Tasker in the Gray's Ferry section of South Philly, had extended without pause onto the bus, and had consumed large portions of the toll roads of three states.

ND Harvey, who usually makes four or five additional pilgrimages per season to Notre Dame on his own, is the kind of man who naturally elicits intense affection and fidelity among his friends. This seems to derive largely from his passion for Notre Dame.

"To know Harvey is to love Harvey."

"So you've met Harvey? Harvey is God."

Of middle height and weight, forty-seven years old, a computer analyst for DuPont Chemical, ND Harvey has sandy brown hair and a brown mustache. In both appearance and demeanor he resembles the comedian Denis Leary. A gold chain hung around his neck. At first glance I assumed it held a crucifix, but when he withdrew it from his shirt, a miniature, golden Notre Dame leprechaun depended from the chain. ND Harvey is actually a nickname, given to him as a boy by his uncle—a Notre Dame devout who passed his fanaticism down to his nephews in the 1960s. Harvey's real name is Bob Sumner.

Despite his post on the Internet message board, ND Harvey today was not keeping the faith. He predicted a loss against Michigan, perhaps severe, perhaps similar to the 38–0 drubbing that Notre Dame had suffered last year at Ann Arbor. Harvey had had a tough time coping with that one, but, then again, he had a tough time coping with any Irish defeat, regardless of the fact that nearly ten years of awful football tended to atrophy the expectations of even the most optimistic fans. He said, "It took me three days to get over the BYU loss last week."

The 2004 season opener had actually occurred the previous Saturday, on the road against Brigham Young University, a game that Notre Dame's athletic department had rescheduled so as to provide the Irish with a warm-up match before taking on the Wolverines of Michigan. Hated, secular, land-grant Michigan, ranked No. 7 in the nation. Despised neighbor-state Big Ten Michigan, which had, early in the twentieth century, successfully lobbied for Notre Dame's exclusion from the Big Ten for reasons having to do with the applicant school's mode of backward Catholic education. "The matter seems to have been settled on theological rather than athletic grounds," Notre Dame's vice president said at the time. Michigan is a game no one can stand to lose, no matter the odds, and so BYU, believed to be highly undermanned, was stuck there at the front of the schedule—the warm-up game. In theory, it not only provided a satisfying victim given BYU's own religious affiliations—though, of course, no one would publicly admit to that feeling—but it was also seen as the perfect team on which to exorcise any lingering demons left over from a radically disappointing 2003, in which Notre Dame had lost seven games and won five, the team's third losing season in five years. Even in the midst of that downward spiral, Notre Dame had easily defeated BYU. Almost no one, therefore, believed the Irish could lose this season, and almost everyone thought that Head Coach Tyrone Willingham would use his relatively talented and veteran team in this, his third year on the job, to reclaim some of the momentum he had created in 2002, his first season, when he had led Notre Dame to victory in its first eight games. As it turned out, the unranked Mormons used their trademark unorthodox blitzing schemes to warm up the Catholics, 17–20.

Everyone here at Harvey's tailgate wore a kind of uniform—the same custom-made blue-green T-shirts.

ND Harvey's
27TH ANNUAL PILGRIMAGE
South Philly to South Bend

"We always call it a *pilgrimage*," said George Sumner, Harvey's brother, standing among the Philadelphians. "And we always have a theme. In 2001, because of 9/11, we called it The Patriotic Pilgrimage.

Another time it was 'Faith, Family, and Friends.' This year, as you can see, it's 'God, Country, Notre Dame.' " The T-shirts also pictured a Celtic cross, a U.S. flag, and the Notre Dame trademark leprechaun, each above their corresponding terms—*God, Country, Notre Dame*—a sequence of words that has become epigrammatic in the mythology of the institution, suggestive of a method for ordering one's core values. They appear carved into the limestone archivolt above the east door to the transept of the Basilica of the Sacred Heart.

Eleven o'clock in the morning, and elderly men in blue blazers, the Basilica's volunteer security detail, closed that very entrance to the public. The door beneath its carved slogan is a memorial to Notre Dame alumni killed in the First World War, and through that portal on every home-game Saturday, an hour and a half before kickoff, the football team and the coaching staff, in street clothes, enter Sacred Heart for an accelerated twenty-minute pregame Mass—in and out. As always, the coaches entered first, with the head coach at the lead, showing the way. A small man, trim as a tightrope, Tyrone Willingham wore a dark suit and a somber expression. Embattled, criticized, condemned, and death-threatened (by an opposing-team fan, it bears remarking), he may have welcomed the few moments of solace here in the quietude of Sacred Heart. Two years into his tenure at Notre Dame and he had already experienced the antipodes of the position, among the highest profile in all of sport—near deification after winning those first eight games of his first season, which produced a nonfiction book and a series of T-shirts and many articles in the sporting press all entitled "Return to Glory"—and then near damnation after compiling last year's record, which grew full of ignominious thrashings at the hands of Notre Dame's bitterest rivals (0–38 to Michigan, 0–37 to Florida State, 14–49 to Southern Cal). It amounted to an abridged history of the football program's run of mediocrity and worse, which extended back ten years, included the tenures of three head coaches, and seemed to indicate a set of institutional problems that both rose above the head of the current coach and fell squarely atop it.

Now, as he took his seat for Mass, Willingham and his players faced the prospect of taking on a powerful Michigan team in the wake of the previous week's humiliating display. The fan base, meanwhile, had gone bipolar. People were calling for Willingham's immediate dismissal; others were desperately praying for him to succeed. "A bank of candles were lighted, ten rosaries were said, all for the coaching staff," announced one fan on an Internet message board. "May Touchdown Jesus guide us through the dark forest of our opponents."

The team Mass is celebrated in the apse, in a section of the church called the Lady Chapel, roped off and guarded by the elderly security detail, and at a thirty-yard remove from the fans who congregate each home-game Saturday for a glimpse of the players in their suits and ties, sitting their listening to the scriptures. Outside, from the east transept all the way to the stadium tunnel a half mile away, a corridor of humanity forms, and when the players emerge from the church following Communion, the crowd erupts in a roar, and down this pathway walled with football fans the team parades from Lady Chapel to locker room.

All through Saturday, before and during and after the Mass, the multitudes rotate through the Basilica. Years ago, the sacristy staff attempted to count the number of people who entered Sacred Heart on a home-game Saturday. They lost patience and quit after their clickers clicked many thousands of times. To achieve basilica status—an honor bestowed only by the pope—a church must meet several criteria. Among the more important, it must prove itself to be a legitimate place of pilgrimage. Notre Dame didn't have a tough time with that one. They needed only call attention to the number of people who visit Sacred Heart in the fall, and who happen also to couple those junkets with three-hour observances inside a nearby stadium. After more than a hundred years of application, Rome finally did the deed and basilicated Sacred Heart in November 1991. The next year the Irish ended the regular season undefeated.

Through Sacred Heart, the crowds make a prescribed circuit. Into the main entrance, through the narthex, they dip their fingers into a granite font the size of a birdbath—the basin gurgling with circulated holy water—make the sign of the cross, and they move deliberately up the nave, eyes lifted to vaulted ceilings fifty feet in the air. The ceilings bear the figures, frescoed on fields of gold and blue, of Old and New Testament scribes, cherubim and seraphim, a communion of saints, all afloat on cartoon clouds—heaven above. Rainbowed light slants through the stained glass. It casts pictures onto the floors and pews and up vertically onto beveled stanchions thick as tree trunks holding the whole place aloft. When first-time visitors enter the church, there is often an audible cooing. Flash photography is discouraged, but prayer in the pews is not. And neither is confession. When the carved oaken doors swing shut, the sinner enclosed inside the confessional, a green bulb goes off and a red bulb lights up. Every so often, overwhelmed by the scenery, a lapsed Catholic will see the green light and follow it in. Among Holy Cross priests it is well-known that game-day contritions often entail taut, prolonged moments of renewed introspection. "Bless me, Father, for I have sinned—it's been thirty years since I've taken the sacraments."

After parking their cars and arriving on campus and before doing anything else, the pilgrims of Notre Dame will likely visit a man-made cave called the Grotto, situated behind Sacred Heart, down a flight of granite steps and cut into a slope of steep pitch—a terminal moraine left by a glacier twelve thousand years before. Deep and dark in the permanent shade, it resembles with its stonework an exhumed catacomb. At a one-to-seven scale, the Grotto is a replica of Our Lady of Lourdes, the Marian shrine in southern France where She appeared to a peasant girl in 1858. Famed for its healing waters, Lourdes attracted pilgrims in such multitudes that religious tourism may well have been invented there. At Notre Dame, its replica has acquired a portion of that luring power. Aside from the stadium, it is the most-visited shrine on campus, and every year its cavern will receive a quarter of a million pilgrims. Filled to its fieldstones with candles set into iron racks, the Grotto gathers prayers. A black cube in the middle of the cave accepts bills through a slot—a sign on top says OFFERING. People push in their money like votes. With long wooden tapers, they light their candles. Today, as always, a thrumming host stood outside the Grotto, the bodies queued up, five- and six-deep, waiting for their turn inside, before moving over to the long wooden kneeler that fronts the cavern— hitting the rails, they used to call it. Shoulder to shoulder, about fifty people can fit on the kneeler at any one time, and heads bowed, they direct their pleas to the university's titular Our Lady. Above the cave's maw, resting in a cavity the size and shape of a mummy case, stands a statue of the Virgin Mary. In her hooded, peaked cloak she's narrow as a rod. Her eyes point skyward and on her face there is a look of ardor. She appears ready to transmit.

Away from sacred ground and all over the country, millions of fans were preparing themselves in their small individual ways, with their small individual rituals, tuning their televisions to NBC for a 4.0 Nielsen share. Portraits of St. Patrick came off walls and were placed next to TV sets. The heads of dogs were rubbed for luck, dogs named after former Notre Dame head coaches. In Niagara Falls, New York, Eddie Gadawski, for more than fifty years the proprietor of an eponymous tavern, readied his bar for the arrival of Notre Dame fans from around the region—from Buffalo city and parts suburban, from the Falls on both sides of the border. Not surprisingly, given that Niagara Falls is 60 percent Catholic, Eddie Gadawski has converted large segments of the local population into Notre Dame fans (the process of becoming an ND partisan is usually phrased in the language of conversion). This development is also not surprising given the manner in which Gadawski has gone about representing Notre Dame at his tavern. It is possible that, outside one or two local establishments in South Bend, Gadawski's is, on a national scale, the ne plus ultra of Notre Dame bars. Its walls and cabinets and backbar and doorways and windows and ceilings—every surface horizontal and vertical—have been layered with Notre Dame memorabilia, acquired piecemeal by Gadawski over the decades. Its interior has the texture of the Carlsbad Caverns. It is an elaborate rococo homage to one man's passion, a shrine away from the shrines.

Eddie Gadawski has attended so many Notre Dame games over so long a time he has trouble remembering just when he may have first experienced a game on campus. He was eighty-four years old, and this season he would make it to Notre Dame for only one pilgrimage—his lowest total since the era of Ara Parseghian.

Not many fans share Gadawski's record as an annual pilgrim. ND Harvey for instance, made his first trip to Notre Dame in 1977, a year in which, he is proud to say, the Irish won a national championship. Individually he travels to just about every home game of the season, but his annual communal pilgrimage with his busload of friends is by far his most important of all. He and his friends sometimes refer to themselves as the Boys of Gray's Ferry, since most of them of a certain generation all grew up in that section of South Philadelphia, at one time the city's principal Irish enclave. Only a few of the boys still live in the old neighborhood. "Gray's Ferry, it's not the same anymore," Harvey said. "It's kind of dying now. But our bus trip every year to Notre Dame, this brings us all back together." He slid a palm down his face. "It kind of breaks me up a little bit." Harvey now lives in south Jersey. As a way to bind the clan in the wake of diaspora, Harvey and the entire group have made it a point not only to organize this trip every year, but to bequeath to those of the next generation their absolute devotion to Notre Dame. As one of Harvey's friends has said, "My kids are Notre Dame fans, and now, my grandkids, they're fucking Notre Dame fans too."

Of the forty men on ND Harvey's bus pilgrimage, just one was a Notre Dame alumnus. Class of 1975, Captain Bill Fisher now worked for the Philadelphia Police Department. Thick in the belly and the jowl, with enormous aviator sunglasses worn under the bill of a navy blue ballcap stitched with the ND monogram in yellow-gold, with a beer in his hand, he had the aspect of a tailgating MacArthur. Surveying the chaos around him—forty-odd South Philadelphians, a good quarter of them belting out another lewd version of the Michigan fight song—the captain said, "I oversee protests and civic affairs in the city. So I know a thing or two about crowd control."

Aside from Captain Fisher, everyone on Harvey's bus trip belonged to a class of fan known as subway alumni, followers of Notre Dame football who have no educational affiliation with the school whatsoever. Their fanaticism tends to flow from team to institution to religious devotion to a reverence for the textured mythos that the whole amalgarn has acquired over the years. The origin of the term dates to a series of games played against Army in New York City between 1923 and 1946. According to popular history, so many working-class, immigrant Catholics emerged from their tenements and spilled into the subway tunnels for transport to these games that a clever reporter coined the term, and the term entered the lexicon. Sui generis in the sportive world, these original Notre Dame fans paid for tickets and listened to the games' radio broadcasts in such numbers that they could be said to have invented big-time college athletics. Other teams with large-scale followings who were not educated by the sponsoring universities have since appropriated the term. The reasons why these prototypical subway alumni made their short pilgrimages were easy enough to discern: they felt a deep affinity for this team made up of Catholic schlumps just like them—Irish and Polish and Italian, mostly—for whom they could root against the West Point Black Knights, a team and an institution that defined Establishment. Embedded in discrimination against their religion and ancestry, forged by clannish tendencies imported from the Old World, their passion for all things Notre Dame grew almost nationalistic in its fervor. When Catholic enclaves in the big cities were still intact, whole neighborhoods became Notre Dame backers—South Boston, South Philly, the outer boroughs of New York, the South Side of Chicago. Inasmuch as Ohioans root for Ohio State, Catholics rooted for Notre Dame. That feeling has never really gone away, but has, over the decades, as Catholics have entered the mainstream and left behind their proletariat past, morphed into something else again: veneration of the American-immigrant bootstrap ethos of hard work and Catholic faith, and the notion that the two entwined can only produce the good life. With each victory on the field, the team and the university not only came to represent that life, but seemed as well to confirm its possibility. It proved a potent combination, and devotion to Notre Dame, passed down through the generations, has become a religion in ways that exceed metaphor.

Millions in number, the subway alumni now dwarf Notre Dame's actual alumni population, which stands at about 110,000. They constitute a fan base larger than that of any other college team, larger than those of most professional franchises. In surveys conducted by the market-research wizards at the Harris Poll, on polls conducted online by ESPN, subways consistently make Notre Dame the most popular college team in the country, despite that the Irish have not won a national championship in sixteen years. As an audience, they have made it possible for Notre Dame football to remain independent of any athletic conference, to bargain with NBC for an exclusive contract to televise all Irish home games, to garner more press coverage than any other college team, thus begetting even more fans, and to have a licensing arm of such financial magnitude that university officials would rather not talk numbers. Well before television, the income these fans generated—from ticket sales and merchandise sales and even straight-up donations—helped endow the university.

"Let me tell you," Captain Fisher said. "I'm an alum, and I can't match their love for Notre Dame."

I had first met ND Harvey and his group at the pep rally the night before, which takes place inside the basketball arena. Wading through the crowds, trying to find seats, Harvey's brother, George Sumner, a burly man with dark hair and a thick mustache, walked in front of me, throwing blocks. At last we found seats in the bleachers, and George reflected on the oddity and profundity of his Notre Dame zeal. "I saw a sign on a pub in Northern Ireland once that got about as close to explaining our obsession as anything I've ever seen. It said, 'For those who do understand, no explanation is necessary. For those who don't, none is possible.' " The sign, he said, was in reference to the Troubles of Northern Ireland. "It's a weird thing. Nobody understands it, really. I graduated from Temple University, but this . . ." And with a sweep of his arm he indicated everything—the fans crowding into the arena, a group of students hollering the fight song, the campus outside with its spire and dome and mosaic of Christ with his arms raised. The rally had grown loud, and George shouted over the noise, "This is the only thing there is! I always relate it back to that sign in that Irish pub, because none of this makes any sense. I mean, *none of us went here.*"

Game time approached and the greensward in front of the Main Building had become a scene of agitation. Thick with mature trees, this was the oldest of Notre Dame's quadrangles, containing at its perimeter both the Basilica and Mary atop the dome. It had come to be known as God Quad, and by now it had almost zero standing room. A sea of fans crammed into the areas between the trees and the religious statuary. Children had climbed up into the branches of the trees. People were sitting on each other's shoulders. Digital camcorders by the hundred were aimed and recording. The marching band had assembled before the steps of the building, and in a burst of sound, brassy and reverberant, they fired up the "Victory March" and moved in precise ranks away from the staircase and along a path headed south. Called the band "step-off," another Notre Dame game-day ritual, it essentially marked the beginning of the day's sport. In a hustling, jostling human migration of a thousand yards, the fans followed the band en masse as it advanced loudly through God Quad, continued out across the great open plain of South Quad, and marched east toward Notre Dame Stadium, entering the tunnel, threading the needle, a last flourish of sound hanging over the mob now arrayed on the concrete esplanade underneath the facade of the coliseum.

Up on the fifth floor of the press box, in a large hall called the VIP level, the VIPs had begun to gather, Friends of the University. An enormous bank of windows overlooked the field high above the fifty-yard line, and they encompassed an IMAX of sky and stands and, at the far left side, the upstretched arms of Touchdown Jesus. Trustees and big-check benefactors and the like had just begun the afternoon of mingling with university officials, all the provosts and deans and endowed-chair academics and university vice presidents and Holy Cross priests casually dressed. Fr. Edward "Monk" Malloy, president of Notre Dame, entered the elevators and rode up to the fifth floor. The noise of the crowd and the music of the marching band as it entered the stadium beneath the press box barely reached the VIPs, perhaps only as a structural vibration, and through the windows they could watch the stands gradually fill with Notre Dame fandom. Thirty minutes to kickoff.

Vegas favored the Wolverines by thirteen points, a large margin, and down in the parking lots, as the tailgates started to close up shop, not many people would have laid bets on a Notre Dame upset. An ancient dictum, that of the ND "home dog," states that one should never bet against the Irish if the Irish are underdogs at home. But these were extraordinary times, and the old rules no longer seemed to hold. Almost everyone expected defeat today, citing the extreme ineptitude displayed by the Irish in Utah, an offense that produced eleven net rushing yards for the entire game. That—as almost anyone would tell you—was *not* Notre Dame football, and if 2004 was meant to exorcise the demons of 2003, the demons still had possession.

George Sumner was as pessimistic as anyone, and he voiced an opinion shared by many others, speculation that expanded out from today's game and over the long term. He said, "I'm not sure they'll ever win a national championship again. That doesn't mean I'll stop hoping and praying. But everything is against them." He listed a set of familiar complaints, complaints that arise every time the Irish struggle on the field. He spoke of Notre Dame's academic rigor—which, he quickly added, as nearly all Irish fans will, he'd never wish to see diminished so that the university might attract more and better athletes, for this among other things is what makes Notre Dame "special"—and he spoke of an overall shift in the culture. Eyes on the NFL, the best high school athletes would rather skim through a few semesters of dumbed-down curriculum on a palm-tree campus among gone-wild coeds and, essentially, play their college ball semipro.

George backtracked a bit, however. "I won't say they'll *never* win a championship again, but it could be a while. But, no, it won't change anything for me." Win, lose, abolish athletic scholarships, and drop the program to Division III, and George Sumner would still be as rabid as ever. "We'd just get teased a lot more when we get back home. Because believe it or not, not everyone is a Notre Dame fan. As impossible as that sounds."

The fear that Notre Dame might never again compete at a high level had lately escalated in the minds of Irish fans all over the country. Like George Sumner, many of them were getting used to losing. Others had become enraged by it. It had been ten years—going on eleven—since the Irish had ranked among the elite, let alone won a national title, and ten years of middling football had convinced many fans that Notre Dame's leaders had capitulated to the idea that running a university with elite academics could not withstand the demands of running a university with an elite football program. Many believed that the Notre Dame administration had designs on *de-emphasis,* an ancient term peculiar to American higher education, the only university system in the world to play amateur athletics at a level of popularity equal to professional athletics, and thus the only university system in the world that hems and haws and worries and agonizes about the *overemphasis* it places on its sports teams—an emphasis, they fear, that has made a joke of the term *student-athlete,* and thus the educational mission as a whole. The NCAA owes its very existence to this sort of agonizing, and no other individual university in the country agonizes about it more than Notre Dame, for no other university in the world is so defined by a game, by a single endeavor, as this one. Football had always been

Notre Dame's blessing as well as its sin, and the university, many people feared, wanted to escape once and for all what had defined it.

To do so would have all kinds of ramifications. Over its history, Notre Dame together with its football team had become that powerfully persuasive symbol: It represented all those working-stiff strivers of generations gone who toiled and sacrificed for the future of their children. The credo of the university, "the Notre Dame way," as it has been called, articulated over the decades by a series of Notre Dame plenipotentiaries, was to strive for excellence in all things and thus bring glory to God. Football had become not just the most visible example of the credo—it had helped to create it in the first place. For many fans, then, to abandon football excellence would be to abandon the essence of Notre Dame.

Whether or not the leaders of Notre Dame purposefully wished to "de-emphasize," the last ten years pointed to a fundamental cultural shift occurring within Notre Dame that seemed to mirror the wider one spoken of by George Sumner. It had been occurring for forty years. For forty years there had been talk of a "New Notre Dame." All the way up until the early 1960s the university had largely drawn its students from the same groups that the Fighting Irish had drawn their fans—the Catholic working classes—so much so that to divide Notre Dame fandom into alumni and subway was a little tricky. Sons, and then daughters (ND went coed in 1972), of devoted subway alumni matriculated at their dream school and went off to get their Catholic education, learning to strive, but with a sense of difference inherent in their spiritual devotion. They wove the Notre Dame community together, and that community became known as the Notre Dame Family, which, all at the same time, is a business network, a fraternal organization, a charitable foundation, a clan, a club, and an audience of football fans. If you could combine elements of the Knights of Columbus with a dash of the Century Club and the fan culture of Manchester United, you'd have something close to the Notre Dame Family.

But as the children and grandchildren of Catholic immigrants climbed the ladder of prosperity, so had the university, until its academic programs began to compete with those of the best universities in the country—universities that had all gone secular. And slowly, glacially, Notre Dame's student body shifted profile as well, from working class to middle class to privileged class. By the turn of the last century, this change had reached a point that people began to make connections: De-emphasized football, with the 2003 season and the BYU loss representing the leading edge of that decline. A seeming desire to ape in all ways the great secular academies. Football, over time, had got all bound up at Notre Dame with Catholic identity. Losing the first was a symptom inherent in moving away from the second. With elements of nostalgia, the fans looked back on an older Notre Dame that played superb football, an older Notre Dame that, they believed, played such football without shame. Among the fans, both alumni and subway, there was a growing sentiment that the newest New Notre Dame had lost itself, and that this development had its origins at the very top.

The day after the BYU game, ND Nation, the most prominent of the Fighting Irish Internet fan communities, collectively suffered something close to a nervous breakdown.

"I bought a black ND hat over the Summer . . . and now I finally get to wear it. In mourning for my beloved, lost football team."

"I have two tickets to every home game . . . I'd be willing to buy them and burn them versus going to any home game—until this mess is fixed."

"The longer this goes on, the more I see me straying toward apathy. I worry about apathy . . . I've always seen Notre Dame's role as the noble samurai."

"The end of optimism is official."

"Success is not inevitable. . . . Tradition doesn't win football games. Winning football games builds a tradition. Without a constant commitment to excellence from the top to the bottom, Notre Dame will quickly fade from memory as a football powerhouse. I'd rather we just quit playing than let this happen."

"We've become 'Fat Elvis.' A wheezing, money making parody of what we used to be."

"The emperor is stark naked."

"I believe that the next few months are going to be hell for all of us who love ND and especially the football program. But I believe battle lines will be drawn in what will soon be ND's own civil war."

"Finally, say it like it is: Ty is out of place here. Wrong guy for this program and its history. . . . I've been a part of ND (self and family have five ND degrees and have donated a small boatload) for 35 years and have met and personally spoken with Ty on more than one occasion. In my opinion he is an arrogant and condescending jerk. Other than PC, he has nothing going for him as regards the world of ND football."

"Racist pig."

Mike Coffey, under a canopy at the ND Nation tailgate, sipped from a bottle of Sierra Nevada and discussed the state of Notre Dame football from behind a pair of sunglasses. The consensus, as elsewhere, was that the possibilities of an upset today over Michigan approached absolute zero. Notre Dame class of 1991, Coffey is one of four men, three of whom are Notre Dame alumni, who operate and administer the ND Nation Web site. Collectively known as BoardOps, they preside over a community of about five thousand registered members. Theirs is a free board, open to the public. On a day such as the Sunday after the BYU game, traffic at the site can swell to twenty thousand visitors. And on a day like the previous Sunday, the ranting can take on such hysteria that the BoardOps will "wipe," "flush," "nuke" the slate clean like electroshock. The perception among outsiders is that the boards, and ND Nation in particular, are hothouses of vitriol and angst and rage—fans of the sort who need a constant and immediate fix of Notre Dame news, gossip, and rumor, but, most important, a venue on which to vent. A mix of alumni and subway alumni, the posters of ND Nation are thought of as one-dimensional, hard-core, zealotic, right-wing. In cases of defeat, they are believed to be the ones who die the hardest. If the Internet fan communities form a sub-subculture of Notre Dame fandom as a whole, ND Nation is thought of as the lunatic fringe. One Notre Dame official told me, "On the message boards, you're either a blasphemer or a child of the light. It's like a kind of unexamined fascism."

But, as Mike Coffey is quick to point out, "the board is monitored well." In addition, he says, the Web site's membership rolls contain a number of large-scale Notre Dame donors, former athletes, and university faculty and staff. The athletic department in particular is full of avid lurkers, and employees of the Sports Information Department use the site, as much as they may deny it, as a means to take the temperature of the masses. As it stood now, a few minutes before kickoff on the first home game of the year, the temperature of the fan base had reached the malarial.

Coffey comes from a long line of Notre Dame graduates; his father and grandfather are alumni; his mother went to Saint Mary's, the all-girls college across the street from Notre Dame. His handle on the boards is El Kabong, an allusion to the alter ego of Quick Draw McGraw, the Hanna-Barbera cartoon character. For the game today he wore a gray T-shirt that said NOTRE DAME BASKETBALL. He speaks emphatically, as if putting into speech a message-board post that succinctly dismantles another poster's bad logic, as his posts often do. As it turns out, his line of work is logic—he's a database-software programmer, and he splits time between Chicago, where he was born and raised, and South Bend. Last January, he had appeared on television in Chicago, on a local sports show, to explain the position of an alumni letter sent to every member of the Notre Dame board of trustees. Motivated by fears that the university's leadership, through incompetence or design or both, was allowing the football program to die a slow death, the letter had voiced as well as summarized all those profound anxieties that had come to permeate the fan base. Bearing the signatures of 412 alumni, the "Call for Change" letter, a title soon acronymed on the message boards to C4C, began its argument with a set of premises. Notre Dame had achieved its greatness based on "three pillars"—rigorous Catholicism, rigorous academics, and championship football, though not necessarily in that order. Demolish one of those pillars, their argument seemed to run, and the weight of the roof would make rubble of the other two.

The only other BoardOp here today was John Vannie, handle of Jvan. A key framer of the C4C document, he was, at the moment, mixing a batch of margaritas, the recipe for which is evidently famous among the ND Nation set. In from San Diego, a manager in the fighter jet division of Northrop Grumman, he was graduated from Notre Dame in 1975, in the era of Ara Parseghian. He carried a cell phone in his right hand attached by a cord to a hands-free headset plugged in his ear, into which he would break into ghostly conversation at irregular intervals. Vannie is responsible for the pregame and postgame write-ups that appear on ND Nation. He concluded his BYU "postmortem" with gloom. "This opener was in many ways a painful reminder of the 2003 season, and it will be nothing short of disastrous if that comparison can be made again next week."

A few ND Nation members had convened at the tailgate today, but no true regular posters. One of those regulars, a 1988 Notre Dame graduate and an attorney in St. Louis, was supposed to be at the game today, but he had canceled his trip after the BYU game, enraged by the result. For his part Coffey had decided to watch Michigan's evisceration of Notre Dame from a TV plugged into a generator right there in the parking lots. His tickets remained in his pocket.

Kickoff neared, NBC commenced its coverage with its slow sentimental rendition of the "Victory March," and Eddie Colton sat at home on Staten Island with only his fiancée. If not on campus, which he travels to regularly during the season, he prefers to watch the games without distraction. As he puts it, "Normally I can't have anything within arm's reach. I get into the games a little bit." New York City police sergeant, member of the Emerald Society, the national club of Irish Cops, Colton learned to love Notre Dame from his father, who learned to love Notre Dame from *his* father, the font of it all, who had come upon this small, obscure Catholic college and its football team in the newspapers circa 1917, before radio, in the days when Rockne was still a student-athlete, in the days before the team was known as the Fighting Irish.

For the last ten years, Colton has been a sergeant in the First Precinct, which covers Lower Manhattan from Houston Street to the Battery, and the date of the 2004 Michigan game carried a significance that tended to make him a little less enthusiastic than he might normally be for a football Saturday. Had the calendar not been so vicious, he would have caught a flight to South Bend and been at the game right now, perhaps having a word with Fr. Edward "Monk" Malloy, a friend of Colton's. "I didn't wanna go out there for 9/11. I didn't wanna leave here . . . outta respect, you know?" So instead he tuned his television to NBC. He got up from his seat, walked into the bedroom, and moments before kickoff, as he always does, he laid his hands on a two-foot ceramic statue of the Blessed Mother. His grandmother had rescued it in the 1920s from the curbside of a house in her neighborhood. Someone had set it out with the garbage. He then touched a strand of rosary beads hanging from the statue and said a prayer of remembrance for his father, with whom Colton used to make his pilgrimages to Notre Dame and who had succumbed to heart disease eight days after 9/11. He blessed himself, and by the time he returned to his chair, the coin had been tossed. Michigan elected to defer.

2

Getting It

Tyrone Willingham appeared on the dais like a conjurer. One moment the seat on the stage behind the microphone was empty, and the next moment the head football coach of the University of Notre Dame occupied his position overlooking the reporters. They were seated in funeral chairs, and they were murmuring amongst themselves. Apparently he'd been up there for some time.

"Very little reaction from this group," he said. His voice emerged from two black Eon speakers flanking the stage. A few uncomfortable laughs emerged from the press corps. Someone cleared his throat. No one said anything, and quietly, soberly, in his characteristic monotone—creaky like an old door hinge, but full of bass profundities—Ty Willingham recited his opening monologue to the 2004 football season.

"Thank you for taking the time to join us. Obviously I'm very excited to begin this season. I think that's almost an everyday circumstance for me, because I do enjoy what I do, coaching the game of football and working with the young men I have to work with.

"There are a lot of exciting things and great prospects for our season, and our young men have come back in great-looking shape. We'll find out exactly how detailed that condition is a little bit later. But I think they are prepared to have an excellent season and do some great things this year.

"With that, I'll entertain any questions that you might have."

At first, there wasn't much in the way of entertaining. The head coach sat alone on the dais, a yellow-gold curtain behind him, a blue skirt hanging from the table, fake yellow flowers on either end. He stared out over the heads of the corps, his arms folded on the table, huge and boardroom size. It made him look small. Six TV cameras were trained on Willingham from a platform amid the folding chairs. The Joyce Center climate-control system droned from inside the walls like an immense vacuum cleaner. Assistant athletic directors in ties and shirtsleeves stood at the perimeters like Secret Service agents. The only sound was the building breathing. Inside the field-house portion of the Joyce Athletic and Convocation Center, a big open room the size of a factory floor, at the first press conference of the season, just before the start of fall practice, on Media Day, August 9, 2004—and the media appeared to have nothing to ask. Moments passed. The cameras waited. The assistant athletic directors waited. Ty Willingham waited and continued to stare. It was a stare similar to the one he used on the sidelines at particularly tense plot points during games. He was famous for it. When he was head coach at Stanford, they called it The Look. Among Notre Dame fans too it had become a much-commented-upon mannerism, interpreted either as a kind of Rasputinish Zen-gaze capable of summoning thunder, or a mask designed to camouflage incompetence, depending on the attitude of the fan, optimist or pessimist.

Breaking the silence, Willingham said, "That is consistent with what I got earlier."

Again mild laughter, and the questions began.

"Can you talk about the team's transition on the field?"

As a rule, the Notre Dame press corps appeared to favor golf shirts tucked into khaki trousers. About fifty chairs had been set out, but they were barely a third full. Willingham answered the questions almost by rote and in a kind of academic style—his phrasing peppered with such constructions as "things of that nature" and "I'm hopeful that"—and the occasion had the air of a breakaway discussion panel on the last day of a convention of actuaries. The press corps royalty had all arrived with their tape recorders and notepads. There was Jim Doyle, of the *South Bend Tribune,* now semiretired, the elder statesmen of the Notre Dame beat, Notre Dame class of 1949, whose career had spanned seven head coaches and fifty years, beginning in 1953 with Frank Leahy. He didn't stay at the press conference long. His reporterly duties now entailed a once-a-week column of purely historical content, his vast repository of Fighting Irish trivia and anecdote dribbling piecemeal onto the page each week here in the coda of his career.

There was Jeff Jeffers of WNDU-TV, the "dean" of the local sports anchors, who cohosted Willingham's weekly football-season television show—*Inside Notre Dame Football*. There was Tom Coyne of the Associated Press and John Jackson of the *Chicago Sun-Times*, and Jason Kelly, former sports page editor of the *Observer*, Notre Dame's student newspaper, and now the lead sports columnist for the *South Bend Tribune*. There was Avani Patel of the *Chicago Tribune*, the only female member of the press corps, other than Allison Hayes, the blond anchor for the local Fox affiliate, and also, at twenty-nine, one of the youngest. She sat in the front row and took notes in a three-subject spiral notebook.

There was Tim Prister, Notre Dame class of 1982, senior writer for the fanzine *Blue & Gold Illustrated*, established in 1981, the oldest of four Notre Dame fanzines still in business. Over the last five years, *BGI*'s circulation had fallen from fifty-five thousand to forty thousand, either from competition from Internet sites, or from a lessening of interest in the whole business of Notre Dame football, or from a lessening of interest in *BGI*. Prister's most incendiary piece had appeared on January 1, 2002, the day Notre Dame had introduced Lionel Tyrone Willingham as its new head coach. "The vocal segment of Notre Dame fans who are apt to publicly express an opinion about the hiring of a football coach are bitter, disappointed and, in some cases, downright irate about the naming of Tyrone Willingham as the next head football coach," Prister wrote. "You see, despite all the progress we've made as a society, we still are—as a whole—a racist country. There are thousands upon thousands of Notre Dame fans today who are angry that Willingham has been named head football coach at Notre Dame, and they're going to hide behind Willingham's record at Stanford as the reason for their anger and disappointment."

After seven seasons as head coach at Stanford, Willingham had amassed a record of 44-36-1, and a winning percentage of .550, which did not on the surface compare favorably to Bob Davie, his predecessor at Notre Dame, who had attained a winning percentage of .583 over five years. Willingham had suffered three losing seasons (5-6, 3-8, 5-6) against four winning ones (7-4-1, 7-5, 8-4, and 9-3), and his greatest achievement had been guiding Stanford to the Pac-10 championship in 1999 and into the Rose Bowl, where his team lost to the University of Wisconsin, 9–17.

As most football coaches will, Willingham had conducted a peripatetic career, with stints at Michigan State (his alma mater), Central Michigan, North Carolina State, Rice, Stanford, and three years in the NFL with the Minnesota Vikings. Before ascending to head coach in Palo Alto—hired out of Minnesota, where he oversaw running backs— he had never been an offensive or defensive coordinator, had never held an assistant's job above that of position coach, though his experience in that role was wide, encompassing defensive secondary, special teams, wide receivers, and running backs. In the coaching profession, it is exceedingly rare for a man to jump from position coach to head. Like executive vice presidents in the corporate world, ambitious coaches are, generally, first groomed for promotion in coordinating roles, where they have responsibility over a full offense or defense. This fact, along with Willingham's rather ordinary career winning percentage, did not escape the attention of those Notre Dame fans who keep track of such things, and, suffering from résumé angst, they did indeed, for the most part, receive rather coolly the announcement of Willingham as the next Irish head man. His knowledge of game-planning and strategy was viewed as suspect. He was seen as a "CEO coach," perhaps just shy of figurehead, his success dependent, more than is the norm, on the tactical abilities of his subordinates.

For the skeptics, matters did not improve when Willingham brought along from Stanford nearly his entire staff. It was believed that he would use his new position to attract assistant coaches of the highest caliber possible, since this would behoove a man without coordinator experience. As it stood, more résumé angst ensued when the skeptics glanced at the assistants' CVs and noticed a bit of CFL, of Arena League, of lower-tier Pac-10, of obscure collegiate Mountain West.

At least one member of the Bay Area press agreed with Notre Dame's skeptical sect. "Tyrone Willingham is making a huge career mistake," wrote Glenn Dickey of the *San Francisco Chronicle,* also on New Year's Day, 2002. "At Notre Dame, he will be exposed for the mediocre coach he is."

But the fans had so despised Bob Davie that, as they learned more

about their new head coach, their pessimism reversed course and optimism grew all through spring and into the summer and fall. He had
something of a pedigree, having trained under Dennis Green, a student
of Bill Walsh, the guru of the San Francisco 49ers and winner of four
Super Bowls. Willingham thus brought with him from California a version of the so-called West Coast Offense, a fashionable strategic philosophy, first developed by Walsh, that favored intricate passing patterns
and precise timing routes—a pro-style offense that seemed, in light of
the confused offenses Bob Davie had run, like the coming of an Age of
Enlightenment. In addition, Stanford's offenses under Willingham and
his coordinator Bill Diedrick scored a lot. They averaged 37 points and
451 yards per game in 2001, though the skeptics pointed out that these
figures had been amassed against Pac-10 competition historically disinterested in defensive prowess.

Then there was the man himself, who had an interesting biography, with elements suitable for the backstory of a deity—but only if he
should go on to win a national title. Immediately the fans plumbed
Willingham's past for this sort of stuff. They wanted, and needed, to
find reasons for optimism and hope. With no other program has the position of head coach grown into such a looming reverend presence.
American football itself is peculiar in its veneration of the coach as
field general, drill sergeant, chief executive, motivational mastermind,
Svengali, soothsayer, minister, idol—and the head coach of Notre
Dame stands alone in this regard, perhaps because Knute Rockne was
the first coach to generate, largely by design, such veneration. Each
successful coach from Rockne onward has heightened that veneration
until today, the instant a Notre Dame head coach is hired, he creates
his own cult. The cult is either dismantled painfully after the coach
tanks or is expanded into legend after he succeeds.

In the meantime, in early 2002, the fans isolated the details and
held them in abeyance. Anecdotes were available from Willingham's
life story that over time and through much retelling were burnished
into something close to metaphor. They indicated the right sorts of
traits—the "intangibles"—for achieving success as Notre Dame head
coach. He grew up in Jim Crow North Carolina, in a town called Jacksonville, the son of a contractor and landlord. His mother was a
teacher. At his introductory press conference he said that as a child he

would sneak out of Sunday church, Methodist, to watch the day-after highlights of Notre Dame games, a program televised nationally. (In the dismantling process that occurred after 2003, the fans judged this particular anecdote to be, perhaps, apocryphal.) An undersize quarterback in high school, well below six feet, 150 pounds, not especially fast, not especially strong-armed, recruited by no one, he enrolled at Michigan State University in 1972. He walked on, he pulled a Rudy, he earned a scholarship. He never had a drink, never a cigarette, nor, evidently, any vice at all. He outworked everyone else. He started six games under center after the first-string quarterback went down with injury. The team voted him "most inspirational player." He won scholar-athlete awards. He went into coaching immediately after college—major: physical education—and he impressed his bosses with a list of übercoach attributes, the kinds of things that might also be found under bullet-points in the brochures of a corporate-leadership retreat: "attention to detail," "self-discipline," "work ethic," "precision," "consistency," "preparation," "perfectionist." He was the first to arrive at the office, the last to leave. When he became head coach at Stanford he forced players who had broken team rules to run wind sprints at six thirty in the morning. He kept himself in such physically exalted shape that he ran the sprints along with his players. They puked, they required IVs. He kept on running. He scheduled his practices and the lives of his players down, pretty much, to the second. To improve player focus, he prescribed the use of a metronome. In team meetings he used Microsoft PowerPoint. He was as punctual as the railroad in Switzerland. His wife once showed up a few minutes late for the team bus. The bus left her behind. He believed in concision. He chose his words carefully. With players at practices and in games, he spoke only when necessary. They leaned in low, close to his mouth, to hear him deliver his wisdom. He perfected The Look, also known as The Stare, which in the media and among the fans took on mesmeric qualities. His eyes smoldered, his brow furrowed, his players said, "Yes, sir!" This seemed to indicate that he was a motivational mastermind, a legitimate head-coaching Svengali. He believed in leading by example. Off the field he dressed like Cary Grant in *North by Northwest,* and he imposed codes of appearance on his team. He appeared in classrooms unannounced, startling the professors, to make sure his players weren't cutting class or arriving late or sitting in the back row. He continued to sit and take in the lectures in honest intellectual curiosity. With his players, he counseled and offered life advice. He often used the phrase "our young men," as in "the development of our young men as human beings." His players seemed to adore him. To reporters they said things like "For me, it's a horrible feeling to think I've let him down" and "He has taken me so far as a person and a player, that I want to do my best for him." He was a "molder of men," a "father figure." The cult of Willingham was ready for use.

Four games into his first season, when he opened his Notre Dame career with eight straight wins, *Sports Illustrated* ran a cover story on Willingham at Notre Dame—deploying all the tropes of the Irish head-coach cult. "Return to Glory," read the head. "What a difference a coach makes," read the tagline. "The Savior of South Bend," read the inside header. After Willingham's hiring and the electrifying start to the season, Notre Dame's athletic director, Kevin White, was quoted as saying, "Devine intervention at its best. That's what this represents to me and, more importantly, to Notre Dame and Notre Dame football . . . Thank God he is here." Equanimity was hard to come by in those heady times. Eight-game win streaks following the grim incompetence of Bob Davie constituted a moment of paean. For his seeming resuscitation of Notre Dame football—the team ended the season with a 10-3 record—Willingham won several coach of the year awards. (But, then again, so had Bob Davie, just two years earlier.) Alan Grant, a former player under Willingham at Stanford and now a correspondent for ESPN, had spent that first season "on the inside." Grant titled his book, of course, *Return to Glory*, and it arrived in bookstores a few weeks before Willingham would begin his disastrous 2003 campaign. In retrospect, those first eight games of 2002 appeared more than flukish. Many were won on razor-thin margins by exceptionally proficient defensive play, which had caused an implausible number of turnovers and had masked an offense that did not score a touchdown in its first two games, a trend of incompetence that did not abate through most of 2003. There were other ominous signs, including lousy special-teams play and game-day blunders that had grown into frustrating patterns. There were penalties late in the season for twelve men on the field and strange personnel decisions, such as the withholding of tailback Julius

Jones from the starting position for the first five games of 2003. The Dallas Cowboys would go on to select Jones in the second round of the 2004 NFL draft. He would start for the Cowboys immediately and lead the team in rushing.

In October 2002, Notre Dame defeated Florida State 34–24, at Doak Campbell Stadium in Tallahassee, a vicious place for opposing teams to play. This would mark the biggest win by far of Willingham's Notre Dame career. After that game, the Irish ascended in the polls to No. 4 in the nation, but in the very next contest, they collapsed at home against a lackluster Boston College team, final score: 7–14, BC. They lost by thirty-one points to Southern Cal in the final game of the regular season, and by twenty-one points to North Carolina State in the Gator Bowl. Since the Florida State victory, Notre Dame had seven victories against ten losses, many of which were double-figure blowouts, and the legend of Willingham declined as fast as it had risen.

Eleven queries into the Media Day press conference, a veiled but substantive question at last arose. It concerned the "Call for Change" letter of the previous winter.

A reporter said, "A lot has been written over the off-season. How difficult is it to separate yourself from that?"

Willingham said, "You're speaking of . . . ?"

The reporter cleared his throat. "Speaking more about the alumni."

A pause. "Okay. Just wanted to make sure I'm on the same page, because people say things about my golf swing, et cetera."

The reporter made a nervous-laugh sound.

Willingham had indeed seen a copy of the letter, and he responded to it now with high diplomacy. "If you guys have been around this program the last couple years, you recognize by now that what I focus on is the positive. Whatever is said, you take it and you learn from it and you make yourself and the program stronger. If there were good things that came out of any of those comments, I want to make them an advantage for us. I believe we listen, I believe we look at those things, and I believe we've done that. But in terms of the pressure aspect of it, if you're going to tell me that the pressure on Coach Willingham was any different today than the day he arrived, then it's news to me."

Willingham and the media shared a curious relationship. You couldn't call it icy, you couldn't call him aloof. He was approachable, but once approached, his guard went up. He had cultivated a mode of speech that offered about as much quotability as a midlevel bureaucrat at the Department of the Interior. The word most often used to describe him was *stoic*. This, to some degree, was euphemism. Compared to the blunderings of Bob Davie, who came across as lumpen to such an extent that he had earned the nickname Boob, Willingham was seen as a regular intellectual.

Careful and measured and a bit elusive, he said such things as "Modern football is all about the quarterback. But, at the same time, it's also not about the quarterback." At first, the fans generally embraced this sort of thing, thinking it an example of a fine analytical mind at work and a relieving change of pace. But when it came to forging a public persona, Willingham did not occupy even the same universe as Lou Holtz, the nonpareil, and to whom all modern Notre Dame coaches will forever be compared, whose wit and virtuosity made him rich on the public-speaking circuit. Fans would flock to the Quarterback Club luncheons on the Fridays of home-football weekends to hear the one-liners drop from Holtz as he gave his addresses. To the fans, he was Mark Twain in a headset and a Notre Dame pullover. With Willingham, however, there was a knot of language that grew even knottier when the team played poorly. In good times and bad, many people described his speech as "cryptic," and as with his sideline stare, it either indicated a depth of meaning cunningly obscured, or a method for disguising a deep lack of answers.

This characteristic had begun to grate on both fans and reporters alike. If a coach starts to fail consistently on the field—and for most Notre Dame fans, Willingham's record of nine losses in the last fourteen games qualified as failure—any persona at all will begin to grate. The Willingham cult was beginning to suffer. Yet the press also seemed a little intimidated by him. For the most part they treated him with kid gloves. This led to a lack of confidence when asking press-conference questions. Maybe through sheer contagion, their phrasing grew as convoluted as the coach's.

"How close are you to your academic standards that you want and the levels you want to achieve in those other aspects?"

And, in turn, Willingham's press conferences became exercises in avoidance. Every Tuesday in the fall, head coaches across Division I

conduct their weekly pressers, and a certain type of fan will parse the
Q&A transcripts with an almost hermeneutical rigor. Inside Willingham's texts, posting their findings on Internet message boards, often
enough these fans were chasing after wind.

During the Media Day press conference, a reporter queried with
uncustomary directness, "You talked about staying positive. You talk
about the championship being a cornerstone of your foundation. But
yet last year, you lost three games by more than thirty points, you lost
another one by twenty-eight. How can people believe that you can win
a championship at this point?"

After a moment of thought, Willingham said, "It's always difficult
for fans to have confidence in teams when things go poorly. I think I
was home—if I might draw some kind of parallel—I was home and I
was listening to one of the talk radio shows, and you have to understand, I don't do that very often. But I was listening to it. And this particular host was calling out to the audience for people that had given
up on the Cubs—and did they learn anything from that. Well, to me
you can draw some parallels there, okay? Yes, we got beat. Yes, some of
the scores were sizable. But unless we're wrong, it is truly only one
loss. And if we can come back and win this year—then I think that will
vindicate everything. Fans are very often quick to praise or perish—I
think I can use that. Coaches see things over the long haul and see
things more as they are."

In the transcript eventually compiled and distributed by the Notre
Dame Sports Information Department, Willingham's answer broke off
after the words "vindicate everything." Perhaps the most pertinent response to the most pertinent question of the entire Media Day sympo-
sium had been censored.

The reporter said, "It's been a long ninety-six years for Cubs fans,
Coach."

The press corps laughed. Coach Willingham laughed. He leaned
into the mike and his voice boomed through the Eons. "Are you telling
me you have a lot of reason to be pessimistic?"

"Yes, in terms of the Cubs—*not* for your team."

"Okay then," Willingham said. "Thank you."

A little while later, the coach decided to add something, possibly uncomfortable with his metaphor linking Notre Dame to the Chicago Cubs, a team that had last won a championship in 1908, hexed famously by a tavern owner and his billy goat.

"I don't mean to put a jinx on us or anything."

How Willingham defined *long haul* was open to interpretation. To review the long haul of the last ten years—which would have been an unpleasant ordeal for any Notre Dame fan—you would not necessarily consult the *2004 Notre Dame Football Media Guide.* Handed out to reporters and sold in bookstores for twenty bucks, coming in at 464 perfect-bound pages, it was a four-and-a-half-pound slab of statistics, trivia, rosters, bios, anecdotal sidebars, action photos, big-game play-by-plays, historical arcana, former coach and player hagiographies, and guidebook-style blurbs of the Notre Dame campus sites. You won't find much in there about the bad times. You would, however, on page three, under the headline "Irish Football Boasts Unmatched Record of Success, History and Tradition," which is printed right at the beginning of every season's media guide, find an abstract of the program's celebrated achievements. Stacked there altogether in the same spread, they might have produced a goose-bump tingle in readers of Notre Dame bent, which was certainly the aim. Eleven consensus national championships, more than any other team. Seven Heisman Trophy winners, more than any other team. Thirty unanimous first-team all-Americans, more than any other team; 177 total all-Americans, ditto. Forty college-football hall-of-fame inductees, more than any other team; ten NFL hall-of-fame inductees, tied with archrival Southern Cal for the most of any college team. Five hall-of-fame head coaches, more than any other team. A total winning percentage of .746, the highest for any college team—at least at the time of the *Media Guide*'s publication.

Although certainly impressive, this numerical litany did not alone add up to what is known as the Notre Dame *mystique,* the word most often used to describe the team and the university's uncommon allure. Coined in 1891, younger than Notre Dame's football team by four years, the word has become the linchpin of the Notre Dame Brand. More than anything else, the Notre Dame Mystique involves Catholicism, the university's status as a sacred place, and the ways in which a winning football team seemed to prove, or at the very least enhance, the rightness of the school's religious dedication.

For decades, part of the Notre Dame Mystique had revolved around the idea that the team had won at the highest levels without also submerging itself into the sump bog of college-football malfeasance. Compete at the highest levels in football without cheating or otherwise rendering *student-athlete* an outright oxymoron, and prove to the world that such an endeavor was possible. There was a religious component to this, of course. Notre Dame had become the "conscience," the "moral compass" of intercollegiate athletics, and both the university and its fans were often criticized, and hated, for being righteous, arrogant, hypocritical, and sanctimonious. But their identity as Notre Dame fans had found its source in just this kind of Christian ethic.

Notre Dame's publicity people, however, shied away from any direct reference to religion when talking about mystique. They preferred a more secular understanding. Hyperaware of its function as a "branding opportunity," in the lexicon of modern PR, the *Media Guide* had a blurb ready to attempt a definition of the Notre Dame Mystique, under the label "Intangibles." It said, "Maybe the most prominent characteristic of Irish athletes and teams has been their indomitable spirit. As former Irish quarterback Joe Theismann once said, 'If you could find a way to bottle the Notre Dame spirit, you could light up the universe.' "

But lately that spirit seemed unfit for a bottling line, and lately the margins of that "unmatched record" had been eroding. Streaks were forming that would not find coverage anywhere in the *Media Guide*. Taken as a body of work, the last decade had amounted to a sequence of failures and humiliations unprecedented in the university's sporting past. In terms of purely wins and losses, it was actually better than the other decade-long stretch of piss-poor football in the school's history, the ten years between 1954 and 1964, bookended by Frank Leahy's departure and Ara Parseghian's arrival, two coaches, two multiple-title winners, now bronzed in the Fighting Irish pantheon. Over that midcentury span, the team had amassed a .515 winning percentage, including three losing seasons (2-8, 2-8, 2-7) and three break-even seasons—which, at Notre Dame, then as now, are tantamount to losing seasons. First Terry Brennan and then Joe Kuharich and then interim figure Hugh Devore (who took over for Kuharich after his resignation and served only a year in 1963) coached the Irish during this span. If ever the death of Notre Dame football seemed imminent, it was in the early 1960s. But, in this case, the dead did not rise slowly. The university hired Parseghian in 1964, and in that year he promptly went 9-1, resurrecting the team, founding his legend, and furthering the concept of the Messiah Coach, the Savior Coach, the Chosen One, who would lead Notre Dame back to where it belonged, the Promised Land of the national championship.

By comparison, from 1994 to 2003, Notre Dame had a .632 winning percentage, somewhere in between the program's historical win rate of .746 and the true mediocrity of the Brennan-Kuharich-Devore era. Still, the parallels were in place. Three losing seasons (5-6, 5-7, 5-7) in five years, including 2003. To put that in perspective, prior to those three seasons, the Irish had a total of seven losing seasons *since 1892.* Fifteen years had passed since the last national title, in 1988, Holtz's one and only. Sixteen years marked the longest championship drought the Irish had ever withstood—from Leahy's last in 1949 and Parseghian's first in 1966. Five times since 1993 Notre Dame had ended the season unranked, out of the top twenty-five. Six times between Leahy's departure and Parseghian's arrival did ND finish the year with the same fate. The first defeat of more than twenty points at the hands of an unranked opponent since 1960 occurred in 2003, against Syracuse, when by all accounts Notre Dame's players surrendered late in the third quarter, the defense limp-arming tackles and the offense standing around watching as Orange defenders waltzed through their nonblocks. The Irish lost 38–12. By chance, I watched that game at a bar in Chicago with Larry Conjar, a star fullback under Parseghian in the middle 1960s, now a real estate developer out of Evanston, Illinois. As a player he was revered by fans for his wild-man intensity. Toward the middle of the fourth quarter, he quit watching. He said he felt physically ill.

This was Willingham's latest contribution to the expanding anthology of decline. There were other indicators as well. Notre Dame had not won a bowl game since January 1994, and under Willingham, the team had been shut out and defeated by scores in excess of thirty

points three times, twice in 2003 alone, more than during any one season in ninety-nine years. To many fans, Notre Dame indeed seemed
jinxed. In retrospect, searching for origin myths, people pointed to a
single game.

Late afternoon, November 20, 1993. Twilight has fallen, and the
Irish defense has gone into prevent. A week earlier, second-ranked underdog Notre Dame had defeated the No. 1 team in the nation, Florida
State University, at home in ND Stadium, in what was billed as yet another Game of the Century. The hype was such that, according to
Nielsen, 50 million people tuned in to NBC. Florida State was said to
be unbeatable, perhaps the best college team of all time. The Sunday
after Notre Dame's victory, a huge sign in the shape of the numeral 1
with lightbulbs all around it lit up on the roof of Grace Hall, a high-rise
dorm on campus. Students mobbed outside the dorm to watch the
thing ignite, like the New Year's crowd in Times Square. This was the
last time Notre Dame was ranked number one in the country, and it
lasted seven days. For those seven days, a twelfth national championship appeared imminent, with one game left in the season, against
Boston College, a team rather new to the schedule, an afterthought
team that Notre Dame had disemboweled a year earlier, 54–7. Saturday
afternoon arrives and I'm in the student section, a freshman, half-
drunk on the liquor someone smuggled into the stadium, and half-
drunk, like everyone else, on euphoria. There's delirium up here in the
student section. Notre Dame has apparently iced its win against
Boston College, having miraculously awoken from a twenty-one point
deficit, madly scoring in the fourth quarter to take the lead. Through
two-thirds of the game, Notre Dame played lifeless football, no doubt
having decided to take a little time off against this jejune opponent
after last week's rousing victory against the best team of all time. The
lead is one point, 39–38. Less than a minute is left in the game. After its
go-ahead touchdown, Notre Dame kicks off. Down the field Boston
College moves the ball, a swing pass, an out pattern, complete and
complete. The prevent defense yields its yards. Almost without anyone noticing, BC achieves field-goal range. Five seconds remaining.
The lasting image I have of the game comes from this last drive of BC's.
A Notre Dame linebacker named Pete Bercich leaps and stretches for a
poorly thrown pass, his arms up, raised high, his hands forming a kind

of cup, and the ball noses softly into the cup, and the students are climbing up onto one another's back, mouths wide-open, a deep, silent shriek seizing everyone inside the moment, anticipating victory and the end of this lunacy and the all-out V-day drinking that's about to occur, and the ball somehow dislodges from Bercich's hands and falls to the ground, and the BC kick goes into the air and through the up-rights, and Notre Dame football has never been the same.

That's the origin myth, anyway. All of it—the prevent defense, which "prevents winning," as the saying goes, the lackluster play for two-thirds of the game, the dropped interception by poor Pete Bercich, whose name lives in near–Bill Buckneresque infamy (though touched with sadness rather than rancor), the inexplicable collapse on the verge of triumph and greatness. The next year, Notre Dame went 6-4-1, at the time a record of unfathomable tragedy. Three years later, after the 1996 season, Lou Holtz would resign—Holtz, yet another Messiah Coach, who had resurrected the team after a relatively brief five-year stint of mediocrity under Gerry Faust—Holtz, the final head-coaching hire of Fr. Theodore Hesburgh, CSC, the celebrated Notre Dame presi-dent—Holtz, who had led the team to its last national title in 1988—Holtz, the motivational mastermind—Holtz, the small, elderly-looking man with the highly imitable lisp and the self-deprecating charm—Holtz, the most famous football coach in America, with the appear-ance of a person whose only athletic ability may have been mowing lawns, a line he may or may not have used himself—Holtz, the Fight-ing Irish fan since birth, the Catholic subway alumnus with the Notre Dame out-clause built into all of his previous head-coaching con-tracts—deified, glorified, larger-than-life Holtz.

Holtz "got it." To really achieve the pantheon of Notre Dame leg-end, a man must "get it," a phrase coined and used by Notre Dame fans as a historical gauge of coaching success. Dan Devine, for instance, who followed Parseghian, won a national championship in 1977 and had a winning percentage one thousandth of a point worse than Holtz's. In the minds of Notre Dame fans, however, he failed to "get it." No real definition exists, but as best as I can surmise, it combines a rev-erence for Notre Dame as deep and loyal as any subway alumnus's and a whole lot of winning. But more than that, it's a recognition of how these two things are connected, and an ability to communicate the idea with the charisma of a Churchill. Dan Devine seemed to have deficiencies in his passion for the school. Faust, also a devout Catholic and a subway alum, known to urge his players and assistant coaches to pray Hail Marys on the sidelines for third-down conversions, to no good effect, had major deficiencies in the winning category. Holtz did not. For "getting it," he perhaps set the all-time standard. Holtz once made a preseason speech to his players that, luckily for Notre Dame fandom, someone recorded. A portion of it reads:

> It's important that I express my thoughts about this university— which you may or may not agree with. This school was founded by Father Sorin in 1842. It was founded as a tribute to Our Lady on the Dome. I believe the overwhelming majority of our football team believes in Jesus Christ. We may have some whose religious beliefs are such that they do not recognize Jesus Christ. That's fine. I don't wish to change anybody's religion or philosophy.
>
> But this school was built as a tribute to the Blessed Virgin, the mother of Jesus Christ. I firmly believe that if you really look at this school, you realize it has been blessed. The people who attend this school are blessed. Father Sorin said it best in 1842. "I've raised Our Lady aloft so that men will know, without asking, why we have succeeded here. All they have to do is look high on the Golden Dome and they'll find the answer."
>
> When we do what is right, we bring glory and honor to Notre Dame. When we win in football, we help this university. To reach our potential, you must learn to love this university. Put your faith, confidence, and belief in Jesus. That is what this university is all about. It's your decision, but I firmly believe that Our Lady on the Dome will watch out for you. Spend some time at the Grotto and you'll discover that this school is special. There is a special mystique about it. You are special for being here, a student at Notre Dame.

The speech was delivered before the start of winter conditioning, 1988 (and published in the first chapter of *The Fighting Spirit*, Holtz's account of that season's title run). No wonder the fans nearly worshiped the man. As his audience extended from his players in that meeting room out to Notre Dame fandom as a whole, he was preaching to the converted.

Like this speech, much of the minutiae and detail of Holtz's career at Notre Dame, his rise with the team, his peak in the early nineties, his decline and ultimate resignation, has trickled out into the Notre Dame fan community like a set of fables.

Many of Holtz's problems—and, by extension, the seeds of the ten-year decline—can be traced back to 1991. When he arrived at Notre Dame from the University of Minnesota in 1986, his Notre Dame out-clause at last put into effect, he brought along with him a young, ambitious graduate assistant named Vincent "Vinny" Cerrato. Not that much older than a college student himself, Cerrato had a chunk of dark, back-swept hair and a photogenic smile and a verbal dexterity nearly as acute as his boss's. Cerrato had the gift of sales. Traveling the country and paying visits to the best high school athletes in the nation, Cerrato would always be closing. He was Notre Dame's recruiting co-ordinator, he was hated by the staffs of opposing teams, and he became so good at his job that the NCAA created rules in response. Most fa-mously, from the sidelines of the 1990 Orange Bowl, he spoke with re-cruits over a giant early-generation cell phone—you could be here too. It is a practice that the NCAA has since outlawed.

For four consecutive years, 1987 through 1990, Cerrato at Notre Dame assembled the nation's No. 1 recruiting class, according to the sporting publications that rank such things. Nine of those recruits ended up as first-round NFL draft picks, ten ended up in the second round, and forty-six were drafted overall. At least one is a lock for the Canton Hall of Fame—Jerome Bettis of the Pittsburgh Steelers. The day after signing day, Cerrato would fly to Florida, where, at the home of a Notre Dame alumnus, he would lounge in the pool and conduct con-gratulatory interviews with sportswriters from around the country. And get started on the next year's recruiting. From 1988 through 1993, Notre Dame had a record of 64-9-1, including one undefeated season and three one-loss seasons, and if you ask Notre Dame fans, they'll say their team was robbed of two additional championships in those days when the title rested solely in the hands of the human polls, poisoned with anti-Catholic, anti–Notre Dame bias.

Cerrato's role in this near-dynasty was unmistakable. In 1991,

however, he and Holtz ran into some trouble with the admissions department. By many accounts, a territorial war had developed along
age-old lines—athletic department vs. academe. Some may have felt
that Cerrato and Holtz held too much sway, offering scholarships to
athletes without first consulting anyone at admissions. To this day, on
campus Cerrato has an unseemly reputation. Officials will wince at the
mere mention of his name as if confronting some malignant sin they've
yet to come to terms with. One priest described him to me as "the Dark
Side." The perception seems to be that Cerrato recruited boys of lesser
"character" than Notre Dame was accustomed to—"thugs" as people
like to say—and that Cerrato was interested in athletic ability only, as
if the two were mutually exclusive. In any student body, students fail
for a variety of reasons, and in the Holtz years that rate of failure was
neither higher nor lower than in any other period under any other
coach, and always among the best in the country. Outside of campus,
among the fans, Cerrato is generally looked upon as one of Holtz's
minor heroes, and every once in a while the rumors will fly, based
purely on hope, that Cerrato is returning to recruit again for Notre
Dame. But, in reality, that would never happen. He made some ene-
mies in the Main Building as well as the athletic department. Rumor
has it that Monk Malloy may have unofficially banned him from campus. It all came to a head in the winter of 1990–91, when admissions
went on a "purge," as some have called it, nixing for scholastic reasons
a host of world-beater recruits that Cerrato had lined up. This resulted
in a less-than-Cerratonian class, and, not long thereafter, the recruiting
coordinator departed from the university. He became a talent scout for
the 49ers, owned at the time by Eddie DeBartolo, Notre Dame class of
1968. Those players from the purge year would come of age in 1994,
the year the Irish achieved that lackluster 6-4-1 record. This marked
the true beginning of the long haul.

Meanwhile, as admissions did battle with Cerrato, it was well-
known on campus that two reporters were nosing around, making inquiries. Douglas Looney, a *Sports Illustrated* reporter, and Don Yaeger,
a career ghostwriter of sportsmen's autobiographies, published a book
in September 1993, before the start of the season that would end with
the loss to Boston College. Deploying that hoariest of all anti–Notre
Dame metaphors, it was entitled *Under the Tarnished Dome: How*

Notre Dame Betrayed Its Ideals for Football Glory (a Simon & Schuster title, same as this one), and it is a text about as reviled by Notre Dame fans as the *Satanic Verses* is in certain quarters of Islam. Safe to say that it did not receive the imprimatur. It inspired, instead, a figurative book burning. An indictment of the Notre Dame football program under Holtz, it involved a host of allegations, the most important being that the coach had permitted steroid use—despite the fact that Notre Dame appeared to have had a rigorous drug-testing policy in place, beyond what the NCAA required. The book was roundly critiqued in an article entitled "Tarnished Pen," published in *Forbes Media Critic,* a quarterly media–watchdog magazine. The article maintained that Yaeger and Looney had based their findings almost solely on interviews with former players who had been kicked off the team and expelled from school for one reason or another, including, indeed, for failing random drug tests. None of this mattered, though, when the book went best-seller and was the subject of an entire episode of *Nightline* with Ted Koppel. Looney, in his own contribution to the acknowledgments page, admits that he had previously had a deal with Holtz to cowrite a Notre Dame book in the rah-rah genre. But Holtz backed out, and the book drips with a strangely vitriolic rhetoric, thick with the patina of resentment. Notre Dame is widely hated, along the same lines as the New York Yankees, though with an added dash of vestigial anti-Catholism, and *Tarnished Dome* represents the paragon of anti–Notre Dame tracts—and anti–Notre Dame tracts sell.

It must be said that Holtz did have a somewhat compromised reputation coming out of his other college head-coaching jobs, at Arkansas and Minnesota, both of which underwent NCAA sanctions after he left, and some on campus at Notre Dame felt that Holtz's ambitions led to the recruitment of players who did not "fit" at the university. And all of this—the supposed fiefdom Holtz had erected over in the football offices, Yaeger and Looney's hostile screed, Holtz's expanding celebrity—caused unknown hours of heightened discomfort up on the fourth floor of the Main Building, inside the university's uppermost administrative offices. Holtz, some people felt, had become "bigger than Notre Dame," a notion that Holtz himself denied many times in that very language—"I'm not bigger than Notre Dame"—thereby reinforcing it. Holtz, many believed, had achieved the cult of

personality. Control was allegedly retracted, especially when it came
to the players Holtz could recruit. A new athletic director came into office in 1995, a strange hire, since he had no previous experience in collegiate athletics administration. His name was Mike Wadsworth, he
had played football under Parseghian, and he had pursued a heteroge-
neous career. He had been a player in the Canadian Football League, a
sports columnist, a trial lawyer, a corporate executive with a Harvard
MBA, and the Canadian ambassador to Ireland. Among Monk Malloy's
appointees, the most prominent were Wadsworth and executive vice
president Fr. William Beauchamp, whose duties included the oversight of athletics. Together he and Wadsworth were said to have
created an unfriendly atmosphere within the entire athletic department—money-grubbing, parsimonious, cold, in allegiance with only
the bottom line. Perhaps following instructions that had come down
from on high, Wadsworth allegedly told Holtz in 1995 that he needed
to start recruiting student-athletes who better fit the Notre Dame
"mold."

Event into gossip into legend, an anecdote has made the rounds:
As Holtz lost support among his bosses in the athletic department as
well as the Main Building, he became frustrated and he would walk
into Wadsworth's office every so often and half-jokingly toss his
keys—to his own office, to the practice field, to the locker room inside
Notre Dame Stadium—onto Wadsworth's desk. I'm finished, it's over,
I'm done, Holtz would say. Oh, c'mon, Lou, it's not that bad, Wadsworth would reply, and the keys would fly back toward the coach. This
happened again and again until Holtz one day performed his histrion-
ics, expecting the same response out of Wadsworth. The keys remained on the desk. A few days or weeks later, depending on the
storyteller, Holtz officially resigned. After the penultimate game of his
Notre Dame career, in November 1996, reporters asked him about rumors of his impending resignation. He used one of his favorite lines,
which seems to have been a paraphrase of Winston Churchill. "If you
want to know something, don't ask the monkey. Ask the organ grinder.
I'm just a guy at the end of the chain. Other people play the music; I
dance and pass the cup around."

Holtz never really gave a reason for his decision to quit, leaving an
empty mold of ambiguity into which the fans poured the contents of

the story. It has been said, for instance, that if Notre Dame had made Holtz some kind of verbal overture of support, he would have stayed. For the rest of his life Wadsworth would carry the burden of being the man who forced out Lou Holtz, at least in the eyes of the fans. At the time of Holtz's retirement and over the next few years, Wadsworth would state again and again that he had made it clear to the coach that he could stay at Notre Dame as long as he wanted. No one really believed him. In April 2004, a few days after the annual spring Blue & Gold Game, Wadsworth died. He was sixty years old.

There's a joke, a bit of braggadocio, that Notre Dame fans like to tell. The three most difficult jobs in the world rank in this way: president of the United States, mayor of New York City, and head football coach at the University of Notre Dame. Undeniably, like all other successful coaches in the school's history, Holtz had exhausted himself under the celebrated stress of the job. A year before resigning, he had undergone surgery to relieve pressure on his spinal cord—a kind of medical metaphor for the rigors of coaching at Notre Dame. Parseghian popped prescription pills, and his doctors had to instruct him to retire. Twice Leahy collapsed in the locker room during halftime. Friends and colleagues essentially performed an intervention to convince him to quit. Rockne suffered from a blood clot in his leg that almost killed him. He coached from a wheelchair. Fandom's demands take a physical toll. In the spring of 1997, a farewell banquet for Holtz was put together. It was called *Roast the Coach*. Regis Philbin emceed. Speakers included Father Joyce and Bill Clinton, in a videotaped message from the Oval Office. Per roast protocol, Holtz got the last word. His remarks, most of which came across almost as a homily, closed in un-homily-like fashion: "When they get ready to bury me, I hope they bury me at Notre Dame—just like the alumni been doing every Saturday. Thank you very much."

For all intents and purposes, it seems that Notre Dame conducted no real outside search for Holtz's successor. They took a brief look at Gary Barnett, then the coach at Northwestern, but a conversation with Gary Barnett convinced Notre Dame that it would be best if Barnett remained at Northwestern. Bob Davie, defensive coordinator under Holtz, hired by Holtz out of Texas A&M in 1994, was viewed as the safe choice, a man whose personality would not very likely lead to a cult, a man whom the administration felt they could keep under control. The fans received his introduction even more tepidly than they would Willingham's. Davie had no head-coaching experience. He had no perceptible affection for the university—the gravest sin next to losing. Groomed at A&M under R. C. Slocum, he cited Aggie traditions rather than Irish. In all ways he failed to "get it," and the fans turned on him almost immediately. The day before his head-coaching debut against Georgia Tech, he gave an oration to a crowd of twenty-five thousand fans inside Notre Dame Stadium, which had recently been expanded to eighty thousand seats from about sixty thousand. A giant shell now entombed the old stadium, the House that Rockne Built, an act, some felt, of architectural vandalism. His voice echoing into the stands, Davie declared, "This is the start of a new era," and the fans, thinking of Holtz, reacted with a collective groan. Davie would prove himself true.

If Notre Dame's leadership felt it could avoid football-related embarrassments with Holtz no longer heading the program, they were wrong. By the end of Holtz's tenure, the football office had become a rather insidious place, a pit of vipers, full of finks and moles and backstabbers and as infighting as Rome in full-blown decline. It all gradually emerged in campus gossip, then quickly emerged in public testimony under oath a year later, in July 1998, when a lawsuit filed by Joe Moore, Holtz's longtime offensive-line coach, came to trial. A chain-smoking drill sergeant of the old school, not afraid to punch an underachieving player in the chops to the point of bloody lips, Moore was another of Holtz's minor heroes, venerated by the fans as perhaps one of the best line coaches the world has ever known. Moore had recommended Bob Davie to Holtz, and Moore was subsequently fired by Bob Davie. At the time Moore was 64 years old, and his effectiveness as a coach may legitimately have waned; Holtz and Moore were reportedly not on the best of terms, either. But the plaintiff's attorneys had as their star witness an offensive lineman, still on the team, who testified that Davie had indeed told the team that Moore was too old for the job—the smoking gun. That the university didn't settle out of court causes bafflement all over campus to this day. In the event, many Notre Dame fans sided with Moore against the very institution that is the source of their fanaticism. Five days of testimony from coaches and players and athletic department functionaries unleashed an inventory of sordid facts all over the news media, not the least of which was what many people interpreted as the internal politicking of Bob Davie. Testimony revealed that, at one point in Holtz's ND career, Davie questioned his boss's mental stability. Moore won the trial, though he received just $86,000 of the $1.3 million his suit had sought. (He went back to high school football and died in July 2003.) From the courthouse steps, microphones and tape recorders thrust in his face, Mike Wadsworth stated the obvious: "It's not one of our proudest moments."

Pride was about to leave the premises altogether. At about the time of the trial, letters were going back and forth between various offices at Notre Dame and the headquarters of the National Collegiate Athletic Association. The university's first ever sanctions at the hands of the NCAA were about to come to light, the result of a vulgar and rather absurd affair all flowing from a twenty-eight-year-old woman overeager for the attentions of football players. A jock-sniffer, as the saying goes, her name was Kim Dunbar and she embezzled a million dollars from her employer (for which she eventually went to jail) and used a portion of her earnings to fly the players to Las Vegas for Holyfield-Tyson fights and to give them such gifts as a $5,000 charm necklace. She eventually had a child by one of the players. Because she had paid $25 in fees to become a member of the Quarterback Club, a low-grade booster outfit that hosted the luncheon on home-game Fridays, she was also, technically, "a representative of the university's athletics interests," in the language of the NCAA. Over a three-year span, from 1995 through early 1998, Dunbar broke rules prohibiting boosters from giving gifts to players. The NCAA deemed the affair a "major violation," the university elected not to appeal (many believe that the NCAA's charges were trumped-up, and certainly not "major," and therefore a decent attorney could have defeated the sanctions), and the NCAA placed Notre Dame on two years' "probation"—a penalty that amounted to one football scholarship subtracted in each of those years. As a result, the university abolished the club and all other boosterlike organizations.

Because Notre Dame had long attempted to stake out a place on the moral high ground of collegiate athletics, the sanctions came as an acute embarrassment. News of the NCAA's judgment went scrolling across the digital zipper in Times Square, and heads rolled on campus. Mike Wadsworth lost his job. Fr. William Beauchamp, executive vice president, lost his oversight over athletic affairs, and Father Malloy took control. Eventually, the religious leaders of the Holy Cross congregation would transfer Beauchamp out of Notre Dame completely, to teach at another Holy Cross–owned institution, the University of Portland, in Oregon, long the place of traditional banishment whenever a CSC priest has somehow failed.

The penalty of two lost scholarships could have been worse. It was meant to blunt the "competitive advantage" the Irish had gained by playing athletes that would otherwise have been ineligible, but competitive advantage under Bob Davie was a rather rhetorical concept. In his third year, the same year that Leahy, Parseghian, and Holtz had all won their first national championships, Davie went 5-7. In his fourth year, 2000, his team went on a win streak, finishing the season with seven straight victories against Notre Dame's weakest schedule in recent memory. Kevin White, the new athletic director, rewarded Davie with a five-year contract extension. The fans and alumni howled their disapproval. This was several weeks before Notre Dame played Oregon State in the Fiesta Bowl, which Notre Dame lost 41–9—a game now known, unofficially of course, as the Fiasco Bowl. A month after his contract extension, Davie was put on notice. And at the end of his fifth year, a 5–6 campaign, he was fired, much to the satisfaction of the Notre Dame fan base.

He was replaced by George O'Leary, who now ranks as the briefest head coach in Notre Dame history. He lasted in office about five days. Born and raised Irish-Catholic on Long Island, another subway alumnus coach with a Notre Dame out-clause, O'Leary had been head man at Georgia Tech, where he had achieved decent success. A platoon of Notre Dame representatives had flown to Atlanta to interview O'Leary, yet no one thought to double-check the last page of his curriculum vitae. Hoopla surrounded the announcement of his hiring. A pep rally took place in the Joyce Center basketball arena, attended by students and high Notre Dame functionaries and the marching band blaring the "Victory March." In a rhetorical shank that he must now gravely rue, Kevin White said, "He's right out of central casting." T-shirts were printed and distributed that said BY GEORGE, IT'S O'LEARY!—which are

now collector's items in the vein of erratum baseball cards. He resigned in shame after bird-dogging sports reporters from the *New
Hampshire Union Leader* and the *Eagle-Tribune* (Lawrence, Massachusetts) began making inquiries into O'Leary's varsity-letter playing
days at the University of New Hampshire, and discovered that the
coach, in fact, had enjoyed no playing days. More damningly, a
master's degree in education from New York University also proved
fictitious. While O'Leary attempted to recede from public scrutiny,
while the derisory headlines unspooled over every media outlet, Notre
Dame had to scramble for another head coach.

Yet another disaster, and Notre Dame fans everywhere were asking, when would this all end? Eight years of humiliation, public-
relations calamity, internal backbiting, historically dreadful football,
and expanding fan discontent—from Tarnished Domes through NCAA
sanctions through résumé doctoring and an apparent dearth of competence at the highest levels. Mystique had given way to an almost programmatic mortification. The brand had taken a hit. The press reports
were all the same—football's "glamour" gig no longer, who would
want the job? At the time, in many people's eyes, Tyrone Willingham
came to the rescue. This time around, Kevin White was a little less ef-
fusive. At Willingham's introductory press conference he said, "I'm
proud of the football coach we just hired. I realize we've got a lot to
prove."

3

Call for Change

Four head coaches, three athletic directors, two executive vice presidents, and countless numbers of understaff had all done time in the Notre Dame hierarchy through those ten years, but one man alone oversaw the whole long parade of misfortune. Fr. Edward "Monk" Malloy, CSC, president of the university since 1987, had had the unenviable task of succeeding the legend. Johnson after Lincoln, Johnson after Kennedy—Malloy had to work from under the long, deep shadow of Fr. Theodore Hesburgh, who reigned over Notre Dame for thirty-five years and transformed the university from a parochial college with a powerhouse football team and a few decent academic departments into an institution of international caliber. He had help from another Notre Dame legend, Fr. Edmund Joyce, whose name was applied to the edifice that houses the basketball arena. As Hesburgh's executive vice president, Joyce had absolute domain over Notre Dame athletics from Leahy's last years through Holtz's first.

When he fired athletic director Mike Wadsworth in early 2000 in the wake of the NCAA sanctions, Malloy, attempting to do the deed gracefully, said, "There is no denying that problems often lead to accomplishments being overlooked." The same observation could be applied to the president himself. Right or wrong, he had become by the end of his tenure in the fall of 2004 perhaps the most vilified university president in the history of Notre Dame. The sentiment was widely held among Malloy's most vocal constituencies, the football-fan alumni and the subway alumni, but he had also encountered problems with the faculty and the student body. And, according to campus rumor, he had a strained relationship with Hesburgh himself—some insiders claimed that Malloy's administration had kept Hesburgh unreasonably out of the loop.

In August 2004, as Willingham's team started fall training camp, Malloy was a lame-duck president. He had occupied the office for seventeen years, and as the football program flopped about for more than half his presidency, the university as graded by debits and credits had expanded like an unusually acquisitive corporation—an operating budget that had risen from $173 million in his first year to $700 million in 2004; an endowment with gains of 558 percent, $456 million to a little over $3 billion. (Income from football constituted but a fraction of this intake.) It was, by far, the richest Catholic university in the world. But these were the footnotes to Malloy's career, framed in the sidebars that were annexed to nearly every story published in the aftermath of his resignation. There were other, worthier accomplishments, what money will buy you, not the least of which was an ever-improving faculty. But the facts flowing from the football offices and football fields remained in black and white, and for better or worse these were the most public and the most scrutinized of any of the university's endeavors. Such is the ancient dilemma of a school that in many ways originated the business of college athletics. "It may be amusing to speculate how the university's history might have been different without the phenomenon of football," Malloy said in a public address in October 1993, when the team was ranked No. 2 in the nation, "but I for one am happy to accept the legacy as is."

That, of course, was before the ten-year decline had begun. After it had begun, he talked a lot about sin and resurrection. When the NCAA probation came down, after Malloy had assumed control over the athletic department, he gave a series of interviews to the press. To a beat writer named Joe Tybor, who had started the first subscription Web site dedicated to Notre Dame football, Malloy said, "One of the things I say is, I'm a priest, I'm an ethicist, and I'm a confessor. And I deal with human failings, including my own, and sinfulness all the time. I never imagined that any person or institution is immune from sinfulness and human error, and I think we discovered in this particular set of events a need for atonement and for a spirit of repentance that things have gone wrong. And that members of our community have violated our sense of what we want to hold each other to. Having said that, I also believe in Easter. There's a Good Friday, but there's also an Easter."

By the start of the 2004 football season, Malloy was already sharing duties with his successor, Fr. John Ignatius Jenkins, CSC, a condition that would last until the official handoff of power on July 1, 2005. According to the university information office, the two were getting along amicably, with Jenkins playing understudy, traveling the country and learning to glad-hand with high-grade donors to keep that endowment humming along.

But the campus was still abuzz with the events of May 2004, when Malloy had announced his retirement. The exact terminology used to describe his exit was open to interpretation. He had asked the board of trustees, a fifty-seven-person body, to review his presidential performance and come to a decision about his fate. His public remarks made it seem as if he could take it or leave it. "I have no idea myself how it'll go," he told the *Observer,* Notre Dame's student newspaper. "I'm happy with whatever the outcome is." He would, in other words, have been more than happy to stay. Because no unanimous successor had surfaced, it was fairly well-known that, despite his ambivalent public stance, the president wished to remain in office another five years.

Malloy's remarks to the *Observer* went to print on Friday, April 23, a week before the trustees collected on campus for their three-day quarterly meeting. Malloy's head was on the docket. The week passed. The private jets landed. The dark SUVs rolled in from the airport and their passengers debarked outside the Morris Inn. Patrick McCartan, Andrew McKenna, Fritz Duda, Philip Purcell, Joseph O'Neill III, Dick Notebeart, J. W. Jordan, the big shots, the men whose names were etched into the facades of dormitories and classroom buildings, the Fortune 500 chief executives, the managing partners of thousand-lawyer law firms, the multimillionaires. On Wednesday night, a series of premeeting meetings took place in huddles in discreet corners of the lobby or up in the expansive corner suites of the Morris Inn. The first official sessions convened the next morning, and sometime on Thursday, twenty-four hours later, Malloy informed the board that he would "step down," as the press releases termed it.

This was something of a shift from his idea of a week earlier, to go ahead and let the board thrash it all out, highlight the pros, grumble over the cons, and come to a reasoned conclusion. "While Malloy believes the decision will be announced in upcoming weeks, he said he was uncertain whether the board would deliver its decision at the

April 29–30 trustee meeting," the *Observer* had reported. Now, evidently, Monk had made the decision. The university PR office did not release the news until Friday the thirtieth, and it coupled the news with further news—the announcement of Malloy's successor, Father Jenkins. In the ensuing press conference, Malloy said he had undergone an extended period of "discernment." He had prayed. He had sought advice from "a variety of individuals," a group of advisers that may or may not have included some of those private-jet big shots, who may or may not have communicated to Malloy some suggestions regarding his future. At his press conference, Malloy said, "Ultimately it was my decision," and he gave the floor to Jenkins. Patrick McCartan, chairman of the board of trustees, was, interestingly, not at the press conference.

But he did later comment on the situation to *Notre Dame Magazine*. According to McCartan, Father Malloy had informed the board, way back in the fall of 2003, that he'd *always* intended to step down at the end of his term—a piece of information that not only contradicted Malloy's statements to the *Observer,* but also seemed to render a little redundant the necessity of conducting a lengthy period of discernment in the weeks leading up to the April 2004 trustees' meeting.

What shocked everyone on campus, however, wasn't that Monk Malloy might have been denied another five years, but instead the swiftness with which the board had announced his replacement, and that the board had winnowed its candidate list—which university by-laws declare must contain Holy Cross priests and no one else—until only John Jenkins remained.

According to those who were handicapping the affair this time around, all the money, both smart and dumb, had been laid on David Tyson, the provincial of the Indiana Province of the Congregation of Holy Cross, the Congregation de Ste. Croix—CSC. In this position, which effectively had a term limit of six years, he gave the orders and issued the assignments to the priests of the community, and as such he was a kind of clerical dispatcher—you to the missions in Kampala, Uganda, you to head up the parish in Colorado Springs, you to teach mathematics at a Holy Cross preparatory school in suburban Chicago, you to get your Ph.D. because we might need you in the future to run several billion dollars' worth of Catholic university. He wielded the vow of obedience. He had been a university president already, at the University of Portland, and word had it that he knew how to handle a board full of trustees full of a lot of personal notions on how a university ought to be run.

Jenkins's CV, on the other hand, included a supremely rarefied education—three master's degrees and a doctorate in ancient and medieval philosophy, the last obtained at Oxford. It included a tenured position in the philosophy department, a lot of publishing rather than perishing in his field, and, in his most recent assignment, four years as an assistant provost. A good CV to be sure, but not one that approached David Tyson's. One Holy Cross priest said to me right after the election, "I'm sure he'll do fine, but I think it'll be hard for him. He's quiet. He's sort of an introvert."

It just so happened that in the days surrounding Monk's retirement, a number of other meaningful and mournful events occurred. A day before the trustees convened, Mike Wadsworth died at the Mayo Clinic. Two days after the trustees convened, Fr. Edmund Joyce, the master tactician, the old warrior who had, with Hesburgh, presided over the formation of a lay board of trustees, died in his sleep at eighty-seven years of age. Hundreds of mourners filled the Basilica for his funeral Mass. Monk gave the eulogy. Among other things he said, "Little did Ned know that he would spend most of his priestly ministry looking over accounting books and writing reports and running meetings and raising money and giving talks and doing what we would call administration. But the funny things is, if you go back and read Paul's first letter to the Corinthians, it talks about the different gifts of the spirit, and how the church or the body of Christ will prosper only when each is willing to give from the storehouse of the gift of the spirit—over which we have little control."

Up on the fourth floor of the Main Building, in the hall just outside the door to the Office of the President, No. 400, there hangs a full-length portrait of an aged priest, his hair steel gray, a white pocket square peaking from his black suit jacket. It is Fr. Ted Hesburgh, painted upon his retirement in 1987, and on his face is a small but imperious smile, as if he were contemplating the breadth of his conquered domains.

Through door No. 400, past a double-storied receiving room, inside an office neither large nor small, sits the lame-duck president. With its varnished cherrywood moldings and pediments and fanlights, with its blue, plush carpeting over floorboards that creak with age, it resembles the rooms of a junior congressman in the Longworth Building on Capitol Hill. He has skin pale as bathroom marble, made more so by his priestly blacks. He has a long, gaunt equine face and protuberant ears. On top of his head is a pure-white swatch of hair that matches without flaw the white of his Roman collar. When he moves he is stiff-backed, his spine like a flagpole, narrow shoulders resting high on the column. They appear to be permanently shrugged. He's as tall as his basketball-playing days would suggest—six foot three, shooting guard, fifty-five scholarship offers coming out of high school, in an era, 1959, when colleges were just beginning to involve themselves in tactical, organized draft-board recruiting. Tendonitis has lately crept into his shoulders, and this is the cause of his robotic deportment. It has also forced him to quit playing basketball. Twice a week for twenty years he conducted a famous late-hour pickup game, known across campus as Monk Hoops, in which he would go up against students who were, toward the end of Monk Hoops, a third his age. He had a quick release and excelled at the perimeter and took his shots only when the percentages were high. His controlled but physical court demeanor made him appear to be the kind of hustling player who seethed on the inside, a sentiment that expands into a description of his personality beyond the paint and among his closest observers, the brotherhood of the Holy Cross religious community.

"He's a low-key guy. You don't see it, but he hates to lose. *Hates* it. He hates to lose in *anything.*"

"Monk will never tell you how he feels. He may talk about his thought process, but never his feelings."

"He hates to lose, but he puts it in perspective. He doesn't show his emotions. Monk is so stoical—I swear, if a rabid dog were chewing on his leg, he'd say it doesn't hurt."

On the topic, Malloy has said before, "Emotionally I'm very much engaged in what's happening. But on the basis of my athletic experience, I do not manifest the kind of quick emotional response. Coach Willingham and I have a lot in common in that way."

It is widely believed that Malloy received his nickname while in the seminary, or as an undergraduate playing on the Notre Dame basketball team, because of his wan, withdrawn, methodical, prayerful, solitary, and possibly lonesome qualities—"monkish." But this is the result of a misunderstanding. The moniker dates to his grade-school salad days, when Malloy received the name from another kid on the block, "Bunk" Collins, for no other reason than "it rhymed with Bunk and was alliterative with Malloy," the president has explained before. "I like it. I never have tried to change it." Like dog owners who somehow come to resemble their pets, it is possible that Monk grew into his nickname.

His calling to a life in service to Jesus Christ came without epiphany in the kind of place generally reserved for the bolt of lightning, the explosive glimpse of Wisdom, the scales falling from the eyes—on top of a mountain, this one in Aguascalientes, in Mexico, at a pilgrimage shrine called Cristo Rey. He was twenty-one years old. It was the summer before his senior year at Notre Dame, and he was there on a service project. "For whatever set of reasons, on that mountaintop I had a calling. I didn't have any visions or hear any voices or anything. The only thing I can say was, I had an experience of a call." He has described it elsewhere as a "sense of certitude." Measured as that rugged terrain of interior Mexico is not, he decided on the mount that he should become a Holy Cross priest, the culmination of a long, deliberate process of thought, an inclination that had first presented itself in high school when he had decided upon Notre Dame. At that time he chose basketball instead of the seminary, but he chose to play it at a place where the religious vocational office recruited as hard as the sports teams.

Unlike many other Holy Cross priests, Malloy did not come from a family with Notre Dame connections—no alumni, no subway alumni anywhere in the tree. Malloy may have watched an Irish game on black-and-white TV once or twice as a boy; he can't quite remember. He had never seen the campus before his first recruiting visit. During the fall of his senior year in high school, he and a friend and their fathers drove to Pittsburgh to watch Notre Dame play Pitt. They camped on the outskirts of town. "But that was as much because it was a different sort of thing to do, with two fathers and two sons, than because it was specifically Notre Dame. I have no idea who won the game, for example." With eleven seconds on the clock, Pittsburgh kicked a field goal and Notre Dame lost.

Malloy's undergraduate years, 1959 to 1963, coincided with that first period of football malaise. This biographical detail has not escaped Malloy's detractors, who presume that his experience as an undergrad may have dampened his interest in winning football. Malloy himself likes to point to that period, but always in the context of the team's subsequent revival, almost as if in defense of the program's disappointments under his watch as president. Turnarounds are always imminent, he seems to be saying. "When I was here, we had the worst four years in Notre Dame football history, under Joe Kuharich. And I hate losing—but we never had a winning season in my four years as an undergraduate. Father Hesburgh was always being criticized for stressing academic excellence as a detriment to athletic success. But it didn't sour anybody. I mean, nobody left Notre Dame in my class, that I ever heard of, just because we weren't winning football games. They came, they loved the place, they regretted that we didn't win more games, and they had opinions about the coach. But they didn't think that was the end of the world, either."

Malloy, in his black shirtsleeves, is sitting in a straight-backed chair in the small living-room portion of his office. With few outward signs of emotion and fewer signs of the personal pressures involved, he has been considering the tensions that inhere in his job. His status as a fan is peculiar, bifurcated into public and private. He is both a fan and not. He cannot and will not comment publicly on his feelings toward the team's performance. To do so would be to make judgments on personnel that must, by institutional code, remain private. As the boss, he talks around the issue. He says, "There's a lot riding on it now. I mean, I pick the coaches, and I want to see the athletic program succeed. But, in the end, it's up to the players. I don't play the game. I can be happy when we win, I can kind of put it into perspective when we don't—since I have had some experience as an athlete. And I think I know a lot about football as a game. I follow the sport and I watch the games on television. I think I can tell you who the best programs are at any given moment, what kind of offense they run, what kind of defense. Which conferences are good and which aren't. I mean, I think I know the game pretty well. There are a lot of presidents who don't know anything about football."

He says, "If I didn't think it was possible for us to play national-championship-level football, I'd recommend that we get out of it. The lingering question is, what would satisfy the expectations? The winning records of Knute [he pronounced the name, correctly, "Ka-nute"] Rockne in the twenties and Frank Leahy in the forties have never been duplicated. Yet there are Notre Dame–related people who would expect to go undefeated and win every game by thirty points. When Ara was here, people would get down on him because we only won by ten points. Or the year he had no quarterback, they were unhappy about that. Or when they don't think the offense is interesting enough, or when the defense doesn't keep the other team from scoring. There are people whose expectations will never be met. Do I think we can have a consistently strong program and abide by our standards? Yes. And the criterion that I would apply is pretty consistently to be in the running. To win the national championship or play in the national-championship-equivalent game, you have to have everything come together for you in a given year. I guess I think it's possible, but . . . It's going to be a challenge. It's a different era in history."

Though at times he seems to have swallowed his personality whole, he occasionally exhibits a sense of humor almost Anglican in its drollery.

"What do you do on game day?"

"Which day is game day?" A dry Monk joke, delivered so drily you needed a drink.

He has said before, "Watching games on TV by myself I'm very vociferous. But that's not my style in public settings." He prefers to watch Notre Dame games alone, the better to focus his concentration on the proceedings. For the president of the university that the team represents, this is not often possible. Home-game weekends are essentially fund-raising drives and Malloy's role is to be everywhere, the face of Notre Dame to the Friends of the University, who fly in from all over to take in the idiosyncratic ball-game hoopla of the place to which they might be signing out checks. On home-game Saturdays, in a room in the South Dining Hall, Malloy hosts a brunch, closed to the public. An easel carries a sign that says PRIVATE UNIVERSITY FUNCTION. Between four hundred and five hundred people are in there scooping up eggs. "Honored guests," in the parlance of university development, they are trustees and members of advisory councils and large-scale benefactors, plus everyone's family and friends. By all accounts, Malloy does not enjoy these encounters, since, quid pro quo, the attention he must pay them means attention they must pay him. "If you ask me do I like fund-raising," he once told the *Indianapolis Star,* "the answer is no."

During the game, Malloy hosts a somewhat smaller group of honored guests inside the president's box, up on the fifth floor, the VIP level, in the stadium press-box superstructure that rises like a citadel high above the field. A plate on the door says PRESIDENT. Others with private boxes include Hesburgh (PRESIDENT EMERITUS), Patrick McCartan (CHAIRMAN, BOARD OF TRUSTEES), and Kevin White (ATHLETIC DIRECTOR). The windows to all of them are smoked glass, one-way. It's as if the stadium, the crowd, the players on the field, the game—the whole thing—is being interrogated. The president's enclosure is spacious but spartan, with a wall of glass overlooking the action, cantilevered out over the edge of the student section. Here after kickoff, the president sometimes bottles the conversation, corks the fund-raiser. "I'm very attentive to what's going on on the field during game time." He doesn't like to chat. There might be a dozen people in there. Malloy as a fan has been seen watching games with his hand on his chin. He is mostly wordless. He is ponderous. He folds his arms. "If Notre Dame isn't doing well, sometimes my box empties out." Since Notre Dame mostly hasn't been doing well, the visitors slowly leave, in pairs, one by one. Someone might approach the windows and flap open the casements to let in the crowd noise. The opposing team scores. Chill air moves inside if it's late in the season. More people leave—"Maybe they don't want to curse around me or get flustered or out of control. I don't know"—and the box finally empties completely of Malloy's constituents. The president is at last alone. A tree falling in the woods, no one else around, who knows what Monk Malloy does then?

When the news of Father Malloy's abdication became public, a banner headline went up on the fan Web site NDNation.com: HERE COME

THE IRISH. The news sent some portion of the Notre Dame fan population into raptures, none more so than the group of enthusiasts who
posted regularly on Rock's House, the football-specific message board
on ND Nation. It was as if the serfs had slain their overlord and taken to
the streets with pitchforks and ale. It was like Berlin in 1989. Many of
them saw Malloy as the enemy of not just football at Notre Dame, but
the enemy of Notre Dame. The debate had taken on something of a
Cold War cast, with ND Nation as the resistance. Left wing and right
wing—when football was the discourse there were no shades of gray.
Indeed, since the beginning of the Bob Davie years, ND Nation and the
university seemed almost to have staked out opposite sides of an ideo-
logical dialectic.

Malloy was aware of the phenomenon. On the subject of football,
he would later say in an address to the faculty in October 2004, "It's an
area where passion reigns extreme. And it's something we need to
keep in perspective." He had a term of his own for the Internet fan
community: the *mobocracy.*

Sometime during 2003, the mobocracy itself had bifurcated into
pessimists and optimists. They referred to themselves as Cassandras
and Pollyannas, the latter group still believing that Willingham could
turn things around at Notre Dame if given enough time. This was their
rallying cry: "He needs more time."

But by reading the boards and talking to alumni and fans, it was
easy to discern that a large number of them believed that Malloy had
placed one item above all others on his presidential to-do list: de-emphasize football. Evidence came from several directions, but it was almost all anecdotal. Malloy, for instance, went a little cold whenever
fans or alumni or benefactors queried him on the team's prospects. He
was known to redirect the conversation and use it as an opportunity to
describe Notre Dame's other endeavors. But Hesburgh was famous for
doing this as well—and, after all, one might expect such behavior from
any university president. Perhaps more tellingly, Malloy's administration seemed to exude an attitude of disinterest—that mediocre football
did not really concern them—and, the logic went, this attitude of disinterest led to all of the miscalculations of the previous ten years. It
was perhaps a matter less of designed "de-emphasis" than neglect. The
decision to fight the Moore lawsuit in court was said to be Malloy's de-

cision alone, for example. And the decision to kneel before the NCAA
and submit to its sanctions, ditto.

Much of the vitriol directed at Malloy seemed to erupt out of the
wider culture wars—fey, politically correct, relativist academe vs. la-
tently sexist, thug-machismo football. Malloy, of course, was allied
with academe. He and others in the administration had said that one of
their goals was to raise Notre Dame to the level of its "aspirational
peers," a common phrase in higher education but one that, among the
fans, had become tantamount to surrender.

They took it to mean that Notre Dame under Malloy pined to be
among the Stanfords of the world, with their big reputations and middling football, and that Malloy was pushing the university in the same
direction as many universities before it—Harvard and Yale and Princeton, for instance, which had renounced their football programs long
ago, making the conscious decision to let them fade into obsolescence.
A running joke from Irish fans amid the decline advocated a bold
move: if Notre Dame was looking to join a collegiate athletic conference, it ought to think big and make a bid for the Ivy League.

The fans sensed that Notre Dame, like many other colleges, had
grown to lust after the rankings of *U.S. News & World Report.* The university had been stationed at No. 18 for a number of years, tied with Vanderbilt. It is worth noting that only five other schools on the *U.S. News*
top-twenty list play Division I football—Duke, Stanford, Rice, Vanderbilt, and Northwestern—and none of them are any good at it. If Notre
Dame wished to continue its pursuit of elite-research-institution status,
a pursuit begun by Hesburgh in the 1950s and expanded in a major way
by Malloy, then for many fans it had become altogether unclear whether
elite football was compatible any longer with that pursuit. "We talk
about several different publics," Lou Nanni, Notre Dame's vice president of public affairs and communications, was quoted as saying to the
Observer in April 2002. "For example, how the alumni might perceive
Notre Dame football might be very different than how our aspirational
peer universities perceive football." A "disconnect," as one alumnus
described it, appeared to have developed between the Malloy administration and some portion of Notre Dame's alumni. It could also be described as a miscommunication. Lou Nanni, for instance, says his
words were misrepresented in the *Observer* article. A handful of peo-

ple, mostly alumni and including some benefactors, even complained to him about the quote. The article had made it seem as if Nanni and Notre Dame's leaders worried to a disproportionate degree about how outsiders viewed the university and its football. But the fans interpreted the *Observer* story—coupled with their experience of the ten-year decline—as a tacit admission that the sport had become nothing more than an irritant to the Malloy administration. It was almost as if, in a roomful of their Ivy League peers, Malloy and his crowd would be embarrassed by their football team—or so many fans came to believe. According to Nanni, nothing could have been further from the truth.

In the history of Notre Dame, this is an ancient conceit. Ever since the university had first become dominant at football under Knute Rockne in the 1920s, it is well-known that guilt over the success of the team had periodically beset the priests who ran the school. They braced at the reputation their school was acquiring. More than an institution of higher learning, Notre Dame was a "football factory." But fan and alumni intensity for the Irish being what it is, the administration had always relented, and the team had always bounced back.

Everyone knows that maintaining a winning football program today comes with high risk, both financially and in terms of reputation. Unseemly (or flat-out illicit) recruiting practices. Millions of dollars thrown at pursuit of a dubious value. The treatment of "student"-athletes as semipro chattel, used for their four-year eligibility and discarded without concern for what the institution ostensibly exists to do—educate. These are the old arguments against big-time college football, as old as the sport itself, and they remain valid today. To win big at football, the conventional wisdom goes, a college program must bend the rules and spend money and look for ways to make even more money. The Faustian deal must be struck. Therefore, if a college team wins a lot, people tend to assume the worst, and the school becomes tarred with that undesirable cognomen *football factory.*

Under Malloy, all of these concerns seemed to have risen to the surface once again. With its recent history of NCAA sanctions and the rest, perhaps Notre Dame no longer had the stomach to risk with its football what it had so far achieved in academic stature. And some people said, who could blame them?

On the other hand, Notre Dame had long had its credo, its motivating ideal—excellence in all pursuits. As one alumnus wrote on ND Nation, lamenting the ten-year decline, and hoping for a return to the Notre Dame of old, "We are academically excellent, unapologetically so. And we will continue to be the most unassailably clean football program in an increasingly rotting landscape: we will kick your ass on the gridiron, then shake your hand afterwards."

Malloy's regime had also come under fire for reasons not having to do with athletics—at least on the surface. Just as the Ivy League schools had shed their football programs, so had they long ago shed their religious affiliations and gone secular. It is worth noting, as well, that no institution in the *U.S. News* hierarchy has a meaningful religious identity. For decades, since at least Vatican II, many Notre Dame people feared this kind of secularization. It was an ancient and evergreen debate. Each year on campus, symposia and colloquia seemingly by the dozen reprised John Henry Newman and inquired again and again, "What constitutes a Catholic university?" This was an open and difficult question, but for many Notre Dame people, the secularists were almost always threatening the gates. Father Hesburgh steadfastly defended Notre Dame's academic freedom against the designs of Rome—which periodically moved to assert control over all Catholic universities—and so had Father Malloy. Radically non-Catholic professors were hired to teach in Notre Dame's academic departments, most controversially in theology and philosophy. Ecumenism at the school had run riot, some said. A traveling troupe performing *The Vagina Monologues* was permitted to monologue on campus. A homosexual film festival was approved for screening. Both brought censure from the local bishop, and therefore Rome. Notre Dame, the purists believed, had thus tacitly encouraged the moral desuetude of the secularists and had gone against the teachings of the Church. Examples such as these piled up, and the feeling in certain quarters was that Notre Dame was moving away from its roots—all in the hope of joining its elite "aspirational peers." Not every fan or alum who suffered because of the university's substandard football believed that Notre Dame was becoming "secular." But both issues raised a similar ire. Over time, traditional Catholicism and traditional powerhouse football had become allied in the minds of many fans and alumni. Both Catholic identity and elite football represented a traditional Notre

Dame, and any move that seemed to contradict either of these qualities indicated that the university's leaders were surrendering Notre Dame's core mission.

A rift had therefore widened between those who believed Notre Dame *required* a winning football program, and those who believed that what Notre Dame required was a football program that knew its place. It all came down to whether you believed this was a false dichotomy: superb football, superb athletics. Was it an either/or or a both/and? The official university party line still maintained that Notre Dame could do it all without any compromise. "The university is committed to excellence and success in all that we do," Monk Malloy wrote in an op-ed piece in the *New York Times* in April 2004. "We dearly want to win consistently in football. It is a major part of our heritage and our tradition." But those were just words and no one knew if even Notre Dame's leaders truly believed them.

In December 2003, not long after the abysmal end to that season, capped by the blowout loss to Syracuse, a group of about twenty alumni, drawn together by the ND Nation Web site, began contemplating a formal protest to the status quo at their alma mater. Their protest had precedent. In 2000, toward the end of the Davie years, this same group had sent a letter to the board of trustees voicing concern about the football program, and of course Bob Davie.

Four years later, after Willingham had flunked his second season, with the football program in possibly terminal disarray, they again saw an opportunity; they knew that Malloy's term had come up for review. Much as with their previous missive, the idea was to compose a letter laying out their arguments and suggesting ways to resuscitate a football program that meant more to them and all of Notre Dame's followers than any sports team could possibly mean to any other university.

The core group of twenty consisted mostly of middle-aged men. They were relatively affluent, and they came from Philadelphia, Chicago, Milwaukee, New Orleans, St. Louis, Kansas City, Denver, Los Angeles, Portland, Seattle, and South Bend, among other cities. They were attorneys and doctors and accountants and bankers and insurance executives and miscellaneous managers—by and large they occupied the professional classes. They had been undergraduates at Notre Dame during the eras of Ara Parseghian and Dan Devine and Lou Holtz and even Gerry Faust, the statistical outlier. Most of them as students had experienced championship seasons and had therefore benefited from an unofficial standard, articulated by Holtz, that all Notre Dame students are entitled to one national title in their four-year curriculum.

Around Christmas, John Vannie, the Northrop Grumman executive out of San Diego, ND Nation's resident scribe, began composing the protest letter. He based it on conversations with the rest of the group. He went through twelve drafts. He shared the result with everyone else, and new suggestions went into the pile. After five or six weeks, on January 26, 2004, the "Call for Change" letter, the C4C, as it soon became known, was ready for the mail. It read like a manifesto.

> We are writing this letter because we believe that the pronounced and persistent deterioration of the Notre Dame football program requires a concerted response from concerned alumni. We are appealing to you, the members of the Board of Trustees, because you bear the ultimate responsibility for protecting Notre Dame's traditions and maintaining the University's place as an icon of American culture. Part of that responsibility is to take the necessary steps to restore the excellence of the football program.
>
> Our concern is that the importance of Notre Dame football as a source of spirit, pride, and energy for students and alumni is no longer valued among those who are currently in positions of leadership. Notre Dame football provides a legacy that has inspired millions, from aspiring students to admiring subway alumni. It is the basis of a tradition that crosses generations to bind alumni to one another and to the University. We fear that through years of neglect this bond is eroding to the point that current and future generations will lose their rightful link to our University's storied past. . . .

They decided to send a copy to all fifty-seven trustees on the board. John Vannie said later, "The most important thing in the letter was to reiterate that football is an integral part of the university, and something that's in danger of being lost. It's part of our heritage. It's not something to be embarrassed about. It's suffered from ten years of neglect, and the trustees, we thought, were the only people who could change that. They had to step in. If you want to say we called them out, I guess you could."

Mike Coffey, aka El Kabong, ND Nation BoardOp, was in the core group. He said, "It was really a lack-of-trust issue. A lack of trust in the administration that they knew what to do. Notre Dame needs to decide what it wants to be. Stanford is held up as a model. But Stanford is good at sports not many alumni or fans care about. Notre Dame has always been good at fencing, for instance, but fencing doesn't bring in eighty thousand fans six times a year or three-inch type in the *Chicago Tribune.* There's a pecking order, and there's nothing wrong with that. And, hey, I'm a big basketball fan, so I want them to do well. But if being good at those other sports means throwing football under the bus . . . It's not okay to be ashamed of what got you where you are. It's a nouveau riche attitude that makes me sick. Notre Dame's achievements should be based on our own standards, not the standards of other people."

. . . Catholic identity, academic excellence, and championship football are the three pillars on which the University was built. Remove one of those pillars, and Notre Dame ceases to hold its unique place among American universities. If the football program continues to wither, the University will lapse into a crisis of identity, destined to remain perpetually eclipsed by ill-chosen "aspirational peers." . . .

They used ND Nation to broadcast the letter's existence. It circulated among alumni circles around the country, mostly to the drafters' friends and families, about 600 people total. Phone calls were made. Forwarded e-mails entered the in-boxes of those who did not frequent the Web site. Had the drafters also approached subway alumni, they could have added many thousands of names to the dotted line. But they gently let the subways know that this time around such numbers might dilute the impact. Too easily, they thought, could the trustees dismiss such a letter as the ravings of an Internet subset of fanatics, their priorities out of whack, their loyalties only to Irish football. In the end the drafters collected 412 names. They were not disappointed with the number. "It was about what we expected," said Mike Coffey.

The demographics of those signatories matched to a large degree the demographics of the group of twenty. On the list were a few relatives of trustees, several former football players and other athletes, and several substantial Notre Dame benefactors, though no one on the scale of a dormitory underwriter. Almost fifty people expressed interest in signing, but declined for fear of "reprisals." They had children applying for admittance, or they did business with the university, or they were concerned about the status of their season tickets, which Notre Dame had been known to revoke. Such was the state of paranoia and tension out there among the fans, whether alumni or not. Coffey himself thought these people were being a little overwary. "I never believed that sort of thing would happen. It hasn't affected my relationship to ND, nor have I yet to talk to anyone who it has happened to, either."

The letter went out, and ND Nation waited. A week passed. Two weeks passed. "We put our contact information at the bottom. We pledged confidentiality," John Vannie said. "No one really gave us the time of day." A third week came and went, and silence their only response, the drafters decided to take the next step. They sent the thing to Avani Patel of the *Chicago Tribune*. Within two days it was national news.

> . . . *We are mindful that the last decade has seen Notre Dame make significant advances in such areas as facilities, overall academics, and non-football athletics. These are laudable achievements. It is dismaying to us, however, that the same Board of Trustees that has overseen so much positive development could remain unmoved in the face of the precipitous decline of the institution that has done so much to elevate the visibility and reputation of Notre Dame. . . .*

Unsurprisingly, the letter was met in many quarters with disdain and, in other quarters, with sheer boredom. Eyes tended to roll whenever anything related to Internet fandom was brought up in conversation on campus, especially among staff and faculty and CSC. They lumped such dispatches together. A seasonal nuisance, the letters and e-mails arrived in droves game to game whenever the team did poorly, addressed to everyone from Monk Malloy to the athletic director to the head coach. Pooh-poohed and dismissed, this was just another group of alumni who cared too much about football, trying to boss the university around. "I love Notre Dame, *I'm* an alumnus," one trustee told me. He shook his head and laughed and shrugged. "But it was probably a bunch of alumni getting together one night who had too many beers and wrote this letter up. I mean, that's just immature. The days of dominance are over. What I hope is that Notre Dame can be competitive. But to get back to how we were in the old days, when we went so many years winning national championships, that's just not gonna happen. You hope we're still in there, but there is no instant formula for winning football games."

"They had well-intentioned purposes, but it backfired," said Fr. Bill Seetch, CSC, Notre Dame class of 1974. As traveling chaplain of the football team, his duties entailed celebrating the team Mass for every away game. As rector of Corby Hall, the CSC residence on campus, he sits on the board of trustees. "That letter directly harmed some of our recruiting efforts. Kids saw this dissent coming from our fans and were turned away. In this day of the Internet, if a coach is at the airport in Des Moines, Iowa, or if he belches, it's on the Internet and in fifty thousand homes. The alumni are self-appointed experts."

The athletic department, meanwhile, did some vetting. They took the list of 412 names to the development office and cross-checked it with the donor rolls. They were not impressed. An older Holy Cross priest with a long connection to the football program said, "Just between you and me, only very few of them are big contributors."

> . . . *Under your watch and that of your immediate predecessors, those whom you have entrusted with the day-to-day management of football have proven incapable of running it in a manner worthy of its heritage. Their record of mismanagement is evidenced by a series of mediocre and poorly vetted coaching hires, the subordination of winning to revenue generation, a reluctance to reinvest in the program, NCAA probation, and an alarming transfer rate among scholarship players. . . .*

Among the letter's most strident critiques involved the seeming eye the administration had for vulgarly commercializing at every opportunity the Notre Dame name. "Revenue whoring," as the purists have called it, though this phrase did not appear in the "Call for Change" letter. The university, the drafters argued, was content to milk every penny out of the cash cow of the Fighting Irish brand—and therefore Fighting Irish fandom—while ignoring the team's performance on the field. This led to several unsavory developments, including corporate tents rented out to the likes of Xerox, Adidas, and other NBC advertisers and sponsors that were part of "Team Notre Dame," talk of JumboTrons being installed atop each end of the stadium, which would serve as electronic billboards for the crowd, and other schemes offering canned game-day experiences, a kind of Disneyfication of Notre Dame football.

But the most egregious of these developments was yet more talk of Notre Dame ending its independence and joining a conference in football, the merest suggestion of which incites bloodlust among Irish fans. In 1999, Notre Dame had discussions with the Big Ten about joining the league, which would have enabled Notre Dame to take a share of bowl revenue even if Notre Dame made no bowl. Ultimately, Notre Dame decided to remain independent, but promised, in Kevin White's words, to continue "monitoring the landscape." As recently as the fall of 2003, conference rumors began anew, this time involving the Atlantic Coast Conference. The "Call for Change" letter did not shy from threats.

> . . . *It would be a grave mistake to assume that those alumni would remain passive and compliant if this option were presented as a fait accompli. Such a decision would be met with intense resistance and evoke various methods of protest, including withheld financial support.*
>
> *That Notre Dame's independence is even subject to negotiation betrays the current athletic administration's mindset that the purpose of the football program is to produce revenues. Rather than address the program's present woes, they prefer to come up with stratagems that exploit Notre Dame's storied past. Squeezing revenues from a struggling brand is not a substitute for rebuilding an elite football program. When the football team is strong, ample revenues and a commanding post-season bowl position have always followed.*

"I'm so sick of this!" said the Holy Cross priest with connections to the football program. "I think we have the worst fans in the world. They're so bitter when we lose. All they want is to win. They're *spoiled.*" Most of the people whose eyes rolled, including this particular priest, had not read the letter. He believed, for instance, that it had been addressed to Willingham. Indeed, many people on campus thought the same and therefore found the letter insulting. Separating the man from the performance of his teams, many faculty and staff had come to hold Willingham in the highest regard.

"There have been a lot of coaches through here, but the best one by far is on campus right now. And you can quote me on that. As a guy—no contest."

"He's a wonderful, wonderful man. And he's got a wonderful family."

"He really is top-notch. He cares about his athletes. He's at Notre Dame for a reason, because of the higher standards of this place. I mean, he likes to win. But he also knows he's in the business of developing athletes as individuals."

At any mention of the "Call for Change" letter, with its hard-boiled calculus of wins and losses, these people recoiled. They seemed to have received most of their information about the letter from newspapers and talk-radio shows and TV sports channels, which mostly interpreted the letter as a call for the head coach's head.

> *. . . This is not a call to fire Tyrone Willingham. Coach Willingham is a fine leader who represents Notre Dame well, but he has yet to demonstrate the high level of competence that this demanding job requires. Although we continue to support him and hope he succeeds, his performance, marked by unprecedented and humiliating defeats, deficiencies within his coaching staff, and his inconsistent record as head coach, indicates that he may not. Absent significant progress in 2004, a coaching change will become necessary. . . .*

Subtlety upon subtlety, it was, instead, a call to fire Ty Willingham not at this very moment, but if he should go out and flunk one more season.

The letter concluded with suggestions for improving the program, the most important of which was to overhaul the process of searching for a coach. Essentially, the kitchen had too many cooks—a huge selection committee that seemed to include every member of the campus community save the Morris Inn bartenders. Even more essentially, the letter suggested that priests should step aside when football was the subject. People with no business in the kitchen nixed candidates for nonfootball reasons. There were suggestions from ND's administration that football acumen did not hold equal weight with other considerations. During the search that led to the truncated hiring of George O'Leary, an official within the Malloy administration allegedly expressed a sentiment that leaked into alumni circles, causing bewilderment: "Notre Dame doesn't need a great coach to succeed," implying either that Notre Dame could make mediocre coaches great, or that Notre Dame needed to redefine what it meant by "succeed." But, evidently, here again was the disconnect, the miscommunication, occurring between the fans and the administration. One Notre Dame official who was in the kitchen during the post-Davie coaching search said he had never heard that statement uttered by anyone. "In fact, I'd say it was just the contrary." Everyone inside the administration, the official said, firmly believed that "to have a great football program comes down to how great your football coach is. The single most important variable is the leadership at the top." But, the official went on, "The tough part is finding a great coach."

Before the hiring of Willingham, the university had a chance to bring in Jon Gruden, then the head coach of the Oakland Raiders and at the time the NFL's latest coaching wunderkind. He had grown up in South Bend. His father had coached defensive backs at Notre Dame under Dan Devine. He was another head-coach subway alumnus, an Irish fan since birth. Gruden, despite portrayals in the press after the fact, had more than passing interest in the job. He met with White and members of the search committee, and the parties negotiated in extreme secrecy. There were some sticking points, however, none larger than Al Davis, owner of the Raiders, who indicated to Notre Dame in no uncertain terms that if talks proceeded he'd pursue legal action, one member of the search committee told me. Notre Dame dropped out of the talks. The party line at ND appears to be that Gruden was never seriously considered for the job. David Haugh, then the lead sports columnist for the *South Bend Tribune,* spent a good amount of time attempting to uncover the story only to write, finally, in 2003, that it "remains one of those stories cloaked in enough mystery and intrigue to interest Oliver Stone." He went on, "The most trusted account, based on instinct and information culled over a year from reliable sources, involves Notre Dame and Gruden agreeing in principle to build a future together," with Al Davis at the last second putting the kibosh on the deal. After the O'Leary affair, Notre Dame allegedly had a second chance at Gruden, but here the situation grows even murkier. Some Notre Dame people are adamant that Gruden's Al Davis/contract difficulties had cleared up later in the season after O'Leary had resigned, and that Gruden again wanted to be considered for the Irish job. This time, however (according to those adamant tipsters), there were further sticking points. Gruden, it was well-known, had the sideline demeanor of a roustabout. He was not afraid of the oath. He had a big, fiery personality and he very much liked to win—visions of Holtz and cults of personality. Malloy had taken a larger role in the search following O'Leary, and Gruden went to the Tampa Bay Buccaneers, where the next year he won the Super Bowl.

The next candidate was Willingham, lately of Stanford University, aspirational peer. Kevin White actually had Willingham high on his list of prospects. He contacted the Stanford coach even before O'Leary's name emerged, but after a preliminary interview, White concluded that Willingham did not exhibit the requisite passion for the job. Then came the O'Leary fiasco, and then, with Gruden nixed, the search committee went back to Willingham. The searchers reviewed the case. Jesse Jackson had already done so, issuing a press release making this very suggestion to Notre Dame. Willingham's high moral rigor, his embodiment of the father figure, apparently won over the committee. There was also, probably, a good deal of desperation. After O'Leary, after the NCAA scandal and the labor lawsuit, after the personality cults that had led to hatchet-job artists writing books with tarnished-dome metaphors in the title, Willingham was deemed an "institutional fit."

In his long opening remarks at Willingham's introductory press conference—possibly the largest number of words the university president had ever dedicated to football in public—Malloy said, among many other things, "This is a kind of occasion which has the potential to be described entirely as a kind of social statement, and surely there's an element of that to it. What I want to say very straightforwardly is that the reason that Coach Willingham was chosen after a very exhaustive search was because he was the very best coach who was appropriate for Notre Dame and all it represents."

The first black head coach in any sport at Notre Dame, one of only four black head coaches out of 117 football teams in Division I-A, Willingham was universally hailed by the media as the wise and progressive choice. With the hire, those observers felt that Notre Dame might have gone some way toward repairing the breach its reputation had suffered over the last eight years.

We regret the football program has declined to the level that required us to submit this letter, but we fear our silence may be interpreted as tolerance. As alumni who understand football's irreplaceable contribution to Notre Dame's greatness, we could not remain idle as the University's vital third pillar crumbled. We ask you as Trustees to fulfill your responsibilities in this area.

Sincerely yours in Notre Dame,

No trustees availed themselves of the contact numbers printed at the bottom of the letter. But not long after the *Chicago Tribune* ran its story, John Vannie and his group received the desired dope. Through an "intermediary," they heard that several trustees, some of whom were in positions of great authority, sympathized in all ways with the spirit of the letter. The intermediary had spoken privately with Philip Purcell, Notre Dame class of 1969, then chief executive of Morgan Stanley. He was also chair of the board's athletics committee. The intermediary gauged Purcell's reaction to the letter, and what the C4C alumni heard was "Yes, we've read it. Yes, we're working on it. Yes, it helped us." John Vannie says, "I think the issues we raised got a lot of discussion. The letter brought a sense of urgency to these things. Once we found out that there were people on the board who felt like us, we were heartened."

Three months later, Father Malloy announced his retirement, and ND Nation went into its raptures. The enemy had been vanquished.

4

Charism

In *Sports Illustrated*'s 2004 college football preview, James Carville, of all people, addressed what currently ailed Notre Dame football. None other than Don Yaeger, coauthor of *Under the Tarnished Dome,* conducted the interview. A diehard fan of Louisiana State football, Carville nonetheless hit the mark more than perhaps he knew.

"Notre Dame's problem is that no one in the athletic department ever took a class in the history department. They don't realize what happens when hubris and arrogance take control. All that arrogance usually leads to you getting your butt kicked, and that's what's going to happen to Notre Dame. For all those years they had their NBC contract, and they had all the nuns praying for them. Well, there aren't as many nuns as there used to be."

Sister Jane Marie and Sister Helen Minich, in their gray habits, walked up the ramp to the upper deck of Notre Dame Stadium just before kick off on September 11, 2004, Notre Dame vs. Michigan. I was with a group of young Holy Cross seminarians, picking our way through the mob on the way to our seats, when we espied the nuns. Pausing amid the rumbling crowd, Sister Jane said, "We don't think Notre Dame is second to any university in the world, let alone the country!" Small as a figurine, sixty-seven years old, she is a member of the St. Francis convent in nearby Mishawaka. Sister Helen, sixty-six years old, the local superior of the mother house, is by all accounts the most strident Notre Dame fan on the premises. The rest of the convent, the hundred or so nuns not lucky enough to have tickets today were back at the house, clustered in covens around the TV sets in their cells. "When the Notre Dame game is on," Sister Jane said, "you can hear screams coming from behind the doors of all the rooms." "It's like a tailgate party in the convent," Sister Helen said. "Without the alcohol of course." By their reckoning, a lot of prayers go up in the house, if not precisely for victory, then for the prospects of the world's greatest university and, by extension, the world's greatest team. Before each game, Sister Helen will pray a special intention at the convent's morning Mass, asking for protection for the players and saying, rather democratically, "may the best team win—and hopefully it's Notre Dame." The nuns see nothing the matter with this, no frivolous use of God's time. "Well, you need the spiritual in every part of your life," Sister Jane said as the bodies swarmed around her. "It's all about the Mother on top of the dome." The nuns had good seats, on the forty-yard line, and they waddled up to an usher and flashed their stubs and vanished into the assembling congregation.

Nate Farley, first-year professed, lately having taken his temporary vows, sat in a section of the stadium—four rows, a dozen seats across, high up near the rim of the bowl—given over to those who live communally in Moreau Seminary. Named for Basil Moreau, the French priest who founded the Congregation of Holy Cross in 1837, the building sits separated from the rest of campus by the expanse of St. Joseph's Lake. It was built optimistically in the late 1950s at the height of a boom in priestly vocations, and it has enough cells to house 150 seminarians. But in the 1960s the boom quickly became a dearth, and today, twenty seminarians live in Moreau, across five classes at various stages moving toward their Holy Orders. The extra rooms in Moreau are used for visiting scholars and visiting priests and a few permanent CSCs, but the vast majority of Moreau's living quarters sit vacant, unless it's a home-game weekend when, for a $45 "donation" per night, the rooms are rented out to fans and alumni. Moreau becomes a kind of pilgrim's inn, and six times a year there is no room at it.

Basil Moreau, as superior general of the religious community of his own invention, ordered one of the first priests he'd ordained, Fr. Edward Sorin, across the Atlantic on a missionary expedition that ended on a tract of wilderness in northern Indiana, where Sorin, twenty-eight years old, established a log-cabin grammar school that he rather grandiosely named L'Université de Notre Dame du Lac. He also established on the American continent a bloodline of CSC ordination, priest coaching seminarian into priest through 160 years and a thousand fathers until the very vanguard became occupied in the current day by

Nate Farley, professed seminarian. If everything goes according to plan, Farley will receive Holy Orders in 2007. By the time he is ordained, he will be the same age as Sorin when the great man first laid eyes on the piece of Indian territory that would eventually sprout the steel-and-concrete hulk now holding Farley aloft over a football field.

On the field, the Notre Dame marching band had arrayed itself into ranks, playing first "America, the Beautiful" and second "The Star-Spangled Banner." The seminarians in chorus sang the songs, and sang them well. On key, they hit the high notes with aplomb, holding on to the difficult "rockets' red glare" bit so well they might have been seated in a choir loft.

Farley has a sharp nose and small blue eyes and dark, Caesar-cut hair already flecked with gray. When he smiles, which is often, braces appear on his teeth. Around his neck at all times he wears a medallion—the cross-and-anchor seal, in imitation silver (real silver would conflict with the vow of poverty), of the Holy Cross Congregation. The anchor represents the stability of home. The crosses are obvious. Only after professing vows for the first time, before the third year of seminary, does a seminarian receive the medallion. Today, around Nate Farley's neck, it tapped against a T-shirt of kelly green. Known as The Shirt, it is a garment produced each football season by the student body, for the student body, but sold to the public at the bookstore, the proceeds to charity, and everyone at a Notre Dame game seems to have one on—seminarians included. It commemorates each season, and each year it has a different color and different design. The 2004 edition pictured on the back a 1970s-era quarterback in midthrow—many speculated that it was Joe Montana, Notre Dame class of 1978—with the words, "The cheering thousands shout their battle cry," a line from an obscure alternative Notre Dame fight song called "When Irish Backs Go Marching By." (Over thirteen previous years, The Shirt's designers seemed to have exhausted the lyrics from the standard "Victory March.") The Shirt binds Notre Dame fandom into one sartorial groove, and because of its affiliation with the undergraduate population, it has become a way for alumni and subway alumni to feel a part of the scene.

Most of the seminarians who sat with Nate Farley went to Notre Dame as undergraduates. Class of 2001, Farley had spent his four years not sitting up in the student section, but standing down on the field amid the giants in shoulder pads. Adept with tape and ice and the bandaging of cuts, he assisted in battlefield triage. In hot weather he carried around bottles full of water and Gatorade. He was a student trainer for the football team, and his autumn Saturdays were hectic and intense and stressful enough that, in his memory, his four years' worth of games have blurred into one long, indistinguishable quarter. "A lot of that stuff I guess I've blocked out." He remembers slinging the sprained shoulder of Grant Irons, a defensive end. He recalls taping the sprained wrist of a young option quarterback, Arnaz Battle. The weight of his responsibility as trainer seems heavy on him even today, recollecting those times. "It was big stakes—Division I football on national television. Careers were not *in* our hands, but they were in the balance." Running to and fro, following the orders of doctors and staff trainers, getting bellowed at by coaches every once in a while, he had no chance to pay attention to the plays developing on the field. Instead, he videotaped the games on TV and watched them the next day. His career encompassed the Bob Davie epoch, 1997–2000, and some of those tapes were tough to review. He used a lot of fast-forward. Like many of his generation, he had grown up entranced with the dominating teams of Lou Holtz. His earliest memories of Notre Dame come from football and NBC and 1988. He was nine years old, and as he watched this team continue to win and advance toward its national title, echoes awakening, the desire and the daydream quickly rose in him to attend the university that it represented.

He grew up in a family of "basic Sunday Catholics," not markedly devout, and went to public high school in Dover, Ohio, a city of thirteen thousand situated thirty miles south of the Cleveland-Akron-Canton corridor. Other than Nate Farley, his family consisted of no Notre Dame fans. His father went to the University of Dayton, a Catholic school founded by the Marianists, and was mostly ambivalent toward Notre Dame. Nate Farley's family of Ohioans preferred the Buckeyes of Ohio State, a Big Ten team whose fans often do not take kindly to the Fighting Irish. In essence Nate Farley was an isolated, individual, self-made subway alumnus.

He visited Notre Dame just once before applying, during the off-season, in the spring, and the outing inspired a reaction so common

among first-time visitors that there are people who cite the supernatural. It is often described as a "feeling," a "sense," an intuition of
"home." He says, "As soon as I set foot on campus, I knew this was
where I had to be." He matriculated and pursued a course in premed,
which led him, along with his enthusiasm for Fighting Irish football,
onto the sidelines and into the locker room to tape up and ice down
wounded athletes. Notre Dame also opened the door to God. Sometime
during his sophomore year, an inkling grew into a notion, and the notion eventually bloomed into full-scale intention. He started attending
daily Masses, he had conversations with priests. It all took him a little
by surprise. Until he arrived at Notre Dame, he had no special interest
in religion, let alone the idea of taking vows. "The thought of being a
priest would never have occurred to me." It did when he witnessed the
work of a few younger CSCs, "dynamic" and "energetic," who had a
"charisma about them and how they served." Farley saw his calling as
pastoral. Missionary, parish priest, high school teacher—he wanted to
go out into the world, like a doctor conducting permanent pro bono.
Drawn to Notre Dame as an enthusiast of its football, he ended up joining the seminary. Notre Dame had converted a fan into a priest.

The seminarians had seats at about the twenty-yard line, up in the
new portion of the stadium, erected in 1997. Each of them receives free
season tickets with the ability to purchase more should he wish to invite guests, and many had brought friends and relatives to the game—
a ticketing deal that exists nowhere else outside the Holy Cross
community, with its vow of poverty. Full-blown Holy Cross priests sit
at the fifty-yard line in a section underneath the press box, shielded
from the elements, across the field from the seminarians on the other
side of the stadium. Elderly fathers have an area all their own, and it's
known as Cardiac Row. Of late, however, the newly outsize stadium
and its larger crowd have mostly kept the oldest priests away. The im-
mediacy of the live game experience also has its dangers. Hearts weak-
ened with age, some of the retired CSCs stay away under orders from
their doctors, who wanted to keep the row innocent of cardiacs. Those
who don't make it to the stadium watch the game on television at Holy
Cross House, the community retirement home and hospice center,
next door to Moreau.

All in all, Farley and these future CSCs and leaders of the university had excellent seats, with views of both end zones and the full sweep of the field, preparing them, perhaps, for the press box or, much later on, for Cardiac Row—if, that is, the football team that then existed would be worth having a heart attack over.

Michigan had won the coin toss, had deferred, and now amid the rotating arms of eighty thousand fans, all bellowing in unison a prolonged "Go," the Michigan kicker sent the ball into the air. At impact—foot to leather—everyone yelled, "Irish!"

As the ball arched, Drew Gawrych said, "Alright! Touchdown, baby!"

The kickoff fell into the hands of the receiver, whose dash upfield ended seventy-six yards short of a touchdown.

"Alright!" Gawrych yelled. "Touchdown this play!"

Drew Gawrych, twenty-four years old, had short brown hair, a full but well-trimmed beard, and the spindly frame of a cross-country runner. He had taken his initial temporary vows two and a half months earlier. Chastity, poverty, and obedience, they lasted a year and then required renewal. Or not. This was a process, a slow one, everything measured and taken in steps, with plenty of outlets. The first year of seminary, called the candidate year, consisted of course work in theology and philosophy, as well as full-time residence at Moreau, getting a taste of religious life within the Holy Cross community. In the second year, the stakes escalated—the half-dreaded, half-anticipated novitiate year. Both he and Farley had already done their time, had spent those twelve months in deep seclusion at the Holy Cross novitiate in Colorado Springs, cloistered in a manse halfway up Pikes Peak. On the other side of the mountain is the Air Force Academy. On some other portion of the mountain is the high-altitude training facility of the U.S. Olympic team. The seminarians, meanwhile, are meant to use their time on the mountain as a period of what they described as "intense discernment," to engage in "extended conversations with God," to test their mettle and find out if they have what it takes. The novitiate is indeed a kind of religious training camp, physically rigorous, psychologically demanding, monastic, and austere. Here they enter the profession. Manual labor and long, silent intervals of prayer almost totally occupy a novice's waking hours. Like SEAL boot camp, like the Harvard Law School, attrition is high. More than half of those who enter end up quitting, but both Farley and Gawrych came out the other side of Pikes Peak with their callings intact.

Notre Dame class of 2002, a year behind Farley in the seminary, Drew Gawrych grew up in Kansas, the son of a history professor; his father taught at the Command and General Staff College, Fort Leavenworth. While he wouldn't call his family "devout" exactly, he says they nonetheless had a strong sense of spirituality. They prayed together each evening before meals and each night before bed. "I grew up in a family where faith was integral to our lives. Faith came up in our discussions. My parents were always looking to apply the Gospels to daily life. If my dad had a tough day at work, for instance, he'd throw in his two cents from the Gospels. But it wasn't forced. It was natural. It permeated all parts of our family life. It was a faith that lived." He had his first inklings of a calling in high school. He calls it a "curiosity." But he put it aside in looking for a college—small, private, with challenging academics. The summer before his senior year, he visited campus and had an experience that paralleled Nate Farley's. "Within forty-five minutes I had fallen in love. I knew this was the place for me." He mentions the "history." He mentions the student atmosphere, the dorm life, the palpable Catholicism. He mentions "the tradition," which necessitates a caveat—"but not just football tradition. The word I sometimes use is *aura*. There was a feeling I had about the campus; it just made me feel at home. I could sense the spiritual dimension of campus. It was alive for me, and real. That's why I could turn to my dad right then and there and say, 'I'm coming here' with conviction. It wasn't just some whimsical 'Oh, I really like it here because the campus is beautiful.' It was deeper than that. It was the conviction that I had come home." By his senior year the feeling was strong enough that he applied for a spot in the seminary. A little mysterious and somehow inevitable, it was almost as if both he and Farley were called first by Notre Dame.

Of the seminarians, Gawrych was perhaps the most knowledgeable about football, the most prototypical fan. "Wow," he said at one point, looking down at the field as Notre Dame's offense lined up in its formation. "Four wide, the tight end offset." The result was a pass to a wide-open receiver, first down.

On its first offensive series, Notre Dame went three-and-out, and after punting, with Michigan on offense, the band struck up the "Imperial March" from *Star Wars,* and the cheer in this instance was a chant. "Kill! Kill! Kill!" With each downbeat, another "Kill," and with each downbeat, a chop of the hand. The seminarians all did it with gusto. I remarked that this must be some new thing. No such cheer was performed during my student days.

"Yes, that's right," said one of the seminarians. "And it's not very Christian either."

Sitting in the row above us was Eric Ufheil, who wore a sleeveless, green The Shirt. Forty-eight years old, visiting from Annawan, Illinois, a supervisor on the third shift at a U.S. postal service depot in the Quad Cities, a former truck driver, he was the father of a seminarian. He had thick arms and a flat growl of a voice and a mien that grew ever more demonstrative the more the Irish messed up on the field. Like many fans, he would publicly address the Irish sidelines with his judgments on the play of the team and the strategy of the coaches. When things went badly, he appeared to censor himself here among the novices. Had he been sitting in some other section, his words might have been a little choicer. "It does help you to be good," he said of the seating arrangements. Ufheil lurked on ND Nation, checked it out about once a day, and posted every so often. A week earlier, in the wake of the BYU loss, the "Call For Change" people had opened up the letter to subway alumni, and Eric Ufheil had added his name to a list that swelled from the original 412 to more than 4,000.

His son, Seth, Notre Dame class of 2004, had not yet arrived. "I don't know where he is," Ufheil said. "He might be somewhere in the stadium. He might be elsewhere. For all I know, he might be in the chapel *praying.*" During a long TV time-out, the kid showed up. He was tall and skinny as a pew, with blond locks under a white Notre Dame ballcap, the brim curved severely like a frat boy's. He had entered his candidate year just a few weeks earlier.

The day before, the Ufheils had gone to the pep rally, and Gawrych wanted to know about Ty Willingham's demeanor, considering the performance at BYU, the terrible game-planning, the embarrassment, the ill-prepared team he had brought onto the field that night in Utah. Gawrych was interested in the psychology of the enigmatic head coach. Did Willingham come out of his shell at all? Was he in any way expressive, angry, emotive?

"Yeah, more than usual," Ufheil said. "He was really worked up. Probably because he knows his job's on the line."

Nearly twelve thousand people, a capacity crowd, including the Ufheils, filled the Joyce Center basketball arena for that Friday-evening pep rally, where they'd spent an hour being cajoled to "raise the roof" tomorrow at the Michigan game. According to some purists, these pep rallies, a Friday tradition since anyone could remember, had become tourist traps—canned, fake, trite, soaked with sports cliché and vacant boast and hollow predictions of victory in the midst of great decline. "We are a family!" Chuck Lennon had bellowed from the floor at the rally. Director of the Alumni Association, Notre Dame's chief of rah-rah, he was a small, white-haired man in his midsixties with the jumpy vim of a Jack Russell terrier. He strode around the court hollering and waving his arms, with a microphone clipped to a navy blue cardigan, a big gold ND monogram on the breast, a letterman's sweater circa 1950. "The students, the team, the faculty, the alumni, and the fans—*we are a family.* And a family . . . a family is always there for each other! There will be tough times, but a family never gives up, never gives in, and we're gonna beat Michigan tomorrow!"

At the podium now in the middle of the court stood Ty Willingham. He wore a trim gray suit of English cut, pure Madison Ave., and his team, eighty-odd players in all, sat in folding chairs around him, dressed like boys on the way to a semiformal. Willingham said into the microphone, "Only Notre Dame understands what Notre Dame is all about," and after a short speech that had as its theme the history of the ND-Michigan series, Willingham at the podium would now test the crowd in what he called its "unity skills." It was a drill the team performed each practice. He explained what to do. The head coach would wait for silence from the crowd. Then he would raise his hands, holding them high above his head. Then, as a signal, he'd yank them down and shout, "Hit!" almost as loud as he could. At the signal, the people in the arena would clap their hands once and only once, in unison. Twenty-four thousand palms slapping together at the same instant would, in theory, produce a tight, cracking booming sound like a thunderpeal.

Willingham raised his arms. The crowd fell silent. The crowd waited. His arms aloft like a semaphore, the coach yanked them down. "Hit!"

Overeager claps arrived prior to the hit, lazy applause sprinkled like hail on a roof long after—anarchy and disorder, these fans were a bunch of freethinkers.

"That was the preseason version," Willingham said. "Okay, let's try it again, let's go." His arms came down like an ax—"Hit!"—and again an awful result, and Willingham in mock-frustration said, "We're working on our *lesson skills* here."

He tried a third time. His arms went up; the crowd recovered its silence. "Hit!" Crack from the fans, big, booming, and tight, and then a double crack, a stutter—atrophied reflexes reacting a second too late. But maybe that one had been good enough.

"Wait, wait, wait. We're not there yet." His arms up, the crowd dead, the coach waited and waited some more. His hands pointed high toward heaven. "Hit!" And crack!—one discreet, reverberant strike— unity achieved. The crack echoed into the nosebleeds and the rafters and dissipated up there among the NCAA Tournament banners, and the fans paused as if stunned by their success. They appeared to consider it; they appeared to decide that they were pleased with themselves—and then the crowd roared.

Willingham lowered his mouth to the mike amid the general pandemonium. Calmly, quietly, in inverse proportion to the crowd's reaction and almost under his breath, he said, "Let's go Irish."

Six to nothing Michigan on two Michigan field goals, and the crowd seemed almost bored. Notre Dame's offense so far had reprised its performance of a week earlier, short passes of the dink-dunk variety, no running game to speak of. Echoing the dissatisfaction of a good portion of Notre Dame fandom, the Ufheils expressed their disgust with Willingham's offensive coordinator, Bill Diedrick.

"It's frustrating. His play calls are frustrating," said Seth, the son.

"He's gotta go," said Eric, the father. "He's got to go."

"But on this drive," said Mike Lewis, a seminarian, "on this drive we go ahead!"

At the start of the second quarter, a running back named Darius Walker entered the game. A freshman, a highly recruited athlete out of

Georgia, he wore the No. 3 jersey. No one knew who the player was except Drew Gawrych, for Gawrych is something of a recruitnik, a breed of fan that follows recruiting almost as intently as the regular season. To see Walker out there lined up in a single-back set behind Brady Quinn, the quarterback, was an exciting development indeed, and Gawrych brought it to everyone's attention.

On his first collegiate carry, Walker gained one yard. Third down and four to go. Get this first down and the game's momentum, as the saying goes, might swing in the direction of Notre Dame.

"Alright," said Eric Ufheil. He paused and cleared his throat. " 'Hail Mary, full of grace, the Lord is with thee . . . ' " He did not finish. The running back, not Walker, but the putative starter, Ryan Grant, took the handoff, squeezed through a scrum of linemen jostling at scrimmage like drunks in a bar scuffle, and found four yards of space, which he leaned across and fell on top of. First down Notre Dame.

The crowd roared and Eric Ufheil rose to his feet and looked around and lifted his arms to the sky in triumph. "Alright!" The seminarians cheered for him almost as hard as for the team now huddling up before the next play.

Ufheil sank back into his seat. "It's pretty sad when you're prayin' for first downs!"

The drive crossed the fifty-yard line and ended after two incomplete passes. Another Notre Dame punt, another Michigan punt, booting balls back and forth. And then a wide-open Irish wide receiver named Maurice Stovall, six foot five with track speed, loped down the field and dragged a pass out of the sky—a forty-nine-yard gain and the place erupted. On the next play, Walker took the toss on a sweep, turned the corner, thirteen yards to the eight-yard line, Notre Dame first and goal. On the next play, Walker took the toss on a sweep, the identical play, and a defensive lineman crawling on all fours got behind the line of scrimmage. He swiped a paw at the back's ankles. Tripped up before he could turn the corner, Walker lost two.

Unenthusiastic about this kind of predictability, Ufheil directed his voice to the press box high above, where the offensive coordinator sat calling plays.

"Diedrick! Figure! It! Out!"

After an eight-yard pass, a touchdown now seemed imminent.

Walker up the middle for a yard. Fourth down and goal. The seminarians rose to their feet and chanted in unison, "Go! Go! Go!" And Ty
Willingham elected to go. The handoff went to Ryan Grant, up the middle. No gain, zero points, and the Irish lost the ball on downs. The
crowd fell to its seats and went dead as a mausoleum.

Drew Gawrych said, "Michigan is pinned on the one. I like the
call!"

And father Ufheil said, independent of Gawrych's remark, "That's
bullshit! Diedrick is *terrible*!"

The band struck up the "Imperial March," and again the chant
"Kill! Kill!" Ufheil ignored it; the seminarians threw their enthusiasm
behind it.

Deep in its own territory, Michigan did not extract itself. Notre
Dame's defense held and Michigan punted, and on the second play of
ND's next series another tall wide receiver named Jeff Samardzija ran
his route, turned around, and put his hands into the air. The ball arrived where his hands were. It bounced out of his hands and into the
arms of a Michigan defender. Interception.

Ufheil said in a kind of angry singsong, "You gotta catch those!
That's what we're *paying* you for!"

Gawrych was calm, the voice of reasoned optimism. He was
preparing for the confessional. "That's alright. We have time to get the
ball back and score before the half."

Earlier in the day, just before kickoff, Gawrych had proclaimed,
"It's victory today for us. This is going to be a big W." Incredulous, I
asked him, "You really think they have a chance?"

"I always do at the start."

Against the odds and flouting the conventional wisdom, both he
and Nate Farley and many of the seminarians predicted a win against
No. 7 Michigan, and they weren't just saying it. As Farley sat up in his
seat some distance from the rest of us, he felt the sun beating down on
his face, and a kind of intuitional confidence descended over him, perhaps due to the lack of weather. So good did he feel that he discounted
BYU completely and believed a good season was in the works. "It's
frustrating to have these seasons—up and down, up and down," Farley
said. "But you're always hopeful."

The seminarians' status as fans was typical of the CSC community at large—so typical that it had perhaps congealed into a kind of party line.

"I prefer winning, but if we lose, I'm not going to take that to the extreme; it's not the end of the world," Gawrych said.

"I wouldn't call myself a superfan," Nate Farley said. "I love Notre Dame football, I enjoy the games, but my life doesn't rise and fall with it anymore. After so many years of the team being up and down and inconsistent, and with me being a trainer—I won't say I've been desensitized, but it's given me a little perspective. Being a trainer gave me a little more knowledge of the inner workings of the team. And I've been around Notre Dame for seven years now, from being an undergraduate to the seminary. I think I like Notre Dame football in a different way now. I have a hard time saying my interest in the team has increased or decreased. It's just not the wide-eyed wonderment that it once was."

Both Gawrych and Farley were only vaguely aware of the "general wave of discontent," in Gawrych's words, swarming around Father Malloy, his presidency, and Willingham's burgeoning place within the ten years of decline. Word of fan and alumni grumbling, if not specifically the "Call for Change" letter, had made its way indistinctly to the tables in the Moreau refectory, where the seminarians were most likely to discuss the football program. But Gawrych said, "In season, it's important that you unite behind your team. That's part of being a fan. Especially in college athletics. Those are kids down there playing on the field, after all—teenagers. And they're playing for my school, my alma mater. Maybe you haggle over a call here or there, but during the season is not the time for those kinds of criticisms. After the season, then you take stock. Then you can ask some of the bigger questions." About the criticism leveled at Malloy, he said, "I don't share those opinions. And I'll leave it at that."

Farley said, "It doesn't really matter to me what those people think about Notre Dame football. A lot of the opinion comes from people who don't understand the inner workings of Notre Dame. You need to take it with a grain of salt. It's one of those things where you have to trust the people making the decisions."

Now, preparing for a life in a religious community that controlled a university and, as well, a football program of enormous dimensions, they seemed to have acquired, along with their vocations, the gift of "perspective." For the Congregation of Holy Cross, Indiana Province, it might as well have been a fourth vow.

Perhaps the two most incisive, if not well circulated, remarks concerning Notre Dame and its football were uttered by Edward "Moose" Krause and Frank O'Malley.

Krause was athletic director from 1949 to 1980. Born in Chicago, Notre Dame class of 1934, both a football and basketball all-American, hired as AD by Hesburgh when Hesburgh was still executive vice president, he had long ago entered Notre Dame's sporting hagiography. If Holtz set the modern standard for "getting it" for head coaches, Krause set it for athletic directors. A bronze Moose, life-size, sits with his legs crossed on a bench outside the Joyce Center, a cigar between his knuckles, a look of deep contentment on his face. Having been around Notre Dame so long, Krause understood the fundamental, if subtle, dynamics at work inside this unusual institution. Intensely loyal to his bosses, always trusting their intentions but sometimes not their judgment, he was known to say in private, as reported by Moose's biographer, Jason Kelly, "The priests at Notre Dame are great people, but they don't know much about football."

Frank O'Malley, Notre Dame class of 1932, was professor of English at his alma mater for forty-three years. A campus icon, one of Notre Dame's last "bachelor dons," he lived out his life in a campus dorm and at Leahy's, the bar at the Morris Inn. Revered by his students, he was described as "elusive," "mystical," and "devoted to place, not the profession." That place, of course, was Notre Dame—and here, again, was a man who "got it," though in his own idiosyncratic way. Inevitably, football metaphor was used to further O'Malley's legend. According to *Newsweek,* he was "the Knute Rockne of Notre Dame's academic faculty." This piece of hyperbole may have contained at least a kernel of truth. Perhaps a bit maliciously, O'Malley often scheduled his lectures for home-game Saturdays. His classroom was always packed. Unmaliciously, he ended his teachings in time for kickoff.

O'Malley's view of Notre Dame and its football was cranky, droll, refractory, contrarian. According to Tom Stitch, another bachelor don, almost on par with his colleague in terms of legend, someone once re-marked to O'Malley that he didn't seem to be much of a football fan.

"Sure I am—I've got nothing against football at Notre Dame," the don is said to have replied. "It's the only thing we do really well."

Together these quotes from Krause and O'Malley amount to a con-cise history of Irish football and its relationship to its guiding pres-ence, the Congregation of Holy Cross. Both men, of course, were being a little facetious. Most of all O'Malley, who was playfully alluding to the fears of several generations of CSC.

But in the space between their remarks lies enough material to fill many hundreds of pages of written matter. When Murray Sperber, an academic from Indiana University researching American intercolle-giate sports, descended into the university archives in the basement of Hesburgh Library, he rooted around and blew the dust off several boxes full of private correspondence untouched since a secretary had made the carbons and cleared out the letter writer's office files. Inside the boxes were the collected epistles of Knute Rockne, and with this discovery the academic himself entered into Notre Dame legend. The volume Sperber composed out of the letters was *Shake Down the Thunder: The Creation of Notre Dame Football* (Henry Holt), and it il-luminates the uneasy and, at times, wholly antagonistic relationship between the great, ambitious head coach and his bosses in the CSC, a relationship that not only created tension, but also seemed to reveal like nothing else before Notre Dame's lasting raison d'être—excellence in all pursuits for the glory of God. The tension created in those early days has survived, and the last words of Sperber's book are prescient: "Notre Dame's struggle with its athletic culture and its academic aspi-rations will likely continue well into the next century."

It came out, coincidentally, in 1993—the same year as *Under the Tarnished Dome*—the same year, the last year, that Notre Dame seri-ously contended for a national championship. Notre Dame fans largely received *Shake Down the Thunder* with affection. To this day Sperber receives emails almost on a weekly basis from fans wishing to praise the book. The university administration seems to have embraced the volume as an antidote to, as Sperber has put it, "the slash-and-burn job" of the Yaeger-Looney partnership. Sober, objective, with 134 pages of endnotes, it was researched as if the man had rolled out a cot at the Hesburgh library and lived there five years, and it demythologized some of the university's most nostalgia-fogged myths.

A country in the midst of a boom; the emergence of mass communications capable of moving voices through the air; the tycoon publishers who invented the sports pages and paid a new category of stylist to fill them with purple prose; the American immigrant experience; a small Midwestern college with a peculiar mission to send out educated Catholic men into a stridently anti-Catholic modernity; a college with little money to fully realize such a mission; and a man named Knute Rockne—all of these things converged at the same explosive alpha moment in the 1920s to produce what we have come to know in this country as football. Its rise at Notre Dame between 1918 and 1931 was both accidental and deliberate. Within that span the sport had become a profession, an adjunct to show business, a campus-advertising tool (a true "branding opportunity"), a tactic for proselytizing, a public-relations boon and nightmare. Notre Dame with its football success had suddenly become involved in high commerce. Notre Dame was suddenly famous. Before 1918, the sport at the school was less organized than your average bar-sponsored softball league. In those innocent times, Notre Dame's schedule included opposing teams fielded by the Illinois Cycling Club, the Chicago Physicians and Surgeons, the Missouri Osteopaths, Englewood High School, and North Division High School, Chicago. There were, however, no schools for the blind, no Sisters of the Holy Rosary. By the time Rockne died thirteen years later, in 1931, his football program had reached a level of sophistication that the general managers and PR directors and talent scouts of a modern NFL franchise would not have found alien. By the time Rockne died, Notre Dame had a national reputation, a peerless revenue stream, and a fan base of uncommon intensity that stretched from coast to coast.

Before Rockne, the priests of Notre Dame generally thought of football as a rousing good game capable of lifting the spirits of the student body, binding them together, and offering them a little recreation. The CSCs were all for expanding the program. Long before he became president of the university in 1922, Fr. Matthew Walsh, CSC, made it a point during freshmen orientation to tell football stories. Already he was assembling the lore. In 1909 touchdowns counted as five points, goalposts still rose directly from goal lines, and Notre Dame defeated Michigan for the first time. With the freshmen gathered before the start of each fall semester, Walsh liked to tell of how a fullback named Pete Vaughn scored the winning touchdown from the red zone by somersaulting over the Michigan defense and into the goalpost so hard that he broke the post. With the anecdote, Walsh was giving his freshmen an example of the Notre Dame "spirit," the origins of the current "mystique." It had been part of the school's culture since the beginning, when Fr. Edward Sorin—who, like all Notre Dame legends, had the gift of sales—scrapped, clawed, and conned on behalf of his grandiosely named boys' academy. Today Sorin would be called a workaholic, and in him there was a bit of the tyrant. He schemed and gambled, an entrepreneur in perpetual need of seed capital. He once dispatched a few CSCs to the California gold rush. Bearded as a Viking, tall and broadshouldered, he was physically intimidating. He entered America with six Holy Cross brothers in 1841, and on his overland trip from New York to Indiana, he repelled three highwaymen who had posed as guides and were now threatening the religious with loaded revolvers. Sorin stood there, looked them in the eye, and dared them to make a move. They looked back at the priest and thought it over. They holstered their guns and escorted Sorin the rest of the way. If anything is surprising about this anecdote—all of it according to legend—it's that Sorin didn't convert them. The real origin of the Notre Dame "spirit," however, probably didn't become fully realized until 1879, when much of the school burned to the ground. Sorin toured the ruins. As Sperber relates, many other colleges met a similar fate in the nineteenth century, and most of them remained ruins. Sorin, however, amid the embers, turned to another priest and reportedly delivered a line that could have been struck in coin: "If it were *all* gone, I should not give up."

Perhaps Sorin was at that moment thinking of some famous words from the constitution of the Congregation of Holy Cross, which are often related to this day in homilies by priests during Masses on campus, sometimes in the Basilica after football games. "But we do not grieve as men without hope, for Christ the Lord has risen to die no more. . . . All is swallowed up in victory." From the ruins eventually rose the Main Building that exists today, among the most famous campus structures in the country and the world. Synecdochical of the university, its symbol and its brand, it is a weird compote of architectural modes—Renaissance Revival, Second Empire, neoclassic, and neo-Gothic. With its yellow marl-brick facade and Gothic-arch lintels, with its rambling mansard roofs and crosses like antennae rising from every gable, with its gilt state-capital dome and sixteen-foot Virgin Mary standing sentry on top, the whole thing looms over the campus like an edifice from Assisi as conceived by a promoter of world's fairs—fantastical, holy, and somehow naive.

The frontier campus began to attract the sons of poor immigrants—not all of them Catholic, but mostly—from the big urban centers of the Midwest, a demographic that fit nicely with Sorin's dogged, practical, gambling character. Together it produced a milieu in which competitive sport naturally flourished—boxing was big, baseball was big. Knute Rockne was one of these kids. Prayer and athletics and academics were all integrated into daily, ordinary life. It was an ancient tradition, sound mind and body and soul—the "whole man." From this pool of sturdy immigrant stock, athletic and rough-and-tumble, the football team gathered the players that would constitute its first championship-caliber teams, and from the same student body, the Holy Cross congregation recruited its priests. The priests produced by the Notre Dame milieu, like its lay graduates, tended to be tough and pragmatic, with the addition of being relatively learned, though in a continental and medieval way, with its focus on Latin and the ancients and the early Christian thinkers.

In Catholic theology, a charism is a special gift of the Holy Spirit, quite literally bestowed by the Holy Spirit and, therefore, by God, to a person or a group. It is meant to be used for the benefit of humankind. Every religious community or order has its own specific charism. Basil Moreau founded his congregation in the Ste. Croix neighborhood of Le Mans—thus its name—a couple decades after the French Revolution had pretty well routed the Catholic Church from France. But because Catholic parishes had run most of the nation's schools, a crisis in education as well as faith soon developed. Thus, the charism of Moreau's religious community became missionary teaching. In the rural neighborhoods of France, his Holy Cross priests would also reestablish the sacraments, which, for Moreau, was synonymous with education. In the words of the Holy Cross constitution, its priests are "educators in the faith, . . . supporting men and women of goodwill everywhere in their efforts to form communities of the coming kingdom."

The greatest and most prominent and most famous example of the Holy Cross charism would, of course, reside just outside South Bend, Indiana, USA. The big idea was *not* to cloister these Catholics from the world, but to prepare them for entrée into the establishment, and therefore to "make an impact in the world," as Fr. Peter Rocca, the current rector of the Sacred Heart Basilica, has put it. But it was more radical even than this, for the goal was to *convert* an establishment hostile to their basic Catholic beliefs, whether that establishment was French libertine or American WASP. It was, they believed, a sacred enterprise, a gift, after all, from God.

Not long after World War I, Fr. James Burns, CSC, initiated the university's first strategic, long-term fund-raising drive. The first Notre Dame president to have his doctorate, he wanted, at last, to endow the institution. His stated ambition was to start Notre Dame on a track that would make it, as he said in private correspondence, the "Yale of the West," except Catholic. No one knows how Notre Dame fans of the time would have responded to this early articulation of an "aspirational peer." Academic ambition descended on the university's leaders at about the same time that their school started to play nationally elite football.

No wonder, then, that the CSCs blanched at the attention their football venture had suddenly acquired under Rockne. Prompted by Notre Dame's sporting success, outside, reform-minded groups studied and investigated big-business football programs and what role they played within the ivory tower. These studies, when published, never explicitly named Notre Dame or Knute Rockne, but anyone literate or sentient enough could read between the lines. They questioned Notre Dame's institutional values. Meanwhile, the Big Ten snubbed Notre Dame three times in its bid to enter the league, frozen out on theological grounds. Publicly, the Big Ten claimed that Notre Dame did not live up to the conference's high ethical standards. These win-obsessed Catholics played dirty, they said, mostly by shirking the rules of player eligibility. The newspapers covered the Catholics unevenly—the Gee

Whiz school glorified, the Aw Nuts school attacked, and myths developed both positive and negative, the Four Horsemen and the indefatigable Notre Dame Spirit on the one hand, and a football factory of devious papist intent on the other. By and large, anti-Catholic prejudice created not only KKK rallies outside Notre Dame's front door, but also double standards. The press and the reform groups ignored the corruption of the teams in the Big Ten and at the same time attacked Notre Dame.

By 1923, the university had become, in the minds of many, a pure football factory, a term invented sometime during these years by the sports press, and a term that would subsequently enrage many generations of CSC, including both Hesburgh and Malloy. ("It's the only thing we do *well.*") W. O. McGeehan of the *New York Herald-Tribune* once set out for a trip to Notre Dame so that he could "investigate the rumor a university was located there." (Rockne schmoozed him to such a degree that McGeehan thereafter became a staunch Notre Dame defender.) The reputation has indeed lasted up until the present day; many otherwise knowledgeable people seem to believe that Notre Dame's student body is land-grant size, football-factory size, when in fact it has an undergraduate population of eighty-three hundred, compared with twenty-four thousand at Michigan, sixteen thousand five hundred at Southern Cal.

With this sort of reputation developing, football threatened to overshadow not just the higher-learning portion of the institution, but the sacred enterprise—the Holy Cross charism itself. But, of course, football could also be used to further the charism, and Notre Dame's double bind was created. On the one hand, the CSCs strove to stem the power of the expanding program, and on the other they embraced it. Largely from gate receipts, money poured into the endowment to fund the university's mission. The proceeds helped Notre Dame remain solvent through the Depression. Revenue from football covered its costs and reached a half million dollars a year. The Irish once drew 120,000 people to Chicago's Soldier Field. They filled Yankee Stadium each year against Army—79,000, standing room only. They made a deal with Southern Cal to play the Trojans every year for, according to Sperber's well-researched conjecture, around $100,000, which would amount to almost $11 million in today's dollars. Flush, the university went out and poached European scholars looking to escape fascism. Flush, the university built the vast neo-Gothic quad that stretches on an east-west axis and, intersecting the main quad, forms a giant cross. To do it, they put off building Knute Rockne's stadium, under great protestation from the head coach.

Reading Sperber on the squabbles between the CSCs and the peerless Knute Rockne brings to mind Ecclesiastes—nothing new is under the sun. Notre Dame class of 1914, Rockne wanted to play national schedules—which led to less time in the classroom for the players, and which in turn led to charges that gate receipts meant more to Notre Dame than courses in Latin and Thomas Aquinas. The CSCs let him play those national schedules, knowing that this was what created the fans and, therefore, ticket sales, but Rockne wanted more. Bowl games were vetoed. The extra revenue from these matches, originally created by local chambers of commerce to bring tourists to town, would have made Notre Dame look even more moneygrubbing. Save the Rose in 1925, the no-bowl statute would hold fast until 1970, the middle of the Parseghian period. Rockne was also his own athletic director and wanted, of course, more money to buy equipment—the football arms race. He wanted as many players as possible, and he wanted sole oversight over their academic progress. Their grades in class were somewhat secondary. Giving and taking, he and the CSCs haggled constantly over their eligibility. Rockne was the first to convince Notre Dame to grant athletic "scholar" ships, a practice then in place for decades at most schools. Less than almost all of the teams of the Big Ten, which were far more corrupt, Rockne bent what recruiting rules existed, but bent them so intelligently that additional rules were created to thwart him—Vinny Cerrato on the phone from the Orange Bowl. He wanted a stadium of suitable dimensions and believed it should have priority over everything else. After everything else went up, the CSCs gave him his stadium. A body was created, staffed mostly by CSC academics—the Faculty Board of Control of Athletics—with orders to curtail Rockne's influence. Rockne despised them, called them "effete," and brought in high-powered alumni to help with his cause. The "Call for Change" letter versus Monk Malloy and PC academe— nothing new is under the sun. When Rockne didn't get what he wanted, he wrote letters of resignation and entertained the overtures of other colleges—first Iowa, then Southern Cal, then Columbia (the job he came closest to taking), then Ohio State, and then, finally, a new Jesuit school then being built in Los Angeles that would be called Loyola Marymount. In short, he exhibited all of the qualities of a modern college head-football coach, except that he did it first.

Even the team nickname became a metaphor for the whole problem, and its solution. The Ramblers, the Rovers, the Nomads, the Hoosiers, the Wandering Irish, the Catholics, the Papists, the Dumb Micks, the Dirty Irish, the Fighting Irish—all these nicknames and more were applied to Notre Dame until the last one stuck and Walsh, throwing up his hands, made it official when a New York reporter called for clarification in 1927. All of the nicknames, the CSCs felt, were pejorative, since they either slurred the school ethnically or indicated the team's penchant for travel, and thus Notre Dame's status as a factory of football.

Out of these clashes between Rockne and the administrations of two presidents, Fr. Matthew Walsh and then Fr. Charles O'Donnell, Notre Dame forged a policy toward football that has extended right up to Nate Farley in the grandstands. They would incorporate football into the charism.

Through public comment and private statement, the CSC presidents articulated their emerging strategy. Many Irish fans hold to the notion that the university always made its own rules, lived by its own standards. Though this is mostly true, Notre Dame under Rockne no longer resided in a vacuum. Walsh wrote in 1925, "Long experience with athletic conditions at Notre Dame has convinced me, beyond any doubt, that our standing in the outside world is determined, not so much by the number of victories that we gain as by our strict adherence to what reputable colleges consider the proper standards." Because censure coming from the outside world threatened that standing, the CSCs decided to do those standards one better. In 1929, new president Charles O'Donnell said in a speech in New York, later quoted by the *Times,* "We deplore the excessive and almost exclusive eminence of Notre Dame as a place where a football team is turned out."

In 1933, after Rockne's death, with no Rockne to contend with, Fr. John O'Hara, later cardinal and archbishop of Philadelphia, ascended to the presidency and gathered the experience and thinking of his forerunners into one coherent long-range plan that Sperber termed "Fortress Notre Dame." As Sperber summarizes, "His strategy was simple—on the ethical heights he would construct 'Fortress Notre Dame' and render it impervious to the charges and rumors that had long plagued the Catholic school." Staking out the high ground, rising to the mount, O'Hara decided that Notre Dame would become the standard-bearer of intercollegiate sport—pure as the university's titular Our Lady. Six years later, when Frank Leahy was hired, O'Hara's successor called the Fighting Irish football team, and by extension its huge fan base, "an apostolate for the working of incalculable good." Over the years Notre Dame's position as the "moral model" of college athletics has become less a matter of policy than a de facto condition of its institutional existence.

Within the persona of Fr. John Cardinal O'Hara, the Notre Dame double bind was made flesh. He knew what dangers championship football presented, but he understood as well the many rewards of winning. Foundation money was at stake, since the secular intellectuals who oversaw its allocation publicly questioned the seriousness of Notre Dame's academic enterprise, what with its football. To a degree this motivated O'Hara's Fortress, but it also angered him enough that he once publicly pointed out that he'd rather have an endowment funded by football than an endowment funded by the spoils of robber barons and assorted tycoons—Carnegie of Carnegie Mellon, Vanderbilt of Vanderbilt, Stanford of Stanford, Duke of Duke, Rockefeller of the University of Chicago, and all of their leftovers into the trusts of the Ivy Leagues schools and, soon enough, Notre Dame as well.

O'Hara was, of course, a fan himself. Before becoming president, he was prefect of religion and at the players' request, chaplain of the football team. As such, he administered last rites to George Gipp. He often supported Rockne against the meddling of the Faculty Board. The charism clearly at work, he presided over Rockne's conversion to Catholicism in 1925. In 1921, with the team on its way by train to West Point for the annual game against Army, they stopped at Albany and trekked out to another grotto, another Lourdes replica, to celebrate Mass. O'Hara made sure that reporters and photographers were there to capture the scene, and from that moment on the team's game-day

Mass became another famed Notre Dame ritual. Two years later, at Notre Dame's first matchup against Army in New York City, an Army publicist had arranged for a Broadway starlet named Elsie Janis to ride into Ebbets Field on a mule, and then to perform a ceremonial kickoff. O'Hara countered with Joan of Arc. After Communion, at Mass, he distributed to the team medals imprinted with the image of the saint. On the back it said PRAY FOR US. The players sometimes affixed the medals like sigils to their pads, to their uniforms, for protection against injury, and again O'Hara made sure that the media knew about it. To the press corps he said, "Elsie Janis will kick off for Army; Joan of Arc will kick off for Notre Dame." Notre Dame won 13–0, and the tradition of handing out Saints' medals to the players has continued to the present day. Intaglio on each game's medal is a different saint, usually corresponding to the feast day nearest on the calendar. O'Hara viewed football as an opportunity to proselytize, to educate in the faith, and the more popular the team became, so much the better. He put his vision in print, writing a campus circular entitled the *Religious Bulletin.* Not only did it go to students, but alumni, faculty, coreligious at other schools, and the Catholic press. It eventually had a circulation of six thousand, and it contained statements like "Notre Dame football is a spiritual service because it is played for the honor and glory of God and of his Blessed Mother. When St. Paul said, 'Whether you eat or drink, or whatsoever else you do, do all for the glory of God,' he included football." To O'Hara, Notre Dame football was "the red-blooded play of men full of life, full of hope, full of charity . . . who believe that clean play can be offered as a prayer in honor of the Queen of Heaven; Notre Dame football is a new crusade. It kills prejudice and it stimulates faith." O'Hara believed that the larger the number of Notre Dame students who took daily Communion the week before a game, the better the odds that Notre Dame would win. In his bulletin, he drew up charts to prove it—a statistical analysis. When the Jesuits read this kind of thing, they looked down on it over the lengths of their bookish noses. They scoffed. They called it O'Hara's "football theology." Everyone else loved it, and the fans, the subway alumni, the immigrants in their neighborhoods, the nuns in their nunneries, took O'Hara to mean that victories—not just playing the game—meant glorifying God. And if that were the case, then they ought better to pray for Notre Dame wins. When Notre Dame won, it vindicated everything. All was swallowed up in victory. The beads came out before kickoff, and the Grotto filled up. According to O'Hara, football at Notre Dame was also a gift from the Holy Spirit, and as the team continued to win, it would, in a sense, form a community of the coming kingdom.

Father Hesburgh, president emeritus, has a suite of rooms on the thirteenth floor of the immense library that bears his name as well as the giant mosaic officially titled *Word of Life*. The largest such mosaic in the world, 129 feet tall and 65 wide, it portrays Christ the Teacher and is, essentially, a visual depiction of the Holy Cross charism. It consists of precisely seven thousand pieces of granite in 171 colors; the artist, Millard Sheets, had to travel to sixteen countries to find the geology necessary for the palette. To fashion the pieces for Christ's halo, the stonecutters had to invent a method for cutting the granite in curves. It had never before been done. The idea for the mosaic was Hesburgh's. He had seen the one on the facade of a building on the campus of the Universidad Mexicana in Mexico City. He has said, "We needed something spectacular to take this enormous building in the middle of a prairie in northern Indiana and not have it look like a grain elevator. I had no idea of its juxtaposition with the stadium; it never crossed my mind." It crossed someone's. The precise etymology has been lost, but almost immediately after its unveiling in 1964, some campus wit or other created the nickname by which it is now colloquially and universally known. He or she should have taken out a copyright. Almost nobody knows its real title. Jesus posing in a gesture of instruction— He might be midparable—has been converted into a touchdown.

Cataracts in both eyes have nearly blinded Hesburgh, who is eighty-seven years old. His unfixed gaze seems to pass through the person he's talking to and into the space beyond. Like any blind person, he looks oracular. Gray hair has grown a little ragged in the ease of his retirement and is swept back from a balding scalp. He has a lantern jaw that's grown a little jowly and fleshy bags under his eyes. His overall aspect is leonine. The clubbish odor of cigar smoke attends him from room to room up there on the thirteenth floor, and when visitors arrive, he asks if they mind, and he lights up another torpedo. In his study, a

huge circular rug in blue-gold weave bears the Notre Dame seal. A
black TV set the size of a small automobile looms against the far wall.
The rest of the walls are bookshelves. Near his desk, a west-facing window looks across campus and frames the dome of the Main Building.
He is fond of saying, "Any time I need help, I look out the window and
say a prayer to the Blessed Mother. And that's it. Problem solved."

Hesburgh has said before, "Notre Dame has a constant story to tell,
and too many people see in it things that are more superficial than in-
spiring." He was addressing Notre Dame fandom with that remark, and
he expands on it now when he says, "We've got some people that—it's
almost a religion to them. I don't buy that. I *do* think it's an important
exhibit of our school's spirit. And although it's lasted over the years,
it's gone up and down. But it's something that is very real, almost palpable. On the other hand, it's something that grows from the essence of
the place. Football doesn't create that essence. It's something much
deeper—which is that this is the greatest Catholic university in the
world, in my judgment. When you look at the university from a distance, you see first the spire of the church. Then you see the golden
dome of Our Lady. Then you see the upper stories of the library. And
then you see the stadium over there. That picture says something very
important. The church, of course, is central to the whole endeavor. If
all you saw was the stadium, which is true of some universities of comparable size, you'd have a false notion of the place."

As far as the sport of football itself goes, and team competition in
general, Hesburgh could leave it all mostly alone. Up on the VIP level
of the stadium press box, down the hall from Malloy's suite, Hesburgh
has his own private room. According to his biographer, Michael
O'Brien (*Hesburgh: A Biography,* 1988), during tight games, oblivious
to the action, Hesburgh has been known to ignore the field and engage
the people sitting near him in conversation on, say (if it was the early
1990s), the problems post-Tito in the former Yugoslavia. He has "perspective." Again according to O'Brien, Hesburgh once told a colleague
after a defeat, "When you get up in the morning, the clock will be going
around, and the sun will be coming up. The world didn't end today."
But he also follows the team closely enough to know the rosters and
the two-deep, to be aware of team strengths and weaknesses. He told
me toward the end of the 2004 season, "The guys on defense are not in

position. The secondary is playing too far off the ball." In describing his status as a Fighting Irish fan, his friends and confidants sound a lot like the friends and confidants of Monk Malloy describing Monk Malloy. "He hates to lose. He likes to win at everything we do, including football," Father Joyce once said. Football aside and football included, Hesburgh simply roots for Notre Dame the institution.

He has, after all, staked his life on it. He has been described as the twentieth-century version of Father Sorin. The gift of sales—so prevalent among Notre Dame's leaders both CSC and lay that it, too, might have arrived via the Holy Spirit—may never have been more fully realized in a Notre Dame president. He was a fund-raiser nonpareil. He was a master marketeer. Even more than *mystique,* the word most often used to describe Notre Dame is *special,* without further explication. Hesburgh often spoke of the university's "specialness," and in doing so, he appears to have coined its ND usage. He once said, "I *am* essentially a salesman. I sell the university and the good news of the Lord." Before soirees with university benefactors, including up in the press box, VIP level, he would warn his subordinates that if he ever caught them talking amongst themselves, he would not be pleased. They were not there for their own entertainment; they were there to schmooze.

Like Malloy, he steers conversation away from the football program and parks it elsewhere, sometimes in an area near the Knight Commission, a group formed to study and make suggestions on how to fix intercollegiate athletics, another in a long line of such studies, one of the earliest of which, of course, targeted Notre Dame and Knute Rockne. In 1989, another major wave of scandals had swept over college sports, and Hesburgh cochaired the committee. He feared athletic scandal at his own school. If the NCAA ever found Notre Dame in violation of the rules, "it would kill me," he once said. It would be "the worst thing that could ever happen to us." He delegated management of the athletic department—and the school's business affairs—totally and without meddling to Father Joyce, and Father Joyce in turn delegated day-to-day operation of athletics to Moose Krause. They all three smoked cigars together like Chicago sportsmen putting in the fix. Hesburgh, not surprisingly, was a stickler. He obsessed over graduation rates for the football team, and he wanted all players to graduate in four years. There were no jock majors. There were no jock dorms.

There would be no training table; the jocks would eat their dinners in the dining halls side by side with the geeks and the preppies. All athletes were students, and that was that—there would be no class distinctions, in both senses of the phrase. In return, Notre Dame would offer massive tutorial support to its athletes and would not revoke scholarships—as they sometimes were, and are, at other universities—if players suffered career-ending injuries. Assistant coaches were paid well below the industry mean; it was assumed that having Notre Dame on the résumé more than made up for a salary cut. For a long time, Hesburgh refused to let the head coach's salary grow to more than that of the faculty's highest-paid professor.

For reasons not altogether clear, he insisted that all Notre Dame head coaches receive five-year contracts. During this window, if they ran a clean program but fielded weak teams, "I'll keep the alumni off your back." Hesburgh said this to Gerry Faust, who coached the Irish from 1981 to 1985, five seasons. The record in his fourth year was 5-6. After the window closed and if the team remained weak, the deal expired, and the coach ought to "resign." If he didn't resign, he would be fired. This informal, unspoken policy congealed into precedent, and it too became a de facto condition of Notre Dame life, as if written into the university bylaws. It fit squarely into the Fortress idea. Many people considered five years far too long to give a failing head coach. It was axiomatic in the coaching profession that by year three you knew if the coach would succeed or fail. Ara Parseghian even stated as much. But as Hesburgh wrote in his memoirs about Faust and his guaranteed five seasons, "We took a lot of heat for not buying him out after four years, but in the long run I don't think it hurt us. It showed people that when we made a contract, we stood behind it, and that while winning was important to us, it was not the only thing we cared about." This policy seemed as much about image ("it showed people") as it was about integrity, and in that sense too it was of a piece with Fortress Notre Dame. Hesburgh believed that it would last forever. Again in his memoirs, he wrote, "That Notre Dame precept of hiring coaches has not gone out of style, nor, I trust, will it ever."

Born in Syracuse, showing an early aptitude and appetite for spiritual vocation, Hesburgh was recruited by Holy Cross priests, including Fr. Tom Duffy, visiting his parish from Notre Dame. He was in eighth grade and an altar boy. Prior to meeting Duffy, Hesburgh had known about the university not through its priests but via its football. "All the Catholic kids were fans in those days," he says, and so was he. He corresponded with Duffy all through high school. "I remember writing him a letter on December the second, 1933, and it said, 'Two big things happened today. I finally got a brother'—my brother was born that day, on December second—'and also, Notre Dame beat Army.' " At Yankee Stadium, the Irish won by a point, 13–12.

Hesburgh entered the Holy Cross seminary at Notre Dame in 1934. As a seminarian and then as a doctoral student, Hesburgh was part of an expanding gestalt that would eventually bring about the Second Vatican Ecumenical Council—Vatican II. Bits of Hesburgh's doctoral thesis were quoted in documents that arose out of the Council. Vatican II was, of course, a massive reform movement. It was "apostolic." It was an *aggiornamento,* an updating. It advocated that lay people participate in the Church and the Mass in ways the Roman hierarchy would never previously have approved—which, in turn, would bring the Church into the modern world. Secularism had split the world in two—religious life and all the rest—politics, business, education, art, and, yes, sports. Among the goals of Vatican II was to infuse the religious and the spiritual back into these perceived secular arenas, to bridge the gap with the help of the Catholic laity—the Church of the People of God.

Vatican II treated the modern world on its own terms, and these ideas informed Hesburgh's thirty-five-year career as Notre Dame president, during which he conducted an *aggiornamento* of his own. He raised admissions standards across the board (1960), which led to the rejection of alumni children for the first time in school history, and which also made it tougher to bring in less scholarly athletes. It was his stated goal to rid Notre Dame of some of the sentimental schlock of old-school Catholic devotion. "We do not hold that piety is a substitute for competence, but it should not be divorced from competence," he told an interviewer early in his presidency, a position perhaps at odds with some of the earlier O'Haran traditions, with their pious mathematics of sacrament and gridiron victory. He abolished the Mass requirement for students (1961), he made the school coed (1972), and he transferred ownership of the university from the Congregation of Holy Cross to a board of trustees that was all-lay (1967), thus insuring the school's "academic freedom," by which Hesburgh meant interference from Rome. To many in the CSC, especially those of older vintage, Hesburgh had just, as some of them put it, "sold the farm." Hesburgh's reforms also enraged a good many older alumni, who believed that what Hesburgh had done to Notre Dame was de-emphasize religion.

This, of course, is not the case. Hesburgh's goal was to strive for excellence in all pursuits, and "excellence" was a word he used so often that it has since become a kind of credo for Notre Dame. The credo depended, of course, on the charism, and Hesburgh's views on Notre Dame's Catholicism could be summed up in this way, from an essay by Bishop Daniel Jenky, CSC, a Notre Dame–trained priest, now bishop of Peoria: "To be homogenized into the undifferentiated academic culture of American universities would constitute a colossal loss of nerve and a shameless betrayal of the academic tradition of our faith. Because of the Gospel of Jesus Christ, Holy Cross schools should not be like everyone else. They should be better."

Nonetheless, angry missives poured into the presidential office. Letters to the editor appeared in the alumni magazine. "There is another trend in progress. . . . It is the growing official sanction of secularism and spiritual decline among students and faculty. Or perhaps it should be expressed as a more or less conscious departure from Catholic orthodoxy and worship. This, I think, is almost satanic."

The complaints were as heated as anything directed at Monk Malloy—and the crux of the criticism was nearly identical. Traditional Notre Dame was under attack. Notre Dame's cultural shift had begun. High academic achievers and strivers out of high school were replacing the sons of alumni in the student body. The Notre Dame Family was being unraveled. Among Hesburgh's constituencies, there was distrust, as there had been since early in his presidency, when he was also charged with de-emphasizing football.

"Not true," Hesburgh wrote in his memoirs. "I never deliberately did anything to cut back on football. My belief is, and always has been, that the university ought to do everything—academics, athletics, you name it—in a first-rate manner."

When he first took office in 1953, he wrote a letter to the Ford Foundation in application for a grant. A summary of Notre Dame's institutional condition pre-him, it was, all at the same time, an analysis, an indictment, a diagnosis, and a plea. "Our student body had doubled, our facilities were inadequate, our faculty quite ordinary for the most part, our deans and department heads complacent, our graduates loyal and true in heart but often lacking in intellectual curiosity, our academic programs largely encrusted with the accretions of decades, our graduate school infant, our administration in need of reorganization, our fund-raising non-existent, and our football team national champions." The punch line makes a reader wonder. What Hesburgh had just described was a football factory. His claim that he did not de-emphasize football was an argument of semantics—he believed that football at Notre Dame had been overemphasized.

Frank Leahy, author of four national championships, was then head coach, and so many wins did he oversee that the press had revived the football factory cognomen, thus initiating a cycle of sports-media coverage that will likely last as long as Notre Dame plays the sport. In the hyperbole typical of a genre not well-known for the intellect of its practitioners, when Notre Dame does well and wins championships, it has "sold out" its high standards, thus destroying the Fortress idea of Notre Dame as "moral compass" for college athletics. When it does poorly, Fighting Irish football, once and for all, is "dead."

Prior to becoming president, Hesburgh, as executive VP, had already disassembled Leahy's hegemony over the athletic department, mostly by naming Moose Krause athletic director—Leahy, like Rockne, had been his own AD—and limiting the number of scholarships to thirty per year. By the time Hesburgh wrote his letter to the Ford Foundation, Leahy's health was failing, his teams were not living up to his own postwar standards, and Hesburgh convinced him to retire. As Leahy's replacement, Hesburgh hired Terry Brennan, twenty-five years old, Notre Dame class of 1949, a halfback under Leahy and head coach of a Catholic prep academy, Mt. Carmel, Chicago, a Notre Dame feeder school. In addition to setting scholarship limits, Hesburgh also raised academic standards for incoming athletes. By Brennan's third season, that first ten-year period of decline had begun—the "Years of Pennance," as Francis Wallace, a Notre Dame alum and sportswriter, has called them—the mirror image of the present one.

There were other hints about Hesburgh's attitude toward the football program. When the new president made a West Coast speaking tour in 1952, hardly anyone showed up except sportswriters. They asked him about the team. He asked them if they were interested in hearing about education. They said no. He said, "Well, then, this news conference is over." Another story exists, perhaps apocryphal: Upon his inauguration, in 1952, one reporter or other asked Hesburgh to pose with a football for a photo to accompany the story. A version of the tale has the reporter asking the president to hike the ball between his knees on the field inside the stadium. *No way in hell* was the response.

Whether Hesburgh's moves were part of a purposeful strategy of football de-emphasis, Brennan, today, from his home in a suburb north of Chicago, cannot say. "That's an ancient topic," he says. He *will* say, however, that Hesburgh was "trying to make a real statement that he was going to be an educational president. I wouldn't call him a close friend, but I respect him greatly. He wasn't really a sports guy. He was an intellectual, he speaks eight languages, and he wanted to improve Notre Dame academically and make it into a world-class university. And he *succeeded*."

When Brennan's five-year term ended with a combined record in his last three seasons of 15-15, Notre Dame fired him. The timing was difficult—the university released the news a few days before Christmas. Hesburgh has claimed that he and Brennan agreed to the timing of the announcement beforehand. Others have claimed that Brennan didn't want to be fired at all, and Hesburgh delayed the announcement until the school had another head coach in the bag. Some felt that the tougher academic standards had unfairly condemned Brennan to failure. Remembering the furor that this caused from the distance of eighteen years, Francis Wallace, Notre Dame class of 1923, a former press assistant to Rockne and later sports columnist for the New York *Daily News,* wrote in one of his many ND football histories, "For the only time in my memory, the Notre Dame family was divided." The ever-vigilant sports press, meanwhile, came out in full attack, and their reports seemed to combine both major Irish-baiting themes at once, and thus contradict themselves. Only a football factory would ever behave like this; Notre Dame has surrendered its moral high ground. Academic standards are way too high; Notre Dame football is dead. "The Brennan guillotining was mishandled with the impersonal cold-bloodedness of one of those colleges that are known in the trade as a football foundry," intoned the *New York Times.* The story remained in the headlines for two weeks. *Sports Illustrated* ran a long, censorious article on the firing, and in a rare public reaction to this type of criticism, Hesburgh wrote a letter in defense, and the magazine published the piece. Among other points, the president denied that alumni pressure, in the form of withheld donations, had induced Brennan's firing, and he went on to note that precisely two alumni had contacted him to complain about the directions of the football program.

Certain lines from the letter have entered the Notre Dame canon, cited by Irish fans to this day whenever media criticism again rains down. Hesburgh took on both Irish-baiting themes at once. "I think it somewhat an inversion of values that a university can appoint twenty distinguished professors, make broad and significant changes in personnel to achieve greater excellence, without attracting more than a slight ripple of attention. But let that same university make a well-considered change in athletic personnel for the same reason, and it sparks the ill-considered charge that it is no longer a first-rate academic institution and must henceforth be considered a football factory. . . . There is no academic virtue in playing mediocre football and no academic vice in winning a game that by all odds one should lose. . . . There has been a surrender at Notre Dame, but it is a surrender to excellence on all fronts, and in this we hope to rise above ourselves with the help of God."

Five more years of even worse football followed, under former Washington Redskins head coach Joe Kuharich, Notre Dame class of 1938. Fan anxiety at the time reached the pitch of hysteria, and Hesburgh in this situation got out of the five-year guarantee when Kuharich resigned after his fourth season. According to uncomfirmed campus gossip, a group of moneyed alumni attempted to buy out the remainder of Kuharich's contract—possibly a kind of proto-C4C—but the administration had refused the overture. The *South Bend Tribune* quoted Kuharich upon his resignation: "This insatiable appetite to win has become so strong it is ludicrous. The day of invincible college football teams, year after year, is gone." (Nothing new is under the sun.)

But Ara Parseghian's hiring was not long on the horizon, and with his entrée all became right with the world. "It was in about 1964 that Father Hesburgh, I think, felt that the academic reputation of the university was such that football could be re-emphasized," says Bishop Jenky. *Time* magazine ran a cover story on the Parseghian turnaround in 1964 (Notre Dame won its first nine games of that season), and the article hinted that significantly decreased football revenue might have spurred the university into hiring an accomplished head coach and granting him the elbow room to succeed. Of the pre-Parseghian ND, *Time* reported, "Now, when the cost of Notre Dame's sports program was deducted, there was barely enough left over to pay the coal bill for an Indiana winter." Hesburgh, however, has always maintained— Occam's razor—that Notre Dame owed its football renewal from 1964 onward to nothing more than a good coach becoming available for hire (Parseghian actually contacted Notre Dame about the job opening), and a good coach working hard to succeed. CSC priests who have been around a long time support Hesburgh's view—there was no purposeful de-emphasis, and, therefore, no purposeful re-emphasis. "Any mediocre coach we had was a mistake," says Fr. Tom McNally, Notre Dame class of 1949. "I remember one of our priests campaigning hard for Joe Kuharich. He was singing his praises. 'This is the coach who's going to lead us out of the jungle.' But Kuharich was something of a disaster, and, boy, did we get on him, this priest, because of it. To this day, I still remind him of that whenever he complains or voices an opinion about the present coaching. 'Oh, you wanna bring back *Joe Kuharich?*' "

Meanwhile, with Parseghian safely in office, Hesburgh continued to draw funds into Notre Dame's bank accounts, and as time moved on, and further national championships arrived, the fans forgave Hesburgh his moment of "de-emphasis," both football and Catholic, and then seemed to forget all about it.

Hesburgh has become in these intervening years a living icon on par with the statuary and the shrines. Fans drop his name and describe their chance encounters with him on campus, in airports, outside hotels. It has become almost a badge of one's eminence as a fan to say that you've met, or that you "know," Father Ted, as many people call him. His autograph appears on footballs and photographs displayed in the Notre Dame rooms of career Irish fans all over the country. It's dead even whether fans would rather have Hesburgh's signature or one of Notre Dame's Heisman Trophy winner's. He was perhaps the most famous university president in the country, if not the world. With all his high-profile committee work—civil rights, nuclear proliferation, etc.—with his third-world social-justice adventuring, he has lived a life in the public eye. He was, in a way, Notre Dame's John Paul II. Today, an unending sequence of visitors fills his daybook behind the receptionist's desk on the thirteenth floor. Of his undeniable status as a Notre Dame legend, he says, "I don't think of myself as that," and he laughs. "But I'm here, I'm on campus, I've been around a long time. They even put my name on the library, which I didn't want them to do. They called a board meeting. They didn't invite me, or Father Joyce. I didn't know what was going on till I came over here one day and saw the workers tapping the letters of my name up there. I told the board, 'You don't want to put people's names, living people's names, on buildings. If they move off somewhere else, then you've got to take it off.' They said they weren't worried about that."

Most Notre Dame fans would deem Hesburgh a heretic if they were to sit down with him and discuss the current direction of the football program. "We've had more than our share of national championships," he says, and he takes a drag from his cigar, and the blue smoke drifts. "We've had more than our share of Heisman Trophy winners. We've had our ups and downs because that's normal in any sport." And he steers the conversation in the direction of the Knight Commission, of graduation rates, of Notre Dame's exemplary record in graduating its players, the need for penalizing renegade programs, football factories . . .

Every day he says three rosaries and a Mass, and he is proud of this. "I've maybe missed four times in sixty-one years as a priest. But some days I've said three or four Masses, so I can literally say I've celebrated Mass many more days than I've been a priest." He lives now in the Holy Cross retirement home next door to Moreau Seminary, and most often he celebrates the sacrament there. But he also uses the chapel in his suite on the thirteenth floor, a room flanked at its perimeter with shelves displaying his many awards. (He holds the world record for number of honorary degrees, and he once posed for a photograph in his office ensconced in academic hoods.)

Every football Saturday, about thirty minutes after the game, he celebrates a Mass in his office chapel, which doubles as a sitting room. Friends and alumni and just plain fans take the elevators up, pass through the book stacks, and enter his suite. There might be seventy people squeezed into the whole place, and they sit on the floor and on the couches and stand at the rear and spill out into the other rooms. The door to his office is wide-open, and they wander in there for a view of the Dome alight in the darkness. They pull out digital cameras and take discreet pictures. Some of them carry bags of merchandise from the bookstore. Everyone looks exhausted from the game, and children squirm. A hush falls over the audience, and Hesburgh appears in full white vestment. His voice registers in the lower octaves, he talks quickly, and people strain to hear his words. Their attention is so tightly focused it's as if, indeed, they've climbed the mount and are sitting at the feet of the oracle. "When we come here to campus, we come in and out, and we have our fun and our heartache and the rest," he says. "But remember that this place is special. This place is blessed. Thanks be to God for this blessed place dedicated to Our Mother, the Virgin Mary, Our Lady on the Dome, Notre Dame."

The sun had sucked everyone's energy. Halftime had passed, Michigan was now up nine to nothing on three field goals, and on its first possession of the second half, they gained thirteen yards on a running play. Mike Lewis, in his candidate year, yawned. The seminarians in the stands talked among themselves, noting that nine–zip was way better than twenty-one–zip. Eric Ufheil had a different angle on it. "Michigan should be ashamed. Nine to nothing against *us*."

Notre Dame forced the punt, and a drive developed. Darius Walker, the freshman tailback, gained good yards on back-to-back plays and appeared to be guaranteeing that every story in tomorrow's papers would include the words *freshman phenom*.

Walker again on a toss-sweep, and the measured, calm-minded postnovitiate Drew Gawrych rose to his feet and seemed to switch personae. He bellowed down and onto the field, "Get to the corner!" Walker got to the corner—first down—and Gawrych said, "We've had trouble with short yardage all game." On the next play, quarterback

Brady Quinn took his five-step drop and, no pressure, scanned the downfield situation. He reared back and unleashed one toward the end zone, forty-six yards away. The seminarians rose as one to their feet. Matt Shelton, the streaking receiver, was beneath the ball in the end zone. He almost plucked the thing off his helmet. When he landed, touchdown. The seminarians high-fived a little hysterically. There was an edge now in the afternoon, and the crowd roared as if it hadn't been expecting to behave in this way. For the first time in the 2004 season, people all over the stadium went up into the air horizontally, lifted up on the arms of other people for a set of fake push-ups, seven times heaved into the air.

Michigan kicked another field goal, and it was twelve to seven Michigan. Now the third quarter, now Walker with more carries, six yards and one yard. Gawrych did not like what he saw on the last play. "Finish the block! C'mon! You gotta stick that block!"

Third down and three to go, and then a TV time-out.

A seminarian said, "That's a very Trinitarian scoreboard." He pointed, and everyone followed his arm up to the board. Time-outs: 3. Down: 3. To go: 3. Ball on: 33. Quarter: 3. Everyone was silent for a moment, and then everyone laughed.

"Holy shit."

"Wow."

"Now that's interesting."

"That means the Trinity is with us. Good things are gonna happen."

As it turned out, those good things were for the moment deferred. Walker took the pitch on another toss-sweep, bounced around, could find no room. He was tackled a yard short of three.

The drollery of this seminarian's comment was typical of the group as a whole. Intimately familiar with the overlap of religion and sport at the place that was training them for the priesthood, they had grown a little ironical, sometimes cynical—as do the students and the faculty and everyone else on the inside at Notre Dame. At the communal table in the Moreau refectory for breakfast or lunch or dinner, the ironical comments pour forth.

A seminarian relates a quick story. A new building on campus, the Performing Arts Center, contains an enormous handmade pipe organ, carved from ancient timbers and built at a cost of a million dollars. It is meant to perform only sacred music, and it is contained in its own concert hall inside the building. At some point during a recent football weekend, the seminarian saw two Notre Dame fans enter the organ room, gaze up at the 2,551 German Baroque pipes climbing the wall to the ceiling three stories above, and genuflect.

"I wanted to say, 'Dude. It's an organ.' "

During the Ara Parseghian years, to get away from the hubbub on campus on home-game weekends, the football team would take up residence in Moreau Seminary on Friday nights. On Saturday mornings, they would celebrate their pregame team Mass inside the chapel at Moreau. (The pregame Mass in the Basilica was a Lou Holtz innovation, and the team now stays in a hotel downtown on Friday nights before home games.) As part of their duties, the seminarians helped prepare and serve the team its meals, clean up their guest rooms and turn down their beds, and set up the chapel for the pregame Mass. Often they would hang around and observe the service, the dispensation of the medals, and the recitation of a shortened version of the Litany of the Blessed Virgin.

Jenky, ordained in 1976, was a seminarian during the team's Moreau days. He says, "When I was a cynical seminarian, I have to say, we used to kind of sneer at all that. We thought, 'Oh, well, they're in there doing all this hocus-pocus before the game.' Because you think you know *everything* when you're a seminarian."

Before Rome plucked Jenky for promotion to bishop, he "pinch-hit" at Notre Dame for the regular football-team chaplain, Fr. James Riehle, who had suffered a knee injury that sidelined him for two years, 1987 and 1988. Noting the years, Jenky says, "I told Monk once, 'The last time we won a national championship, I was chaplain,' " and Jenky makes a sign of the cross. Burly as Claus, Jenky is fifty-seven years old. He has a light in his eye, an easy laugh, and a full red beard going gray everywhere but the goatee. Born and raised on the South Side of Chicago ("inelegant dese-and-doze country"), he sits on the Notre Dame board of trustees. As a bishop, he's something of a big shot, and a few times a season he travels to campus and goes to the VIP level in the press box to glad-hand with benefactors and "work the room." "It really is a working occasion. I mean, they have me go around the press box, kissing trustees' wives. 'This is Bishop Jenky.' I swear, at Notre Dame they think I'm Pope Jenky." He does not do this simply at the behest of his CSC brothers. Notre Dame class of 1969, he is, as well, an ardent fan. The worst part about being a bishop, he says, is that now he can no longer make it to every home game. "Cut me and I bleed blue and gold. Trust me. I have a room at Notre Dame at Moreau Seminary— on the Dome side. So when I go back, I can have my Dome fix." When the glad-handing subsides, he will sometimes sneak up to the roof of the press box, a popular area for anyone with a VIP pass, where he will look down at the game from the highest possible vantage. Lately he has been forced to avert his eyes more than he'd like. "If things are bad, I can't watch. So I go and stand on the other side and look toward campus." Outside his office in the chancery in Peoria, two framed photographs hang from a wall. The lower photo pictures Jenky on game day with the Irish Guard, the undergrads in kilts and high bearskin shako hats who parade martially in front of the band and throw interference as the musicians march to the stadium. The upper photo pictures Jenky and Pope John Paul II, taken during a fifteen-minute audience with the pontiff at the Vatican several years ago. "I figured it would probably be better if I put the picture of the pope on top," Jenky says. "I did invite him to Notre Dame, of course. And what do you think he did? He pointed at himself and said, 'If they let me.'"

Jenky's experience as chaplain perhaps added to his perspective and helped demolish his young man's cynicism. As chaplain, part of his duties included saying the team Mass, and naturally, he composed his homilies with the competitive athlete in mind. The Notre Dame chaplain also stands on the sidelines with the team during the game, and players would sometimes approach there. New to the gig, he did not feel at ease, conscious that he was not Jim Riehle, who had been the team chaplain since 1966 and who had become something of a Notre Dame fan icon himself. Jenky says, "I'm standing there, and the coaches are so intense, and stuff is going on, and someone would come along and say, 'You know, I really liked what you said in the homily this morning.' I'm thinking, one of these minutes Lou Holtz is gonna turn around and . . ." Jenky laughs, does not finish the thought, and moves on. "If you're in a dorm or in a classroom, you're used to students talking theology. But it really did happen *on the sideline.*"

This, in Jenky's words, is the "Notre Dame system." Worship joined to everyday life—the Holy Cross charism at work. He and almost every other CSC priest is fond of saying that Masses and prayer at Notre Dame occur in the most mundane situations as well as the most profound. "It's a pretty common part of university life. And, I would say, part of the genius of the system at Notre Dame is that it ties the life of faith more closely to the ordinary life of the student. It doesn't make it seem unusual. There's this old Holy Cross father's trick. A student's grandma dies. The guy's all upset. You offer to have Mass. Whenever that happens, you make sure everybody knows that this guy is upset because he loved his grandma, and you get his whole dorm section to come to Mass. And you make sure his girlfriend knows—get all those girls from *her* dorm to come over. So then, at a daily Mass that might normally have six people or something, instead you've got forty people. If you do that often enough, before you know it the dailies look like a Sunday Mass. This is something one Holy Cross father passes along to another. That's the system at Notre Dame. To tie prayer and service and community—and I think fans—into the life of the university. And therefore, that there is a Mass, and people pray, before a national football game on NBC, this is just part of what we do.

"I'll bet there isn't a student in theology in the entire world, who right before they're having to defend their dissertation, isn't probably praying, '*Please,* God, don't let this guy ask this question.' But somehow as a cynical seminarian, you didn't transfer that—and that's all that the team was doing. It's not some magical thing. I don't think they're praying for, 'If we do this, this, or this, we're gonna beat Michigan on Saturday.' I think it's more the basic Christian walk of faith—walking in your faith. You try to put your life in God's hands and do your best."

At the start of the fourth quarter, with Notre Dame in the red zone, Drew Gawrych said, "Sweep to the right, maybe?"

Walker took the pitch on a sweep to the right and entered the end zone untouched, pointing at pay dirt and high-stepping across the line—freshman phenom, 14–12 Irish. The crowd went into paroxysms. The seminarians were alternately high-fiving and crashing into one another. On Michigan's next series, Notre Dame held, and when Michigan punted, Notre Dame blocked the punt. Jerome Collins, a big tight end, emerged from the line and threw his body into the kicker in midkick, and the ball hit his chest with the sound of a cannon report. A moment later Walker took the handoff, moved toward the corner, eluded a tackler, stuttered, eluded another tackler—a man walking in place in a dream—then burst for the end zone, touchdown, 21–12 Irish. More paroxysms. The flurry of action made everyone punch-drunk. Drew Gawrych yelled in a fit of alliteration, "If it wasn't for Walker, we wouldn't be winning this game!" A Michigan punt, a Notre Dame fumble, a Michigan fumble, and a twenty-seven-yard pass from Notre Dame's Brady Quinn to Notre Dame's Rhema McKnight, and the seminarians were standing on their seats. Next play: a pass to the full-back in the end zone, 28–12 Irish, and the seminarians tumbled into the aisles. A blowout seemed in the making. Around the collar, Eric Ufheil's The Shirt was dark with sweat. Eyes lit up, the smile of a wild man on his face, he looked as if he'd been lunching on manna. The student section had devolved into a mosh pit. People were on top of other people and getting thrown into the air. Your ears rang. No one paid attention to the field. The seminarians lifted someone's adolescent-age brother into the air for a set of twenty-eight push-ups, and his eighty pounds quickly grew heavy. Dumb jokes yielded slaphappy, hysterical laughs.

"Play the seniors!"

"Play Rudy!"

Initiated by the student section, a wave developed inside Notre Dame Stadium, and the seminarians' focus shifted from the game to the wave—watching it, analyzing it, commenting on its virility as it moved from the gung ho students through patches of elderly and middle-age alumni and rabid subway alumni and around the bowl to the seminarians, who rose with gusto and flung their hands in the air.

Meanwhile, Michigan scored a garbage-time touchdown, 28–20 Irish, and attempted an onside kick, which was recovered by Maurice Stovall, the big wide receiver, point man on the Irish "hands team," game over and upset complete.

Eric Ufheil said, "Looks like Willingham saved his job."

The student section poured from their seats and rushed the field and surrounded the players, who held their golden helmets aloft, one hundred plus miniature Domes. Divots of sod flew into the air. The seminarians stood and watched as students drained from their section like an overturned hourglass. The band played the "Victory March" and then the alma mater, "Notre Dame, Our Mother." It is tradition that alumni—and all Notre Dame fans for that matter—link arms for the playing of the song at the end of each game and sway to its slow dirge of a rhythm. Tears will often emerge at this point from the most emotional among the fan base. As the band started, Gawrych was on his way out of the stadium. "Ope—forgot about the alma mater," and he returned to his row, and the seminarians all put their arms around one another's shoulders and swayed.

They did not know—no one yet knew until the *South Bend Tribune* printed the anecdote several days later—that a Notre Dame fan had brought to the game a vial of dirt from the gravesite of George Gipp, laid to rest in Calumet, Michigan, and handed it to a priest standing on the sidelines. The priest, Fr. Brian Stanley, Notre Dame class of 1984, was the alumni chaplain of the Notre Dame marching band—an informal, volunteer position. Among other things, he celebrated Mass in the band room after the game. A trombone player as an undergraduate, Stanley had spent six years as a Holy Cross seminarian, but had left the congregation before taking his permanent vows as a diocesan priest near his hometown in Michigan. The fan had some instructions for Father Stanley: sprinkle the dirt onto the field. At halftime, Stanley did so, in the northwest endzone, directly in front of the student section, onto a spot over which Darius Walker would later run for the second of his three touchdowns. Stanley then murmured the words, "In the sure and certain hope of the resurrection of Jesus Christ from the dead, may the soul of George Gipp know the peace of Christ and enter into His Kingdom. In the name of the Father and the Son and the Holy Spirit," and he withdrew a vial of holy water from his priest and poured a few drops over the dirt, and the water mingled with the molecules of Gipp and seeped into the field of Notre Dame Stadium, sacred ground—magic.

"Could the Gipper's ghost . . . have altered Irish fortunes Saturday?" posited the *South Bend Tribune* in its story. A week later, Father Stanley was no longer alumni chaplain of the Notre Dame marching band. The band director had called him up and said that some in the university's administration "disapproved of what I did. They did not want me on the sidelines. They did not want me celebrating Mass in the band room anymore." It was the age-old dilemma of Notre Dame translated to modern times. Religion inhabiting sport—this was too much hocus-pocus. "They said I had embarrassed the university. The last thing in the world I'd ever want to do is embarrass the university. I thought I was honoring the memory of George Gipp. I said a blessing as I would at his grave. I did not attribute anything supernatural to the gesture—it was just a gesture of prayer. If anything, I say that what happened in the second half of the game was a happy coincidence. And if anyone wants to attribute it to something else, well . . ." Later, in a telephone conversation with a Notre Dame administrator, Stanley heard a different, more practical reason for his dismissal. "The university has no problem with what you did," the official said. Instead, because the priest was not on the university payroll, he was not insured to be standing on the sidelines.

5

The Neighborhood

About two weeks before the start of the 2004 campaign, a post appeared on ND Nation, seat of the mobocracy. It said, "This season is the first in my 30-plus years of following the Irish that I will have to do so without my dad. He died in March after a pretty quick and sweeping illness. I just can't seem to get excited about the season. . . . I have no doubt that our mutual love for ND football was a major factor in the close relationship he and I had."

Seeking a kind of spiritual counsel, the poster went to the message board. His handle was NDave. He wanted to know if anyone had ever undergone similar torments—how could he "get the passion back" for Notre Dame football without his father to share it with? There ensued a thread of responses that would be almost unimaginable coming from the fans of any other sports team—commiseration, advice, invocations of faith, and at least one argument for the existence of God [all *sic*]:

"Last year was my first year without my son. We were both ND nuts. . . . Navy will be the first game I'll go to without him since he was in the third grade. Hang on to the memories—I always imagine Kevin is up there somewhere watching with me."

"He's probably up there watching with NDave's Dad too! Probably the biggest gamewatch with the most important Host!! God bless the Notre Dame community."

"Continue in your same routine and make it down to ND. You'll find that your dad's spirit is there."

"You can feel what you wish for at The Grotto, and I'm not convinced it's all 'in your imagination.' When 80,000 beings . . . feel the exact same emotional wavelength at the exact same moment, for a play that defies physics, as the band kicks up—can't you feel the magic and the power coursing through the crowd, at a speed that leaves 'light' shaking its head in wonder. Isn't that a clue that Life, and we . . . are spiritual? How can the apparency or importance of 'physical ailments', or barriers to one's dreams mean much in the face of You?"

"My Dad died, surrounded by his family, right around kickoff of the Navy game, 10/30/82. . . . Mom recalled hearing the radio broadcast of the Pitt game the following Saturday, when Faust's team knocked off then #1-ranked Pittsburgh and how she reacted: 'Well, we know he's in Heaven now, for sure!' . . . When I drove down and visited the Grotto last Tuesday, he was very much with me, very much 'there.' Notre Dame was his dream, and it was because of him and Mom that it became mine."

"Do you have a child? If not you may want to borrow one (niece, nephew, big brother volunteer program, etc.) at least on Saturdays in the Fall and spread your Dad's passion for ND, so that it lives on. . . . As for your Dad, I suspect he'll be an important addition to the magic now. We always need that."

"This is why we need to be great again. Quickly. I don't think there's any question that there are less subway alums in my generation (early 30's) than in older generations. As those older men and women begin to leave us, ND's continued struggles on the field make it harder to pass down that love and appreciation through the generations. Some of my most cherished memories regarding my time at ND involved my father (a true subway) and many of our working class relatives and friends from my hometown who were in awe every time they set foot on campus."

"My thoughts and prayers are with you. He'll be watching Old Notre Dame with Leahy, Rockne, and all the ND greats by his side. . . . If you're not in South Bend, I think a trip to ND would help. There's nothing like making a trip there to remind you of the first time you saw the Golden Dome, which is, for everyone on this board, one of the best days of our lives."

An unknown percentage of the 80,795 tickets issued for each Notre Dame home game ends up in the hands of subway alumni—collectively and by reputation the most zealous and most reverent of all Irish fans. Large numbers of subway alumni have never seen campus except in photographs, have never seen the Fighting Irish play except on television or from the stands of alien stadia—*in partibus infidelium.* Except on an extremely limited basis, there is no sale of tickets to the general public. After a complicated allotment system dispenses the seats, every game is a de facto sellout and has been since October 7, 1964—the fifth game of Ara Parseghian's first year—except once. (A game against Air Force played over Thanksgiving weekend, 1973, came up short by about two thousand fans.) A scarcity of tickets has therefore developed over the decades, despite the expanded stadium.

Demand from alumni alone would fill a stadium the size of Michigan's—117,000 people—for each of the six games on the home slate, probably more. After allotments to the vestigial season-ticket holders, sixteen thousand of them still around; after allotments to the students, faculty, and staff, all of whom receive discounts; after the VIPs get theirs—seventy-five hundred total to trustees and advisory-council members and various Friends and benefactors of anywhere from Sorin Society ($1,000 a year) to building-underwriter—after all this, somewhere between two hundred and three hundred tickets per home game remain unsold. Because most of the rows in the stadium contain thirty-seven seats, and because people generally buy tickets in pairs or groups of even numbers, a precious few single tickets form an exiguous surplus, and the university puts them on sale every August during the first week of fall training camp. A press release goes out. A post on UND.com, the official Web site of the Notre Dame athletic department, announces the day and time of the sale. E-mails and phone calls shoot around Notre Dame fandom, among the subway alumni. At the will-call window outside the Joyce Center a line begins forming a day before the sale. People drive from as far as Pennsylvania and New York and bring tents and food and beer. Tailgates develop. They spend eighteen hours in line. By the time the windows open at nine in the morning, four hundred people might be standing outside. The tickets are gone by eleven thirty. Meanwhile, all day the telephones in the ticket office do not stop ringing, even after the singles have long sold out. The office brings in help, adds lines. "We'll have people answering phones in any closet we can find," says Josh Berlo, director of ticketing. "We'll have people over in the hockey offices, by themselves, to take calls. We'd love to answer every call, but even with unlimited resources, I'd bet that's impossible." Ten thousand calls, twenty thousand calls, forty thousand calls, sixty thousand—so many calls that they bounce out of the queue and engulf the university-wide telecom-munications grid. In August before the 2002 season, Willingham's first, the fans overwhelmed the system and bogged it down until no one on campus could receive voice mail. Now, the ticket office gives fair warning to the university telecom department, which will instruct the phone company to beef up the grid.

Some of those people not lucky enough to get singles will send pleading, heartfelt letters and e-mails to the ticket office. Often they will make appeals to the university's Christian sensibilities. This sea-son, a boy wrote on behalf of his grandfather—a World War II vet, a Purple Heart recipient, a lifelong fan. The boy wanted to fulfill the old man's dream of seeing a game in Notre Dame Stadium. He sent two let-ters, for two different games. The ticket office found him a pair for ND vs. Stanford, for which there were an uncommon number of returns, mostly from Stanford people (the opposing team receives an allotment of around five thousand tickets). The ticket office does not maintain a waiting list—to do so would quickly become unmanageable—and therefore they do not take down the names of those fans who call every day during the season to see if any tickets have been returned. Every day the same people call in, and the agents begin to recognize voices. Word will spread of the availability of returns, which the university will resell at the will-call window on game-day mornings. In good weather and bad, the lines begin forming in the wee hours. For a No-vember game against Boston College in 2002, the last game of the eight-game win streak, thirty-seven tickets were returned. When Josh Berlo arrived at will-call early that morning, the temperatures were sub-freezing. "The line went almost halfway around the stadium. I couldn't find the end of it." The cashiers went out and warned every-one that the office only had thirty-seven tickets to sell. Expectantly, hopefully, a little desperately, most of the fans remained in line. On oc-casion fans will take far more drastic measures. Once, a man posed as Skip Holtz, the son of Lou and his onetime offensive coordinator at Notre Dame. The call moved up the chain of command.

"Skip Holtz is on the line for you."

"Who?"

Once the fan had reached high enough up the chain of command, he changed his tactic.

"Skip Holtz told me to call you. He said you might be able to help me—"

"That's funny, I've never met Skip Holtz."

A customer-service person was once offered a car if she could get the fan on the other end of the line season tickets. She declined the offer. Fans will see ticket-office employees interviewed on television, somehow locate their home phone numbers, and call them there. Some years ago, a fan showed up, uninvited, at the house of an agent, beseeching him for game-day entrée. Nothing, thankfully, came of that episode. As with all athletic department employees, those at the ticket office are advised to keep their home phone numbers unlisted.

Relative to the number of Notre Dame fans in the nation with no connections to the university, rare are the subway alumni who make one annual pilgrimage to campus, rarer still those who make multiple games, and extraordinary the fans who travel to every home game on the slate. The most exceptional breed, however, are the subways who have somehow obtained season tickets, for new season tickets are no longer sold to anyone. Unless, that is, a person has the means to cut checks of many digits to Notre Dame and in the memo line write *unrestricted gift*—thus becoming a Friend of the University. Calls are sometimes placed to the development office, and the voice on the other end will say, "So, to get season tickets . . . how much do I need to donate?"

In addition to *subway alumni,* they have also been called, in earlier periods, *synthetic alumni* and *assistant alumni* and *curbstone alumni,* the last of which seemed most appropriate now. Tracy Hallahan, curbstone/assistant/synthetic/subway alumnus, a general contractor out of Cincinnati, Ohio, holder of season tickets, has not missed a home game in eight years, and stood on the pavement in a parking spot near a curb outside Notre Dame Stadium. He was surrounded by a mob of undergraduates, all of them wearing The Shirt. A huge photo shoot had developed, the kids huddled up, with Tracy Hallahan ensconced in the middle like a Little League coach amid his team after the last inning of the championship game. Coeds ran up and handed their cameras to an arbitrary tailgate-goer standing nearby, who happened to be me. Designated the moment's photographer, I had cameras under my arms and coming out of my pockets and resting on the ground. I went through them all and took each shot. Flashes illuminated the scene.

Tracy Hallahan was the de facto boss of a tailgate party that sprawled across a half acre of pavement. The whole thing combined groups of friends from Cincinnati, Pittsburgh, and South Bend. They had all met while tailgating separately nine years earlier, when they began aligning their half dozen cars and vans and SUVs in the same spot in the same corner of the vast parking-lot system that surrounds the stadium—a bank of Porta Potties strategically close by. They called the aggregate the Neighborhood of Hope.

Hallahan had talked and shouted so much through the morning that he had a voice like a 1980s heavy-metal rock star's following a five-night engagement, though his hair was military-short and clapboard gray. He wore white running shoes, denim shorts, a sleeveless green sweatshirt, and wraparound sunglasses. His head was covered by a straw farmer's hat, the brim curved up. On his left shoulder he had a tattoo of the Notre Dame leprechaun, and on his right the crisscrossed flags of Ireland and the United States surrounded by the words MY COUNTRY and MY HERITAGE. Withal he looked like a customer toughened by the kinds of experiences that occur only on shore leave. When Hallahan saw me, he turned from his secret-recipe chili, heating on a propane grill, and gave me a bear hug as if we'd seen action in the same platoon. I had met him only once before, at Notre Dame's annual spring intrasquad scrimmage, but this was his nature. When not welcoming old friends after the long off-season, or lobbing beers in their direction, or leading chants, or foisting over chili in Styrofoam bowls, he was introducing strangers and escalating the party. Toastmaster, ringleader, facilitator, host—if there are six degrees of separation, Tracy Hallahan could be Kevin Bacon.

In South Bend, at the Neighborhood of Hope, Tracy Hallahan is universally known as the Sheriff. So ubiquitous is the moniker that most of the undergraduates did not know his real name. Freshmen, sophomores, juniors, seniors, the kids had come down from all over the lots, from other tailgates, from their dorm rooms on campus, and made their way to the white van in Joyce South. Every year he recruits a new pool of Notre Dame students into his circle, and he's been coming to games long enough that the Neighborhood could now form an alumni club. Some of them had brought along their parents to see if the Sheriff might grant them an audience. While other fans moved through the Basilica, knelt at the Grotto, took pictures of the Frank Leahy statue outside the stadium, visited the Main Building, and stood on God Quad awaiting band step-off, these students had trekked out to Joyce South en masse to idolize the Sheriff.

"Hey, Sheriff; hey, Sheriff! Can we get a picture with you, Sheriff?"

"Sheriff! You're a great man, Sheriff! A *great* man."

"You need a beer, Sheriff? Lemme get you a beer."

As replete with perfunctory titles as the Chicago patronage system, the Neighborhood also has a mayor. His name is Bob Wentroble, subway alumnus, a labor-union negotiator out of Pittsburgh, and he has missed precisely one home game in thirty-eight years. In 1996, for Lou Holtz's last game, union business kept him away. His son has now overtaken him for the longest streak of consecutive home games in the family, stretching back nine years and encompassing fifty-six games. But Wentroble's total number of contests long ago eclipsed two hundred, making him the Neighborhood's most senior member and allowing him a distinct advantage over all other claimants to the office of mayor. It has a singular prerequisite, instituted by Wentroble. "In order to run for mayor," Hallahan once explained, "you had to hold the position the year before."

The Neighborhood also has its various other deputies and, of course, the Sheriff. The exact nature of Hallahan's responsibility as gendarme is not exactly clear, but he seemed to understand it well enough. He led rousing renditions of the "Victory March," including its lesser-known first verse, which begins, "Rally sons of Notre Dame..." About a dozen times during every pregame, and another dozen times post-, Hallahan gathers a group of tailgaters around him, a bottle of Jameson in his hand, for a performance so regular that everyone knows what's coming. It's called the Four Sins Toast, and it's declaimed like a responsorial psalm. Now, realizing that a student had brought his parents out to the Neighborhood, Hallahan addressed the tailgate at large. "Excuse me!" he shouted, and his roughshod voice emerged as if projected from a bullhorn. "All you Notre Dame students! C'mon over here! I wanna show that you guys have learned something this year!"

The students formed a tight circle around him. He held the Jameson bottle aloft, and he yelled from deep in his lungs, "Are you ready?"

"Yes!" was the collective response.

"How many sins of an Irishman?"

"Four!"

"And what are they?"

"Lying! Cheating! Stealing! Drinking!"

"And if yer gonna *lie?*"

"Lie in the arms of your lover!"

"If yer gonna *cheat?*"

"Cheat death!"

"If yer gonna *steal?*"

"Steal a kiss from a pretty girl!"

And Hallahan suspended the toast, leaned over to the student's mother, who stood there agawk at what her son had been learning and gave her a peck on the cheek.

"Hey! That's my mom!"

"And if yer gonna *drink?*"

"Drink with your friends!" The students bellowed the last line in unison—well trained, well oiled—and sent up a volley of cheers, pleased with themselves. Girls hooted, boys roared, everyone applauded. Completing the toast, the Jameson bottle made its way around the group. Each person swigged, a few grimaced, and they all passed it along.

The Sheriff turned to the kid's parents. "And you thought they were stupid," he said. "They're geniuses." After the whiskey had completed its circuit, Hallahan made sure to take the bottle back. Both for their own protection as well as to maintain the economy of his liquor supply, he stashed it in his van. He knew from experience that if he didn't, the kids would chug the bottle empty within a quarter hour.

The Neighborhood of Hope has been around long enough to see its share of tragedy. Before last year, it was called simply the Neighborhood. But George May, a South Bend native and Neighborhood citizen since he first hooked up with Hallahan and Wentroble nine years ago, lost his wife to breast cancer after the 2003 season. Her name was Hope. Over the Neighborhood's nine years, its people have grown close as college classmates. For all the undergraduates who visit the tailgate, at least the same number of subway alumni come by to pay homage to the Sheriff and the Mayor and George May and the rest. It is a way station, a port of call, a ticket exchange, a corner tavern, and the subway alumni form the core.

"I didn't go to college," George May said. "I'm one of the dreaded subway alumni."

"Dreaded?"

"Well, usually subway alums are the ones who bitch and whine the most."

The Mayor made his first pilgrimage forty-one years ago, at age seventeen. After high school the following year, he did not become a freshmen. He got a job as a welder, and he got married. Eventually he worked on the floor of the Westinghouse plant in Pittsburgh that built the hulls of Trident nuclear submarines, and he eventually became a negotiator for the IUECWA: International Union of Electrical and Communications Workers of America. He said, "No offense to the alumni, they're nice to us when we're here, but the subway alumni are the real backbone of this university. Because I think they put more into this place—other than money, of course, though they do that too—than anyone else."

The Mayor pronounced his o's in the manner of his native city. When he said no, there seemed to be a w in there somewhere. Among the subway alumni in general there is a panoply of accents, and to walk through the lots on a game day and chat with the fans is to take a primer in phonetic anthropology—diphthongal Brooklynese and outer borough in general, round-voweled Jerseyan and lax-voweled Philadelphian, the wicked good non-rhotics of Boston and New England, the rotated short vowels of the rust-belt Great Lakes, the Mason-Dixon twang of the Ohio River Valley, Wentroble's palatal western PA, Da Bears Chicago, and the flatland monophthongs of the upper Midwest—wherever Catholic immigrants settled and clustered and merged their speech patterns with the already present dialects of American English, they also gave rise to subway alumni.

Rich Rozmarynowski, a Neighborhood regular, was a retired South Bend cop whose beat on Saturdays included the tailgates. From 1988 to 1994, toward the end of his active-duty career, he guarded a room inside Notre Dame Stadium where bags contained $35,000 to $40,000 in small bills, revenue from the sale of game-day programs. Gleaned from his experience among the tailgates, what he said today seemed to combine the observations of both George May and Bob Wentroble. Notre Dame's subway alumni, he said, had remained loyal to the university through all the down periods, even if that loyalty came with instances of high vocal lament. He was also feeling a little underappreciated. He said, "Notre Dame doesn't give the ethnics enough credit. Because in the fifties, when the team was losing, the Chicago taverns would take busloads of people to the games. Buses of people would be grilling and drinking out here. And they'd all be from the taverns in Chicago and Gary. And from Pennsylvania and Ohio too. They *all* had tickets— *season* tickets. But you don't see that no more. They took all that away. These are the people who supported this university through all those lean years. But all those people lost their privileges."

Robert Vahalik stood at the perimeter of the Neighborhood, quietly drinking a beer. Small, flinty, gray-haired, 76 years old, Vahalik owns a two-hundred-acre farm in ruralest Ohio near a burgh named Amsterdam. His primary crop is hay, and he sells most of it for $6.50 a bale to the Chesterfield Racetrack in West Virginia. "That's a good price when you think I only get a buck a bale back home," he said. His father was not a farmer, but a coal miner in the Mahoning Valley of eastern Ohio, an immigrant from Slovakia, as was his mother. Though his parents were not especial Notre Dame fans, they listened to the football games on the radio with their children, glad to see that they supported what appeared to be the only Catholic college in the United States. Vahalik is a fan of atypical hardiness. "I've set through rain, I've set through snow. I been comin' to games forty years." Over that period he has missed precisely two home games, when, for the first time, he traveled to his homeland. "I went to see all my family in Slovakia the one year," he said, "aind they all wanted to come back to America with me." Vahalik is a member of the Sorin Society, the Notre Dame benefactor circle, which requires of its fellows a thousand per annum. The Society has 9,860 members total, out of which 1,250 are non-alumni, out of which most, like Vahalik, are subway alumni. Among other privileges, Sorin membership gains a person entry into the ticket lottery for every home game and pretty much guarantees a win for all of them, about the closest a fan of relatively modest means can get to season tickets today. Vahalik has known the Sheriff for going on ten years, having first met him at a tailgate before a game no one otherwise recalls. At the Neighborhood, the Sheriff likes to show Vahalik off. "Hey! Come over here and meet the Silo Man!" he says. "This is what Notre Dame's all about, right here!" "Hey, have you met the Silo Man yet?"

"They call me the Silo Man."

From his wallet, Vahalik removed a laminated card that said on the back SILO MAN. On the front was a color photograph of a grain silo.

"My nephew at the time worked on silos," Vahalik explained. "I had the roof made special and he put it up there." The roof of the Silo Man's silo is a dome, a statue of the Virgin Mary rises from its peak, and the entire edifice from base to Blessed Mother has been spray-painted yellow-gold.

"Someplace out here in South Bend I picked her up, and she's hollow. She's about four and a half feet tall. I fit her on a pipe and she's been up there thirty years. Hasn't moved. No matter what kind of wind or weather, she's still up there."

On one side of the dome, stenciled in block letters of Madonna blue, are the words NOTRE DAME, and in this way Robert Vahalik's silo dome deviates from the original.

I asked Silo Man what gave him the idea.

"I's just a *Notre Dame* fan," he said. "They got theirs up there. I figured I'd get one of my own down here. This way I don't have to go clear to South Bend—I can stay at home aind see my *own* Golden Dome."

From the other end of his outstretched arm he peered at his laminated card. He grinned as if laying eyes on the edifice for the first time, and he let out a laugh. "It is somethin', ain't it? *Oh,* my."

Down there in Buckeye country the Silo Man has occasionally had problems with his neighbors. "You oughta see them Ohio State fans. Comin' down with helicopters tryin' to lasso the thing."

"With helicopters?"

"Yeah!" He laughed his wheezing laugh. "They did not succeed. She's still there!"

Over in the heart of the Neighborhood, the students broke into the fight song, led by the Sheriff. He led them in a chant of "Go, Irish! Keep rolling!" He was well on his way to running out of beer—eighteen cases—for the first time in many tailgates. Springsteen and Mellencamp and Sam Cooke, three of Hallahan's favorites, pumped from speakers sitting atop his van. Two Notre Dame coeds Irish-danced,

clogging in tennis shoes to Michael Jackson's "Billie Jean" and then to
rousing applause. Here at the Neighborhood of Hope, you would have
no idea if the Irish were in the middle of a national championship run
or on their way to another losing season. All was swallowed up in the
party.

As it happened, the team had pulled out its victory against Michigan, astounding everyone, on September 11. The next week, the Irish
had traveled to East Lansing and defeated Michigan State, 31–24, in a
game that ended up much closer than it could have been. And today,
the team was about to take the field against the Huskies of the University of Washington. By the end of the first half, doubt about the outcome would leave the stadium. Four first-half touchdown passes by
Brady Quinn eliminated the Huskies, who would end the season with
one win against ten losses. Final score, 38–3. Optimism had made a
comeback among the fan base. The "Call for Change" alumni looked
antiprophetic. The Brigham Young fiasco had been the outlier. Seemingly vindicated, full of gusto, the Pollyannas asked, what if Notre
Dame won out? The Cassandras, meanwhile, retrenched. With a
streaking Purdue team up next on the slate, they looked to that game as
a test. As one Cassandra wrote on ND Nation, "This is Ty's last chance
with me."

The Cassandras also cited disturbing rumors that had made their
way to the message boards. The scuttlebutt concerned Notre Dame's
assistant coaches, most of them imported from Stanford when Willingham had taken the Irish job, and most of whom had spent their careers
at universities in the Pacific Ten conference. Allegedly, the assistants
had greeted their colleagues from Washington, a Pac-10 team, after the
game and complained about their employer. The scrutiny was suffocating, the fans a bunch of nutcases, the climate cold, the sky often
gray rather than blue, the long tradition a yoke around their necks. The
rumors led to a single conclusion among the Cassandras: Willingham
and staff most definitely did not "get it."

Were Hallahan an ND Nation poster, he would have voted Cassandra, but Hallahan does not generally surf the Web for any reason. He
hasn't the time. At home after work at eleven at night, he and his wife
do the books for the business over a cold beer. Like the Cassandras,
however, Hallahan had his doubts about Willingham, given the 2003

season and all the blowout losses, but he was content to enjoy the wins and let the coach prove that he was "the answer," as Hallahan says.

"I was interviewed again by TV today," he said after the Washington victory. For some reason, the local South Bend TV sports reporters, whenever conducting their postgame man-on-the-street interviews with fans, often isolate the Sheriff at his bailiwick. "They asked me if I thought Ty would win us a national championship. I said, 'You're not gonna hold this against me, are you?' They said no. So I said, 'No, I don't think Ty is the answer.' I said, 'Any win we get, I'm happy with. But I've been watching this team forty years, and I don't know what this is—but I know it's not a Lou Holtz team. I know it's not an Ara Parseghian team. It's not even a *Dan Devine* team. There's no cockiness, no yelling and screaming when they're coming out of the tunnel.' "

Whenever Hallahan gets on this subject, it will often initiate something close to a rant. He believes that Holtz did not resign, but was pushed out, was fired. At the time, this tested Hallahan's faith in Notre Dame the institution, and the intervening years have not altogether quelled his anger. Spinning his theories, he often works himself into a furor. Once, I was with Hallahan in his van in Cincinnati, going from one job to the next, when he launched into a heated monologue on the subject. So involved did he get in his oratory that he missed his turn. In 1997, when Davie took the podium at the pep rally inside newly expanded Notre Dame Stadium, Hallahan was sitting in the stands. "Davie comes in there and says, 'It's the start of a new era.' I said, 'A *new era?* The fuck it is!' " Hallahan enjoys listing Holtz's accomplishments—coming in after the Faust disaster and three years later going undefeated and winning the national title. In 1989, he was one "bullshit clip call" away from a second title. And in 1993, Holtz again was jobbed out of a third. "Holtz got the university their NBC contract, he filled that stadium, he won what shoulda been three national championships. And what does Davie do when he comes there? He stabs the guy in the back, he weasels his way into the head-coaching job—and Notre Dame lets him! Bob friggin' *Davie*. He was just a fucking idiot. That was the start of the whole thing right there."

Hallahan's wife, Diane, has suggested that all of this has resulted in a mellowing of her husband's fanaticism, except when someone mistakenly brings Bob Davie into the conversation. His feelings for the team and the university have shifted into something else. "I don't think he's so crazy anymore, where he loses his life in the team," Diane says. "I'm glad he's not as upset by losses as he used to be. When Lou Holtz was there, oh my God. He'd get teary-eyed at wins and losses. He's just so sentimental about it. And then when Lou left, that broke his heart. He didn't think they treated him right. So, he's not *as* emotional about it now. I think he just enjoys the people at Notre Dame and being there with them. He works so hard—it gives him time to play hard."

Sober Tom and Boston Tom, sophomores, stood near Hallahan's van in sunglasses and ballcaps and shorts that hung baggy from the hip. High school chums from Brookline, Massachusetts, Boston Tom with light hair, Sober Tom with dark, they stood the exact same height—six foot three. Rarely not seen in each other's company, they had, as a distinguishing mechanism, acquired their nicknames early in freshmen year. Sober Tom especially was steeped in Notre Dame legacy. Five of his immediate family had attended Notre Dame, including his father and grandfather. His grandfather, now deceased, was the last living member of Knute Rockne's final team, 1930. Already veterans of the Neighborhood, both Toms made sure to spend a good portion of their game-day mornings and afternoons drinking beer with the Sheriff. By word of mouth, passed down through select portions of the student body, or by simple serendipity—walking past Hallahan's party on their way someplace else—new freshmen arrived at the Neighborhood every year before the first game of the season. Sometimes, Hallahan would accost an unsuspecting group of youngsters, easily noticeable in their green The Shirts, ambling wide-eyed and probably buzzed through the tailgate madness. He'd haze them into the Neighborhood.

Hallahan had recruited the Toms in this way, and they had grown closer to the Sheriff than most everyone else. They were his favorites. They even knew his real name.

Now, at the Neighborhood, Sober Tom stuck a dorm key into the side of a Natural Light, thumbed a hole into the aluminum, hoisted the can to his mouth, pulled the tab, and triggered the shotgun. All the way back he tilted his head until he faced the sky. He wasted no fluid; no plumes of beer geysered from the corners of his mouth. After a four-second count, can empty, he let out a roar and a subterranean belch. Then he crumpled the can in his fist, and chucked the thing like a jump shot into a garbage barrel ten feet away. Swoosh. He wiped his mouth with his hands and said that he and Boston Tom and four other freshmen had been walking past the Neighborhood last year, before the first game of the season. They did not make it past. A voice had emerged from somewhere, gravely, loud, and a little startling.

"Hey! You sons of bitches don't have beers in your hands!" They looked down at their hands and saw that the voice was right.

The Sheriff said, "You know the words to the fight song? If you can sing the fight song to everyone at the tailgate, you can drink here for free the next four years."

"And we did," Sober Tom said now, recalling the story. "And we're here." He grabbed another Natural Light from a cooler of ice and turned to the rest of the Neighborhood, filled not only with students, but with Hallahan's friends from Cincinnati—every one of them a sub-way alum. In a kind of toast, Sober Tom raised the can to the heavens and bellowed as loud as he could, "I! Love! Tracy!" No one paid him much attention. He turned back to us and said, "I want to be the Sheriff when I grow up."

The size of Hallahan's arms made you comprehend the character of his work. He had fingers thick as one-inch rebar. From a couple decades hauling cinder block and pounding nails, his palms near the thumbs had calluses like mushroom caps. He owns his own one-van contracting company, Main Street Building, and mostly he takes on home renovations and home additions and new home construction, averaging about a house a year. He runs a crew of about six guys. He juggles big jobs with "side jobs," taking on other work at nights and on weekends to supplement his income. At the moment, among several other smaller engagements, he was performing a gut rehab on a four-story Victorian mansion in Bellevue, Kentucky, up on the bluffs and across the Ohio River from Cincinnati. He could also build a nice back-yard deck. He could build an exquisite basement bar, from rec-room countertop to full-on Irish-pub replica—his true and natural specialty. Dozens of his pieces decorate basements all across greater Cincinnati. Hallahan's home, a spilt-level structure of his own design in a suburban development thirty miles from downtown, contains a pub as well.

Tucked in a corner of the lower level, in deeply stained oak, it has fluted columns and a glass-case backbar and overhead racks and oak wall paneling and, of course, a Notre Dame theme. It is the Hallahan iteration of the Notre Dame rooms that exist in the houses of fans all over the country, built to contain the mementos of a passion, and it is the pride of his current residence. Every house Hallahan has lived in for the last thirty years he has built himself, footers to shingles, electrical to finished carpentry, at night and on weekends after he's finished work at his main jobs.

Once, a student came up to Hallahan as he packed his equipment into his van just before kickoff. The student pulled out a twenty-dollar bill and tried to press it into the Sheriff's palm. "Hey, Sheriff. For the beer."

"Put your money away. Put your money away."

His words a slur, the student had been well served. He protested, but Hallahan would hear none of it. "Ah right, ah right," the student said. "But next time wheel get you a box of *Jameson's*!"

"That's all right, don't worry about that. What you *can* do is do me a favor. Get outta here so I can clean up. And make sure you come back after the game!" Hallahan slapped the kid on the back. "Now get in there before you miss kickoff!"

Hallahan has said before, "I love my job, I really love it. But I work every day from six a.m. till ten at night, seven days a week, and earn my money just so I can afford to come up here to Notre Dame." When the Irish travel and the Sheriff does not travel with them, he will work on Saturdays until an hour before kickoff, then head to the bar with the friends he has long ago converted into Irish fans. On gas and beer and miscellaneous tailgate provisions and equipment upgrades and hotel rooms and nights out, he spends about $7,500 for a season. He accepts money from no one. He is the leader of a cavalcade that migrates from southwest Ohio to South Bend six times a year. The pilgrims shift with each game, but the Sheriff remains, behind the wheel of his 1990 Chevrolet 2.0 van with the hand-painted tire cover on the back that says IRISH.

• • •

Like almost all subway alumni, he has a view of Notre Dame student-hood that approaches idealism—and to be among the undergraduates appears to be one of the major reasons he makes his pilgrimage week after week, year after year. In loco parentis, he feels a sense of obliga-tion toward them. "You guys study hard all year to be here at Notre Dame. This is the time for you to have a good time, and not worry about anything, and blow off some steam." He has said to me before, "If I can give them a good time and take their minds away from grades and fi-nals and whatever else they're worrying about for four years—if six times a year I can make it a little easier for them to forget the real world—that's the goal in life, isn't it?" Sometimes Hallahan offers parental advice to his undergrads, conferring with them closely in se-rious tones. "I didn't get a chance to go to school. I want you to work hard. I want you to do good. Now grab a beer."

Notre Dame undergrads are, above all, "good kids," by which Hal-lahan means built at the core of the stuff that Hallahan holds most dear—trustworthy, generous, hardworking. To Hallahan, with his sixty- and seventy- and eighty-hour workweeks, this is what Notre Dame as a whole means to him. He says that the school and its football team have inspired him to work hard, to raise a good family, and in this way Notre Dame seems to have become his ethic.

But for many subway alum, it goes beyond even this. For many of them, their dreams of youth were to matriculate at the university and perhaps as a consequence, a kind of saintliness hovers over their con-ception of the Notre Dame student. When asked why they didn't go to Notre Dame, subway alumni will often respond, "Oh, I wasn't good enough." Doubtless their idealization arises out of what they believe to be the studiousness necessary for admission, and the pious inclina-tions necessary to be attracted to the Catholic school in the first place. With its single-sex dorms and its parietals, Notre Dame has students who are not oversexed. These Notre Dame girls do not go wild; instead, they go to the library. Their politics do not exist and seem to be con-fined to pro-life rallies, which at Notre Dame is like making sure that the coal has been shipped to western Pennsylvania. Oriented to their goals, a bunch of go-getters, there are no goof-offs here, and therefore their degrees from Notre Dame will certify lifetimes of success. The sins of the student body are limited to a predilection for quantities of beer. But they attend the sacraments, and they confess to these sins. "Notre Dame kids," I have heard subway alumni say over and over, "they're different—they're just *good kids.*"

But Tracy Hallahan, transformed into the Sheriff at South Bend city limits, has his own particular sense of obligation to the Notre Dame student body—and here he is, helping them blow off a little steam. "If you don't have a good time, it's not my fault," he likes to say. "It's the American ideal. I create the opportunity, but it's up to you to have the wisdom to take it."

Two coeds, small and blond, fixed themselves vodka drinks in red Solo cups from the bar spread at the Neighborhood tailgate before the start of the Washington game. They had high helium voices. They had rolled the sleeves of their The Shirts up onto their shoulders, making them into tank tops. Courtesy of the Toms and not through the normal near-harassment, they had been introduced to the Sheriff. All through the season they would come back to the Neighborhood, at least for some of the time.

"Because we're girls, we have other obligations—like visiting our parents' tailgates," one of them told me.

"That means we can't drink there."

"Apparently the Sheriff has some kind of connection. I think he knows the police or something. So when we're here we know we won't get arrested."

Two rent-a-cops, middle-aged women in dark blue uniforms, basked in the sun on lawn chairs close by the Neighborhood. Every home-game Saturday, when he arrives in the parking lots at seven thirty in the morning, Hallahan presents the rent-a-cop women with a bag of breakfast sandwiches bought from McDonald's—Value Meal baksheesh. This keeps them on his side, and this is the extent of Hallahan's "connections." When the Toms first met Hallahan, they heard his nickname and reasoned that the man carried a badge, sheriff's office, St. Joseph County. There have been other misconceptions as well. Normally when freshmen first encounter the Sheriff, they figure him to be an alumnus of particular zeal, and with sufficient means to finance such a party through the season, week after week. They seem surprised to learn that he is "just a fan," but it does not concern them, and they go right on drinking their beer, no questions asked. They're vaguely aware that he lives somewhere not so far away, but not so close, either—perhaps Ohio. Disabused of their law-enforcement notions, disabused of his educational history, no one seems, nonetheless, to know what exactly draws Hallahan to the place. Like Sober Tom, some of the students are legacies with ancient Notre Dame histories. Others chose Notre Dame simply as an alternative to other elite universities. Either way, almost all of them come from affluent families—middle-middle and upper-middle. In the student parking lots sit Volvos and Saabs and leather-interior SUVs. When the university still drew its students from the proletariat masses (up until the late 1950s and early 1960s, as Hesburgh's changes took hold), about the only thing that separated a subway alumnus from an actual one was a framed Notre Dame lambskin. No longer. As Catholics moved out of the ghettos and in among the WASPS, the economics of Notre Dame studenthood shifted. And when Notre Dame became an elite college destination, today sanctioned by *U.S. News,* the "meritocracy" at work, it began to draw more and more of the relative elites. *Subway alumni,* formerly an expression familiar to all at Notre Dame, now draws blank stares from the students drinking beer at the Neighborhood of Hope. Not one of them has ever heard of the term.

John O'Hallahan of County Cork immigrated to the United States in the late nineteenth century; no one knows the year. Somewhere along the line he dropped the *O* from his name for the typical reasons. Since Irishmen need not have applied, he obtained a fake birth certificate, converting his native city into San Francisco, no trace of Cork. He hid his brogue, but for John O'Hallahan this was no trouble at all. He had a talent for voices. He was a song-and-dance man on vaudeville stages from Broadway to Los Angeles. Shortening his name even further for the stage, he was one half of Hallen n' Day. He married a magician's assistant whom he'd met on the circuit. Her own mother was a vaudeville fan dancer. For the first five years of Tracy's father's life, he knew as his home only trains and hotels. John Patrick Hallahan also took to the stage, and an old family photo exists of him at perhaps five years of age, bowing gallantly to a vaudeville audience. During the Depression, when not traveling, the boy and his father (John Sr. was separated from his wife, and he took custody) lived in an apartment in the back of a theater in downtown Chicago. Touring about the nation in the twilight of vaudeville, John Sr. at one point became aware of this Catholic school in northern Indiana with the football team nicknamed the Fighting Irish and coached by the Chicago-raised immigrant Knute Rockne. All of this was too much to resist, and Saturdays in the fall soon became ritualized.

Tracy's father eventually entered the family trade as a dancer and a musician. He grew to be six foot two inches tall and 320 pounds, but he was nimble. "He taught ballet and tap till the day he died," Tracy Hallahan says, which makes you wonder what John Patrick could have done in Notre Dame Stadium as an end for Frank Leahy. He also played banjo and piano and trumpet and organ in a succession of five-piece Lawrence Welk–like bands. After the war, which he spent in the Pacific theater, ordered there to entertain the troops, he settled in Chicago and commenced a career as a Notre Dame subway alumnus as well as a superintendent for the Chicago Transit Authority—subways and el trains. On Saturday afternoons in the autumn, he would gather his household around the radio and force his sons and daughters to pay attention to what was being said. (The voice belonged to Joe Boland, the lead broadcaster for the Irish Football Network, who was at that same moment creating subway alumni all over the country, since his voice belonged to the only nationally transmitted college-football broadcast.) On those afternoons, the Hallahan family room grew almost as crowded as the Neighborhood of Hope. Some of them have since died, and the last time the whole family convened in the same place at the same time was 1979, the day of Tracy Hallahan's wedding. Before moving out to softer climes in the suburbs when Tracy was about five or six years old, the Hallahans made their home in a three-room walk-up in a tenement building on Kenmore Avenue, just west of the Loop. In one room slept mother and father. In the second room, big sisters had dibs on the mattress, while little sisters got tucked into the open drawers of a dresser. On the floor of the living room, the brothers spread out on blankets. In each of the rooms hung a crucifix.

Out of this rabble Tracy is the tenth eldest. Not one of them attended Notre Dame, but all of their number are Notre Dame fans. Another Hallahan brother, Terry, died in a motorcycle accident twenty years ago, and at the wake, over the body in the coffin, his siblings draped a Notre Dame T-shirt and placed atop the shirt a Notre Dame ballcap. They have spread their devotion across the generations. "I have eighty-four nieces and nephews running around," says Dan Hallahan, one of Tracy's brothers. "And I think they're all Notre Dame fans." Tracy has made an Irish devotee out of his son, Matthew, a redheaded twenty-one-year-old, who is said to resemble John Patrick Hallahan. He weighs in at 250, stands six feet two, and for a time in high school played defensive tackle. Everyone calls him the Beast due to an incident of competitive behavior on a basketball court many years ago. With a bowler on his head he'd not be out of place in a Chicago gangland photograph from the 1920s. So freckled is the Beast that his complexion resembles mortadella. He often travels to games with his father, and his devotion to the team is such that he, also, has tattoos. Blue-green lettering in a Gothic script runs down each of his forearms, which look like albino footballs. On the left arm it says FIGHTING and on the right it says IRISH and you can almost imagine the bar brawl—in left-right, fighting-Irish combinations. On his left shoulder is the O'Hallahan family crest.

But no one in the clan has reached a more zealous attachment to Notre Dame than the Sheriff, Tracy Hallahan. When he was a younger man, Irish defeats occasionally induced violence. "I gotta tell you, I busted three stereos over the course of my career." At a party in 1978 celebrating his parents' thirty-fifth wedding anniversary, the family gathered around a radio playing Notre Dame's loss to Southern Cal on a last-second field goal, 25–27. After the ball sailed through the uprights, the radio sailed into a wall. Party over. As late as 1998, in Bob Davie's second year, when Michigan State routed Notre Dame, 23–45, Hallahan stormed out of a friend's house where people had gathered for a game-watch party. Everyone thought he was kidding. He stormed back into the house. "Diane! Get your goddamn stuff! *We're goin' home!*"

As Diane has said, the years have mellowed Hallahan a good deal, but the process by which he was mellowed did not come easily. "Let me ask you," he said to me once. "Have you ever been so passionate about something that it was more important than anything else in your life? Man, it was like that for me. Notre Dame, they were the best, the most feared team in the country, and to watch that go away over the years— it's like it slowly tore away . . . It's like it tore out your upbringing."

Sometimes he talks like a recovering addict. "I got stupid over Notre Dame football. I say stupid because, I mean, it's only a game. When they lost, I took it personal. I shouldn't have, but I did. It was like, how could you *do* this to me?"

He attended his first home game in 1984, the Irish vs. the Buffaloes of Colorado, Boulder. His father died fourteen years later, never having made it to a Notre Dame game with his son. When Hallahan told me this, I was reminded of the thread of posts that developed on ND Nation about fathers and sons and Notre Dame fandom. But unlike those people, bucking the trend, Hallahan did not seem concerned about never having joined his father on a pilgrimage.

"He hit first and asked questions later," Tracy Hallahan says. No uncertainty surrounded the question of who ruled the Hallahan clan. In Tracy's experience, his father displayed no emotion except when expressing displeasure, disappointment, anger, and fury. His temper lit fast. "Quick story. My dad bought a new car, and he brought it home. He was very proud of it. A neighborhood cat got into the car somehow and left paw prints all across the upholstery. My dad was convinced one of his kids had let a dog inside it. He picked three of us at random. He said, 'Who put the dog in the car?' None of us answered. He said, 'Somebody better speak up or you're all gonna get it.' *Get it* meant the belt."

Such experiences, of which there were more than a few, bound the Hallahan children together. Notre Dame football did as well. To an extent, Notre Dame Saturdays provided common ground, with the paterfamilias presiding over the scene. To a greater extent, Notre Dame Saturdays offered escape from the paterfamilias. "The most embarrassing times in my life were because of my dad. The best times in my life were because of Notre Dame football—hanging out with my older brothers, watching the games. I was so young I didn't really understand what was going on. You were screaming and yelling because everyone else was screaming and yelling. The wins and losses didn't make any difference when I was young. It was the atmosphere, watching the games, being with my brothers—all the guys together in the house with the Notre Dame game on. Stop and think about that. Let's say you're on the road, and you stop and watch the game at a bar with nothing but strangers, but they're all Notre Dame fans. And everyone is screaming and yelling. For a little while you forget about politics, about your job, about money, about what happened at home. You feel part of something, you feel something in common with these people. I'm passionate about a lot of things, but nothing more than Notre Dame. It's been dear to me since I can remember."

All of this goes a long way toward explaining Hallahan's demonstrative nature, and the community he has created in the parking lots. "Probably ten times a day I tell my kids I love 'em," he says. "My dad, till the day he died, never said those words to me. I owned my own company, I was in business for myself, busting my ass. He never gave me praise for anything I'd ever done in my life. As I got older, I tried to understand why my dad did what he did. Maybe I appreciate it a little more now that he was trying to raise sixteen kids. But he went overboard, I think. I've gone overboard the other way." He says, "I'm a hugger. I hug everybody." Male, female, friend, acquaintance, a stranger he just met, Hallahan moves in for the embrace. His two children adore him on the level of an older and wiser friend, a role that sometimes worries Hallahan—perhaps, he thinks, he should be a little sterner with them. He sheds tears at the merest breeze of sentiment or nostalgia, especially when it comes to either Notre Dame or the United States of America. "I'm so pro-America it's not even funny," he says. Yellow-ribbon stickers, SUPPORT OUR TROOPS, adorn all his automobiles. And if the two are ever combined, watch out. Before a home game early in the 2004 season, an alumnus of Notre Dame and an alumnus of the Neighborhood, class of 2000, visited Hallahan's tailgate. He wheeled his wheelchair up to the Sheriff. An army Blackhawk helicopter pilot, he had some months before gone down with his ship in Afghanistan and ripped up his legs and almost died. (He would walk again, but he would require six operations.) When Hallahan heard the story, he was beside himself. "He's my hero," Hallahan said. "He's what America is all about. If it weren't for him, we wouldn't be drinking beer here right now."

Hallahan seems to live by the words *God, Country, Notre Dame*, with the notable exception of the first of those elements. He has never set foot inside the Sacred Heart Basilica. Aside from photographs and postcards, he has never laid eyes on the Grotto, a circumstance so rare among Notre Dame fans that it would be almost as strange for a person to visit the Grotto on game day but not the stadium. When he brings newcomers to Notre Dame, he does instruct them to take a walk around campus, to drink in the aura of the place—Grotto and church, the sacred regions. But for Tracy Hallahan, his six-times-a-year pilgrimage is purely secular. He says that his duties as Sheriff, as tailgate host and ringleader, serving his guests and maintaining the party, keep him away from the campus sites. There is, however, another possible explanation. Though confirmed Catholic, he has no religion now, lost many years ago for perhaps quite specific reasons. Of his father, Hallahan has said, "Every Sunday, he'd come to church late, on purpose, so he could march to the front and show everyone in the congregation that John Pat Hallahan—here he is—comes to church with all his kids. John Patrick Hallahan, good Irish-Catholic father."

Hallahan seems to have replaced the Church with the Neighborhood. At the close of a postgame tailgate, saying his good-byes, distributing his bear hugs, he looks around him at the fans mingling behind his van—students, alumni, subway alumni, everyone having a good time—and says, full of beer and goodwill, "This is what Notre Dame is all about." The phrase rises above cliché as the emotion rises in Hallahan's face. Others seem to appreciate it as well. One night, bidding everyone at the Neighborhood farewell till next time, Silo Man said, with some amazement, "This here's more important than the *game*."

Just before kickoff at the last home contest of the 2004 season, a group of freshmen and sophomores, Neighborhood denizens since only the Michigan game, called Sheriff Hallahan over to their group and solemnly present him with a gift, an album full of photographs from the previous five Neighborhood tailgates of 2004. Thirty undergrads surrounded Hallahan as he leafed slowly through the album. He laughed and he jawboned and, finally, as he reached the last picture, wiped his eyes. "You guys are assholes," he said. "You guys, I'm tellin' you. You rotten motherfuckers are gonna make me cry." He looked around at his admirers and he was suddenly without words. "There it goes," he said. Girls cooed as Hallahan teared up. But he quickly pulled himself out of it, and the kids erupted in cheers, and someone said, "Get 'em a beer!" and Hallahan said, "Alright! Are we ready? One! Two! Three!" And he led the Neighborhood in a song.

Rally sons of Notre Dame,
Sing her glory and sound her fame . . .

In 1998 Hallahan was about to leave for South Bend—Notre Dame against Michigan—when he received a call from one of his brothers, who would be joining him for the weekend pilgrimage. John Patrick Hallahan had died. He was seventy-eight years old.

"What are you gonna do?" his brother asked.

"I'm going to the game," Tracy said. "I'm not changing a thing. What are *you* gonna do?"

His brother paused, weighing the decision. "I'm comin' to Notre Dame."

And Tracy Hallahan said, "Good choice."

John Patrick had never been part of his son's Notre Dame pilgrimage, which took on its current regularity when Tracy met a Notre Dame alumnus in 1996. He offered the subway the chance of a lifetime. He was looking to transfer the use of his season tickets to an Irish fan of abiding passion, at face value plus a $2,000 donation to the university, necessary to keep the tickets from expiring. The alum could only make it to one game a year, so why waste? He approached Hallahan, and when the alumnus asked the subway if he liked Notre Dame, a look of astonishment spread across the face of the fanatic. He said, "Goddamnit, Sammy. They're my biggest joy and my biggest heartache."

6

Subways

When Helen "Tudy" Cummings drove her 1948 Plymouth onto campus and parked it outside Walsh Hall, a dorm on South Quad not far from the Sacred Heart church, she might very well have invented the tailgate phenomenon as it occurs at Notre Dame. Tudy Cummings, subway alumna, has been called the greatest Notre Dame fan who ever lived, and such was her influence that, in 1976, she became the first woman—and the first fan—ever inducted into the Notre Dame Monogram Club, the exclusive alumni group made up of every athlete to earn a varsity letter, in any sport. (Notre Dame's first varsity sport for women, tennis, did not get its start until 1976.) A year after her induction, her friends threw a party to celebrate her three and a half decades of contribution to Notre Dame as a fan. Dan Shannon, who played end for Leahy, was the master of ceremonies. Ara Parseghian gave the keynote speech, in which he noted that Tudy Cummings was the first and last civilian (not including players' families) ever permitted to celebrate the pregame Mass with the team. Parseghian considered her presence in the congregation necessary for the fate of his Irish on the field later in the day.

Born in 1913 on the South Side of Chicago, she grew up at a time in a place and among a people that positioned Notre Dame and its football above any other institution outside, perhaps, the Church and the machine of the Democratic Party. In this way, the South Side Irish rivaled the Irish of Hell's Kitchen, New York. Tudy Griffin (she married a Cummings) became a Notre Dame fan simply because that's what one did on the South Side of Chicago. It was as inevitable as the sacrament of confirmation. Perhaps her being a tomboy enhanced her feeling for the team. She owned a baseball autographed by Babe Ruth, but her mother took it away, thinking the object more suitable for her brothers.

"Fifty years later, she still complained about it," her son, Michael, has said. She was a good athlete, and after high school she played for a brief period in a women's semipro basketball league.

Her childhood neighborhood bordered the immense jungle of the Union Stockyard, and her father and almost everyone else's father worked in a packinghouse. With her parents and six brothers and sisters she lived in a cold-water tenement, and she went to a crowded Catholic high school, one of many dozens all over the city. Other Catholic ethnic groups lived in the same neighborhoods—Poles, Italians, Germans, Slovaks. It was an intact Catholic ghetto that, later in the decade, after the Second World War, was slowly dismantled by white flight. The Irish of Chicago have since fled to a neighborhood in the southernmost part of town called Beverly, now the city's principal Irish enclave. Nonetheless, some of the old ways remain. Though their density has somewhat diminished, a lot of them are still Notre Dame fans, and then as now, if you ask where they grew up, they will not say the South Side, they will not say Beverly. They will instead name their home parish—Nativity, First Visitation, St. Rita, St. Sabina, St. Gabriel, St. Leo, St. Ethelrida, St. Killian, Thomas More, Little Flower, Barnabas, Christ the King. Tudy Cummings, of First Visitation Parish, was born into the first generation of Notre Dame subway alumni. About twelve years old when the term first entered the language, sometime around 1925, Tudy as a Notre Dame fan predated the coinage.

There is some dispute over the term's exact morphology. Some historians believe that it derived from the fans in New York who read the sports pages, and thus the Notre Dame football headlines, while traveling to and from work on the subways. The more specific *straphanger alumni* thus enjoyed a brief vogue. Thankfully, for reasons unknown, it died out in favor of the more poetic *subway alumni*. Late in his life, Grantland Rice, of the *New York Herald-Tribune,* author of the legendary purple-prose lead "Outlined against a blue-gray sky," claimed *subway alumni* as part of his oeuvre. But as best as Murray Sperber could find out during his research for *Shake Down the Thunder,* a reporter named Paul Gallico first used the term with regularity. At the time Gallico was the sports-page editor of the New York *Daily News,* a newspaper that, indeed, played a crucial role in the rapid growth of

Notre Dame fandom in the late 1920s, despite the fact that Gallico, part of the Aw Nuts school of sportswriting—cynical, skeptical, with tongues of acid—had an active distaste for Notre Dame, its football, and its fanatics. But the *Daily News* knew where it lived. By design, it had a large working-class audience, and therefore a largely Catholic ethnic audience. At first the paper had ignored football, since the sport had been, like rugby in England, a pastime of the aristocracy, played at its best at Yale, Harvard, Princeton. But Notre Dame, along with the rise of the Midwestern land grants, seemed to have changed this, and while those other schools existed obscurely out in the provinces, only Notre Dame played every year in the media hive of New York. It also helped that in 1927 Notre Dame alumnus Francis Wallace became a columnist for the paper's sports page, where he also helped popularize the nickname Fighting Irish. By the late 1920s, the *Daily News* gave over more inches of column space to Irish football than any of its rivals, in a town that then had about fifteen daily newspapers. (One reason for the paper's expanded coverage of Notre Dame, as posited by Sperber, arose from its discovery that people were laying money on college football as much as they had been on thoroughbreds and boxers.) And so the coverage in the *News* and elsewhere hyped Notre Dame's annual game with Army. Almost always the papers played up the religiosity of the school and its team, and the proximity of these Catholics beating up on the Establishment drew the interest of readers in quantities never before seen—and, the assumption went, how else would they travel to Yankee Stadium but by subway?

The very first game between Notre Dame and Army, arranged by Jesse Harper, Rockne's predecessor as head coach, occurred in 1913, the year of Tudy Cumming's birth. The series would last, with one interruption in 1918, until 1947. Through the first ten years, the site of the game was always West Point, but in 1923, Notre Dame alumni living in New York finally convinced the university's president, Fr. Matt Walsh, to shift the scene of the Big Game, as it was then called, to the big city. After a year at Ebbets Field in Brooklyn, after a year at the Polo Grounds in Harlem, the game found its natural home in 1925 at the Yankee's brand-new stadium in the Bronx—thus hitting all three of the city's most-venerated sporting rialtos. The manager of the stadium, which first accepted visitors to see Ruth and Gehrig that same year, offered Notre Dame a guaranteed $60,000 to play against Army at his new arena. He knew the game would draw.

The Lexington Avenue line of the Interborough Rapid Transit Company, the IRT—today the No. 4 train—emerged from beneath the Bronx at 149th Street and stopped at the Bronx Concourse station right outside the front gates. On game days in the 1920s the IRT platform at Yankee Stadium was not as yet a madhouse of immigrants. To the Big Game, hardly anyone took the subway. Their preferred conveyances sat bumper to bumper in parking lots crammed with late-model automobiles. "The Stadium might have been described as an island completely surrounded by motorcars," reported the *Times* in 1925. Women stepped out of the cars wearing mink and sable and ermine and pearls. The men wore suits, the women dresses—they did not obtain their game-day apparel at any college bookstore. Once in the stadium, to look down from the upper decks onto the crowd below was to see a sea of fedoras and homburgs and bowler hats. Tobacco smoke drifted up in clouds from the building like a giant barbecue. The crowds were largely "non-partisan," said the *Times,* there for the spectacle rather than to root for the team. For the New Yorkers of the 1920s, ND-Army was as heady as the stock market, as fashionable as the nightclubs of Harlem. In the private boxes, there was Jimmy Walker, mayor of New York and such a Friend of the University that some began calling him Notre Dame's unofficial mascot. There was Cardinal Patrick Joseph Hayes, archbishop of New York, and in the regular stands whole squads of lower prelates—Roman collars in such profusion it could have been a conclave. There was Douglas MacArthur and a hierarchy of highly placed West Point graduates and future war heroes, the chests of their uniforms ablaze with stratified ribbons. There were state and federal judges. There was Al Smith, governor of New York, whose candidacy for president in 1928 unleashed a torrent of latent anti-Catholic bigotry around the country. There were Wall Street bankers and Midtown industrialists and Broadway bookies, including Tim Mara, owner of the New York football Giants. There were stars of stage and silent film. There was Babe Ruth and Lou Gehrig, and Gene Tunney, the former heavyweight champ. There was Charles Francis Murphy, head of Tammany Hall, and Joseph Kennedy, bootlegger and father of American scions. (Joe Kennedy would become a member of Notre Dame's board of lay trustees—before Hesburgh signed over ownership of the university to that body—and his son, the future president, would receive an honorary Notre Dame degree. The Kennedys, then, were perhaps the most famous Notre Dame subway alumni who ever lived.) There were enough cops to fill several precincts, and there might have been more mobsters than cops. In short, all the elements that made New York go in the 1920s attended the Big Game in spades.

They obtained their tickets in a kind of patronage system. Although the game took place always in November, tickets were often "sold out" by the previous June. Notre Dame's New York alumni received a large allotment of tickets, many more than they actually needed just for themselves, and they distributed their passes as they saw fit, which was mostly how they saw it befitting their careers. A scarcity therefore developed, and the market bid up prices so high that from scalpers a box seat might cost as much as $300 in 1920s money, the equivalent of $3,000 today. A "general admission" seat would cost you $50—roughly $500 today.

Nevertheless, the crowds at the Big Game nearly always pushed toward eighty thousand and always achieved the highest attendance totals of any sporting event in the city. It was the most popular football game in the country by far. Yankee Stadium and the two schools sometimes received up to 750,000 requests for tickets. Sportswriters called it bigger than the Kentucky Derby, bigger than the World Series (when a New York team didn't make it, that is). To fit that many people into the stadium, seating was added, and the stands seemed to descend right down onto the sidelines and almost up to the team bench. The fans in their hats and greatcoats appeared to be mingling with the players. People in the stands drank from flasks with impunity. It was still Prohibition, but at the Big Game, for the length of two halves of football, the Volstead Act was repealed.

About the only working-class stiffs in the stands got their tickets like everyone else, through the right connections—a chauffeur from his employer, a laborer from his union boss, a campaign volunteer from the local party machine. Through New York's unevenly booming economy, the tickets trickled down. But, for the most part, these original subway alumni stayed at home in their cold-water tenements and, if they could afford a set, listened to the games on the radio. If the fans had no radios at home (the first Notre Dame–Army game was broadcast in 1924, from the Polo Grounds), they gathered outside the offices of newspapers and sometimes bars, in front of huge screens imprinted with football grids. A man on a stepladder charted down and distance with football-shaped spotters. A reporter in the press box telephoned in the plays. The screens were called Gridgraphies, and standing on the street corners, the Notre Dame fans who watched, the Notre Dame bettors who betted, became known as curbstone alumni.

Radio and newspapers conveyed Notre Dame's wins to the masses. Displaying their savvy, Notre Dame and Army let the radio networks—CBS, NBC—nationally broadcast the game for free, so as to create more ticket-buying fans. Only later, in the 1940s, would the subways convey large numbers of working-class fans to Yankee Stadium, and only then would the phrase *subway alumni* truly catch on. Their enthusiasm had by then grown extreme. Even if they could not gain entrance into Yankee Stadium, each year in November on Big Game Saturday they converted New York into St. Patrick's Day and Mardi Gras rolled into one. "Tomorrow is the annual gathering of that amazing clan of self-appointed Notre Dame alumni which will whoop and rage and rant and roar through our town from sunup until long after sundown in honor of a school to which they never went," Paul Gallico wrote in 1934. "There are no self-appointed Colgate or St. Mary's or Tulane or Purdue alumni when those teams come to visit our town. But there is some sweet magic about the name of Notre Dame that annually draws the damndest rabble out of its warrens. There is nothing the proud old University can do about these boorish sons."

The "sweet magic"—that which Gallico could not understand and therefore condescended to—was Catholicism in harmony with a whole lot of winning. Around this same time, there were conspiracy theories afoot and writers arguing in national magazines—*Forum, The Atlantic Monthly*—that Vatican propaganda was the real cause behind Notre Dame's rise in popularity. In these Red Scare times between the world wars, many Americans believed that these arriviste immigrant Catholics pledged their allegiance to the pope in Rome rather than the president in Washington, D.C. In this time between the world wars, the Pledge of Allegiance was invented for this reason. As Notre Dame con-

tinued to win under Rockne, a revival of American anti-Catholicism
had developed. In their immigrant enclaves, these Catholics had for almost a century faced a hard choice: assimilate and ditch their Old
World ethnicity, or maintain their culture and lose out on the American Dream. It's an old story—Americanist vs. ultramontanist. For the
most part they chose to assimilate and ditch. But, in some sense, rooting for Notre Dame perhaps let them have it both ways. A Catholic
school with its Catholic methods—team Masses, team prayers, saints'
medals—was playing an all-American sport at its highest possible
level. It was assimilation through victory. It did not matter if significant portions of the Irish roster were neither Irish nor Catholic. It only
mattered that the university was. (Rockne, after all, was a Protestant
until many years at Notre Dame converted him. George Gipp was a
Protestant. There were also Jews and, in later years, Muslims.) Their
Notre Dame fanaticism was bound up with notions of religion and ethnicity and class—all of which, of course, are venerable methods of arranging identity—and Notre Dame fans defined themselves according
to the success of an *idea* as much as a team: the Fighting Irish as representative of a system of spiritual belief doing battle with a world in opposition to those beliefs. Fr. Robert Griffin, an old Notre Dame priest,
wrote an essay in 1977 that has since become famous, entering the
Notre Dame canon. In it he described his experiences subbing as chaplain for the football team one game day. With a metaphor, he seemed to
hit on the heart of the matter. "The world is out there, waiting to defeat
you: because you are not alone in a hostile universe, you ritualize the
battle. The nameless forces seem arrayed against you on a single field,
but you face it as a team trained in the stratagems of victory." The team
was Catholicism. The stratagems were the sacraments.

As a result, Notre Dame fans were fanatical in the true sense of the
word. To them, Notre Dame football was no metaphor. Despite having
the winningest team in college football history, Notre Dame has para-
doxically throughout the years been deemed the underdog in important games. So when the Irish won, their victories carried the rich and
inevitable patina of Fate. People came to think that instead of superior
talent or work ethic or strategy or even desire, Destiny had caused their
team to win. Deus ex machina, these Notre Dame teams were, in other
words, *ordained* to win.

Catholic publications all over the country published essays on this very matter. From the *Catholic Sun* of Syracuse, New York, 1947: "The Midwest school and its tradition in football is a kind of sacramental, and I speak seriously." From the *Catholic Mirror* of Springfield, Massachusetts, 1943: "I am inclined to believe that God has made use of Notre Dame elevens to spread devotion to the Blessed Sacrament. . . . Certainly it means something when thousands assemble week after week to witness these young men do homage in a humble, rough way to our blessed Lady, whose monogram they wear. . . . The simple facts are that Notre Dame football is played for the greater glory of God and our Lady. The Notre Dame stadium is Our Lady's Field . . . every game in our Lady's stadium is dedicated to her."

Thus, whenever the team did poorly, angry letters poured into the Main Building from fans all over the country. The complaint, of course, was the sin of de-emphasis. They decried the direction of the football program in terms that indicated that to lose games meant to lose favor with God. After Rockne's death in 1931, for instance, when the team began to perform beneath the head coach's rarefied standards, a letter arrived for John O'Hara, who served as president of Notre Dame from 1934–1940. "How, in the hereafter, can you excuse yourself for having willfully voided the prayers of thousands and thousands of Nuns who sit at their microphones each Saturday and fervently pray for victory for Old Notre Dame? You can become a National Hero, Father, by insisting on winning teams and you may be canonized later."

And angry letters poured into the mailboxes of reporters who wrote unfavorably about the Irish. The complainants accused the newsmen of being anti-Catholic, an accusation that Irish fans periodically deploy even today to criticize sportswriters who consistently knock Notre Dame. At times the university has sided with the press. "I think our school has been very unfortunate in some of the synthetic rabid nuts who have attached themselves to us and I sincerely hope that you pay no attention to the crazy stuff they may send you. I hope it wasn't too much." The author of those sentences felt compelled to apologize on Notre Dame's behalf to a reporter accosted with hate mail. The apologist was Knute Rockne.

Even O'Hara, so attuned to football as a proselytizing mechanism, became overwhelmed by the fan base. When he learned that one of the team's star players was a divorcé (he was eventually kicked off the team) O'Hara wrote in a private letter, "If Salvoldi is dismissed we will incur the enmity of our most embarrassing friends, the synthetic alumni (and God be praised if we can get rid of some of them!)."

Ever-intensifying fan ardor even put an end to the Big Game, or at least contributed to it. Notre Dame fans accused West Point of anti-Catholicism in letter after vitriolic letter. Notre Dame received bigoted mail from anti-Catholic Army fans. The academy superintendent felt the heat enough that he voiced his concern to Eisenhower: "In the eyes of a large portion of the public, it pits West Point against the Catholic Church." Church vs. State played their last game in Yankee Stadium in 1946 as part of their annual series. It ended in a scoreless tie.

Notre Dame and its leaders have always exhibited ambivalence when it comes to the subway alum phenomenon. On the one hand they know that such an enormous fan base has proved to be the university's blessing, producing the dollars later spent on improving the academic institution—and in a somewhat guarded way, the university has gone on to embrace its nonalumni fans as a veritable element of the Notre Dame identity. "You need all the friends you can get," Father Hesburgh has said. But he immediately goes on to qualify the statement: "Some friends may overstate the importance of football at times. But if you live here and work here, you know that's not the story by a long shot."

Without such legions following the team and spending their money on tickets and other accoutrements—buying the Fighting Irish product—there would, of course, be no such term as *football factory*. In some ways, the subway alumni go to the root of Notre Dame's historical dilemma. Often they are typecast as typical sports-fan nutcases unhealthily attached to the vicissitudes of a football season, men and women who live vicariously through the exploits of young athletes, and who care only about victories. They are sometimes seen as investing religion to dangerous proportions in an activity that's only a game. At around the same time as the break with Army, some people within Notre Dame began to grow weary, and wary, of this intermingling of religion and sport. Both ND fans and anti-ND fans, wrote Fr. John Murphy, Notre Dame's head of PR in the 1940s, "make the unpardonable mistake of confusing football prowess with apologetics. If Notre Dame wins, the Catholic Church somehow triumphs; if we lose, it is a blow to Catholicism in the United States!" The reputation of the subway alumni is one of emotional intensity and intellectual naïveté—the reputation, of course, of any and all die-hard sports fans—and for the typical subway alumnus, according to this formulation, the academic institution behind the team might as well not exist.

But this, largely, is a mischaracterization. Precisely because the Fighting Irish football team represented a university, the original concept of which was to educate the children of the aristocracy, and Catholic University at that, Notre Dame became a symbol of Catholic striving—of immigrants working and sacrificing so that their children might see better days. Eventually, of course, the economic and social barriers came down, and the sons and grandsons of those bootstrap immigrants moved into the middle classes, the upper-middle classes, the upper-upper classes whose millionaires became benefactors of the Notre Dame endowment. Subway alumni sent their children to Notre Dame. Subway alumni sent their children to Harvard. They went out of the urban ghettos and into the world wars. They made use of the G.I. Bill and graduated into the suburbs. The 1960s came and went. Vatican II came and went. Outright and systematic discrimination against Catholics disappeared, and as throngs of sociologists and historians have posited, the notion of Catholic ethnicity shifted and morphed until Notre Dame and its Fighting Irish became, indeed, a complex metaphor that took memories of intact Catholic communities and the labor and sacrifice of earlier generations and mixed them with loyalties to traditional devotion and traditional obedience. Notre Dame became an example of success in the modern world but not at the cost of the Faith. The resulting sentiment is both sappy and not, and elements of the Notre Dame Family—the very idea of which flows out of this sentiment—express it today repeatedly:

"ND football has always meant more than just football to me," a Notre Dame alumnus wrote on ND Nation. "It is a symbol of a people and a way of life. That probably comes from my father and a story he never ceased telling. My grandparents were Italian immigrants who came to this country in 1917 . . . "

"For my father, Notre Dame really did represent the epitome of a Catholic from the South Side of Chicago getting out and making it," says Scott Engler, subway alumnus, graduate of the University of Delaware, BoardOp of ND Nation. "The Dome was the shining light, the beacon, for all those kids on the South Side—even if my father ended up going to Northwestern."

"My dad wanted me to go here in the worst way," says Jack Arbino, class of 1962. "He was a very strong devout Catholic. People thought he went to school here. He started out as a tailor and then he started his own business, a manufacturing company, and because he had his own business and he was really smart and articulate, and was such a big fan, always coming to games, people just assumed he'd gone to college at Notre Dame. In truth he only had an eighth-grade education. But he was smart, he was a hard worker—he was a *subway alumni*."

"The success of Notre Dame football is a symbol of the presence of Catholicism in the United States, its leavening of the general culture, its aspiration to excellence in this life and the next," wrote Ralph McInerny, a Notre Dame professor of philosophy since the 1950s, in an essay in *Notre Dame Magazine*.

"There's a feeling about Notre Dame in the broader Catholic community—that Notre Dame is emblematic of the Catholic Church making it," said Fr. Ron Nuzzi, a priest and professor at Notre Dame. "And that is very appealing to a certain generation of Catholics. Notre Dame isn't just a symbol of Catholicism, but of the Catholic Church making it in this society, and a symbol of its power or its influence in our society. The Dome announces to the world that Catholics have succeeded in this country. The whole university announces that. It's not an immigrant religion anymore. We've made it and we're here to stay. There's no other reason to gild the Dome, is there? Otherwise it's just money in the sky."

In Rockne's last year as head coach, 1930, before he died in a plane crash over Kansas, Notre Dame went undefeated and won the national championship, beating Southern Cal in Los Angeles in the last game of the season. On the way back to South Bend, the team's train stopped in Chicago. Down LaSalle Street the Irish slowly rolled in Studebakers showered in a blizzard of ticker tape. Tens of thousands of people lined the boulevard. Banners of blue and gold streamed from the windows of skyscrapers. Rockne alone would later receive the same treatment through the steel canyon of lower Broadway, New York. Seventeen years old, a senior at Visitation High School, already a Notre Dame diehard, Tudy Griffin cut class and headed straight to the Loop. She got off at the el station downtown, and she ran square into the chest of the pastor of Visitation parish.

"Gee, Tudy, I didn't know they'd canceled school today."

She made no immediate response. As it turned out, none was necessary. The pastor was there for the same reason as the girl, and nothing ever came of Tudy Griffin's truancy.

She had actually met Rockne the year before. As president of her high school class, she and several classmates and their headmaster, a priest of course, traveled to South Bend to meet with the coach and ask if several Notre Dame players from Chicago might be able to come back to the old neighborhood, after the season, as celebrity guests of a high school dance. Permission granted. Ever since Rockne, who grew up on the North Side, matriculated at Notre Dame without a high school diploma, Chicago had provided a pipeline of raw talent onto the Irish rosters, most of all from the city's Catholic League. The high school players who went on to Notre Dame became local heroes, and even the conventional students accepted at Notre Dame achieved the status of neighborhood celebrities. The base of support for Notre Dame in Chicago cannot be underestimated, and a lot of it flowed out of the South Side. Because of its proximity to campus, Chicago had more influence on Notre Dame than the East Coast with its legions of original subway alumni, and Chicago's Notre Dame supporters congealed into a kind of Notre Dame mafia. The metaphor remains in currency to this day on campus, used to refer to the powerful group of alumni and benefactors who hold a certain amount of sway inside the Main Building—"the Chicago mafia." Tudy Griffin seemed to know everyone in this South Side community of Notre Dame fans, students, alumni, denizens. One of her high school classmates would go on to marry Moose Krause, also from the South Side. Johnny Jordan, who grew up in Visitation around the same time as Tudy, went to Notre Dame on a basketball scholarship and eventually became its head basketball coach. There was Blackie Johnson, out of St. Leo Parish, a coach on Frank Leahy's staff, and there was Joe "Red" Gleason, of Visitation, who would become a Notre Dame halfback. Accompanied by a little-known guard on the Notre Dame team, Tudy once went on a double date with Gleason and his girlfriend. The guard was from South Bend and his name was Joe Kuharich.

Nineteen years old, Tudy Griffin married a Notre Dame fan named Michael Cummings in the fall of 1932. Their wedding ceremony took place on a bye week, and for their honeymoon, they drove around the Great Lakes with the goal of reaching Cleveland and Municipal Stadium to see Notre Dame play Navy. Michael Cummings died in 1950, Tudy Cummings never remarried, and to some degree she seemed to replace her husband with the University of Notre Dame and its South Side community. She was plump and blond and full of energy. As her family's only breadwinner—she had one child, Michael Jr.—she found a job at the Chicago Parks Department, assistant to the assistant parks superintendent, special events, which included Soldier Field. In this capacity she helped organize the annual Prep Bowl, which took place in Soldier and pitted the winner of the Catholic League against the winner of the Public League, a game so popular that it sometimes drew one hundred thousand people. Through her work she came to know almost every football coach in the Catholic League system, including Terry Brennan, player for Frank Leahy, successor to Frank Leahy, and at the time head coach at Mt. Carmel, the fabled South Side Notre Dame feeder school. And she came to know all the best players in the Catholic League, including Johnny Lattner, future Notre Dame halfback and winner of the Heisman Trophy, and many more before and after him. It is safe to say, in this era before the NCAA outlawed such practices, that Tudy Cummings steered her fair share of Chicago talent into Fighting Irish jerseys. She once drove a young defensive tackle named George Connor to campus for a recruiting visit. For some reason, Connor instead chose to attend Holy Cross, the Jesuit college in Massachusetts. This did not please Tudy Cummings, but after serving in the Second World War, Connor transferred back to Notre Dame to become a two-time consensus all-American, a first-round NFL draft pick, a Chicago Bear, and eventually member of the NFL Hall of Fame. Not long after his transfer from Holy Cross, Cummings bumped into Connor one day on campus. She looked him in the eye and took stock of the situation. "Well, smart-ass. You ended up here anyway."

Sometime in the early 1950s, she used her Notre Dame connections to gain entry into Leahy's pregame Mass, which then took place in the chapel of Dillon Hall, a dormitory, one of the school's collegiate Gothic gems, on South Quad. The chapel contained a statue of St. Olaf, the Norwegian saint, dedicated to the memory of Knute Rockne not long after his death, and for reasons not exactly clear the otherwise authoritarian Leahy allowed Cummings and her small boy to stick around, to receive Communion and even the dispensation of the saint's medals. No other fans seemed to know about the Mass. Cummings used the experience as a lesson for her boy: here are your football heroes, here are your tough-guy idols, taking the sacraments and glorifying God and His Mother, Our Lady. Michael Cummings was impressed. "She was a master psychologist with me," he has said. "She drilled me in this stuff. I mean, I was bathed in it." He does not remember his first Notre Dame game, though he remembers a family photo that may have recorded it. In the picture, his mother is changing his diapers in the stands.

At around the same time that she crashed the team Mass, Tudy Cummings began roasting hams in a sherry baste at her apartment in Chicago, putting a couple cases of beer along with the hams into the trunk of her car, and driving it all to campus on the Fridays before home games. She wanted to make it in time for the pep rallies, then held in the old Fieldhouse. Erected in 1898, demolished in 1983, with a dirt floor and high wooden rafters and an arched roof and little else, it resembled nothing so much as a stockyard. Students jammed the premises until it was standing room only except for a bank of bleachers upon which sat the coaches, the players, whatever VIP speakers had been invited to give rah-rah speeches, and Tudy Cummings. On the west side of campus, a little-known access road obscured by trees led to an ungated, unguarded side entrance. Early on game days, Cummings would pull onto the access road and follow it around St. Mary's Lake and up a hill and into a courtyard with a small parking area behind Walsh Hall. Around the corner was the Sacred Heart church, where she and her son would attend Mass at eight in the morning before opening the trunk of the Plymouth and commencing what soon became known to all her friends as Tudy's Trunk Club, the natural antecedent to Tracy Hallahan's Neighborhood of Hope and tailgating at

Notre Dame in general. Before long, the university put up a gate on game day to block traffic to the access road. Meeting the obstacle, Cummings overcame it. She led the passengers in the car—usually a few friends and always her son—in a quick recitation of the Hail Mary. Then Tudy Cummings pulled the wheel hard to the right, and the car went down off the road and into the woods, rumbled over uneven ground between a pair of trees, and rumbled hard left between more trees and back over the berm and onto pavement. All clear, she drove off to her coveted Trunk Club spot. "Let's say a prayer of thanksgiving to the Blessed Mother," she would say. "We got through it."

The term *tailgate* as applied to football pregame parties would not be coined until around 1965. Like football itself, tailgating was an East Coast, recherché, highly WASP development, created at Harvard-Yale matches around the turn of the century so that alums could get together and talk business in a suitably decorous environment before the big game—brandy and punch and canapé. It was late in coming to Notre Dame, at which it was never, for the most part, recherché. Rockne, largely responsible for the design of Notre Dame Stadium, made sure to include a vast parking region—if you build it, they will come. When Cummings came and started her Trunk Club, those lots around the stadium filled up shortly before kickoff and emptied out almost immediately after the clock went to zero. The campus on game-day afternoons was filled mostly with exuberant students, nostalgic alumni, and a few tourists simply wandering around. The band step-off had yet to become popular, there was no massive cheering of the team as it moved from church to locker room, and there were certainly no tailgate parties. The interstate highway system had yet to extend to Indiana. In South Bend there were two hotels. About the only similarity between today's experience and that of the 1940s was the Grotto, jammed then, as now, with prayerful fans hitting the rails—both for God and for team. Nonetheless, enough South Sider alumni and subway alumni came to the games that Cummings's party became an instant social success. Her game-day uniform was a Celtic cross, and skirts and blouses and assorted jewelry of blue and gold. She was the center of her circle. The South Side community transported itself from the parishes to the parking lot behind Walsh. She made up business cards that said TUDY'S TRUNK CLUB, and her guests printed up lapel buttons and bumper stickers that said the same. Eventually they started bringing their own provisions and adding it to Cummings's basic stock. A full bar developed. Beer tubs developed. A card table spread out with finger foods and Tudy's basted hams developed. She carved the ham and served her guests sandwiches. So unique was the situation that passersby mistook Tudy's Trunk Club for a university-operated lunch counter. A man with his wife once came up to Cummings, standing behind her table, the hams and condiments arrayed before her. She gave him a sandwich and he mingled with the crowd. His wife, the whole time, looked anxious, uncomfortable. When he had finished eating, he went up to Cummings and pulled out his billfold. "So how much do I owe you?"

"What do you mean? Nothing."

And the wife turned to her husband. "I told you, you horse's ass! This is private!"

Holy Cross priests would sometimes come by for a pregame highball. Postgame, the players out of Chicago paid visits to Tudy, whom they'd known from their high school days playing in the Catholic League. They would, perhaps, sneak a beer or two underneath their head coach's training rules. There was Donny Hogan and Ziggy Czarobski and Johnny Lattner, out of Fenwick High, and therefore more a West Sider than a South Sider. Nonetheless, he was among Tudy's favorites. He autographed his black-and-white publicity photo with the words "To my South Side girlfriend. If all the Notre Dame teams had your spirit, Notre Dame would never lose." Other players followed Lattner as Trunk Club regulars all the way up through Parseghian and Dan Devine, and increasingly they came from other parts of the country—George Connor, Dan Shannon, Frank Reynolds, Paul Hornung, Jim Just, Jim Colosimo, John Huarte, Jim Lynch, Nick Eddy, Jim Seymour, Joe Montana, and many others. Jim Lynch, especially, replaced Lattner as one of Tudy's favorites. "She really was a big part of my Notre Dame experience," he says today. *Look* magazine once printed an anecdote about his recruitment to Notre Dame, an anecdote—apocryphal, says Jim Lynch now, recalling those times—that nonetheless would have met with Tudy's approval. His brother had played for the Naval Academy, and Jim was waffling between the two institutions. On a retreat, he received advice from a priest who had a partisan view of the situation: "Your family has done its bit for country; now you should do something for God."

By plane, train, and automobile, Cummings trekked to away games—to Southern Cal, Texas, Oklahoma, New York, all the Big Ten matches—and she always stayed in the same hotel as the team, often traveling with players' families. The Trunk Club became a movable feast. She was as friendly with the regular students as she was with the players. When she eventually took her show on the road, she found ways to finance more than a few trips for students who couldn't afford to travel. One of those undergrads, Michael Haggerty, class of 1967, once wrote an essay on Cummings for a Notre Dame fanzine: "She had a way of greeting you that made you feel that she'd been waiting all day for you to walk into her life."

She also brought to campus plenty of South Siders, converting them into subway alum. The most prominent was Chester Jaskolka, an orphan raised by the priests and nuns of Visitation parish. He became a second son for Tudy Cummings, and a subway alumnus almost as vehement as his mentor. He joined Cummings on every pilgrimage, and as she got older, he assumed a role as a kind of bodyguard—Tudy's "heavy," as her son has described him. He was also a Chicago cop, and as such had been known to pull over carloads of kids in Chicago for one violation or another, come to discover they went to Notre Dame and say, "Alright. Say a Hail Mary and get outta here." Along with Tudy in 1976, Chester was inducted as an honorary member into the Monogram Club.

Eventually the university built a new bookstore in the Trunk Club spot, and Cummings relocated her affair to the regular stadium parking lots. For the next twenty years her tailgate, growing in fame and attendance until it swelled with the Parseghian era to well over a hundred fans, was located just north of the Joyce Center, across the street from the stadium, and beside the Aerospace Building, which today no longer exists. Sometime in the early 1960s she bought a beat-up station wagon and had a few workers from the parks district paint the sides Madonna blue, the roof and hood yellow-gold—a customized Notre Dame pilgrimage machine.

By the time she moved spots, in the middle 1950s, smack in the middle period of mediocrity between Leahy and Parseghian, tailgating had started to take off. In game photographs from the time, there are sections in the end zone empty of fans. People thought Hesburgh was taking Notre Dame the way of the University of Chicago, which had killed its onetime championship program just after the Second World War. Notre Dame was so desperate to lift attendance numbers that it enlisted the support of Catholic parishes in all the subway-alum hotbeds—New York, Philadelphia, western Pennsylvania, Detroit, Ohio, and, easiest of all, Chicago. Notre Dame sent letters to parish leaders asking for help, and the parishes received blocks of tickets from the university to sell to their congregations in package deals. Still active in Visitation though she no longer lived there, Tudy Cummings received a few of these letters. Buses and trains took the parishioners to campus for the games. The Grand Trunk Railroad left from the South Side near Midway Airport, and the South Shore line left from the Loop. Both hauled the subways to South Bend in large numbers. Liquor bottles and beer bottles went rolling down the aisles, and large-scale tailgating at Notre Dame was born. Along with their partying, the fans discovered the Basilica, the Grotto, the shrines, the lakes, the campus, and Notre Dame as a home-game pilgrimage site was born.

Anyone at the time could buy season tickets for cheap. Taverns in Notre Dame neighborhoods bought up whole rows for their partisan patrons. Unofficial Notre Dame fan clubs—booster clubs some would call them—bought up whole rows for their members. A few of them tailgated next to the Trunk Club at its new location, and they soon combined their festivities. Out of the West Side of Chicago, there was O'Leary's Upside Down Club, made up almost entirely of union men, the base behind the Chicago Democratic Party machine, the muscle behind Mayor Daley. Boss Daley became a Trunk Club semiregular. There were the boys from McGuire's pub, on the West Side, in Forest Park, who perpetrated a legendary scam. They filed a petition with the NCAA. Somehow the document made it through the system, and the bar received recognition as an institution of higher learning— McGuire's University. For the next four years, until the authorities finally caught up with them, the McGuire administration, as was their plan, received from the NCAA dozens of free tickets to the Final Four. Out of Gary and Hammond, Indiana, there was the Notre Dame 100 Club, so called because it had a hundred original members, made up of

Notre Dame diehards who worked in the steel mills near Lake Michigan. Their leader was a subway alum named Joe Moore (no relation to Holtz's line coach), who over time made relatively substantial donations to the university. He provided other services as well. For Fighting Irish football players, he obtained summer jobs in the steel mills. When Lattner opened a well-known restaurant in the Loop, it became a kind of off-campus headquarters for the Trunk Club—or, rather, the Trunk Club became an on-campus headquarters for it. Lattner famously kept his Heisman Trophy sitting atop the restaurant's piano. He now allegedly keeps it in the trunk of his car. Lattner's partner was Bob Nevers, a Jewish fellow who made book out of the restaurant, and who became a Notre Dame fan by sheer utility and by sheer propinquity. Lattner's was inside the Marina Towers, not far from St. Peter's Cathedral, downtown, and Nevers once said, "They come in here, they drink, they place their bets, and then they go across the street to confession!" Nevers and Lattner would both become part of Cummings's traveling entourage to away games.

On behalf of the Trunk Club, Cummings purchased a small block of season tickets on the forty-five-yard line, row forty-nine. They're still in the family. For a onetime flat fee you could hold your season tickets in perpetuity. But perpetuity ended in the late 1960s with Parseghian lighting up the win column. The school stopped the sale of season tickets and froze the number at around twenty-one thousand. With interest in the Fighting Irish reenergized, with Hesburgh's aggressive fund-raising projects in place, alumni demand increased, big-donor demand increased, and the ticket office rewrote its policy: to keep your season tickets alive, you would now need to make a small per annum donation. As the years wore on, through the 1970s and 80s, the university went through its season ticket–holder lists and revoked seats held by fans who had not contributed. Many companies and organizations also held large blocks of seats, and those too went back into the pool—everything allocated to alumni and Friends of the University. Cummings and then her son went ahead and donated healthily, and the Trunk Club carried on as strong as ever.

Before leaving campus after closing the trunk on game days—indeed, before she left campus ever, no matter the day—Cummings would always visit the Grotto, light multiple candles, and say multiple prayers. Though not an attendee of daily Mass, she nonetheless came from a time in which the "basics" were followed without question—a product of pre–Vatican II parochial education. While driving to games, she and her boy recited the rosary. He says, "No matter where we went, she would never think of eating meat on Fridays. No matter what time of year. On Sunday, if you had to get up at four in the morning to make Mass a hundred miles away, no big deal. In that sense, her obligations to confession and Mass, to not eat meat on Fridays, to give up something for Lent—she didn't think she was anything special in doing those things. If you had two bucks, you gave one away to someone who needed it more than you. And with everything, you said a prayer. If you saw someone on the street who was in bad shape, you said a prayer. Or if something good happened, 'Let's say a prayer of thanks.' " When Michael Cummings received his Notre Dame acceptance letter in the mail for the class of 1964, the first thing Tudy Cummings did was drop to her knees. He had applied, of course, to no other school; such a thing would have been blasphemy.

The idea of integrating prayer into all parts of life—"the Notre Dame system," as Bishop Jenky, CSC, would say—extended, of course, to the football field. Tudy Cummings's mother was a Notre Dame fan less for the football than for what Notre Dame represented. Like many older Catholics who were alive when Notre Dame under Rockne first started winning big, she was not concerned about the niceties of the game. She simply wanted victories, for the glory of Church and Mother and God. When Notre Dame was losing, she would turn off the radio, retreat to her bedroom, kneel down, and say a Hail Mary, waiting a few minutes for her words to ascend. Only then would she return to the kitchen and flip the radio back on. At such moments, Michael, her grandson, then five or six years old, would ask with much agitation, "Did it work?" He says today, "It was like she was waiting for an instant miracle." Tudy Cummings, though not as literal-minded, seemed to follow her mother's example. During tight games, the beads would rattle in her hand. "She did more praying than watching the games sometimes," Michael says. Once, after a tough loss in October, Bob Nevers saw the crestfallen Cummings and tried to cheer her up. He said, "Tudy. It serves 'em right. Any school named after a Jewish lady and plays on Yom Kippur, they *should* lose."

"She was from that generation that thought Notre Dame was over-coming evil. And the other team was that evil," Michael says. "After the game, of course, they were all great sports with the opposing team's fans. But during the game? Not so much. I'm sure some form of realism ran through it for them, but the one feeling was more powerful than the other. I mean, my mother—she suffered until the last play of every game. Her suffering was visible. If Notre Dame lost, she'd sit in the stands and cry. But she'd flip off the emotion immediately. She didn't want people to see her like that. Once she got outside the stadium, she was alright. She would move on to the next week and try to be opti-mistic. She didn't like Notre Dame people to criticize the team, either, if they played badly and got beat. There was no such thing as construc-tive or honest criticism with her. She didn't want to hear it. To her, being loyal meant you didn't criticize. I always thought that was unre-alistic. You can criticize Notre Dame and still love Notre Dame. But not in her house." And if an opposing-team fan expressed criticism of the Irish during a game—woe to that opposing-team fan. Once, during a bowl game in the 1970s, a man sitting behind her in the stadium made a few anti-Catholic, anti–Notre Dame remarks. She wheeled around and slapped him in the face so hard that she broke her hand.

What exactly drove Tudy Cummings to throw herself with so much deep feeling into all things Notre Dame remains a little elusive, as it does with all similarly devout ND fans. Her son does not have a clear answer. "It intensified after my dad died. She wanted to give me a healthy male image and combine that with the religious theme, and Notre Dame football is certainly a good way of doing that. But she never pinpointed a definitive moment. As she related it to me, as far back as she could remember, she was just a fan." Notre Dame was in the culture so pervasively no one gave it a second thought. Perhaps the best explanation is that, in her close-knit, working-class, ethnic neigh-borhood, where family and religion were tightly bound, the people she met through Notre Dame became—like Tracy Hallahan and his Neigh-borhood—Tudy Cummings's family.

At the party in 1977 that celebrated her life as a Notre Dame fan, Cummings received a plaque that also bore a poem. For perhaps the first time, a fan had entered the Notre Dame pantheon, at least for the people who attended the party. The poem's last stanza read,

In the annals of our gridiron greats
Our immortals of football fame
None dare to compare with Tudy
Our gracious lady of Notre Dame.

About a month after the party, Tudy Cummings had a stroke. She was sixty-four years old. She lived another three years, but a series of invisible ministrokes made life difficult. By the end, her mind remained intact, but she couldn't speak. Almost fully paralyzed, she was forced to use a feeding tube. Old friends stopped by the hospital and gathered at her bedside. Lattner sang her the "Victory March." George Connor said, "Hey, Tudy. You remember calling me a smartass?" Lying in the bed and hooked up to machines, she could only look up at the boys and nod. Lattner had to leave the room and fight it back. Sometime during those last years, but before she was permanently hospitalized, Michael tried to convince her to go with him back to campus, just to walk around a bit, to reminisce. Words similar to those once written by Fr. Robert Griffin may have passed through her mind: "There has always been, for me, a beauty surrounding Notre Dame and her people so that if one had only this experience, with neither hope of heaven nor expectation of glory, it would be enough." She refused her son's request. It would be impossible, she said, to handle the sadness of seeing Notre Dame for perhaps the last time.

After her death in 1981, Chester Jaskolka kept the Trunk Club going in the same spot north of the Joyce Center. He held court all the way up through 2003 and including the Michigan game in 2004, the home opener. All the old players and old South Side alumni and subway alumni, those still alive, would come back each game and pay homage to Chester and the memory of Tudy Cummings. Sitting in the stands as Notre Dame held on against Michigan, Jaskolka had a fainting spell that forced him to leave in the middle of the game. He has been diagnosed with leukemia and has not been back to campus since, and the last vestiges of Tudy's Trunk Club have, for the time being at least, decamped from Notre Dame.

7

Nothing but Victory, $16

As a gift from one of her Trunk Club regulars, Tudy Cummings once received a flake of gold from off the Dome of the Main Building. It had just undergone one of its periodic regildings, in 1961, and Cummings felt that the flake had an almost sacred value, up there for thirteen years sucking up the Notre Dame sun. The university had presented the leaf as thank-you gifts to the benefactors of one of its early capital campaigns, and this particular flake had somehow trickled down to Cummings. Indeed, the bits of dome became a kind of commodity within the Notre Dame fan base. As it happened, the Dome underwent another regilding in the spring of 2005, but, due to advances in gilding technology that have since made the process impossible, the university can no longer peel the dome's skin—23.9 karats, three-microns thick—like a giant banana.

It's unlikely that those sections of the Dome from 1961 were ever available for purchase by the wider public at the Notre Dame bookstore. Cummings's flake, in other words, was a limited edition. One can, however, acquire any number of other things, at the bookstore, in bewildering array, emblazoned with the Dome's image, one of eighteen trademarks registered by the University of Notre Dame. If most pilgrims on a home-game weekend stop first at the Grotto and stop last at the Basilica for Mass, then sometime in between these visitations, almost all of them will go to the bookstore.

The Hammes Notre Dame Bookstore at the Eck Complex, as the business is now officially titled, occupies a relatively new building, erected in 1999. It sits just off Notre Dame Avenue, the tree-lined *grand cours* that leads onto campus and approaches the Main Building. An observant undergraduate once noted in *Scholastic,* the student-run weekly magazine, that the entrance to the bookstore does not face campus. Instead it faces south—the direction from whence the pilgrims come. Collegiate Gothic to the point of cartoon, it appears to have been designed in reaction to a few of the confused postmodernist mistakes erected elsewhere on campus in the last fifteen years. It could be a landmark example of the Atavistic School. The front facade is an immense turret with battlements at the corners and a recessed lancet window the size of a screen at a drive-in movie theater. Across a courtyard from the bookstore stands an almost mirror-image building, which contains the Visitors' Center and the offices of the Notre Dame Alumni Association. Frank Eck, Notre Dame class of 1944, a man who made his fortune in industrial drainage pipes, underwrote the spread with a $10 million donation. The whole thing cost $21.5 million. The Eck replaced the old Hammes Bookstore over on South Quad. Despite decades of wear, the old Hammes had long become a game-day shrine of vast financial and human turnover, and the lines even to get inside stretched all the way through the doors and out onto the grass of the quad.

If, in appearance, the old space seemed Woolworth's, the new one is Neiman Marcus. The vestibule opens onto an atrium like the lobby of a boutique hotel. It has cathedral ceilings and sunshine pours in from skylights above and the wall of lancet window. Every Notre Dame icon in the history of Notre Dame icons has, it seems, published his memoirs—coaches and players and priests especially, of course—and on game days the memoirists take turns sitting at tables set up in the atrium to sign books for the fans. On the slate for the weekend of the Washington game were Paul Hornung, Digger Phelps, Gerry Faust (who has been signing his memoirs at the Notre Dame bookstore for something like fifteen years), Monk Malloy, who had just come out with a volume entitled *Monk's Travels,* and the current men's soccer coach, who had just published a coaching how-to. The atrium opens onto the retail floors, and the crowd inside on a home-game Saturday suggests a souk in Tangier on the day of the arrival of the year's largest caravan. Over the sound system plays an endless loop of the "Victory March" set to assorted piano arrangements that varied in tempo and style so much that through the speakers there now seemed to come a slow bagpipe dirge, now an upbeat battle of the bluegrass fiddles, now a nostalgic ballad in Irish trad, now a contrapuntal Dixieland brassfest.

Available for $16, the album is called *Nothing but Victory.* Underneath the music, hangers squeak along their racks as the shoppers hunt for their sizes. There are leather couches, suggestive of an American gentlemen's club, and blue, plush carpets and deeply varnished moldings and baseboards and pediments and cabinetry in custom-carpentered American cherry. The first floor is apparel. The second floor is more apparel—children's, women's—along with novelties. The books in the bookstore are on the first floor, and on home-game weekends they play a kind of symbolic role. The whole place is modular, and workers roll aside portions of the bookstacks to make room for additional cash registers.

If Notre Dame fans have welcomed the new store's increase in space over the old, they also seem to universally bemoan what they perceive as a corresponding increase in prices.

"It's a lot easier to get around in, that's for sure. The old one, they only let a few in at a time. Now, you're paying the price. Everything seems sky-high in there. They got the captive audience, and they got the license to steal. That's what I say. License to steal."

"I used to buy three T-shirts every game. Nowadays, no way—that's sixty bucks right there!"

The checkout line lasts fifteen minutes, says a young "sales associate" in a hands-free headset hooked to a two-way Motorola that squawks. Roped off with ribbons like Departures at an airport, the line weaves through the bookshelves. Everyone has armfuls of T-shirts and sweatshirts. Masking-tape arrows on the carpet point the way. Past Journalism and Media, past Business and How-To, and on through Fiction and Literature, the line progresses nicely, consistently, evenly, the "Victory March" now a piano solo. Around a corner, a lady takes your hangers. At the registers, the bar-code infrared-laser guns beep, and the merchandise moves across the countertop and into the huge, distinctive white plastic bags of the Hammes Notre Dame Bookstore at the Eck Complex.

Notre Dame Talking Bottle Openers—"Hear the 'Fight Song' by the Notre Dame Band when the opener touches the bottle cap"—$8.

University of Notre Dame Wall Hangings—Grotto, Dome, Sacred Heart spire, tapestries in macramé shag-carpet weave, twenty-five inches by thirty-one—$60.

Notre Dame Irish Plush—*I-R-I-S-H* in cartoon letters, stuffed like a pillow, though its intended use is an open question—$20.

A middle-aged woman with high blond hair picks up an Irish Plush and absentmindedly gives it a squeeze. "This is cute."

Folding nylon Notre Dame Tailgate Chairs, Notre Dame Aprons and Notre Dame Oven Mitts and Notre Dame Snack Bowls and Notre Dame Spoon Rests—a tailgate outfitted for $115 total, not including tax.

A woman says to her friend, "I'm surprised you don't have the ND license plate"—$20.

Notre Dame Collector Glasses says a sign underneath a shelf. Notre Dame Collector Glasses by the gross, Notre Dame Collector Glasses in incredible variety, enough Notre Dame Collector Glasses to satisfy the spring-break tequila binge of a midsized college dorm—jiggers and half jiggers and test tubes, with leprechauns and interlocking *N*'s and *D*'s and the seals of the university, *Vita, Dulcedo, Spes*—$6.95 to $8 apiece.

Two middle-aged men clad purely in Notre Dame gear admire the Collector Glasses and ignore the euphemism.

"That one-shot glass is cool—the blue one."

"I didn't see that. Oh, that's eight bucks. Got me one just like it at home."

Notre Dame Rally Beads in blue and green and gold, inspired not by rosaries but pre-Lenten festivals, commonly seen dangling from balconies in the French Quarter to calls of "Show your . . ."—$5.95 a strand.

Notre Dame Rosary Beads on felt in glass cases, your choice of Genuine Malachite Beads, Connemara Marble Beads, or Aurora Borealis Beads, each with sterling-silver crucifix and Notre Dame center medal, the Dome and the Virgin Mary set in intaglio—$49.95, $49.95, and $59.95 a strand.

Notre Dame Snowfight Snowman Snow Globes—a Hummel-like figurine wearing an ND letterman's sweater inside a case that says on the plinth, "University of Notre Dame. Third in a Limited Series. www.memorycompany.com"—$40.

Irishopoloy board games—$24.95; Notre Dame Football Checkers—$19.95; thirty-four-karat [*sic*] Notre Dame Football Chess Sets—

"32 meticulously handcrafted and hand-painted metal alloy figures are mounted on rosewood bases; fine mahogany chessboard stores all figures in hidden drawer," the pawns linemen, the rooks Irish Guardsmen, the castles footballs, the kings quarterbacks, the queens female cheerleaders (and not, as one might assume, Blessed Mothers)—$750.

Notre Dame Metamorphic Coffee Mugs—"A picture appears as a hot beverage is added. Not dishwasher safe," and the picture that evidently appears, according to the packaging, is, on one side, a contemporary football team suited up and running away from the facade of Notre Dame Stadium, and, on the other, a half dozen old-timey leather-helmeted players walking away from the pre-renovation Notre Dame Stadium, pour in your coffee and see the Mystique—$20.

"You told me you weren't going to buy anything in here today," says a wife to her husband. In each hand he carries a bookstore bag bursting with merch. Posters tubed in plastic rise from inside the bags. Sweatshirts fatten the middles.

"How'm I doing for not buying anything?"

"Pretty shabby."

The husband holds up a brown Notre Dame lightweight coat—$89. And the wife says, "Oh, that's beautiful."

A receipt spools with a whisper from a cash register. Four sweatshirts, two T-shirts, a pair of shorts, Notre Dame flags meant to fly from your car, a little girl's cheerleading outfit—$299.69. A woman pays with three $100 bills. She takes her three-C-note bag and heads to the staircase and stops.

"Oh! I forgot to buy something for my dog!"

The retail floor at the Hammes Notre Dame Bookstore at the Eck Complex occupies forty-five thousand square feet. Tiffany's on Fifth Avenue in New York is about the same size. Sixty-two cash registers are ready to go. On a football weekend the whole bookstore operation employs four hundred people—two hundred and twenty at Eck, the rest under tents strewn about campus, satellite bookstores, and at the Varsity Shop inside the Joyce Center. Forty operators answer telephones at a separate facility, the bookstore's catalog and online operation. About forty people work down in the windowless bowels of the Eck, the "back end." During football season the store receives, each day, several dozen semitruck containers' worth of shipments and around thirteen hundred cartons of Notre Dame–licensed "product." Runners carry the product up to the floor as directed by the sales associates through their Motorola radios. "It's pretty much an aircraft-carrier mentality," says Jim O'Connor, manager of the Hammes Notre Dame.

Fifty thousand people cross its threshold over a football weekend, one million over a year—this at a university with 7,700 undergraduates. The Follet Corp., an operator of university bookstores, runs Hammes Notre Dame as well as the outlets at Oklahoma (31,000 students), Florida (32,000), and Florida State (30,000), to name just a few. Out of seven hundred Follet-managed bookstores, no other store receives as much foot traffic as the Hammes Notre Dame. And, correspondingly, no other store in the Follet chain achieves more revenue.

"This is the flagship site for our company. It's often the subject of peer review to seek out best practices," O'Connor says. He wears white shirtsleeves and beige suit pants and a brown-olive necktie in a pattern of ovals. His cell phone is clipped to his belt. With squinty eyes and a near-permanent smile he has the demeanor of a man who has risen quickly through the ranks of the hospitality sector. Forty-five years old, brought in to oversee the shift from the old bookstore to the new, O'Connor has worked here eight years. On a typical football weekend, Thursday through Sunday, he will put in fifteen-hour days, not leaving the premises until around midnight. During football season he doesn't really have an office—for lack of space elsewhere, it has been taken over by racks of children's clothes and office supplies, moved off the floors to make room for higher-selling items. O'Connor is as on-message as a manager of a political campaign. He says, "My paycheck comes from Follet, but make no bones about it, Notre Dame is my boss." When he speaks, he italicizes. "It's wonderful," he says. "It's a great facility. It's a wonderful tool not only to sell more, but to *provide* more to our guests. On home-game weekends at the old store, we couldn't *entertain* like we do now. The soccer coach downstairs, for instance. We're not just showcasing football. This allows us to showcase the *other* sides of the Notre Dame student-athlete. The Notre Dame student-athlete is a very special person. This is a way to show our guests a *different* side of Notre Dame. And, this is an important fund-raiser for the university. The money goes into the general fund of the university, and it furthers and supports the university's *academic mission*."

He says, "It's not just about fanfare. We want to create *memories*." O'Connor stands in the atrium, with its cathedral ceilings and its lancet window and its Monk Malloy sitting at a table autographing *Monk's Travels* for several fans. With a sweep of his hand O'Connor says, "The experience begins here. Nowhere else in college football, or in collegiate merchandising, will you have such a dramatic entrance." He motions toward the glass cases that form a wall behind a bank of cash registers. Crystal vases and goblets and punch bowls are etched with various university trademarks. "This is our high-end case. It's also such a wonderful entrance. How many other colleges do you know that have such a beautiful display of Waterford crystal?"

These, however, are not the most expensive items in the store. That honor goes to the bronze statues of Frank Leahy, replicas of the sculpture that stands just outside the stadium—$1,500. O'Connor estimates that the store has sold around thirty of them.

Of course he will not even hint at what eventually appears on the income statements of the Hammes Notre Dame Bookstore. Myths abound, he says, that both vastly overvalue and vastly undervalue the retail figures. "I've heard some wild numbers over the years," O'Connor says. A man once told him, "I heard you guys did twenty million one weekend," and O'Connor says, "I'd like to get a cut of *that* action." Others, lowballing, have estimated weekend turnover of a hundred thousand dollars. "Well, that might be *a little bit* off." Other than this range—so wide that it has no meaning—he will offer no further clarification. He does admit, however, that victories on Saturday tend to produce in the pilgrim an increased willingness to tithe at Our Lady of Commerce, as the Holy Cross seminarians have cynically titled the Hammes Notre Dame. "Happy people," O'Connor says, "are good customers."

When the Eck Complex opened in 1999, it elicited some strong reactions, especially among alumni, students, and faculty. Some people saw it as the most public example yet of an unseemly trend that they believed was developing within the university—the same "revenue whoring" that so outraged the "Call for Change" alumni.

"Over-the-top and elegant to the point of garish—that's what a lot of people on campus thought about the bookstore when it first opened. Everyone was kind of dumbfounded by the selling of all these other things—Waterford crystal and whatnot. It certainly didn't seem to accentuate books as one thought a bookstore might. The feeling was that they were trying to appeal to upscale visitors. It's not real Franciscan, let's put it that way."

"The old bookstore, it was an experience. It was always jammed, it was kind of dirty and dark and chaotic. There's something to be said for that. The new one has no personality, no atmosphere. It's like someone dropped a Barnes and Noble onto campus. That's not a Notre Dame bookstore. It's just a building."

"There's no evidence of function with these Eck buildings. They were built purely to maintain the fantasy. It's Disney. It's to keep the people coming back so that the university can get their money."

Criticism of the bookstore often broadens along the same lines to criticism of the university as a whole.

"Just because you *can* put an interlocking *N* and *D* on something doesn't mean you should."

"The heart of ND has become a marketing institution with education in the second tier."

"There's lots of talk at Notre Dame now about 'the Brand,' about marketing and protecting 'the Brand.' "

"They're milking the football program for all the revenue it's worth."

Notre Dame officials in the Main Building and in the athletic department exhibit extreme caginess whenever the subject of football wealth arises—the ancient psychological residue of Rockne vs. CSC. High football profits would seem to equal football factory. Secretive as Zurich in this regard, they refuse to divulge numbers, and they take pains to point out that whatever money football draws in, the university plows back into the general fund for student scholarship aid, for endowing professorships, for its academic well-being as a whole. They seem to be contrasting this with other universities, many of which plow their football money back into football.

All this anxiety despite that some portion of this financial information is already public and has been since 1996. Federal law (the Eq-

uity in Athletics Disclosure Act) requires that all colleges and universities that play sports and have students who receive federal financial
aid—which means just about every accredited institution in the
nation—report their athletic income to the government, no matter if
the school is public or private. The law arose out of Title IX, which has
strived for gender equality in college sports, and the government
wanted hard numbers to compare the emphasis universities have
placed on men's athletics against women's. Before the law went into
effect, Notre Dame had released its football accountancy to the public
twice before—once in 1930 and once in 1941—both times in response
to the growing perception that the priests of Notre Dame were lighting
their incense with football-earned C-notes. To quell these football-
factory notions, Notre Dame opened the books, and both times this
"sunshine policy" revealed far smaller gains than anyone had thought.

According to its most recent filing, which covered the twelve
months between July 2003 and July 2004, Notre Dame had football revenue of $38.6 million, expenses of $11.4 million, and a football bottom
line of $27.2 million. This ranks the university at number seven in the
nation in revenue, number eight in profit. After the monsters of Texas,
Tennessee, and Ohio State, however, not much separates the top ten.
Michigan, for example, is about dead even with Notre Dame in all regards. The Longhorns of football-mad Texas, at number one, are the
most adept at prospecting for interesting new revenue streams; their
program reported a top line of $47.6 million and a bottom line of $34.6
million. Ohio State and Tennessee, with their stadia in excess of a hundred thousand seats, are not far behind. Florida, Georgia, and Alabama
are not far behind them. If revenue correlates to the size and intensity
of a school's fan base, this particular piece of sunshine reveals the extent of Notre Dame's, since all the other top schools are enormous public institutions with living alumni that can number a half million. The
small private schools in Division I do not merit comparison, not even
Miami, not even national champion Southern Cal. Notre Dame's profit
alone exceeds their revenue—$23 million for Miami and $26 million
for USC.

Seventy-three years after the death of Rockne, it would seem as
though Notre Dame had grown highly accomplished at the selling of
its Mystique. Counterintuitively, all through the decade-long decline,

football finances expanded—profits are up 80 percent from the 1997–99 cycle the first year to take into account the expanded stadium—and this more than anything else suggests that Notre Dame has gone postindustrial. If no longer known as a football factory, it is good at exploiting its brand. Despite existing for most of its history on a threadbare budget, borrowing from Peter to pay Paul, modern Notre Dame has achieved a reputation, among students and fans and the people of South Bend, for its business acumen, its opportunism, its parsimony. So much so, in fact, that some fans in the South Bend area have suggested a new meaning for the abbreviation of the Congregation of Holy Cross, the CSC—Cash, Strictly Cash.

The Equity in Athletics Disclosure Act defines "revenue" liberally. It encompasses every line of business you can think of, and every line of business the big-time programs have already thought of. Tickets, licensing royalties, corporate sponsorships, JumboTrons, television and radio broadcasting contracts, bowl-game payouts, parking passes, stadium hot-dog concessions, summer camps for high school players, donations. For instance, in 2001, the University of Arkansas (of all places) topped every other university in the nation with football revenue of $66.3 million, boosted a hundred percent above its normal level of around $30 million because of contributions from Wal-Mart richies for the renovations of the Razorback football stadium. But totting all this up is a highly complex endeavor, and with all such numbers, the universities' published athletics revenues are somewhat fictional. Many schools, for instance, often define one or another line of business as not related to athletics and therefore exclude it from their statements. Notre Dame, for its part, does not include licensing royalties, a massive money engine. Some people believe that Notre Dame is deliberately conservative when reporting its numbers—big money equals football factory. Because the law does not require the schools to break out what exactly goes into the revenue line, everything that contributes to it remains a partial mystery, making it impossible to compare meaningfully one college to the next.

Despite all the charges of "revenue whoring," Notre Dame has actually shown restraint in some areas. For big donors and such people, the stadium has preferred seating, with cushions and seatbacks, at the fifty-yard line. Everyone else sits or stands on benches. But Notre

Dame Stadium does not have the luxury private boxes now increasingly common in university coliseums, especially Texas, which require five-figure donations (or more) that go directly into the athletic department bank accounts. Anyone may decide to donate a grand a year to Notre Dame and thus become a Sorin Society member, and thus receive a privileged lottery spot for home-game tickets. But that grand a year goes to the general university fund, not athletics. For rather more aesthetical reasons, Notre Dame Stadium does not contain large-scale advertising of any kind, though this has perhaps been avoided through persuasion rather than any sense of proportion on the part of Notre Dame's leaders. In 2002, the athletic department floated the idea of sticking a pair of JumboTrons onto either end of the arena. At least one university official made a speech to an alumni club gathering, trumpeting the school's new "revenue stream" plans, and the alumni went berserk. Used to show replays as well as TV-style commercials to the crowds, JumboTrons are now ubiquitous across the sporting world. To put such things into Notre Dame Stadium would be akin to staging a Pink Floyd laser-light show inside the Sistine Chapel—or so the alumni made it seem. Via overnight mail, a small-scale "Call for Change" letter went out to Kevin White, the athletic director, warning that if he pursued such a plan, he risked alienating a large number of alumni. Shortly thereafter, the athletic department not only shelved the plan but denied it had ever occurred to them. White has since become the favored quintan of alumni and fans when criticizing Notre Dame for its commercialization, though the whole mind-set is believed by some fans and alumni to be systemic throughout the administration—all the way up, of course, to Malloy.

Kevin White has a coif of such silvery hair he might just have walked out of a Senate confirmation hearing. There are times, under the lights at a press conference, when it looks sprayed on. He is fifty-four years old. Trig and corporately dressed, a true company man, he seems to have stocked his closet entirely with blue and gold regimental neckties. Hired to replace Mike Wadsworth in 2000 in the wake of the NCAA violations, he is a career professional athletics-department man, the first in Notre Dame's history, with the exclusion of Moose Krause, who stayed on so long at the job he certainly made himself into a professional. White, however, has earned graduate degrees in it, including a Ph.D. from Southern Illinois University, where his doctoral research analyzed the effect of Title IX on the Big Ten. Before Notre Dame, White had been the athletic director at Arizona State, and he came to South Bend widely recommended as among the best in the business. His biographical spread in the *Media Guide* reads like everything else in the *Media Guide*—hagiography—and in the absence of football success there are long lists of the many accomplishments of Notre Dame's twenty-five other sports teams under White's watch. As just one example, women's soccer would go on to win a national championship at the end of the 2004 season.

Over the years White has acquired a reputation for possessing a sense of commercial opportunity as potent as Walt Disney's. Of course the athletic department's rather mercantile culture long predated White—ten years before his hiring, the university made its NBC deal— yet he appears to have contributed to it in no small way. With this business sense he has walked square into the teeth of the Notre Dame dilemma: how to achieve excellence all the time in everything without trouncing all over tradition.

Among the fans, it is a massively open question whether White "gets it." Frequently he deploys corporate-speak. Frequently he is forced to defend his moves. "We just made a huge commitment to elevate all our Olympic sports to what we call 'full NCAA scholarship compliments,'" he told the *South Bend Tribune* in 2002. He was defending the increases in football ticket prices that had occurred every year under his watch. "We've also made the commitment to elevate coaching salaries and operational budgets where it would be consistent with our programmatic expectations." Ever since Title IX came into being, it has been his and the university's stated goal to improve the women Irish and all the other teams that end the fiscal year with financial losses.

One way to cover the costs of those sports was, of course, through "revenue whoring." Another way was to field high-quality football teams. The fans made the obvious point: good football is good for business. Make it into a Bowl Championship Series game—Rose, Fiesta, Orange, Sugar—and Notre Dame, because it remained independent, would receive nearly $17 million, the same amount as a twelve-team BCS conference. Miss qualifying for a BCS game, and Notre Dame received zero dollars—high risk, high reward. Over the 2004 season, however, the parties had been quietly negotiating a new deal. It would not come to light until the middle of November. Under this fresh agreement, Notre Dame would receive a guaranteed $1 million each year, no matter whether it played in a BCS game. But in return for this stability, the Irish would get just $4.5 million if they reached one of the major bowls. The sporting media, by and large, interpreted this as Notre Dame once again using its sway to guarantee itself a cut of the action. Notre Dame fans, however, mostly alumni, interpreted this as another spineless capitulation to outside forces on the part of Malloy's administration, or, as one alumnus described it on ND Nation, "the ultimate compromise in excellence." He went on, "I suspect that White and the Administration have an assumption of how often ND will be in the BCS to make the math work for them, and I dare say that it's far from the excellence we've all come to expect. . . . Is a new standard of excellence being created before our own eyes?"

To hear White talk about covering the cost of the nonrevenue sports is to hear a man who seems a little worried about Notre Dame's ability to finance them all. The athletic department sends a hundred percent of its profit "across the street," as the ADs like to say, which means the money goes into the university's general fund, mostly to support academic scholarship. The entire portion of the school's NBC contract revenue moves across Juniper Road, from the Joyce Center to the Main Building for use by the financial aid office. The athletic department, then, must find other ways to fund the loss-leader sports.

When he first came to Notre Dame, White would often say, with some annoyance, "We are not in the athletics fund-raising business," by which he meant that, unlike most other universities, Notre Dame avoided actively seeking benefactors who would make gifts straight to the athletic department. This unofficial policy flowed, of course, directly out of Fortress Notre Dame, the guiding principle articulated by Fr. John O'Hara to keep Notre Dame athletics morally unassailable and "in perspective." To pursue benefactors explicitly for campus sporting emporiums seemed to indicate a lack of priorities. Only reluctantly did Hesburgh ratify the decision to build the Joyce Center, which was underwritten with $9.5 million in onetime donations. He repeatedly shot down various proposals for the construction of a Fighting Irish

Sports Museum and hall of fame. Spire there, dome there, library over here, and that stadium underneath it all. A donor had to be pretty adamant about his or her desire to give money for a sports facility before the university would take the donor up on the idea. And the facility always had to be open to all students.

But through White's influence, the university has now changed this policy, and with it has come a rather large shift in the institutional culture of Notre Dame. Early in his tenure he and the athletic department formulated their "master plan" for a set of improvements and new construction. Architects drafted blueprints, consultants were consulted, and after White showed the documents to the administration, portions of the proposal got absorbed into the university plan as a whole and, with that, absorbed into the next giant overall Notre Dame capital campaign—a supra-billion-dollar fund-raising drive—already ongoing in a covert way, but not scheduled for announcement until who knows when. (It is standard practice for universities to delay going public with such campaigns until they've gathered a sizable sum, thereby creating PR splash and, hopefully, a bandwagon effect.)

For the first time in its history, then, Notre Dame began actively seeking athletic department donations. The first indication of this shift occurred in 2002 with the inception of the Rockne Heritage Fund, which raises money to help the athletic department defray the cost of athletic scholarships (or "grant-in-aids" as they're now styled) in the "nonrevenue sports," that is, the fencing and the 400-meter freestyle of the Olympic-sports set. The second indication occurred in April 2004, when the earthmovers rolled in and the steel I beams went up on the Don F. and Flora Guglielmino Family Athletics Center, ninety-six thousand square feet and 24 million dollars' worth of Fighting Irish football headquarters, rendered in the same cartoon Gothic as the Eck Complex. Because many other buildings on campus have acquired nicknames over the years, the Guglielmino family wanted their building to be known as the Gug (pronounced *goog*), and all press releases concerning the structure have made sure to point out that the new football building has "quickly become known as" or is now "affectionately known as" the Gug. "The Gug was a huge departure for us," said one official in the Notre Dame development office. "Our fear was always that you might divert someone to athletics who would otherwise give to academics. We've always wanted our high-end donors to contribute to a part of the university that everyone could benefit from." Monk Malloy, of course, gave the final approval, and with such rubber-stamping it certainly didn't seem as if he was out to de-emphasize.

White also talks a lot about the "arms race" of intercollegiate football, whereby successful recruiting depends to a large degree on the glistening weight rooms and luxurious lounges and Augusta National-esque locker rooms and huge, pristine practice fields of a school's athletic facilities. The previous football appointments did not compare with those of the other big-time programs around the country, and for a long time many Notre Dame people had an almost literary pride in this fact. But the Guglielmino family and the first piece of White's athletic-department master plan has brought Notre Dame back up to snuff. The training room has a vaulted cathedral ceiling that makes the space resemble the interior of an Anglican church. The weights are accessible only to scholarship athletes. Only the football coaching staff has its offices here. Only football players have access to its luxe locker rooms and a players' lounge with TVs implanted into custom-carpentered, built-in armoires. One Notre Dame staff member and alumnus said, "Now they can seduce eighteen-year-olds with the best." Around the same time that the Gugs made their gift, another big Notre Dame donor, J. W. Jordan, Notre Dame class of 1969, a Chicago financier, offered up some large sum, never made public, for a new $70 million science building. After a freeze on new construction unfroze in early 2004, both the Gug and the Jordan were at the head of the building docket. Notre Dame broke ground on the science building first. As the development office official put it, "We've always been very careful not to send the wrong message."

Notre Dame's most significant lines of football revenue are tickets and NBC. From its famous television contract, which airs every home game nationally, the university receives an alleged $9 million a year in revenue. Somehow the press got hold of this number, and it has been repeated so often over the years that the media now reports it as fact, even though the university has never released it, nor has any university official ever commented publicly on it. The tones in their voices when declining to comment on it publicly would, however, seem to suggest that the number is low. Sui generis in all of sport, inked in 1990 at the height of Holtz's run of dominance, the contract induced immediate denunciation. There were calls of arrogance and greed unrestrained; these football industrialists were at it once again. (Every other school shares its TV proceeds with its conference, which does the negotiating for its members, and those contracts are quite lucrative for each member school as well.) The NBC contract exists, of course, because of the uncommon extent of the university's fan base. Lately, however, the television spirit has slipped slightly away, at least according to Nielsen. The average number of households that tuned in dropped from 3.3 million in 2002 (Willingham's hot-streak first year, when the team was ranked as high as No. 4 in the country) to 2.6 million in 2003, a decrease of 21 percent, and the lowest number since 1991, the first year of the contract. Evidently the threshold has not yet been reached whereby the sponsors—Xerox, Adidas, Coca-Cola, Gatorade, Sirius Radio, otherwise known as "Team Notre Dame"— would quit NBC's ND broadcasts. And evidently the ratings have been high enough that several other networks—most notably ABC and Fox—have hinted to Notre Dame that should NBC waver, they would be more than willing to step in. After the 2003 season, tight on the heels of Notre Dame's third losing record in five years, NBC and the university extended the contract through 2010.

Ticket sales account for more than half the football program's annual revenue as reported to the Equity in Athletics people. In 2003, tickets brought in somewhere between $20 million and $25 million. Every year for the last few years, prices have gone up five bucks until they reached $53 in 2004. But the real money first rolled in after the university expanded and, in some ways, destroyed the House that Rockne Built, in 1996. Piers of steel-reinforced concrete entombed the old redbrick art deco, all but obscuring it, and held aloft a new dish of seating. There is now a weird, somewhat disorienting second concourse—you think you're out of the stadium, but then you're not out of the stadium. Etched into the facade in gold are the giant words UNIVERSITY OF NOTRE DAME, a tawdry addition, some people felt, since it seemed a little redundant. A student in the *Scholastic* in 1997, just before construction finished, said that it appeared as if a UFO had come down from space and landed on the old stadium. An architecture professor at the school said, "Notre Dame has created the world's largest reliquary." With the coming of Bob Davie and ten years of football decline, the meaning of his words have since doubled up.

But, nevertheless, with twenty thousand new seats, the expanded stadium immediately relieved alumni ticket demand—one hundred thousand of them alive, a figure that grows every year as life spans increase and two thousand more graduates come down each May. Depending on their age, alumni must make a minimum donation of between $50 and $100 to the university's annual fund, which will enter them into a lottery for a chance to win the privilege of buying tickets, another method whereby the academy uses football to boost the intake of dollars. But, again, Notre Dame is one of the few universities with big-time football, if not the only one, to use those lottery donations for academics rather than sports.

Merchandise licensing, perhaps the granddaddy of all football-related business lines, including ticketing, nets for the university a sum not reported in the revenue line of Notre Dame's Equity in Athletics accounting. (A small portion of it does go to the athletic department—mostly from the sale of replica jerseys.) It is as highly guarded a figure as any at Notre Dame. The royalty rate is 8 percent, and 8 percent of many, many millions is still many millions. Though the revenue statement in the university's publicly available 2004 annual report contained no line called "licensing, merchandise," it did have one called "sales and services of auxiliary enterprises," which entailed, among other things, bookstore proceeds and licensing royalties. The figure on that line was $130.4 million.

Not surprisingly, the university enforces its eighteen trademarks with batteries of lawyers, with plainclothesmen in the parking lots trained to discern counterfeit product, with the United States Customs Service, with the FBI. It is a war of attrition. "I just took down five sites on eBay today," Mike Low, director of licensing, told me when I visited him at his office. "It's like banging your head against the wall." That morning, someone had been selling T-shirts bearing pirated Notre Dame logos, and a sleeve patch that said FDNY IRISH. It bore a leprechaun altered to look like a firefighter.

Notre Dame's eighteen registered marks include all conceivable derivations of the phrase *Fighting Irish.* "The word *Irish* is actually trademarked," said Chuck Lennon, the Alumni Association director. "But we're pretty lenient with that one." He thus passed over that the school had succinctly and legally subsumed a nationality. They include the Notre Dame leprechaun, an apelike little man in a green suit of clothes and green bowler hat pushed over his forehead, bootees pointed at the toes like a swami's, fists raised, left before right, his chin-bearded face written with malevolence. The same artist who came up with the *C* logo for the Chicago Bears invented the leprechaun for the university in 1964. Notre Dame gave him $75 for it, an investment that likely paid for itself rather quickly. He may have based his character on a famous nineteenth-century British political cartoon that depicted an apelike little Irishman eerily similar to Notre Dame's. The original intent of the cartoon was to portray the Irish as the British thought them to be—belligerent, dipsomaniacal, and less than human—the Fighting Irish. Other trademarks include representations of the Dome, the Sacred Heart church, the university seal, all derivations of the words *University of Notre Dame,* thus subsuming a slightly older Parisian cathedral, and, of course, the school monogram, the transcendent and universally known interlocking *N* and *D.* Notre Dame has been somewhat lenient with that one as well; so far, at least, it has taken no legal action against the University of North Dakota, which uses the exact same insignia.

Licensing revenue fluctuates year to year more wildly than any other football-related business line, and it fluctuates based on one thing: wins and losses. It is, after all, fashion—most of those royalties come from apparel. "The impact of a successful season on licensed product is huge," Low says. "And I hate to say it, but it's especially so at Notre Dame because football is traditionally important here. At other schools that might not happen so much." Since 2003, a firm called the Collegiate Licensing Company, which holds a kind of monopoly over academia, has managed almost all of Notre Dame's royalties and licensing accounts. Every facet of a university's institutional existence seems, these days, to be ranked, and so the CLC puts out a quarterly ranking of the top royalty-producing universities that it represents. Over the short period of its engagement with the CLC, Notre

Dame has fallen from No. 3 to its current No. 7. Also moving up and down the top ten are Michigan, Texas, Georgia, Oklahoma, North Carolina, and Tennessee.

"Notre Dame licensing has certainly been larger than it is today," Mike Low says. "My job is to reposition us in the top three, if not number one in the country." He would, of course, be aided in this endeavor by a winning football team.

But if it wanted to, the university could earn even more from its royalties than it does now, without resorting to football victories. Though perhaps hard to believe, relative to the other top schools, the amount of strange bric-a-brac found on Notre Dame's bookstore shelves is actually somewhat modest. A committee made up of faculty and staff—general counsel, public relations, the athletic department, the bookstore, someone from business operations, though no one, at present, from the Holy Cross community—vets each new licensee and keeps a sharp eye on how potential products might affect the university's image, the Notre Dame Brand. In addition, when approving products for licensing, the university has an unwritten edict. Sporting icons shall not appear juxtaposed with the religious. A few years ago, The Shirt broke the rule and caused a minor uproar on campus and among the Holy Cross community. It mixed the Dome with images of football players—with its Blessed Mother statue, the Dome is considered a religious symbol. After the incident, the licensing office became "sensitized" and is now doubly diligent. "We just don't want to send mixed messages," says Mike Low. "We're a religious school first and a football powerhouse second. They coexist but they're not necessarily blended."

Roger Valdiserri, one in a long line of great Notre Dame football publicity men, the brain responsible for altering the pronunciation of Joe Theismann's name so that it rhymed with *Heisman,* was ND's sports information director since the time of Terry Brennan. Now retired, he also worked closely with Hesburgh on the Knight Commission. He had a policy identical to the licensing department's, though perhaps for somewhat different reasons. "I would never let religion become part of football while I was in my job. I would never let photographers photograph the team Mass, for instance. I would never let them photograph players in religious settings, whether at the Grotto or the Communion rail, because I felt you can't push religion down people's throats and still have them admire the university. I didn't think it was the football team's place to be doing that. I thought the religion of the football team was a private thing. And I felt we had reached a point where that wasn't necessary anymore. Everyone knows the university is Catholic. I told Gerry Faust the same thing when he was hired—in front of Father Joyce, I might add. And Father Joyce agreed with me." A devout Catholic, Faust had sometimes been known to grab a player or two on the sideline just before a key play and coerce them into saying a Hail Mary with him. "I told him to cool it with the Hail Marys," Valdiserri says.

A much subtler blending of religion and sport is now occuring, however. The university will not put its trademarks on anything manufactured in overseas sweatshops—which means no Made in Chinas, no Made in Indonesias. It's called the China Policy, and Low says, "It prevents us from having products that other schools license profitably. It goes to the teachings of the Church. There are some things that money can't buy." In keeping with Fortress Notre Dame, it is the university's ambition, even in something as quotidian as merchandising, to have it both ways—to be atop all forms of ranking, and to do so while maintaining an ethical high ground, the city on the hill.

But this ambition has become so tightly bound up in the Notre Dame Mystique and image and Brand that it too has become a marketing bullet point. It is a kind of residuum left over from the blatant blending of the religious and the sporting that occurred many years ago, and that the university is now so careful to avoid, at least on the surface. Outside the bookstore on home-game weekends, and at several other prominent spots closer to the stadium, a sign hangs from a promotional tent. It says UNIVERSITY OF NOTRE DAME PLATINUM VISA. If you sign up, you get a free T-shirt, navy blue with the ND monogram inside a green shamrock—presumably licensed. On this day, the Friday before the game against Washington, the woman working at the tent said she had signed up more than two hundred people. Over a weekend, she said, all the tents combined typically gather between 750 and 1,000 signatures. Should your credit rating pass muster, you have your choice of designs for your card. One with old-timey players in leather helmets, identical to the picture on the Notre Dame Metamorphic Coffee Mug. A second with simply the ND monogram, and a third with a panorama of the Dome and the Sacred Heart spire as seen from the Moreau Seminary side of St. Joseph's Lake, perhaps the best view on campus. These cards do not mix steeples with old-timey players. But they do mix something else. The university decided to earmark its cut of the profits for academic scholarships—to help ease the financial burden of the neediest potential students—Fortress Notre Dame again at work. The money does not go to the alumni association or to the athletic department, as it does perhaps at all other schools, and Notre Dame is careful to point this out to potential customers. "From Sacred Heart to the stadium that Rockne built, Notre Dame remains a part of you," reads the ad copy for the cards. "Now, you can support Notre Dame every day, and save money, too. Whenever you use the University of Notre Dame Platinum Visa® card, a contribution is made toward academic scholarships. And you get back even more."

Said one person affiliated with the University of Notre Dame Platinum Visa, "Some people might ask, 'Why would I want to give even more money to the school? They've got enough already.' This way, you put them at ease. It's a really nice marketing tool."

8

Benders

State Route 23 comes into Edison Road at a forty-five-degree angle, forming a deltaic slice of property less than an acre square. Situated just off campus, it is a prominent place geographically and in the postgame minds of large portions of the student body, younger alumni, and certain elements of Notre Dame fandom, because on this spot a bar called the Linebacker Inn has done business since 1962. Its sign pictures a martini glass with bubbles rising from its font, and from the top of the sign rises a miniature goalpost. The 'Backer, as it's known, occupies a low-slung cinder-block building, and on non-home-game weekends it contains an incongruous mix of sullen working-class South Bend locals shooting pool, and giddy business and engineering majors jump-dancing to the pop-rock standards of Def Leppard and K.C. and the Sunshine Band. They purchase Jell-O shots and twenty-four-ounce plastic containers of yellow beer and seem to be in constant celebration over having just turned twenty-one. On home-game weekends, however, the Linebacker swells to capacity with nostalgic alumni wanting to relive their student days and visiting subway alumni wanting to participate in the local Notre Dame student culture. They come to rejoice in victories and they come to drown defeats. The Linebacker sits adjacent to Belmont Liquors, the closest liquor store to campus and therefore the principal tailgating outfitter for all of Notre Dame.

On Saturdays in the fall, both the Linebacker and Belmont make their mint, along with all St. Joseph County—$6.3 million spent by the pilgrims every home-game weekend, almost $38 million a season, according to the conservative estimates in a 2003 study of Notre Dame's impact on the region, commissioned by the university. A decade of mediocre football has, if slightly, affected the economics of pilgrimage. The ticket scalpers have reported weaker-than-normal demand for

late-season games against opponents of lesser interest—Navy, Pittsburgh—and it is always true that postgame business drops off if the
team loses an individual contest. Restaurant queues grow shorter, receipts shrink at the Hammes Notre Dame Bookstore, fewer pints go
across the bartops of the South Bend pubs. For this reason, all hotels in
the area maintain a two-night minimum. Depressed after a loss, you
can skip town, but you're still paying for Saturday night.

Nonetheless, at Belmont Liquors, the staff is always run weary by
home-game demand. The workday starts early and ends late. On Saturdays the store opens at seven a.m., when the run begins on vodka
and Bloody Mary mix, and it doesn't close until midnight. The manager, a woman named Mary Beth Lang, begins gearing up for the season
in August, stocking the store and bracing herself. She looked at the
schedule for 2005 and shook her head. "Next season they got five home
games in a row. I may have to retire!"

But developments not related to losing seasons have recently cut
into the store's game-day trade. A few years ago, the university began
cracking down on tailgate parties. Drinking out in the lots during the
game was banned. The parking-lot constabulary increased its numbers. More cops on horses clopped through the tailgates, more cops
wrote tickets and busted underage drinkers. Once a game-day fixture,
the raucous student-sponsored tailgates—with kids up on car roofs
chugging Mad Dog 20/20, fifty and sixty of them standing around shot-
gunning beer—have become a thing of the past, like pep rallies at the
old Fieldhouse, like campus keg parties. And, most substantially of
all, the university banished recreational vehicles from campus, sending them to a field so far north of the stadium that shuttle buses are required to ferry the RV crowd back to the game. The banishment's
precipitating incident occurred in 1993, when a convoy of Florida
State RVs rolled onto campus for that epic battle, No. 1 vs. No. 2. After
their team lost, the Seminoles tore up the joint, overturning trash bar-
rels and setting fires. But the locals of South Bend—often called Benders by Notre Dame students, and a kind of subcategory of the subway
alumni—made up (and still do) a significant portion of the RV crowd.
Many of them did not have tickets to the game and instead watched on
televisions plugged into generators outside their RVs. Their numbers
were large, they consumed in quantities before, during, and after the

contest, and their rowdiness increased to a point that officials in the Main Building decided that they presented an image at odds with the Notre Dame Brand. All these Benders with their beers—this was not a family environment. Each year since the RV banishment and the institution of other "antifun" measures, the fans have complained about the "Gestapo tactics" deployed by the university's tailgate henchmen.

One of those banished RVs, a 1996 Holiday Rambler, remains near campus, slyly parked every game day on the prime real estate in the small parking lot adjacent to Belmont Liquors and the Linebacker Inn. Notre Dame property ends across the street, and thus the RV sits just outside of the Gestapo's jurisdiction. Visible to the north and west is the stadium, about a five-minute walk away. On October 2, Notre Dame vs. the Boilermakers of Purdue University, around 150 people stood beside the RV, most of them Benders. Meanwhile, Linebacker patrons stumbled out of the bar and sometimes brawled. A permanent detail of South Bend cops sat in a prowler parked at the curb and became involved when necessary. A bank of Porta Potties outside the bar received its pissers and, often enough, its pukers. Tailgaters from all over campus moved in and out of Belmont Liquors to restock on cases of beer and bottles of hard stuff, and a huge field stretched on the other side of the Belmont/Linebacker lot—the so-called soccer fields, a traditionally boisterous tailgating area that, because of campus expansion, will cease to exist starting with the 2005 season—and all of it together conspired to make this snatch of pavement perhaps the most besotted district on a Notre Dame game day.

The RV in the Linebacker lot belonged to Dick Schaffer, owner of an auto sales and rental business in South Bend. For $60 a game, he rents the spot from the Linebacker, and he parks his camper sideways across the lot, taking up four or five spaces. On this day of sunshine and mild temperatures, an awning unrolled from the camper's roof cast shade over two big-screen televisions plugged into a humming gasoline generator. The second half of the Purdue game had begun, and hardly anyone had noticed. Outdoor speakers from the liquor store sprayed the Westwood One radio broadcast all over the lot. "Go, Irish!" someone shouted. Folding buffet tables carried an astonishing spread of food. Three Crock-Pots of duck stew, a hundred pieces of fried chicken, a five-pound smoked ham, sixteen turkey breasts, four pork loins, four London broils, and miscellaneous dips and chips and vegetable pieces. People sat on a row of a dozen lawn chairs opened in front of the televisions, where Notre Dame quarterback Brady Quinn overthrew an open receiver. Freshmen phenom Darius Walker was dropped for a one-yard loss. On third and ten, Quinn completed a pass well short of the first-down marker. Still losing 20–3, Notre Dame was forced to punt.

"You need ten yards and you throw a five-yard pass. Nice play-calling."

"So much for halftime adjustments."

The first two quarters had shell-shocked the people. Misfortune and ugly miscues had started in earnest when Purdue returned a kickoff for a touchdown, had continued when Walker fumbled at the two-yard line just before he was about to score (which would have brought the Irish within a field goal, 10–13), and had reached skull-clutching, garment-rending stages of frustration when Kyle Orton, the Purdue quarterback, orchestrated a technical and fastidious evisceration of the Irish secondary. Supra-ten-yard pass after supra-ten-yard pass, Orton moved his team ninety-eight yards down the field from the spot of Walker's fumble for a Purdue touchdown—20–3 Purdue.

Riding a win streak of three games, Notre Dame had come into its annual contest with Purdue harboring dreams of possibly making a run at a BCS bowl bid. But now, less some heroic, improbable comeback in the second half, those dreams appeared to be in ruins. If Purdue, riding its own four-game win streak, had presented Notre Dame and Ty Willingham with a test, they appeared to have failed. Orton out there looked like a multiple Heisman Trophy winner. He would eventually pass for nearly four hundred yards on the day. Quinn, meanwhile, on the current play, was sacked.

"The O-line sucks."

"Well, they're young."

"Fuck that. They're young *and* they suck."

Notre Dame kicked a well-orchestrated punt that pinned the Boilermaker offense deep, on its own three-yard line, and now it appeared that the Irish had them in a tight spot—possible momentum shift. Third and ten and Notre Dame blitzed. Purdue picked up the blitz.

Orton dropped back and stood in his own end zone. He scanned for open receivers and looked off a defensive back. He planted his feet and delivered a short strike to a flanker named Stubblefield, open on the sidelines. When Stubblefield received the ball into his arms and turned upfield, the TV screen at the Schaffer tailgate contained no Irish defenders. Stubblefield launched down the sideline, running and running on a run that seemed to last forever. When he reached the end zone, he dove across the goal, his arms extended Superman-style, 97 yards, the longest play from scrimmage in Notre Dame Stadium history—27–3 Purdue.

"Holy fuck. Not possible."

"How do you let *that* happen?"

"Notre Dame you *suck!*"

"Wait, wait, wait! There's a flag!"

"It's holding!"

"This might be coming back!"

"Please, God, bring it back."

"Goddamnit—it's not holding."

"Jesus *Christ.*"

"Well. I guess Purdue is covering the spread. Deal with it, deal with it. What idiot put their money on *us* this week?"

No one seemed to gather what penalty the referee ended up calling, and the tailgaters turned back to their party.

The core of the Schaffer's RV crowd consisted of a circle of friends, all in their late forties and early fifties, as tight-knit a group as the Neighborhood of Hope. Nicknames were common. There was "Ace," aka "Little Hitler," aka Bobby Acrew, so notorious for complaining incessantly about all things, including the substandard play—and "inept coaching"—of Notre Dame football, that he has annoyed his friends to the point that they've given him this rather unflattering second nickname. He also happened to be on the short side and have a dark mustache. Standing in front of the TVs outside the camper, watching Purdue drive toward yet another touchdown, he said, "I have nothing against Ty. He's a good guy, I'm sure. I just don't think he's the man to put Notre Dame back on track. I mean, *why, why, why* would you hire a coach with a worse record than the one you just fired?"

"That's why we call him Little Hitler."

Judy Schaffer, Dick's wife, seemed to hold the position of tailgate caterer. She worked through the game nonstop. On stoves inside the RV she had Crock-Pots going. She poured toppings onto prebaked cakes, she put turkeys into ovens, she delivered platters of food from the RV kitchen to the buffet tables outside like a waitress.

"You seem to be working pretty hard."

"Every week. Do you need a beer?"

They had all known one another for years, having forced their relationship through the game-day experience here in the lots. Despite the RV banishment, large numbers of Benders still treat the hoopla as an excuse to come to campus, or to the bars nearby, for a good time. Each of the six home-game Saturdays has become a kind of local holiday. They treat Notre Dame as the city's de facto professional franchise, and they seem to root for the Irish more out of local civic pride than any subway-alum-like reverence for the Catholic values of the university. Only about half the Schaffer tailgate was Catholic. None in the Schaffer group had attended Notre Dame. Only rarely did they go into the stadium. Normally, though, they will take the RV to one or two away games a year. This season, for instance, about fifteen people—the core group—had plans to drive down to Knoxville, Tennessee, for the game against the Volunteers, in November. Notre Dame first played Tennessee in 1978, and they've been on and off the schedule ever since. On one previous road trip down there, the Schaffer crowd had befriended a parallel crowd of Tennessee RV tailgaters. Inside a bar in Knoxville, the Benders set up a "jam box" and subjected the enemy to the "Victory March." The enemy responded with "Rocky Top" on a jam box of their own. Dueling fightsong jam boxes brought the groups together, and now every ND-UT matchup has become a long weekend of husbands, wives, golf outings, bar outings, and Volunteer/Irish fanaticism. They do not always limit their trips to the road. Twice in the 1990s Notre Dame played the University of Hawaii, and the Schaffer group chartered an L-1011 jet to take them across the Pacific.

With twelve minutes left in the fourth quarter it was 41–10 Purdue. Earlier, when Notre Dame had cut the deficit to seventeen points, people had said things like "Never give up hope" and "I've seen some crazy comebacks before." No longer. Tommy, another member of the

Schaffer circle, emerged from somewhere. He had a brown mustache and dark eyes, and with the overall inebriety of the Linebacker scene in the background, he looked as sober as a Mormon. He said, "I haven't been watching. I can't take it." The ongoing route had so disturbed him that the age-old questions had risen in his mind. He talked out loud, but he was really addressing no one, and he talked himself into circles, a chicken-egg monologue:

"Who do you blame it on when you lose this bad? The players? The coaches? I don't know. I don't know." His words had the force of metaphysical appeal. He was like a man struggling with the Problem of Evil. He took a contemplative sip from his longneck. "You can have the best coaches in the world, but you need the talent." He looked blankly at the television screen. Quinn let one sail toward the end zone, an attempted long bomb. The ball fell to the earth lonesome of players, and Purdue took over on downs. "We won the last three games. We beat *Michigan.* So was it luck? Were we just playing good? Were the players playing above themselves? Did the coaches have a better game plan those games? I don't know. It's hard to say, really. When you lose this bad, the coaches are on the sideline, the players are on the field—who do you place the blame on? The coaches call the plays. They're supposed to teach the players. But if the players don't execute, you're gonna lose. I guess I should say, the talent is there. They've just been playing with their heads up their asses."

He had posed the eternal, hoary coaching-vs.-talent problem, and he had come to no conclusions. Across Notre Dame fandom, the diehards were doubtless asking the same questions at this very moment, positing parallel theories. Maybe Notre Dame had simply mistakenly hired a poor head coach twice in a row. No, the culture of collegiate football had shifted to such a degree since the prime Holtz years that Notre Dame could no longer attract the talent needed to compete at a consistently high level. No, wrong again, it was a concerted conspiracy on the part of Notre Dame's leaders to de-emphasize.

Doomsday scenarios unfolded among the Benders.

"Well, USC's gonna kick our ass," Little Hitler said. "BC too. Depending on how things break, we'll end up fifty-fifty if we're lucky."

"Are you kidding? We'll lose to Stanford, USC, BC . . . *Navy.* Don't forget Navy. They're pretty good this year."

I asked if the long streak of championship-less football had affected them.

"I guess I'm getting used to this," someone said.

"We bitch and moan and moan and bitch, but then we move on."

"*Unfortunately* we're getting used to it. It's been—what?—five or six years since we were even in a BCS bowl?"

"I think Notre Dame is trying to push football aside."

"I *guarantee* you, when you hire a coach with the same record as Bob Davie, you're trying to push football aside."

Whether or not Notre Dame was actually in the midst of de-emphasis or had merely made a series of negligent coaching choices or had seen the last of its glory days due to environmental circumstances outside its control—nature versus nurture—all of this was somewhat beside the point. In the minds of many Notre Dame fans, de-emphasis was an unassailable truth, and they were both angry about it as well as conditioned to its reality.

On the TV now, late in the fourth quarter, Purdue had the ball and, no kidding, ran what appeared to be a Statue of Liberty play. Orton feinted cocking back to pass, and the ball dropped from his hand and into the arms of a flanker streaking behind him. So far ahead was Purdue that, evidently, they had worked through their playbook all the way to the last pages, the endnotes, the back matter, among the ancient and the esoteric. Insult to injury, it was almost as if they were playing a joke. People watched, but no one commented. They stared on blankly or chatted in groups, disinterested. Purdue had just won its first game at Notre Dame Stadium in thirty years. Notre Dame had just lost its seventh game by more than twenty points under Ty Willingham. At his postgame press conference, Joe Tiller, Purdue's head coach, responded to a reporter interested in his thoughts on breaking that thirty-year losing streak in such dominating fashion. He said, "I'll be real honest. I don't think too much about winning in this stadium."

Judy Schaffer emerged from the RV, her work for the moment complete. She looked as if she'd been released on parole. Large portions of the tailgate had cleared out. Only the core group remained. She said, "What happened to the Irish?"

"We got shit on."

"Well, no matter what, we still have fun, right?" There was no immediate response. "Right?"

Most of the Schaffer party, including Schaffer himself, did not live in South Bend proper, but in the communities immediately to the east, the South Bend "suburbs"—Mishawaka and Granger. In Granger especially the McMansions rise, the many-eaved, newly built monstrosities that sit on parcels of land off culs-de-sac named for species of trees. Lou Holtz and Bob Davie and Ty Willingham all lived here. Some of the developments are gated. Golf courses are laid out among the hillocky woods and overtop the converted farmland. Many Notre Dame administrators and, increasingly, professors live in Granger. Here, as well, one finds the strip malls and chain restaurants and car dealerships and general commercial prefab of Uniform America.

South Bend, on average, is far more working- and middle-class. It has a declining population of one hundred thousand. Postindustrially gutted, it is another scab on the Great Lakes rust belt—the Bayer-aspirin plant, the last steel plant, both shuttered within the last few years. A blot of red, South Bend exists in a state of otherwise pure blue. There is some racial segregation. The grid of streets immediately south of campus and the neighborhoods that stretch west toward the airport are largely black, while Mishawaka-Granger is largely white. Because South Bend abuts the Michigan border, the whole area is known as Michiana. Though Notre Dame is the area's largest employer—with an $833 million economic impact on the region, according to its commissioned study—Michiana is not exactly a company town, but close. As yet, the campus is in no way integrated with the city, situated purposefully on its own plat. It might as well be walled. Edward Sorin, Notre Dame founder, wanted to keep his students away from the temptations of town, and to this day a separateness exists between the academy and its environs. Sorin in his desire for insularity even achieved independence from any local political unit—Notre Dame, Indiana 46556.

South Bend and its suburbs are too large for the university to have subsumed and dominated completely, and too small for Notre Dame to exist quietly amid a wide range of other institutions. Within a hundred miles, until you hit Chicago, there are no other institutions of comparable size or fame. Of course this produces both resentment and pride. Town vs. gown—with the university, the citizens have a love-hate relationship. "Notre Dame acts holier-than-thou, but really they're a bunch of crooks," said one of the Benders at the RV. "When you look at what they're doing around here—you need a school that doesn't try to control the whole state of Indiana!" Monk Malloy made it one of his presidential goals to improve the "town-and-gown" relationship, an indication of how high tensions may have been in the first place. Yet despite his good intentions, Notre Dame is often seen as an enclave of wealth in which the commoners in town are largely discouraged from participating. More and more over the years, it has exerted its influence. It has gobbled up low-income housing in that grid of streets south of campus and reallocated the space to professors or landlords who will rent to students. Notre Dame lobbied for the construction of the College Football Hall of Fame, which it had hoped would become another pilgrimage site. The city of South Bend agreed to contribute some amount to its financing, and the hall is now a taxpayer liability.

Much of the town-gown tension somehow involves football. "Give the peasants a break," read the title of a letter to the editor published in the *South Bend Tribune.* "Face it, folks, Notre Dame couldn't care less about the people of the community. When it expanded its stadium, how many tickets did it set aside for the people of Michiana?" Cash, Strictly Cash, Notre Dame is viewed, indeed, as a fortress, a city-state. Money and power concentrate under the Dome, and the university, to a lot of people, seems to make its own rules, to exist outside the law, a kind of Vatican in the rust belt.

If economically Notre Dame has not quite subsumed its locality, its fame certainly has. The university constitutes the region's dominant culture—both intellectually and with its football—drawing in the scholars, the students, and the pilgrims of religion and sport. For the people of South Bend and Mishawaka, Notre Dame to a large degree defines their hometown, and it is, at once, both highly familiar—part of the background—and yet still the main draw, even for them.

As one South Bend resident told me, "If Notre Dame wasn't here, this city would be dead."

A restaurant called Pat's Colonial Pub is a local Mishawaka institution. Notre Dame memorabilia coats the walls, and a sound system that plays the "Victory March" is triggered whenever someone enters the front doors. On TVs scattered about the corners of the pub's many small rooms, management permits only Notre Dame games. The coaching staffs of many Irish teams often stop by for dinner or a drink, including men's basketball coach Mike Brey, women's basketball coach Muffet McGraw, as well as Ty Willingham and his staff. "The good celebrities," said Jane Hixenbaugh, one of the Schaffer circle. "On Thursday night, that's when you get to see them come in, and when they come in, it's kind of a big deal." The standard flyover-state inferiority complex infects the people to varying degrees, but this feeling is eased by their having Notre Dame. Jane Hixenbaugh said, "Mishawaka is such a Podunk town. If it wasn't for Notre Dame, the place would be totally off the map. But it's weird. Talking to people from out of town, Notre Dame is the glory of their eyes. But for us, you know, it's two miles away."

Many in the Schaffer circle have lived in northern Indiana all their lives, but Sharon Loftus, born and raised in Orange County, California, moved to South Bend in June 2003 solely because she wanted to make a life as close as possible to the university and the football team of which she is a fan. Loftus's settlement here is not as uncommon as it may seem. A class of subway alumni with motives identical to hers constitutes some fraction of the region's population. They come from all over the country.

Loftus, fifty years old, has long, tallow-blond hair and a fair Colleen complexion. About her there is something abidingly matronly. She has a smooth radio voice that would not be out of place interviewing authors on NPR, and she holds a job in the Notre Dame Law School as assistant to six law professors. She is no relation to the Loftus family of the Loftus Center, Notre Dame benefactors of the whale variety. "A different lineage," she says. Her lineage extends back to the town of Newport in County Mayo and more recently to a minute farming village on the hardscrabble prairie of southern Minnesota settled by a group of Irish peasants escaping the potato famine of 1848. They named the place Kilkenny. Today it has a population of 200, Loftuses still live

there, and it is a kind of rural, concentrated Chicago South Side—
nearly everyone in the Kilkenny neighborhood is a fan of Notre Dame.
Sharon Loftus's parents were Kilkenny high school sweethearts, and
shortly after marrying they left the hardscrabble to pursue the golden
dream in Southern California.

"I'm a female version of Rudy," Loftus likes to say. As a girl,
Catholic devotion was omnipresent in her Irish-Californian home. She
attended Catholic grade school and high school. Two of her uncles,
one on her mother's side, one on her father's, joined the priesthood.
Daily rosaries during Lent involved the household telling the beads.
An uncle said a Mass in the living room. "I remember thinking this
must have been like the Last Supper, Jesus saying Mass for the
disciples—not in front of thousands of people, but breaking bread with
friends and family." Though her parents certainly had an affinity for
Notre Dame, her older brother was the first in the family to follow Irish
football with steadfast vigor. "He's the one who got me into this madness," she likes to say. Though in Los Angeles they had gone to many
Southern Cal–Notre Dame contests ("I've been mistreated in the Coliseum for thirty years"), she and her brother would not make it to Notre
Dame for a home game until October 1994. "We walked around campus in tears. It was Indian summer. The leaves were in fall color. It was
perfect. The moment I set foot on campus, I *felt* it. It was like someone
had thrown a damp towel over me. I don't know how else to describe
it. I could feel a physical presence. If you don't feel it when you see
campus for the first time, you never will. Who was it that said, 'I don't
know if I'm in heaven, but I can see it from here'? Well, that's me."

The alumni association has long allowed subway alumni to join
their groups (as much a financial consideration as a democratic one,
since it means more people donating), and Sharon Loftus was a member of the Notre Dame Alumni Club of Orange County. Through the
club, she knew a Notre Dame student, a manager for the football team.
The student took the Loftuses into the stadium while the managers
spray-painted the helmets gold on Friday night, another famous Notre
Dame ritual. He let the Loftuses into the locker room, the sanctum
sanctorum. Mimicking the players' pregame routine, they trotted
down the steps that lead from the lockers to the tunnel, and they
slapped the fabled sign, PLAY LIKE A CHAMPION TODAY, thus fulfilling

perhaps the profoundest dream of any subway alum. Loftus says, "I walked into the stadium and looked around and said, 'This is the most beautiful site these eyes have ever seen.' Just like Rudy's dad. What a nutcase."

Loftus did not attend college. After high school she eventually became a bookkeeper for a Long Beach accounting firm. "All my education came on the job. I'm from the school of sink or swim." She had set for herself two goals in life, two pilgrimages: attend a Notre Dame home game and visit the homeland—the one that's in Ireland. After meeting the first in 1994, she combined pursuits to accomplish the second. She traveled to the Old Sod in 1998 when the Irish played the Naval Academy in Dublin. During football seasons, Notre Dame kept drawing her back. "I just felt so at home here. From the first moment visiting, I felt, 'Yeah, I'm home.' " One game a year, two games a year, three—she became part of a Tudy Cummings–like entourage of traveling addicted subway alumni. In 2002, during Willingham's exhilarating first year, she attended the spring game, five home games, two away games, and, in December, the season-capping football-team banquet. "And I said, 'You know what? Why don't I just move here?' " Other circumstances dictated a change as well. She was in the middle of a divorce. She had no children. Nothing in her personal life was holding her back. Her godparents, two old friends of the family's from Kilkenny, with whom she was close, had died prematurely of illnesses. "I kept telling myself, 'God's plan for your life is perfect.' I kept asking for signs. Something would happen and I'd think, 'Is that a sign?' 'Is this?' 'Okay, Lord, I need a *bigger* sign. Or maybe I'm just dense.' But losing my godparents made me realize, I'm not getting any younger. If you're gonna do this, you better do it now."

She sold her house, quit her job, left her family behind, and moved across the continent. So intently did she want to be part of Notre Dame that she refused to work anywhere else. She was willing to do just about any job; she wanted to join up. (Setting aside Church doctrine on the possibilities of reincarnation, she has said, "If I came back in another life, I'd want to play football.") She met with a woman in Notre Dame human resources. "I told her my whole story. I told her, 'I'm a female version of Rudy.' I told her, 'You can hire me now or hire me later, but you *will* hire me.' "

Notre Dame human resources said, "Are you seeking employment off-campus?"

And Sharon Loftus replied, "Have you heard a word that I'm saying?"

Notre Dame at the time had 208 full-time job openings. For those openings, it had twelve thousand applicants. The applications came from all over the country, and many of them from subway alumni with the same dreams as Sharon Loftus. At any one time Notre Dame is processing sixty thousand applications, excluding academic faculty. In a year it generally has about four hundred job postings. The ratios are such that it is harder to get work at Notre Dame than it is to gain acceptance into its undergraduate programs. (One of the perquisites of Notre Dame employment is free tuition—now around $31,500 per year—for the children of all university staff.) "So many people want to work here so badly, they'll apply for anything," says Erin Smith, the woman who first interviewed Loftus. People have occasionally offered to scrub toilets if it meant employment at Notre Dame. They apply for multiple jobs, rendering many of them overqualified or underqualified for whatever position is in question. Their résumés range from entry-level office clerk and food-service waitstaff to high up in the administrative tree.

Loftus says now, "When Erin told me those numbers, I said, 'Oh my God, what have I gotten myself into?' If I'd have heard those numbers before I moved, I probably wouldn't have moved. I said a lot of prayers at the Grotto, that's for sure." With no jobs available, Erin Smith found Loftus some temporary work, as a clerk at the front desk of the Morris Inn, as an office assistant at Campus Ministry. Six weeks later, she interviewed and landed a permanent position at the law school. "A friend of mine told me, 'You've reached nirvana.' "

Loftus has since built a house in a South Bend development within jogging distance of campus. When offered her choice of brick for the outer walls, she told her builder, "Whatever brick is closest to what Notre Dame uses." The Loftus masons put up a facade similar to Notre Dame's yellowish beige. Inside, she painted her walls a combination of navy blue and Vegas gold, the official pigments of Notre Dame's school colors. On one of the blue-painted walls in her living room she chalked out an ND monogram, three feet tall and three and a half feet wide. She painted the letters with gold leaf. She moved into the house during the summer and only discovered in the autumn, once the leaves had fallen, that through her back windows she could look across the yard and through woods and see the very top of the Hesburgh Memorial Library. In eyeshot of the shrines, she has built her shrine. She says, "Like I've always said, God's plan is perfect. I'm just filling in the details."

Billy Powers, another subway alumnus, came to South Bend in the spring of 2001. He had lived all his life in Yonkers, New York, and he and his wife with their five-month-old son picked up and left to get closer to Notre Dame. After attending a home game with him in 1998, his wife liked the area so much that she suggested to Billy that they look into relocating. New York was too expensive. Northern Indiana would be a fine place to raise a child. A letter carrier for the U.S. Postal Service, thirty-one years old at the time, Powers put in for his transfer.

The idea had already been in the back of his mind. His father, William Sr., first-generation Irish, was also first-generation subway alum. A bartender, a bouncer, a construction worker, he moved around. He had no college degree and ended his career as a trackman for the Metropolitan Transit Authority. After his parents divorced, Billy saw his father on weekends, and game-day Saturdays with the Irish on TV became their only connection. As Billy grew older, their relationship grew tense to the point of acrimony. About the only ambition Billy Sr. had for his son was that the boy matriculate at Notre Dame and study engineering. Short of that, there was indifference. "I didn't even apply," Powers says now. "I knew I wouldn't get in. I was a B student." It seems likely that these circumstances would have produced in anyone else a vigorous hatred for Notre Dame, yet for Billy Powers Notre Dame overcame his father. As time went on, Billy Sr. drifted into alcoholic disinterest in just about everything, and when his son finished high school, their relationship had all but ceased. By the time he moved to South Bend, Billy Powers hadn't seen his father in five years, and about the only thing this father passed on to his son was an overpowering devotion to Notre Dame. Billy Powers made his first pilgrimage in 1996, and as with Sharon Loftus, as with almost all subway alum, it had been the fulfillment of a lifelong dream. For some, however, fulfillment

leads to a need for more. And so Powers came back to games each season until he began considering the possibilities of cutting out the pilgrimage and living at the font. He would bring up his boy—Billy III—as
his father had not. He could bring his son right to the games. He and his
small family would leave Yonkers behind.

When Billy Powers watches a game at Notre Dame Stadium, he
gets into a kind of crouch. As the team breaks the huddle and assem-
bles into formation, he puts his hands on his knees and he leans in,
like a golfer lining up a putt. He will stand for most of the game and
likely be the loudest fan in his immediate section.

On the second Saturday in October, against Stanford, a week after
the ruin of Purdue, this was not difficult to achieve. Here on the other
side of the stadium from the student section, the fans had cultivated a
kind of intellectual distance from the action on the field, with the notable exception of Billy Powers. It was as if they were here to fulfill an
obligation. The normal structured cheering had reached a highly ritualized gloss—all surface and no enthusiasm. A man from Long Island
sat in a row below Powers. He said he was not a Notre Dame fan per se,
but simply an enthusiast of football in general, here for the first time on
a pilgrimage of historical interest to one of the meccas of the sport. He
said, "I'm really surprised at how *quiet* it is."

An elderly stadium usher saw an empty seat. "I think I'll just sit."

A fan sitting in the row behind said, "Yeah, enjoy the silence."

Second quarter, with Notre Dame losing 3–6, Quinn was sacked for
a loss of six yards, and a near-complete hush had fallen over the arena.
As Quinn's back hit the turf, you could almost hear him exhale. Incomplete passes yielded a muttering discontent. A ten-yard scamper
by Darius Walker yielded polite applause. The applause built in volume toward actual cheering later in the game, in the third quarter, as
Notre Dame drove the field until it reached first and goal. But Notre
Dame couldn't seem to punch it into the end zone. Quinn recovered
his own fumble, a broken play that caused the crowd to grumble, complain, criticize, and exchange opinion. It was like a Greek chorus, but a
chorus that was not in concert. The tailback tried it around the corner
but was cut off, forced out of bounds. The fullback tried it up the middle but was stopped—no gain, fourth down—and the chorus found its
voice at last and came together as one: "Go! Go! Go!"

Billy Powers stood the whole time and bellowed and cajoled his section mates into rising along with him. He had assumed the role of choragus. The fans stood, falling in line with Powers. Ryan Grant, the senior running back, technically still the starter to Darius Walker's reserve, entered the end zone. Billy Powers howled like an animal to the moon. The crowd also roared. But flags appeared on the field, and the roar went out of the crowd. The chorus awaited the decision, all faces aimed at the ref, at the players milling back to the sidelines. Arms were folded, stares intent. Face mask, No. 47, defense, and the crowd erupted once again. Notre Dame 10, Stanford 9.

To Billy Powers, this sort of thing proves that fandom has the ability to influence the team's performance on the field. Here he had compelled the crowd around him into showing some kind of spirit, and then the team had scored a touchdown—*post hoc, ergo propter hoc.* Occasionally the person sitting behind Powers and staring at his back will tap him on the shoulder in an effort to get Billy Powers to sit down. "I just ignore 'em. If the students stand and scream the whole game, so should everyone else."

Among the fan base, this very issue has become yet another cause for unrest, a state of affairs bemoaned in many circles. They believe that Notre Dame Stadium has become a golf tournament, an opera house or "Saturday afternoon tea," according to one fan's metaphor. Pick your theory as to why. To the fans it all seems to come down to the overall cultural shift at Notre Dame, the stands now filled with Eighty Percenters, as they've come to be known, those aging alumni, wealthy benefactors, ancient season-ticket holders, and thoroughly gentrified graduates that the school now produces—a bunch of future yuppies. For good measure, throw in a university that has striven to create a Disneyfied Family Experience, and a university with a team on a ten-year slide, and the purists believe that it has all conspired to create a game-day atmosphere—whitewashed, anodyne, canned, simulated—utterly at odds with traditional Notre Dame, a place of spontaneous, instinctual spirit and fight.

Billy Powers has developed his own manifesto on stadium behavior. "We in the crowd should be proactive, not reactive. From the time that ball is kicked off, the crowd should be on 'em every play, especially when ND is on defense. The old people just don't have enough energy. In my opinion it's time for them to step aside and let some of the younger guys have the tickets. Or, they can have their own section set aside. Put the old-timers somewhere where they won't have to complain—because there's plenty of fanatics like me who wanna be a student and share in their spirit."

When he cheers for the team, Powers is in emotional league with a student body he was never able to join materially. It was almost as if, in failing his father's one ambition, he had moved to South Bend to make good. Echoing Loftus, he says, "I'm probably a real-life Rudy. I can relate to what he did. I get emotional every time I see the movie—him getting carried off the field. I can relate to being that kind, wanting to do those things. And I still find myself wanting to be a part of the university as much as I can."

He looked the part of a student anyway. In just over two weeks he would turn thirty-five, but he had a boyish air that flowed from his enthusiasm—earnest, hopeful, eager. He wore jeans and this year's edition of The Shirt and a green ND ballcap, its brim curved like a frown and pulled low over his eyes. He could have been mistaken for a Notre Dame frat boy—if fraternities existed at Notre Dame. Rarely when out of his postman's uniform does he wear anything that does not bear one of Notre Dame's eighteen registered trademarks. His favorite shirt says on the back YOU'VE GOT TO HAVE PRIORITIES / ND FIGHTING IRISH FOOT-BALL.

Next to him today at the game stood a woman named Julie in tight jeans and an even tighter The Shirt. She had high blond hair and a tanning-salon face and square, pink-lens high-fashion sunglasses. Julie, however, was not Billy Powers's wife. Trouble had come over their marriage not long before they left Yonkers—his wife had second thoughts about leaving her mother and family behind. After they settled in Granger, the marriage fell apart, and he took an apartment in a complex called Castle Point—a place mostly given over to Notre Dame upperclassmen living off-campus. At the house in Granger, Powers had to leave behind his bagpipes—he once participated in a St. Patrick's Day parade down Fifth Avenue—and "all my Notre Dame memorabilia. But the way I grew up, I'm not a materialistic person. I grew up with my mom, and economically it was tough; we were on welfare at one point. So not being a materialistic person—and I had some nice memorabilia—I know I can rebuild my collection." Among other things, he left behind a 1977 "national championship football" autographed by Joe Montana. He left behind an official game-day ball signed by Tony Rice, a football signed by all seven of Notre Dame's Heisman Trophy winners, a game-day helmet signed by Lou Holtz and originally worn by Dusty Ziegler (a standout offensive lineman of the middle Holtz period), a jersey signed by Lou Holtz, and a piece of bleacher extracted from the old stadium while it was being rebuilt. His wife has since sold it all. She and Billy III finally headed back to Yonkers for good in March 2004, "on St. Patrick's Day of all days—one of my favorite holidays." Their divorce was finalized in late September, only two weeks before the Stanford game. "She made it difficult to enjoy the few seasons of Notre Dame football I had out here. But she didn't manage to steal my thunder. I managed to make the best out of it."

He got his tickets to the games through any means possible, mostly through friends he had made in South Bend. He had missed only one game so far this season, as it turned out, the best game—Michigan. His connection had fallen through at the last second. Since arriving in South Bend from Yonkers, he had missed only about two games per season. His Saturday mail route in the autumn became expendable, and as he accumulated the personal days, he also accumulated tension from his bosses. "They didn't like the fact that I was always trying to finagle ways to go to the games during the season. More often than not, I found a way. It wasn't easy, but I like challenges."

As the afternoon progressed, the shadow cast by the press box on the other side of the stadium had slowly moved across the student section, eclipsing it. The shadow was angular, like a dagger across the student body. After Stanford had scored to take the lead, 15–10, Darius Walker on first down recovered his own fumble. The crowd grumbled again, and someone sitting in a row above Powers yelled so beseechingly it was almost a cry for the state of the program, a plea directed at the VIP level high up in the press box behind its smoked glass: "*Come on,* Notre Dame!"

Pure Pollyanna, Billy Powers did not feel such angst. Like Tudy Cummings, he equates in-season criticism with disloyalty. He says, "I'm not a fair-weather fan. It annoys me to see fair-weather fans. Every team has 'em, but they don't usually like what I have to say. I think

Willingham is gonna get it turned around. I really do. He's a great ambassador for Notre Dame. He's a good coach and a classy guy. Then
again, I'm the kind of guy, if Gumby were on the sidelines and coaching, I'd be Gumby's number one fan. I'd be Gumby's guy."

The student section has a whole set of cheers that it performs at
various moments during the game, and over here among the civilians,
Billy Powers is about the only fan who cheered along. He did it with a
gusto that drew attention. Eighteen years old in 1988. Holtz's championship year, Powers recalls the feeling of exhilaration that descended
over him all through that season. He wishes that he had been a Notre
Dame freshman, watching that undefeated run from the stadium section cast now in shadow. When he thinks about the kids in their fits of
cheering, doing their touchdown push-ups, he says, "That's what
makes me grin from ear to ear. I'm just as excited—if not more so—than
they are." During TV time-outs, the cheerleaders will break into
groups of four, each group moving to a corner of the stadium. A sign
goes up in the hands of a cheergirl on the shoulders of a cheerguy. Each
corner has its sign: WE and R and N and D. Powers's section had responsibility over the N, and when the cheerleader held up her sign, he rose
to his feet, everyone else remained seated, and through cupped hands
he leaned in, got his body behind it, his face reddened with effort, and
he unleashed a deep-throated, baritone, from-the-diaphragm "Enn!"
So loud did he do this that it vibrated my sinuses.

Notre Dame eventually overcame Stanford and was running out the
clock, the score 23–15. The stadium was a mortuary, but Powers
wanted one more score—"C'mon, boys!" he shouted onto the field—
but it was not to be. As Notre Dame appeared to be icing its win, he
stood quietly. He was attempting to marinate in the atmosphere of what
would likely be his final game at Notre Dame Stadium for who knew
how long. The moment he had learned that his wife was leaving for
Yonkers with their son, he had put in with the USPS for his return
transfer. It had been a rough football season. Not many days before the
divorce had become official, in September, Powers had got word that
his father had died. He did not go back for the funeral. He would be
back anyway soon enough. He had sold all his furniture and ridded
himself of most of his personal belongings. The following week he

would leave for good, and the back of his blue Toyota 4Runner would contain almost nothing except fighting Irish tailgate gear. The Notre Dame experiment had not worked out, and he turned his ambitions to the distant future. "I'll be able to see my son on weekends now. That and work are my top priorities for moving back East. But it's hard to leave Notre Dame, that's for sure. Just like before I moved, though, I'll take a game a season and come out here. And maybe I'll set myself up. If I get myself properly set up, maybe when I retire I'll be what you'd call a reverse snowbird and come in here for the entire football season."

After the game ended, the fans siphoned toward the exits, clogging the aisles. Billy Powers remained at his seat. The Notre Dame marching band took the field and played the "Victory March." Powers clapped along. He said to Julie, "There are a hundred and eighty–plus members of the band, the biggest in the country." They watched without comment, and after a moment Powers said, "They *are* the best band around. I hate to tell you that, but they are."

The band continued through its postgame motions, which included the "1812 Overture." With the song, also famously performed at the end of the third quarter of every home game, the fans salute the Notre Dame head coach. It started among the students during Holtz's reign, and at first it was a simple tomahawk with the arm at each down beat of the overture. Then they began forming an *L* with both hands and with each chopping motion, intoning, "Lou." The tradition continued with Davie—a lowercase *b* with their hands, a "Bob" with their voices, but by Davie's second season many fans refused to do it. It was a kind of protest. Such a salute, they argued, should be reserved for coaches with national championships. When Willingham took over, the salute grew in complexity and the trope was extended to dangerously incoherent levels—a confusing and hard-to-decipher *W* with both hands linked above the head, and, at the downbeat, a "Ty." Now, of course, the coach-salute protest had infected the fans vis-à-vis Ty Willingham. By looking around the stadium during the "1812 Overture" you could take an informal poll of the sentiment of the fans toward the head coach. But Powers would have none of that—he'd form a *G* and say "Gumby" if necessary—and he joined in the Ty homage with vigor. As he moved his arms up and down to the overture, he said,

"Today is win number eight hundred. Did you know that? We're only the second team in history to do that. Michigan of course was the first, and they've been playing for eight years longer than we have."

The postgame motions concluded with the band playing the alma mater, "Notre Dame, Our Mother." Powers embraced Julie at the waist and the two of them swayed subtly to the song, barely moving. He mouthed the words, and when the song concluded, Powers belted the last line like a Broadway singer—"Love thee, Notre Dame!"

And then he just stood there. He stood there as if taking in a mountain vista and contemplating something. His visor was still low over his face and only a small smile was visible underneath it. Julie shielded the sun from her eyes with her hand. He turned to her and said, "I'll be the last one to leave, I can tell you that."

The sun sat above the top of the stadium, as if resting on the lip. The arena, in shade and expanding twilight, had grown cold. The band marched off the field through the bottleneck of the tunnel, playing the "Victory March." Powers clapped. The stands had long been drained of fans. Only gray concrete remained where once there had been a variegated humanity. His arms at his sides, Powers looked about the stadium, and his eyes took him all around the bowl and along the perimeter and up into the sky. From his vantage, you could almost delimit the institution. Down onto the field, up at the press box, toward the Dome's Virgin Mary and the Sacred Heart steeple, both just visible like a toothpick above the stadium rim toward the head and halo and arms of Christ the Teacher, Touchdown Jesus. Julie had taken a seat on the bench below him to wait it out. Only the stadium ushers in their bright yellow jackets appeared to be left, making their way down from the parapets toward the exits. Powers stood there like a sculpture. He hadn't made any move at all when a voice came booming and echoing over the PA system: "All fans remaining in the stadium are asked to leave."

9

The Liturgy and Devotions

Over the loudspeakers during the fourth quarter of every home game, Mike Collins, class of 1967, the Voice of Notre Dame Stadium, takes a moment during a TV time-out to announce the Saturday Mass schedule—thirty minutes after the game at the Basilica of the Sacred Heart, and forty-five minutes after the game at a place called the Stepan Center. People in the stands will check their watches. To find a seat at Sacred Heart, you'll need to hustle. As soon as the game clock unscrolls to zero and the coaches jog to shake hands at midfield, sign of the peace, fans will jump out of their seats and speed-walk across campus to church. Their priorities set to a different clock, some people even start filling up the pews as early as the third quarter. This and all other Masses at Sacred Heart extending through Sunday are uniformly packed from nave to apse—seating for around twelve hundred and standing room for another eight hundred. Fr. Peter Rocca, rector of the Basilica, has said, "We have people on the floor, we have people in the rafters, we have people jammed in all the way to the Lady Chapel. We have to close the doors because we can't fit any more people in. I just pray fire officials don't come around one day and shut the place down."

For the last nine years the Stepan Center has been used to catch the overflow crowds turned away from Sacred Heart, due, indeed, to fire codes. The church in earlier times was packed even more, with people in the aisles Indian-style. A multiuse geodesic dome erected in 1962, Stepan is generally agreed to be the ugliest building on campus—a cross between a flying saucer out of a Roswell photograph and a grain shed. Utility lights are strung along a ceiling that has the color and texture of duct tape. Chunks of it have fallen off here and there, revealing yellow foam, like a couch someone left in an alley. With its cell-structure dome and its neglected shabbiness, Stepan is a kind of ironic comment on the grandiosity of the Main Building. Converted into a church on home-game Saturdays, it can hold twenty-two hundred Catholics in molded-plastic folding chairs, and it almost always reaches capacity.

After the blowout 41–16 loss to Purdue, up on a temporary stage, Fr. Ron Nuzzi gave his homily. Outside, Purdue fans conducted celebratory parties in sacrosanct places—on the lawn just outside the football offices in the Joyce Center, or along Juniper Boulevard, the street that runs next to the stadium, where a strange Purdue vehicle made up like a locomotive slowly moved, Purdue fans dancing and drinking atop it like a parade float. As Notre Dame fans walked to Mass, as Purdue fans hooted and hollered and sometimes cat-called, everyone's ND attire seemed somehow impotent. On the twenty-seventh day in Ordinary Time, the theme of the readings and Gospel and now Fr. Ron Nuzzi's sermon happened to involve the testing of faith and the "strength that dwells within us." Among other things, the priest said in his homily, "I'm uncomfortable with the kind of faith that says, 'I'll believe in God if I get something.' God knows that more than one prayer goes up on this campus for things like"—and he paused for a split second—"victory." A rumbling, under-the-breath laughter moved through the congregation. "Faith isn't getting every prayer answered or getting out of every bind. Faith is loving God whether we're well or sick, whether we win or lose, in good times and in bad. That's what we pray for with the apostle in this week's Gospel. 'Lord, increase our faith.' "

In the same way that one can apply any facet of one's life to nearly any piece of Scripture, the spiritual message of almost every Mass on a home-game weekend will somehow dovetail with the team's performance on the field—win, lose, draw. On the Sunday after Notre Dame rose from the dead and astonished Michigan, the Gospel happened to be Christ's parable of the prodigal son. In his homily Father Rocca said, "When this God of Jesus sees someone who was lost and is now found, or one who was dead and is now alive, there is only one thing to do— have a meal and celebrate."

As Sacred Heart rector, Rocca is also responsible for assigning priests as celebrators and presiders to each Mass on the home-weekend schedule. He says, "Some people I know have two homilies prepared. One if we've won, and one if we've lost." The differences between the two, however, are generally trivial and decorative, having to do with rhetorical devices—a priest might cut an opening joke if the team loses on a last-second field goal—rather than with actual interpretations of Scripture, "the living explanation of the Word." Almost never does a priest directly refer to the game during a sermon. More often they may make a sporting reference in their opening or concluding remarks. "I always make sure to especially welcome our guests from Ann Arbor or, if we're playing BC, Boston," Rocca says a little devilishly. "And if we win, I might pour it on a little. 'Oh, we're *so happy* you're here with us this weekend.' " After a loss, however, he will sometimes feel the need to say something, part pep talk, part admonition. "You may not feel like singing today, many of you, in light of yesterday, but this *is* the Lord's day."

The content of all Catholic Masses—the readings and Gospels for each day of the year—are uniform, supplied by the Roman missal. But, at Notre Dame, with sport dwelling so close to religion, a fan can't help but soak it all up and spell the overlap. "I would have used that line whether we won or lost," said Ron Nuzzi of his Purdue homily. "I think people bring their faith and supply those connections, especially the kinds of people who travel miles and miles to come to Notre Dame games. It would be risky and ill-advised, I think, to base a homily on what happened in the game."

So many people attend Mass during the fall and so hectic are the priests' schedules that the Holy Cross Community has come to distinguish the season from mere Ordinary Time. Instead they call it Football Time. During a typical home-game weekend, there might be a hundred or more Masses in total celebrated on campus, from the largest Basilica pomp-and-circumstance liturgy to the smallest covert tailgate hedge Mass. In addition to Sacred Heart and Stepan, almost all of the university's twenty-seven dorms have Masses in their chapels on Saturdays postgame. Large numbers of fans have discovered this, and they pack the chapels tight, especially at Dillon and Alumni halls, which have the most capacious and architecturally interesting of the dorm chapels. Law school Masses, business school Masses, Masses in the Crypt chapel in the basement of the Basilica, Masses at Moreau

Seminary, Masses at Corby Hall, Masses in the Holy Cross retirement home, a Mass by Hesburgh up in his office suite, Masses conducted by regional alumni clubs who travel by the busload and bring their own celebrants—Friday to Sunday, from seven in the morning through vespers and as late as midnight, so many Masses are said at Notre Dame that it's like perpetual adoration, and a home-game weekend becomes, in a sense, a seventy-two-hour sacrament.

Perhaps not surprisingly, attendance does not drop off after the Irish lose. If anything, it might rise. On occasion, though, tensions do run high. Pilgrims sometimes get irritated when the Basilica shuts its doors and its ushers politely turn them toward duct-tape Stepan. A few seasons ago, a Notre Dame alumnus noticed that a certain group of people had been selected to deliver the offertory to the priest at the altar. They were conspicuous in shirts bearing the insignia of the University of Pittsburgh, Notre Dame's opponent that day. The alumnus strode over to the Basilica staff and in heightened tones made his displeasure known—such an honor should be reserved for the home team. The Basilica staff, however, has noticed a different trend that seems to hinge on wins and losses. After the homily, ushers in green The Shirts go around and collect the offerings of the congregation. Bags of purple velvet on the ends of rods go into the pews, and, after defeats, come out with fewer bills. Father Rocca prefers to think of it in a more positive light. When Notre Dame is victorious, people tend to *increase* their offerings.

In choosing the priests who will preside over Sacred Heart's game-weekend Masses, Rocca looks for homilists with charisma, style, intellect, gravitas. Though he says there is no star system, there is a star system—and this, in turn, results in sermons that often attain oratorical quality. "Those who preach take it very seriously," he says. He also includes the odd celebrity—bishops, archbishops, cardinals, though not yet any popes. In the American Church hierarchy it is evidently considered an honor to say a Mass at the Basilica during Football Time (or any time for that matter). Cardinal Mahoney, for instance, archbishop of Los Angeles will almost always take a Mass when Southern Cal comes to town. If a high-ranking prelate is scheduled to visit Notre Dame, Rocca will immediately send him a letter of invitation to celebrate Mass at Sacred Heart. As a result, the liturgies at the Basilica have reached high style, if not High Latin, though they're about as close as you can get in post–Vatican II Christendom. They do not mess around with their music. The Women's Liturgical Choir sings like a choir of angels. From the loft invisible above the narthex their voices descend to the pews, and their voices have been known to bring people to tears. The priests come in ranks, never fewer than seven, sometimes as many as twenty, and they wear complete vestments—alb, chasuble, stole— handmade by full-time Notre Dame seamstresses. Squads of eucharistic ministers cover the place at Communion time like a SWAT team. Fresh floral arrangements, draperies and banners, candles like staffs, gold-plated tools of the sacred sciences, thuribles, incense—this kind of extravagance is not for the Protestant-of-heart. Rocca says, "One of the attractions of our Mass here, if I do say so myself, is that we do our liturgy well."

Rocca is the master of ceremonies, the emcee, at most Basilica Masses. Before things get under way, he takes the pulpit and makes an announcement. Please turn off your cell phones and your pagers. Please no photography, flash or otherwise. Ron Nuzzi has observed, "When he says that, it clearly communicates, 'This is not a tourist attraction, this is not a media event. This is the heart of who we are, and we take it very seriously.'"

After the Brickyard of Indianapolis, Notre Dame is the most-visited tourist destination in the state of Indiana. Around 673,000 people from outside St. Joseph County visited in the 2001–02 fiscal year, according to the study the university commissioned to investigate its economic impact on South Bend. Nearly a quarter of a million came for football games. Another two hundred thousand were pure religious pilgrims, though of course the former number includes its pilgrims of overlapping motives. All of the numbers are conservative. It is not uncommon for motorists on Interstate 80-90 to see the green exit signs announcing Notre Dame and pull off the highway, not having initially intended to do so. A rest stop about thirty miles west of Notre Dame is called the Knute Rockne Travel Plaza—suitably named since Rockne with his stadium and his parking lots initiated the concept of the automotive pilgrimage. Outside the food court in the lobby sits a rack filled with Notre Dame brochures. Above the rack is a blown-up, illuminated photograph of the Main Building. On campus there is now a Visitor's Center, built in 1999, next to the bookstore in the Eck Complex, with more brochures and an auditorium that holds 152 people and shows a twelve-minute film on the history of the institution. Campus tours start and end here. Many guidebooks have been published— Notre Dame Baedekers—that describe the campus sites. One was written specifically for people traveling to home-football weekends (*Notre Dame Game Day: Getting There, Getting In, and Getting in the Spirit*, Todd Tucker, 2000), which, interestingly, makes no mention of the Basilica Mass, so integral a part of the pilgrimage.

Nor does the book mention the team Mass that takes place in the Lady Chapel a few hours before kickoff. The sacristan of Sacred Heart, an easygoing man in his middle thirties named John Zack, the first layman to hold the position, has roped off the pews in the east transept, just inside the "God, Country, Notre Dame" entrance. He explains, "We used to let people sit there, but the fans figured out that the team walked through that door on their way to Mass." The people would arrive an hour early, and they would fill the pews, pull down the kneelers, clasp their hands, and bow their heads. "They would pretend to pray," Zack says. "They knew we'd never disturb a person in prayer." When the team at last arrived and came through the door, they snapped from their solemnity and became fans once again. They leaned out of their pews and into the aisles. Cameras appeared from pockets and bags. Flashes popped in the athletes' eyes. Game-day programs, scraps of paper, bookstore-bought novelty footballs, football cards, Sharpie pens were thrust into the procession of players for autographing. "The team used to have its Mass at eight in the morning, early, before anyone was even in the Basilica yet," Zack says. "But Holtz changed that to two hours before kickoff. It took the fans three games to figure it out."

Now, on a Saturday in the middle of the 2004 season, the team has assembled in the Lady Chapel, at the far north end of the Basilica. The tourists come in the main entrance, on the south side of the building and ushers corral them over and out the west transept. A family of boys stands on tiptoes on the steps of the main altar. Ropes block the avenues back to the Lady Chapel. To get a look at the athletes in prayer, a fan must peer around the pulpit, over a French Gothic altar and over a monstrous monstrance, all gold, a giant starburst, presented to the university by Napoléon III. Only the backs of the players are visible. Only the murmuring voice of the team's chaplain, a tall, steel-haired Texan named Paul Doyle, is audible. The fans can just barely see the team rise for Communion. They cannot see the distribution of the saint's medals, or the players kissing the relic of the True Cross, venerated since the fourth century, a minuscule piece of wood retrieved by St. Helena from the sepulchre in the Holy City. The fans do not know that Brendan Hoyte, a linebacker and a Jehovah's Witness, sits in the east-transept confessional all through the Mass, alone with his prayers in a kind of meditation. From back in the nave, the fans cannot hear the team's recitation of a shortened version of the Litany of the Blessed Mother. When the chaplain says, "Queen of Peace," the players respond, "Pray for us!"

Arms folded, elderly ushers in blue blazers and gray, uncuffed trousers stand close to the fans as they attempt to take in the proceedings.

"Excuse me, sir. You need to get back."

Men in green football jerseys and green The Shirts point video cameras in the direction of the Lady Chapel. A man in a white Notre Dame jersey, No. 1, wears an Irish baseball cap, khaki shorts, and leather loafers with a weave toe.

"Take your hat off please!" says an usher in a shouted whisper.

A father is with his sons. He has a fanny pack around his waist. He points. "That's the team back there!" Almost everyone carries huge, white bookstore bags tumescent with ND gear. A man has a nametag stuck to his shirt. "MY NAME IS / Uncle Tom."

"Is this the team Mass?"

The chaplain says, "Let us offer each other the sign of peace," and the team stands up. Sounds of high-fiving, hugs, backslapping, commotion and movement that lasts thirty seconds.

The words of Father Doyle are recognizable only because of their familiar cadence. "Lord, I'm not worthy to receive you, but only say the word and I shall be healed."

Communion is now served, and players rise to receive the Eucharist or, if not Catholic, a blessing from the chaplain. A tumult erupts in the nave. The fans jostle for position and a burst of flash photography captures the sacrament on film. A lady snaps a picture with a disposable camera.

"Did you get it?" her husband says.

A middle-aged man in a yellow Notre Dame polo shirt, shorts, mustache, boat shoes, has his hands clasped behind his back. If he wasn't here he'd be practicing his short game. He encroaches onto the steps of the main altar, circumvents the ropes, approaches the French Gothic altar. An usher moves into his running lane, blocks the interloper.

"Can't I just . . . ?"

"This is where the line is. That's why we're standing here."

All the while people in ND shirts sit in the main nave pews, eyes closed, hands steepled and hands linked, not pretending to pray, but praying.

The university's status as a tourist destination has given rise to a somewhat new label for Notre Dame. "It *is* a Catholic Disney World," says Bishop Jenky, CSC, of Peoria, who is the ordination classmate of Peter Rocca. "It is a big center of our faith in this country. I don't think most people outside the university realize—what are there, sixty-four chapels on campus, all of them functioning?—the level of practice at Notre Dame. It's not a perfect place, certainly. But except for the Vatican, I've never seen any place quite like it."

The campus architecture and the campus itself—in some ways as controlled an environment as a bathysphere—lends itself to the theme-park metaphor, as do the many consumer opportunities, most prominently the bookstore, Our Lady of Commerce. But, of course, the metaphor ultimately fails. Where Disney is pure surface, at Notre Dame there is substance behind the manicure, an earnest and genuine devotion that often results in spontaneous outbursts that defy control. Sometimes, for instance, a shrine will develop seemingly out of nowhere.

It was perhaps Edward Sorin's greatest ambition to make his university into a sacred place of worship and learning (of learning *in* worship) that would draw the devout from across the land. He had the notion to create a sequestered Catholic environment, as inviting and cultivated as the garden palaces of Persian kings. The entire campus took shape with this goal in mind, and shrines were erected to provide places at which the students and faculty and campus visitors could perform their devotions. Shrines within shrines within a shrine, the Notre Dame plant is like a Chinese box of Catholic shrines, and today they gather the pilgrims. A small, little-known statue shielded by trees and underbrush sits not far from the Grotto, on the site of a long-gone seminary building. It is the only object left after the university razed the ancient structure. The statue is of St. Therese (1873–1897), a French Carmelite nun, patroness of foreign missionaries, yet a woman who never in her life left her cloister, let alone traveled on foreign missions. She wrote a book, part spiritual autobiography, part catalog of aphorisms, her "little ways," which were teachings that emphasized the sacredness inherent in the small, ordinary acts of daily life done with love for God. Naive in its nineteenth-century French piety, the book struck some as sentimental to the point of sickliness, but her intentions were genuine and earnest to the point of grace and her book struck many other people as beautiful and true. In her own time, she became a best-selling author. It has been said of the writings of St. Therese, you either get her or you don't—and after a home-game weekend her statue at Notre Dame will be surrounded by flowers, votive candles, pebbles, coins, rosaries, holy cards, and religious medals left by pilgrims who have prayed at her feet.

The St. Therese statue began drawing the prayerful spontaneously some years ago. Though it's located in a hidden part of campus, once people discovered it, the snowball rolled. Mike Garvey, class of 1974, who has worked in the Notre Dame information office for more than twenty years, once remarked to me that the shrines of Notre Dame have been made special, and perhaps holy, not because they were constructed or created for that purpose, but because, over time, so many people have come to these places to pray and to find some portion of peace that the sites become sacred. The same can be said of Notre Dame itself, especially on a home-game weekend. By drawing so many people, the place creates a community. Fr. Nicholas Ayo, CSC, has written a book on the subject of Notre Dame's shrines and his experience of them, *Signs of Grace*. In its prologue Ayo writes of the Basilica Mass filled to overflow with its postgame congregation. In entering the church the people have shifted from spectators to parishioners, and "for a moment, one sees and feels what it might be like were the grace of God to spread its wonders in all our lives all the time." What brought this particular community together, was of course, Irish football, and like St. Therese with her "little ways," the divine is evident even in something as quotidian as a community of people watching a game and then going to Mass.

Meaning has a way of doubling up at Notre Dame. Just as *The Word of Life* mosaic has colloquially been rechristened, so have other campus landmarks. A statue of Father Corby, a CSC priest of Sorin times, stands just outside Corby Hall. It captures him at Gettysburg, in a gesture of blessing as he grants general absolution to the troops of the Irish Brigade, for whom he served as chaplain. He has his right arm raised and his left arm over his heart. An identical statue rises from the battlefield in Pennsylvania. Another anonymous campus wit decided that Corby resembled a ref signaling a catch made fairly on the field—Fair Catch Corby. Absolving sins of fighting Irish, keeping the drive alive, Corby at Notre Dame is doing both. A statue of Moses stands in front of the Hesburgh Library. He has his right hand raised, he has his index finger raised—having just descended from Mt. Sinai with the Ten Commandments, he's letting his flock know there's only One True God. The statue has become known as No. 1 Moses, since the top of the rankings at the conclusion of football seasons should always reflect the nation's One True Team. Composed for the occasion of the original dedication of Notre Dame Stadium in 1930, the school song, "Notre Dame, Our Mother," was also written in homage to the Virgin Mary. Bilingually, its title might seem a little redundant. The marching band plays it at the conclusion of every game, and echoing the band, the choir sings it at the conclusion of every Basilica Mass.

> *Notre Dame, Our Mother, tender, strong and true,*
> *Proudly in the heavens, gleams the Gold and Blue,*
> *Glory's mantle cloaks thee, Golden is thy fame,*
> *And our hearts forever, Praise thee, Notre Dame.*
> *And our hearts forever, Love thee, Notre Dame.*

Many people often mistake the song for a hymn, a prayer set to music, and because people think this, it *is* one. A woman once posed this very question to a CSC priest. "Is 'Notre Dame, Our Mother' a school anthem? Or is it a hymn to the Virgin Mary?" And the priest said, "Yes." Reverence for team, reverence for institution, reverence for God—they are each an element of the same feeling. Or, rather, the feelings of reverence slip easily from one to the next, eliding the distinctions that exist between the three.

This kind of mingling of religion and sport—which at times appears infinitely mutable at Notre Dame—makes some people within the university a little uneasy: Roger Valdiserri contra Faust; the licensing department and its dictum of nonblending. Fr. Brian Stanley, the priest in the endzone during halftime of the Michigan game, who performed the ceremony with George Gipp's grave soil that may or may not have embarrassed the university, says, "Notre Dame is constantly sending out mixed signals: 'Yes, we love the tradition and the mystique'— how the wind stopped when Harry Oliver kicked the field goal to win by two points over Michigan in 1980, and all the other strange miraculous things that have happened over the years. Then, on the other side, they say, 'It's just a game. We don't get into all the mumbo-jumbo. God doesn't care about football. Let's keep the two separate.' It's as if they're vaguely suspicious of any kind of religious connection with football. To me and my thinking, you can have your cake and eat it too. It's a *both/and,* not an *either/or.* That's kind of a theological point—one that's used in interpreting scripture. In Catholic theology, if there are two possible interpretations of scripture, it doesn't have to be either one or the other. It's both."

But the blending of religion and football remains, in one way at least, a deliberate endeavor for the priests of Notre Dame. The ancient precepts of John Cardinal O'Hara remain very much alive in the charism of the Congregation of Holy Cross. The notion of pilgrimage has long been part of the university lexicon, and more than anything else, the priests of Notre Dame still view home-football weekends as a conspicuous opportunity to proselytize. Monk Malloy often uses the term *pilgrimage* in his speeches and writings. He has said, "In a sense, the game is an excuse for a fuller experience of campus life." In his typically elusive manner, when Father Malloy says "fuller experience" he means "faith." Coax them in with football, and then show them what's really important. "But," Malloy says, "the use of pilgrimage for athletics is, in my judgment, a derivative concept—although there are people for whom *every* dimension of a home football weekend has a certain status in their lives, and it's ritualistic and full of panoply and established ways of doing things." Indeed the CSC priests of Notre Dame all stress the importance of grasping "the whole package" of the university on a football weekend. Like a diocesan priest with his parishioners, it's almost as if the CSCs of Notre Dame feel a sense of obligation toward the spiritual well-being of their flock of football pilgrims. Home-game Saturdays have become their chance to minister to the fans. "The care we have for the art and the environment of campus communicates that faith is important here," Fr. Ron Nuzzi says. "You can see on any given weekend what a learning experience it is for many people. For the uninitiated or the newcomer, it's some of the best teaching we do." When it comes to Catholic devotion, though, in many cases it seems as though they're teaching to the converted. Rocca likes to point out that attending Mass and attending the game do not compete for the attention of the pilgrims. "One balances the other. And, I'd say, one *completes* the other. Religion provides something that just the secular football doesn't provide. Would all these people be here if there were no football? I don't know. I doubt it." But because large numbers of Notre Dame fans are predisposed to the university's Catholic message, it is equally true that all these people would not be here if there were no religion. In addition to whatever else is being taught, what's also being taught is a devotion to Notre Dame.

Sgt. Eddie Colton of the New York Police Department is known to the cops of the First Precinct in Lower Manhattan as the "mayor of South Bend." Forty-two years old, he is stockily built, with a dark complexion and dark, thinning hair cut close to his scalp, and dark eyes hooded by a thick brow—Black Irish. Even off duty, even at a casual gathering of First Precinct blue at a tailgate in a parking lot outside Giants Stadium before Notre Dame's game with Navy on October 16, his expression does not seem to waver from that of the beat cop on patrol. He could be about to book you. Though he is not the highest-ranking officer in the First Precinct, he seems to have become the undisputed leader of it, mostly due to an air of somberness forged by a series of tragedy and loss, and by his well-placed connections at the University of Notre Dame. He seems to know everyone of importance, and when Notre Dame officials visit the city, he often brings them into his patrol car and escorts them on "ride alongs." Before he proposed to his future wife, at the Grotto, which for Eddie Colton is perhaps the most sacred patch of land outside Palestine, he had Monk Malloy, a personal friend, bless the engagement ring. He wanted to have his wedding ceremony performed at the Basilica, such a popular site for that sacrament that couples book the church solid forty-six Saturdays a year. When Colton scheduled his wedding date, calls were placed to the right offices, and a slot somehow opened for June 2005. The couple held their reception up in the press box of Notre Dame Stadium. They had wedding photos taken at the 50-yard line.

An old friend of Colton's from New Jersey has said, "Seems that everything Notre Dame comes to Eddie. All the places he goes, no matter where he goes. It's astounding. Eddie's story, it's like fiction. No one would believe it."

Eddie Colton knows a thing or two about pilgrimages. He and his father had gone to the Orange Bowl in January 1986, when Miami routed the Irish, 58–7—Gerry Faust's last game at Notre Dame, but not Eddie Colton's. He looked at the future football schedules and vowed to his father that, in 1988, the next time the teams met at Notre Dame Stadium, the Coltons would be there to witness revenge. As the game approached, hoping to work the cop fraternity, Colton placed a call with the South Bend Police Department, trolling for tickets. The woman on the other end of the line laughed at him—the SBPD received fifty such calls a week. (Perhaps not surprisingly—Irish-cop stereotypes withstanding—among police all over the country Notre Dame has always had a potent appeal.) Colton then placed a call to Chuck Hurley, for thirty years chief of Notre Dame's in-house force, NDPD. It turned out that the two men shared many things in common. Irish-Catholics, big families, strong relationships with strong fathers who had served in the Second World War—and, most important, a devotion to Notre Dame. Here was a member of the brotherhood, New York's Finest, a cop from the seat of the subway alumni, looking to bring his aging father on his first Notre Dame pilgrimage—and Hurley was moved to bring out the field passes. "When you get field passes, you run through the tunnel," Colton says. "My father, he cried when we did that. He said, 'I can't believe I'm here.'" An Irish defender swatted to the ground Miami's last-ditch two-point conversion attempt, and the Irish won, 31–30.

Colton has a worshipful attitude toward his father, Edwin Charles Colton Sr., who worked for most of his days in the safety department of a Merck & Co. pharmaceutical plant in Rahway, New Jersey. "Forty-four years he worked there," Eddie Jr. says. "Never missed a day of work in his life." With twenty years on the force, Sgt. Eddie Colton Jr. often takes fifteen-hour double shifts, five in the morning to eight at night or four in the afternoon to seven in the morning ("I'm wearin' myself out workin' too much"), because he wants to make as much money as he can before he retires in the summer of 2005. Late at night, out on patrol, he sometimes likes to talk to friends on his cell phone. From his unmarked prowler, he once told me, "You meet a lotta people working the street. Lotta actors, actresses, so-called big shots. And nobody's ever impressed me that I ever met. Nobody has ever, *ever* impressed me except one person, and that was my father."

In the living room of Colton's boyhood home in Linden, New Jersey, father and son watched Notre Dame on television—the ancient male-bonding method for inculcating love of team into the gene code. To this day, when Colton is not at Notre Dame, he will only watch the game at home in his living room—no bars, no social settings—in deference to his father's ways. Eddie Sr. even seems to have passed down to his son his rooting demeanor. Highly critical, highly vocal, they viewed each failed play almost as a personal affront. Language grew colorful and sacrilegious. Sitting in front of the TV on Saturdays, they lengthened their penances on Sundays. "If they're getting beat real bad or somethin', I'll get up and leave the room. Just like my father, you know? Anytime they were getting beat, my father would get up and go cut the grass, or go outside and start sweeping, or let the dog out, or take a ride to the park with the dog and come back. He could never see 'em lose. And if they did lose, forget about it, don't come near me or the old man. My poor mother. My poor mother—she *knew* when Notre Dame lost."

Colton also learned from his father the prekickoff ritual of laying his hands on the statue of the Virgin Mary rescued from a neighbor's trash by his grandmother, and laying his hands on the rosary hanging from the Virgin Mary's arms. "Here was a guy who lived and breathed Notre Dame," Colton says. "Here's a guy, a devout Catholic. Here's a guy got on his hands and knees and prayed every night of his life. Pope John Paul said that same thing about his father. I read that, I said, 'Holy shit.' That impressed me." Marian devotion ran strong through the Colton household as did devotion in general. "My mother always instilled in me—the Blessed Mother, you pray to the Blessed Mother." Before setting off on trips of any duration or distance, Eddie's mother would, for safe travel, give to her husband and son a small figurine of Mary. Colton carries it to this day on his beat in Lower Manhattan.

By Eddie Colton's own admission, before he and his father made their first pilgrimage to Notre Dame for the Miami game, their interest in the university started and ended with Fighting Irish football. There might as well not have been an educational institution behind the team. About the only thing they knew about the school was that it was Catholic and located, as he puts it, "in the boondocks." Even though their enthusiasm for Irish football had its origins in their Catholicism, their feeling for the school as a site of their religion extended only as a metaphor to what occurred inside the stadium. In 1988, they were going to Notre Dame to see a game.

That first day, Chuck Hurley, chief of the NDPD, took the Coltons on a tour of the Notre Dame grounds. The lore of football ages past swirled in their heads, all those miraculous wins they'd seen on television or read about in books. But as they moved through the greensward quads and up to the steps of the Main Building, when they lifted their eyes to the sky and saw the gold of the dome backlit against a blue October sky, when they genuflected through the hush of Sacred Heart with its stained-glass windows throwing light in rainbows, with its baroque altars and sunburst tabernacle, when they moved outside and down the steps to the quiet arbor around the Grotto and saw the cave aflame and the Blessed Mother hovering above—all through those two hours of touristic ambling, some different feeling had slowly come over both father and son. "I looked at my father, he looked at me, and we knew. My father said to me, 'There's more to this place than just football, boy.' " At the Grotto, the tour's last stop, they lit their candles and knelt at the rail and said their prayers, and at that moment, that initial swell of feeling clarified into a kind of epiphany. Already Catholic, already Irish fans, they were at that moment converted, and Notre Dame—team and place and concept and spirit—coalesced into a Colton devotion all its own.

"My favorite place in the world is the Grotto," Colton says. "That's where I feel most at peace. The Grotto, when I get out there, it's like therapy for me. It's a privilege to me to go out there. It's gonna sound crazy, but many times, down there on my hands and knees at the Grotto, anything I pray for—you know, you don't pray to win the lottery or nothing—but anything I prayed for, it's amazing, but I can't think of anything that didn't come true, any prayers that weren't answered. It's one story after another, one sign after another. It's spooky, you know? Like my friend's father, his son was killed in an accident. Then he went out to Notre Dame a few years ago, went to the Grotto, the Basilica. Now he can't stop talking about the place. You pray for signs. You pray for signs, and he's been getting signs one after another. It's not a coincidence for me, Scottie. Lot of signs, lotta signs. Notre Dame will always have a special place in my heart. I might be out here in July. I just might move out here. I just might. In July, I retire from the police department after twenty years—and I just might."

Seminarians Nate Farley and Drew Gawrych, subway alum Sharon Loftus and Billy Powers, each of them and many more have described experiences similar to that of Colton and his father. And if you talk to Notre Dame fans long enough—fans of all varieties: alum, subway, student, administrative, both lay and prelate—you begin to take note of the trend. Many people seem to have a physical, palpable feeling when they set foot on the grounds for the first time. Fr. Bill Seetch, CSC, the away-game chaplain of the football team, has noted it as well, and he has posed a possible explanation. "In Celtic spirituality, they talk about *thin* places—places that reside at this distance between present reality and the otherworld, places where we most feel the presence of God. In the Celtic Christian world, monasteries and shrines were built at thin places." At Notre Dame there have been reports of "healings." There have been reports of paranormal sightings—as many ghost stories as tales of gridiron heroics. The feeling seems to be ecumenical. Seetch once met a husband and wife, devout Baptists from southwestern Missouri. They took a trip to Notre Dame simply because "they wanted to see what was up here." After a few hours on campus, they told Seetch, "You're right. There's something you can *feel* here."

Father Rocca says, "Many people who have prayed at Notre Dame have experienced something of the divine, a kind of healing. God and the Blessed Mother, I think, must hear prayers in a special way here."

Rocca in particular has recognized a by-product of this draw to the divine—the game-day confession. Unpublicized and unadvertised, one or two CSC priests sit inside the oaken booths in each transept of the Basilica, red bulb and green bulb, from 9 a.m. till noon on Fridays and Saturdays on football weekends. In the past, one of them has been Bishop Jenky. He says, "On football weekends, it's not unusual to have somebody come in and say, 'It's been thirty years since I've been to the sacraments. I'm back here, I've kind of changed around my life, and I want to make a general confession.' There would be *a lot* of that."

"I will hear some very significant confessions on a game day," says Rocca. "All I can say is, there's something about this place and the moment, and they just think this might be a good thing to do. They may not have been to confession in years. And we don't know them from Adam. It's a kind of spiritual healing. They're unburdening themselves. Often it's someone who's been away from the Church for a long time."

By the time Sorin had set up shop near the two lakes outside South Bend, it had been the site of missionary outposts for one and a half centuries. It was a crossroads of conversion. The local tribes, Potawatomi, Miami, Illinois, made business deals, held political conclaves, and received the sacraments from the Black Robes all in the local vicinity. Notre Dame as a pilgrimage site predates Notre Dame football, and the shrine of all shrines has always been the Grotto. The Grotto that now exists, built in 1896, is the successor to earlier Marian shrines at Notre Dame. Sorin made three pilgrimages, the first in 1876, to the Grotto of Massabielle not far from Lourdes, where, just eighteen years earlier, the Blessed Mother had appeared to a rather indifferently Catholic peasant girl named Bernadette Soubirous, now a saint. The Vatican long ago ratified the miracle. The waters of Lourdes are said to contain healing powers. Sorin came away from that thin place so moved that he decided that he needed one of his own. He brought back with him containers of Lourdes water and sold them to raise money for the construction of the current Sacred Heart. In later years two CSC priests brought back two rocks from Bernadette's cavern, now implanted into the south wall of Sorin's. Sorin died three years before construction began.

The site chosen for the Grotto was just behind Sacred Heart's sacristy door, in an area of campus formerly used as a kind of garbage dump, a kitchen midden. The Catholics of the area soon took to this Indiana Lourdes, and parades of devout from South Bend and Mishawaka and nearby Niles, Michigan, hiked to campus to pray, the earliest of Notre Dame's pilgrimages. By the early twentieth century, trains brought the pilgrims from the parishes of Chicago. Students, of course, have from the beginning used the Grotto as a place to find peace in the midst of crises, mostly having to do with midterms and finals. Bishop Jenky says, "It's a place with big arms. I think devotions like it give people permission, in a pretty secular world, to be Christian, to seek out what they believe, to know that there are possibilities in life beyond maybe what they see on MTV or in the Harvard School of Business. It invites, I suppose, a deepening of expectations out of life."

Father Hesburgh once wrote, "I usually get down there in the wee hours of the morning when I leave the office. There is almost always someone down there . . . rain, sleet, or snow. Every university has a place where students hang out for their social life, libraries where they study, and fields where they play sports. But how many have a praying place?"

Over the years the Grotto has taken hold of the collective imagination of Notre Dame fandom like nothing else outside the field heroics themselves. Poems have been written to it. Countless essays have extolled its quiet sanctity. A slim volume has been published called *Grotto Stories,* a collection of vignettes written by people who experienced something of the divine there. It is sold at the Hammes Notre Dame Bookstore, which has classed it, rather strangely, as fiction.

During a week leading up to a game, the Grotto will typically run through nearly ten thousand candles. Norby Wiskontoni, the caretaker of the Grotto, wears a cap that says FDNY, and canvas pants and black leather boots splotched here and there with white wax. He spends a good deal of his home-football Fridays opening a long drawer at the bottom of a rack and exchanging candles in plastic containers for ones in glass. Glass candles are more expensive, but they present a more distinguished air. They're also more durable. In 1985, after the weekend of a game against Michigan State, the heat from fifteen hundred candles melted their plastic casings to ooze, kindled a dangling vine of ivy, and set the Grotto ablaze. So intense were the flames that jets of NDFD water spalled the stones, and great chunks of the Grotto collapsed to the ground. It was repaired in time for the next game on the slate. The small statue of St. Bernadette that stands just outside the Grotto cave collects a collage of offerings from the pilgrims, much like the statue of St. Therese. On a football weekend, between Friday morning and Saturday afternoon, the Grotto's black offering box will receive enough money to make John Zack, the sacristan, a little nervous about divulging the figure. "I plead the Fifth on that one, Senator." He and his staff will go to the sacristy storeroom shortly before kickoff, spread out at a few long tables in front of a television, and count the bills while watching the game.

Eddie Colton told me most of his story in the stands at Giants Stadium, as Notre Dame easily defeated the Naval Academy, 27–9. He had invited me to his tailgate at the Meadowlands and given me a ticket for which he refused payment, but before he did so, he double-checked my credentials. Later, he said, "I wouldn't be talking to you right now if you weren't a graduate of Notre Dame." The clannish tendencies of the police vocation combined with the clannish tendencies of Notre Dame produced in Colton a credo that found its closest analogy, in Colton's formulation, with the Marine Corps, another institution for which he has great admiration. Although never one himself, "Once a marine, always a marine," he likes to say when describing the hold Notre Dame has over him and, as he sees it, all of Notre Dame fandom.

Through numerous small strokes his father's health had been failing for several years when a massive heart attack led to his hospitalization in early September 2001. Eddie Colton's mother had died in

March of that year. Later he would tell me how, since that first pilgrim-age in 1988, their trips to Notre Dame had become less about seeing the game and more about engaging with God. Their trips extended from long weekends to stays of five days, Wednesday through Monday. When in South Bend, they attended daily Mass on campus. They prayed at the Grotto immediately upon waking up in the morning and before heading off to bed at night. In the last few years of his life Eddie Sr. was confined to a wheelchair, but he refused to miss each year's pil-grimage, and his son pushed him around campus. He refused to leave games no matter the weather until the band had played the hymn "Notre Dame, Our Mother" and had marched out of the stadium. "At the Rutgers game one year—it was so cold you froze your balls off— and he wouldn't friggin' leave till it was all over." In October 1996, the Monday after a game against Ohio State, which Notre Dame lost, Eddie Sr. was kneeling at the Grotto rail and Eddie Jr. was sitting on a bench nearby when Monk Malloy and a camera crew and Charlie Rose en-tered the scene. On campus to interview Malloy and Lou Holtz for his PBS show, Rose approached father and son and asked if they were Notre Dame graduates. They explained that they were subway alumni. They were forced to explain to Rose what, exactly, subway alumni were. "And then I said, 'To tell you the truth, Mr. Rose, when we first came out here to Notre Dame, it was just about football. We only cared about the football. But now, it's much more than that.' " Several weeks later, Eddie Colton tuned his father's television to PBS. On the screen, Rose asked Malloy and Holtz, "What brings people out to Notre Dame, like the cop and his father we met at the Grotto?" And Eddie Colton said, "Shit, Dad! They're talkin about us!"

Eddie Sr. lay in intensive care for most of September 2001. His son camped out by his side for nineteen days. The attending doctor wore on his white lapel a pin that bore the seal of the University of Notre Dame. "You gotta be shittin' me," Eddie Colton said when he learned that the doctor was also an alumnus, class of sometime in the 1970s. Colton's hope was renewed. His father showed spirit. The old man flirted with the nurses, including Jackie Valente, his principal nurse. He asked her if she'd ever been to Notre Dame.

"No, sir, I haven't."

"You will be someday."

Eddie Colton paused from his narrative and said, "Trust me, Scott, this is no bullshit. Everything goes back to that place. I'm getting chills just thinkin' about it." Jackie Valente took such good care of his father that Eddie Colton later asked her on a date, fell in love, and proposed to her at the Grotto.

On September 8, 2001, the day of Notre Dame's season opener against the University of Nebraska, Eddie Sr. received last rites. He was conscious. But there were no TVs in intensive care, and he turned to his son.

"Who won the game today?"

"Notre Dame did, Pop. Notre Dame won today."

The game had ended several hours earlier. From the very first play, the outcome never in doubt, Nebraska had creamed the Irish, 27–10. "I lied to him," Eddie Colton said in the stands at Giants Stadium. He then watched a play develop on the field without comment. Finally he said, "It's tough, you know? I don't like talkin' about it. You can understand what I did. . . . I don't know, it was tough. He went to his grave thinkin' Notre Dame beat Nebraska. He's probably lookin' down at me from heaven right now, all pissed off."

For the next eleven days, his father lingered on as the jetliners crashed into Sergeant Colton's precinct. In and out of consciousness, Eddie Sr. didn't see that outcome either.

By the time he went back to work, Eddie Colton had buried his father, and much of the territory of the First Precinct lay buried under the Towers. Five of his cops were in the hospital, one had almost lost an arm, and three had earned the Medal of Valor. The precinct spent the next three months working fifteen- and sometimes thirty-hour shifts, six days a week.

A Blue Mass is celebrated in honor of policemen and firefighters lost in the line of duty, and it follows in the Catholic tradition of the "month's mind," a commemoration of the dead one month later. Through Chuck Hurley and through Eddie Colton, a group of First Precinct NYPD made their way to South Bend for Notre Dame's first Blue Mass, arranged at the request of Monk Malloy. Before leaving New York, Colton pulled down the American flag flying outside the temporary morgue, to which the First Precinct had been assigned, and went inside to find a chaplain of some kind, preferably a Catholic priest. He wanted to have the flag blessed and then give it to Malloy, with whom he had developed an acquaintance since the Charlie Rose episode. The priest he found inside the morgue was Fr. Charles Miller, a Franciscan, Notre Dame class of 1959. ("Trust me, man. No bullshit, you couldn't make this up.") To that first Blue Mass, Colton invited only first-responder cops. For subsequent Blue Masses, which have become an annual Notre Dame tradition, he would work his way down the list. So much the better if they were Notre Dame fans. Among them was Sean McGill, a wiry Staten Island native, a subway alumnus and son of a subway alumnus, who had never been to Notre Dame. Twenty-eight years old at the time, he had been caught on film by the Netau brothers, the French documentarians, using his shirt to douse flames on the body of a woman drenched in jet fuel in the lobby of the World Trade Center. Later, still inside the lobby, Tower No. 2 collapsed on top of him. In pitch-darkness, in extreme heat, he and a few firefighters stood miraculously alive in a cavity that had formed around them amid the avalanche of steel. They saw a streak of sunlight. Through the air shaft they crawled to the surface. It took them six hours. On the breast of his navy blue dress uniform McGill now wears the Medal of Valor.

Sitting beside me at the Navy game, Sean McGill talked about none of this. Instead, he preferred to talk about the Blue Mass and Notre Dame and Eddie Colton. He said, "If it weren't for Eddie, we wouldn't have been there at Notre Dame in the first place." They flew into South Bend on a Wednesday, and by chance it happened that U2 was playing the Joyce Center the following night. Bono said, "Ladies and gentlemen, the NYPD!" and the NYPD found themselves in front of thirty thousand screaming people, led on a stroll around a heart-shaped stage by Bono as the Edge played "The Star-Spangled Banner." "All along the walk, students were high-fiving us, throwing Notre Dame shirts and jerseys at us, and all of a sudden the crowd starts chanting, 'U-S-A! U-S-A!' They treated us like *we* were U2. Nothing was choreographed. All of it was spontaneous. That was one of the greatest moments of my life. It was all set up by Notre Dame and it was unbelievable." On Saturday, the Irish would play West Virginia at home. "Notre Dame told us, 'Whatever you want. You want to be on the sidelines with the football team—no problem.' But we couldn't, you know?" The NYPD had to get back to work.

Prior to 9/11, about half the cops in the First Precinct had counted themselves Notre Dame football fans. After the Blue Mass, Sean McGill says, about 95 percent of them do. One cop told Colton after the experience, "You know what, Sarge? That is sacred ground out there." I wouldn't learn until sometime later that Sean McGill's wife had miscarried two days before 9/11. Of course the entire First Precinct contingent had followed Colton almost immediately upon arriving in South Bend to the Grotto for a little therapy. McGill said a prayer for the health of his wife, that she might be able to have another child, and a prayer of thanks to God for saving him on "That Day." A year later, when another batch of First Precinct cops were heading off to Notre Dame for the second annual Blue Mass, McGill couldn't make it. His wife had gone into labor.

At the First Precinct, in a glass case next to the booking agent's desk, Colton has arranged a modest shrine of his own. The case contains the game ball from the West Virginia contest, October 13, 2001. It contains another football signed by every player on that year's team, and it contains a helmet autographed by the coaching staff and worn by Carlyle Holiday, then the starting quarterback. Colton's workplace shrine is both secular and not. It serves, he says, to remind him, and the pieces in the case have become not only relics of the team, but the university and therefore the pilgrimage site.

Among other things, the Blue Mass experience has reinforced in Colton his love for Notre Dame and his respect for Monk Malloy. From his patrol car he once said to me, "Father Malloy, he's a great man. A great, great man. We felt the prayers. To sum everything up—I felt, and we felt, the prayers from Father Malloy, from Father Warner, from the student body, from the community out there. I *felt* the prayers. I'm not bullshittin' you, Scott. I'm tellin' you right now, I'm a better person. I'm a better person from goin' to that place. We can never, ever reciprocate what Notre Dame did for the city of New York. What the University of Notre Dame has done for us, for the New York Police Department, no dollar amount can ever reciprocate."

At the 2004 Blue Mass in October, Eddie Colton and four members of the First Precinct, including Sean McGill, all in their dress blues, McGill's Medal of Valor dangling from his chest, attended the service in the Basilica and then a brief mingling reception with a few priests and about two dozen members of the Notre Dame and South Bend fire and police forces. At Mass, Monk Malloy gave the homily. Chuck Hurley was there in his civvies. Earlier, before the service, the First Precinct boys had a private audience with Malloy. According to Sean McGill, Monk told them, "As you know, this will be my last year as president. But I'll still be living on campus, and I'll still be affiliated with the university." The pragmatics of the real world had a way of impinging on this particular pilgrimage. "He said he's got to deal with politics just as much as we do," McGill later said at the reception. "He's the kinda guy, he doesn't offer much information. And we're definitely not gonna ask."

Jack Rockne also attended the ceremony and the reception afterward. He wore a beige suede sportcoat and a necktie. Ninety years old, he has white hair and none of the smashed, brutish Norweigian features of his legendary father. His eyes are blue and clear and mischievous, and his health appears completely intact other than that he has no voice box. He communicates with a marker and a white board. A former marine, another vet of the Second World War, he is good friends with Eddie Colton, who says he enjoys Rockne's presence not because of his patrimony but because of his career in the Marine Corps.

Later, the NYPD descended to the Grotto. Night had fallen, and full darkness had enclosed the scene except for the glow of the candles from the cave. Near the concrete esplanade rose a sycamore so high and layered with canopy it appeared to predate the missionary impulse. A breeze moved the branches. On the ground from this and other trees was a carpet of loose, wet vegetation. The smell of burning wicks and candle wax mixed with the smell of damp leaves. The Virgin Mary was illuminated from behind in her mummy case. Ivylike stalactites dangled over the cave's maw. The cops ambled into the cavern. Colton entered last and spent some time in there lighting maybe a dozen candles. He shoved bills into the box. Before heading over to the kneeler, he approached the Lourdes stone, about head high, in the wall of the Grotto. He touched the stone with his right hand and made a sign of the cross, touched the stone with his left hand and did the same. He placed both palms against the rocks on either side of the sacred stone and leaned in, like a jogger stretching before a run, so close he appeared to put his forehead against it. He held the position for nearly a minute, and the candlelight silhouetted his black figure motionless against the stones.

10

A Busload of Pilgrims

A fifty-five-seat motor coach traced the Great Lakes rust belt across Interstate 90—Buffalo, Erie, Cleveland, Toledo—on its way from western New York to South Bend, Indiana, for Notre Dame's October 23 matchup with the Golden Eagles of Boston College. Rented by the Notre Dame Alumni Club of Buffalo, the bus carried around forty people, precisely two of whom were alumni. For the last thirty-two years, Peter McKee, class of 1969, former president of the Buffalo club, had organized this annual trip, but no dispute surrounded the question of who was chief of the bus.

Eddie Gadawski, eighty-four years old, proprietor of Gadawski's tavern in Niagara Falls, New York, had made his first trip to Notre Dame before McKee was born. What Gadawski might have lacked in physical stature—a little stoop-shouldered, pear-shaped, around five feet eight—he more than made up for in the force of his speech. He had the type of old man's voice that worked only if he shouted. Though he had quit cigarettes forty years earlier, he sounded as if he'd been chain-smoking up until this moment. When the bus loaded up outside his establishment just before dawn on Friday morning, a few of his regulars sat slouched at the bar inside, clutching beers and nursing hangovers. Gadawski officiated at the loading of the bus with provisions from his tavern, and when he had finished, he entered the bar, a look of disgust on his face.

"You guys wanna stay here, fine. Everybody *else,* we're goin' to Notre Dame!"

He wore a green polo shirt tucked into pants belted high around his midsection. The pleats in his trousers split over a colostomy bag. On his feet he wore white, blockish orthopedic shoes with Velcro buckles. A ballcap bearing a giant ND monogram rested lightly on his head. He had a fizz of gray hair that, without his hat, stood up on the back of his head like a bird's tail. He wore large, wire-rimmed eyeglasses and had a big-jawed face full of creases and declivities, craggy as the moon. Teeth were missing around a jack-o'-lantern smile. To say that he looked mischievous understated the matter; he had the face of a happy gargoyle.

This was a two-bus convoy, actually, one containing fans from Buffalo, and this one containing fans from Niagara Falls. Nearly everyone on the Falls bus was a regular at Gadawski's tavern. The Buffalo bus carried about a dozen alumni—including a diocesan priest, Notre Dame class of 1974—and it had acquired a reputation directly opposite its Niagara Falls counterpart. "Over there, with them, that's the holy bus," Eddie Gadawski said. "Ours, it's the drunk bus. It's the *devil's* bus."

The front of Gadawski's green polo shirt said, in yellow, on the breast pocket:

> *Boss of Angels*
> *Eddie*

and on the back:

> *Eddie's Angels*
> *Gadawski's Restaurant*
> *Niagara Falls, New York*

Eddie's Angels were four middle-aged women who lived on the Canadian side of the Falls—Barbara Antenson, Linda Hachy, Suzanne Meginnis, and Cindy McAnulty. Barbara Antenson owns the Beachwood Golf Club in Niagara Falls, Ontario. Though she is not Catholic, she learned to love Notre Dame through her uncle, a man named Nin Bruno, from the Italian side of her family, who owned a tavern in Pittsburgh, where she grew up. Nin's was chockablock with Fighting Irish memorabilia and so is the Beachwood clubhouse and grillroom. Ten years ago, Eddie Gadawski had heard that this Canadian woman ran, essentially, a Notre Dame golf course. He took a drive to have a look for himself. The women reciprocated, and whenever not traveling to games, they watch Notre Dame on the TVs at Gadawski's. Soon they were all making pilgrimages of the real kind together, and Eddie had his Angels.

For a good portion of the eight-hour ride Gadawski knelt on a seat and faced the crowd at the back of the bus. For sixty years he had never held a job of any duration other than barkeep, and all that experience had perhaps ingrained in him the need to keep close to his patrons. The bus had broken down into two distinct sections, like a junior-high class on a field trip. At the front, people sat soberly in their seats, snoozing, reading newspapers, or doing nothing at all. The back of the bus, meanwhile, was a hive of activity—the cool kids. The Angels were back there, of course. There was also Don Sweeney, a retired fire captain, a small, white-haired man with a white mustache and a stentorian voice and the air of a brigadier general, an ancient friend of Gadawski's. There was David Nguyen, formerly Kinh, born in Vietnam and adopted when he was nine years old by Robert Gadawski, Eddie's son. His accent carried a strange combination of flat western New York and the inflections of the Mekong Delta. Now thirty-one years old, he worked as a cook at a bar called Brennan's. There was Mike Rhoney, a local undertaker, who had brought along his two twentysomething sons. There was the man everyone called the Judge, also with his sons, and Joe Casales, of Casales Motel, and Larry DeLong, owner of the Portage House strip club, around the corner from Gadawski's. Those who had not grown up Notre Dame fans, Eddie Gadawski had long ago converted.

An enthusiastic game of euchre developed, and whoops went up with each trump. The pilgrims began the trip drinking Caesars—Vodka and Clamato juice—and then, when the Caesars ran out, they broke into the beer. Gadawski had also brought his daughter and his teenaged granddaughters along on the trip, and the girls made continuous routes down the aisles to the back carrying small tubs filled with beer. The drinkers gave them tips. By the end of the road trip, ten cases of Budweiser and Bud Light went from a barrel at the front of the bus and down the hatches in the back. By 10 a.m. it felt like four in the afternoon.

"Mr. Gadawski," Pete McKee asked, irony in his voice, "are you in a better mood? You've been cranky all day."

"Yeah, I'm cranky!"

"Why?" an Angel asked.

"Because I'm pregnant! Whaddaya think I'm cranky for? All *you* people"

At a travel plaza just west of Cleveland, the buses stopped for lunch, where the pilgrims dined on Burger King. Gadawski and David and Sweeney finished their meals and slipped outside to the parking lot and swung open the luggage container beneath the Buffalo bus. The Buffalo contingent had arrived a little late, and all of them were still eating, except the driver. From the cargo hold, Gadawski removed two cases of beer in an effort to replenish the Niagara. The driver leaned against the bus observing the theft. "What's the trade?" he said.

Gadawski loaded the cases into David's arms and looked at the driver. "Nothin'! Not a goddamn thing."

On the TV screens on the Niagara bus, Notre Dame propaganda continuously played. First a documentary on Notre Dame's football traditions called *Wake Up the Echoes,* narrated by John Facenda, the voice of NFL Films, and then a videotape of *Roast the Coach,* starring Lou Holtz, in which Father Joyce, at the podium roasting, made mention of the occasionally unrealistic demands of Notre Dame's rabid subway alumni, "sometimes called synthetic alumni." After the roast came the grand finale.

A chant rose from the back of the bus. "Roo-dee! Roo-dee!"

And then the treacly, sentimental sound track of the motion picture *Rudy* intoned from the speakers of the bus. Released in 1993, some say as an antidote to the PR smear of *Tarnished Dome, Rudy* has become, along with *Knute Rockne, All-American,* the sine qua non of Notre Dame films, the cinematic bible of the subway alumni. Daniel "Rudy" Ruettiger, meanwhile, Notre Dame class of 1976, has become something of a cult figure, with his own personal-inspiration empire, Rudy International, complete with books (*Rudy's Insights for a Winning Life, Rudy's Lessons for Young Champions*) and motivational audiotapes (the *Dream Power* series, the "Best of Rudy CD Pack") and motivational-speaking engagements ("His captivating personality and powerful message of 'YES I CAN' stays with his audiences forever," says his Web site) and corporate-retreat team-building programs on a dude ranch in Mendocino, California.

Applause erupted from the pilgrims as the opening credits appeared and as the bus rolled across the farmland of western Ohio. Planks missing from the sides of barns. Shade-tree clumps in the middle distance gone from green and into fall color. Irrigation pipes rusting in the fields. Cell phone towers rising from the plain. Inside the bus, the pilgrims, transfixed by Sean Astin as Rudy Ruettiger, who delivers the theme in two lines: "You know what dad says. Having a dream is what makes life tolerable."

Rain fell for most of the drive, and as *Rudy* finished, thirty minutes out of South Bend, Barbara Antenson, the lead Angel, said, "As we get closer to God's Country, the sun will come out. It'll be beautiful."

It was at this point that one of the Angels made an announcement. "There's no beer left."

With fright in her voice, Suzanne said, "Are you *serious?*"

The news made its way to the chief. He moved slowly out of his seat, where he'd been snoozing intermittently through *Rudy,* and walked to the rear. He stood in the aisle, facing the culprits, looking down upon them.

"It's all gone, Eddie."

He looked on with no expression. He blinked. "I put a goddamn *case* back here!"

In unison the chorus came, from the Angels, Billy, David, Sweeney, the Judge. "We drank it all!"

"C'mon. What'd you do with all the beer?"

"It's been consumed."

"I, for one, am shocked."

"Yeah, I'm shocked too! That's one of the cases I stole at the last stop!"

"Do people on that bus drink?"

"No," Gadawski said. "They pray."

"It's an outrage I tell you," the Judge said. "An outrage."

"It is. It's a god*damn* outrage. Alright. Everyone's gotta put in. Start a collection, *start* a collection. And buy me back my beer!"

David quickly mixed a Bloody Mary in a red Solo cup and handed it over. For the time being, it seemed to slake the man's thirst. Over the speakers on the bus, the voices of the Notre Dame glee club emerged, slow and nostalgic and a cappella, singing the "Victory March." At that moment, someone's cell phone rang, a series of bleeps pulsing the same melody—digital over analog, the fight songs nearly harmonized.

"We gotta look for the Dome on the left," someone said with excitement.

The sun was low on the horizon and coming directly through the windshield. Gadawski stood in the aisle. He leaned in low and peered through the windows on the left. He caught sight of it first.

"There it is!" He pointed, and people crowded over to his side of the bus, and everyone applauded.

Reports of the rowdiness of the Niagara Falls bus trip had been somewhat exaggerated. "There'll be so many empty whiskey bottles rolling down the aisles, you gotta watch your step," Gadawski's son Freddy had warned. But at eighty-four his father had slowed down a good deal in recent years. He had been diagnosed with cancer of the colon, removed and replaced with the colostomy bag. He still looked like a spark plug of energy, however, and back home at his tavern, he worked almost as relentlessly as ever. He had to maintain the shrine.

In western New York—and perhaps all around the country, given the extent of the contacts Gadawski has made with other Notre Dame fans over three decades of Notre Dame pilgrimage—Gadawski's restaurant is famous.

The proprietor sits behind the bar with a bottle of Molson Canadian. In the evenings, his son Freddy, fifty years old, tends. Eddie's shift is lunch. Now, at night, he has time to jawbone, gab, confabulate, ball-break—always the center of attention. Gadawski's occupies the ground floor of a two-story, flat-roofed, nineteenth-century storefront on Falls Street, at one time the thriving commercial artery of Niagara Falls. Gadawski does not have a long commute. He and his wife, Irene, a tiny woman with a globe of white hair, live in the upstairs apartment. They divide duties; Irene's domain involves the kitchen, Eddie's, of course, the bar. The restaurant consists of two rooms, dining and drinking. The whole place has low, dropped ceilings and utility rugs thrown over linoleum. Its lighting is warm, subdued, ambient—an eternal dusk. On the facade above the front door outside hangs a wood carving on which the artist has rendered a full-color Notre Dame leprechaun. Evidently Niagara Falls lies safely out of the purview of the university licensing department. Over a window beside the leprechaun, a similarly carved sign reads, in green, GADAWSKI'S. Notre Dame stickers are stuck to all the windows. A Notre Dame welcome mat accepts each patron. Inside, the Notre Dame glock overwhelms the eyes. It surrounds you and inters you—Notre Dame posters, flags, banners, bowl-game buttons, postcards, license plates, wallpapers, figurines, Tiffany lamps, athlete photographs, coach photographs, a model of the Dome, a model of the stadium. When the telephone rings, it rings the "Victory March." It's as if you've fallen down the rabbit hole and entered the mind of a Notre Dame fanatic.

Gadawski has made the backbar—heaving with Notre Dame gewgaws and knickknacks among the liquor bottles—the restaurant's shrine within a shrine. To make sense of it all, one needs a guided tour, which Gadawski will freely give, pointing out his most precious pieces. He has, in a sense, been incorporated into the campus itself, a kind of symbolic entombment. "I'm in two sculptures on campus," Gadawski says a little elusively. And he points to two photographs hanging in frames on the wall behind the bar. On one of his pilgrimages he met a man named Jerry McKenna, a Notre Dame alumnus and a monument sculptor who lives in Texas. They became fast friends. McKenna made the Moose Krause bronze and the Frank Leahy bronze that adorn the area immediately around Notre Dame Stadium. Gadawski has a photo of the Krause statue, and it says, "To Eddie Gadawski—Warmest Regards," signed Jerry McKenna, "sculptor." A drawing in the margins of the photo is a detail from the sculpture—the butt of the cigar in Krause's hand. "Hey! Look closely," Gadawski says, and hands over the framed photograph. "What's there, whaddaya see?" Looking closely at the drawing, you see dots like braille that simulate the ash at the end of Krause's cigar. The dots form the letters *E* and *G*.

"Yeah! My initials!"

Gadawski then points out another photograph, this one of a model standing for McKenna as he sculpted the mold for Frank Leahy's bronze. Leahy in the statue has taken a knee and is evidently having a close look at a practice drill, dressed in his coach's casual. Look closely at the photo, what do you see? The model is wearing a gray, hooded sweatshirt that says on the front GADAWSKI'S. McKenna also needed a pair of old high-top cleats to complete the sculpture, and Gadawski had a pair on hand. He sent them to Texas. "My shirt's in the statue and so are the shoes."

To catalog every cameo in the bar would tax the abilities of the librarian of Congress. He has an archive of ancient game-day programs, a bank of ticket stubs. An old, half-deflated pigskin rests in a plastic case atop the cash register, bearing the signatures of all seven of Notre Dame's Heisman winners. "Angelo got me the autographs on this football here," Gadawski says, referring to Angelo Bertelli, Heisman winner, Notre Dame's first, 1943. "You know how many footballs in this country got all them signatures on 'em? *Not many.* Angelo Bertelli got 'em all for me. A very good friend, Angelo is. A *very good* friend." A photo behind the bar pictures a middle-aged Gadawski with a full gut, enormous brown-shaded eye glasses, a thin black tie, a green, three-piece suit of 1960s cut. He is balding and smiling and all his teeth are there, and he is standing next to a smiling Father Hesburgh, about the same age, in Roman blacks. Both with their lantern jaws, they could be related. A painting hangs from the far back wall in the dining room, and a smaller postcard-size print of that painting hangs behind the bar. A cartoon illustration in acrylic, composed by Irene's cousin, it pictures, in the center, the exterior of Gadawski's tavern set within a condensed milieu. The golden Dome rises in the background. The hash marks of a football field stretch to the left of the Gadawski building, and the facade of Notre Dame Stadium completes the frame. Notre Dame transposed to Niagara Falls, Gadawski's transposed to Notre Dame—the picture seems to represent a dreamscape, a wish.

Earlier in the season on a Thursday night, a customer asked Gadawski if he had reconsidered traveling to the game against Stanford over the weekend.

"Not really, no," Gadawski said, sitting behind the bar. "My legs, they're not getting any younger." He rubbed his thighs with both hands. "It's called, getting older! And, ain't getting any younger!"

Not so long ago, Gadawski would travel to the entire slate of Notre Dame home games. The most popular nights at the restaurant have always been Fish Fry Fridays; holding to the rules pre–Vatican II, the family serves no meat on that day. The event has become a local institution, and the place is always crowded. At around 11 p.m. on Fish Fry Fridays during football seasons, Gadawski would hustle his clientele abruptly out—everyone knew the routine—clean the tables, count the take, close up, and lock up. Father and sons and a few buddies, they'd start west on I-90 and drive all through the night eight hours to South Bend. Each year since he'd been diagnosed, Gadawski had reduced the number of games he attended until this season he would only go once—on a bus for the annual Buffalo-club outing.

Almost every morning Gadawski gets up early and goes on one of his "runs," as he calls them, a sequence of errands, before opening up the place for business at 11 a.m. Around his rearview hangs a crucifix and a handicapped-parking decal. I joined him once in October. We pulled out and headed down Falls Street, passing the Holy Trinity Church, an imposing masonry structure with a high spire and a school building no longer in business. Letters carved into a wooden cornice above a door read SZKOLA PAR. SW. TROJCY—School of the Parish of Holy Trinity. This section of town is the old Polish parish, and Holy Trinity is its church. It still functions, with a Saturday and a Sunday Mass, but it is barely functioning. Long ago most of the Polish cleared out. Farther down Falls we passed, on the right, the City Mission soup kitchen and food depot. Though it was nearly sixty degrees, men stood outside on the curb in thick winter coats, smoking and sipping from bottles in brown bags. Every day, a queue forms around noon at the kitchen. People arrive pushing supermarket carts, which come away carrying rations free of charge, and on most days the City Mission attracts a bigger lunch crowd than Gadawski's. The street's most prominent architectural feature has become the vacant lot. Insects chirp in knee-high weeds snagged with plastic bags.

Aimed west down Falls, you see a kind of space needle rising through mist pluming into the sky. The needle is on the vibrant, elaborately gardened Canadian side of the falls. In front of the mist, on the American side, is an art deco high-rise, now vacant, now foreclosed upon, a building no one seems willing to buy. In front of the high-rise is the arched roof of the Seneca Casino. The Indians now control about the only industry left in Niagara Falls with the exception of the trickle of tourism that does not cross the Rainbow Bridge to Canada. "They killed everything in this city with that casino," Gadawski said. "They killed the whole fucking city. They don't pay taxes. They don't pay anything. You realize, the Indians and their casino—the city *gave* them that land? Before the casino came in, business was good. Today, now, the casino took all the people. It's a casino, it's gambling, people lose money. And they don't spend it. Locally, at least. Lotta businesses closing. *Lotta* businesses."

"What about your business?"

"No! No way. Won't close as long as I live. We got our *own* business coming in. All the old Polish people on the fixed income. They come into our place to eat, which is reasonable priced—and that's it. The casino don't take none of that away."

Gadawski made a left onto Buffalo Avenue, the old Niagara Falls industrial belt, now a strip of defunct factories. He said, "They've closed 'em all down so fast it's ridiculous. Lotta money used to be here. *Lotta* money."

Gadawski was born in 1920 and brought up within blocks of his tavern. His parents had emigrated from Poland as adults. His father worked in the Niagara Falls industrial plants, which then thrived like a vision of American know-how, and his mother took care of the house and tended to the Gadawski boarders. To make ends meet as well as help their countrymen, the family rented a room to a succession of Polish immigrant families. Gadawski served stateside on the West Coast during the Second World War and after his service tended bar at the lounge of the Hollywood Park Racetrack, Inglewood, California. In his late twenties, he returned to his hometown and married a girl eight years his junior, Irene Jankowski. Here in the twenty-first century, it is unlikely that anyone would return to Niagara Falls from Hollywood, but when Gadawski was a young man, restaurants, shops, and bars did a flourishing business all along Falls Street, the core of the working-class Niagara Falls Catholic community. Rambling nineteenth-century hotels lined the side streets and collected the honeymoon-tourist trade. Everyone seemed to work on the factory floors, or own businesses that served the industries and their employees. Not long after returning from the West Coast, Gadawski took over a bar owned and operated by his father-in-law, and eventually Gadawski renamed it. His clientele consisted almost entirely of men who came into the bar wearing coveralls covered in grime. They took their shift beers and their shift shots—7 a.m., noon, 4 p.m., 11. Almost everyone was Catholic, but Gadawski's then was not yet a Notre Dame shrine. He built it up over the years, and as the industrial town began its decline in the 1960s, the tavern as a Fighting Irish stronghold began its rise.

When Eddie was about eight or nine years old, his family started following Notre Dame football, notwithstanding the team's new Fighting Irish nickname. One Saturday afternoon, the patriarch tuned the family radio to a broadcast. "That's a good Catholic school," he said to his sons. "You listen to them." He spoke his words in Polish and in the imperative—a command of exclusion. "In other words," Gadawski explains today, recalling the story, "that's Catholics playin', and nobody in this house roots for anybody but them." Like Tudy Cummings of the Chicago South Side, this was the zeitgeist into which Gadawski was reared, community organized around somewhat competitive ethnic enclaves—Italian, Lithuanian, Irish, Polish, and even Lebanese, each with its own parishes and central churches. In the Niagara Falls of Eddie Gadawski's youth and early manhood, Catholics made up nearly 100 percent of the town's population. Today, only about half are Catholic, a percentage that slips each year. As the industry pulled out, so did the ethnics, receding to the Buffalo suburbs or other parts of the country entirely, leaving behind Gadawski's and its nonconformist proprietor, a vestige of a former world.

If an integral Catholic community remains in Niagara Falls, it's here at Gadawski's among the Notre Dame bric-a-brac. Mostly they come from afar, not Niagara Falls itself, and when they open the Gadawski menus, decorated with ND iconography out of a dot matrix printer, they often order the Polish Platter—pierogi, sausage, saurkraut, potatoes—and golombki, cabbage stuffed with hamburger under a tomato sauce—or the beef on wick or the Friday fish. In more ways than one, Gadawski's has become a Catholic preserve, embalmed in Notre Dame fandom.

Notre Dame, not surprisingly, has always weighed heavy on the local imagination. Fr. Michael Burzynski, born and raised in Niagara Falls, is the parish priest of Our Lady of the Cataract, the mother church of the city, and he received his Ph.D. in psychology from Notre Dame. The church sits downtown across the street from the Seneca Casino. When his parishioners talk to Father Burzynski and learn that he received his undergraduate degree not from Notre Dame, but from the University of Buffalo, occasionally they will flash a look of surprise and confusion and say, "Oh. I thought *all* priests went to Notre Dame." Our Lady of the Cataract underwent a recent renovation, and Father Miscamble, CSC, formerly rector of Moreau Seminary, presided over the rededication Mass. This was by design. The present church building was completed in 1873, and to preside over the original dedication Mass, the parish priest brought in an outsider from Indiana by way of France, a Holy Cross priest name Edward Sorin.

Gadawski sometimes talks in a kind of singsong, and he did so now as two customers paid their tab and left the bar. "Thank you!" he called after them. "I'll call you next week. I'm going to the *Holy City* tomorrow!"

It was around 2 p.m. on the Thursday before the bus trip. Gadawski was preparing for the journey and getting ready to close the bar, which would reopen at five in the afternoon for the dinner crowd. He took the edge off his excitement by sipping through the day on a Tom Collins glass filled with Lambrusco and ice and a squirt of club soda sprayed from the soda gun. He scratched a list onto the back of a receipt and from time to time analyzed the shelves behind the bar, arms akimbo. He whistled through his teeth, as he frequently does, from which the melody of the "Victory March" will often spontaneously develop. He couldn't decide whether to bring along a portion of the pickled eggs he keeps in a five-gallon jar behind the bar—a Gadawski's delicacy. Through the day, along with his Lambrusco, he opened the jar and popped an egg into his mouth. He will often consume a dozen during a shift. Hard-boiled, shelled, sunk into a brine mixed with onions and beet juice, the eggs float like eyeballs in their blood-pink marinade. They look like something on the shelf of high-school science class. He appraised the jar and considered the logistics of hauling it along on the trip. He might need his daily fix. He discarded the idea. "I don't need to be carrying *that* shit."

The telephone rang the "Victory March" again and again. Complicated deals were being conducted, a calculus of seating. For the people of Niagara Falls, Gadawski's is not only Notre Dame fan headquarters,

The giant mosaic colloquially known as "Touchdown Jesus" is officially titled "Word of Life." The largest such mosaic in the world, 129 feet tall and 65 wide, it portrays Christ the Teacher and is, essentially, a visual depiction of the Holy Cross charism. *(Photo courtesy of Chestertonlep)*

Fr. Theodore Hesburgh, CSC *(Photo courtesy of AP World Wide Photos)*

ABOVE: Fr. John Ignatius Jenkins, CSC *(Photo courtesy of AP World Wide Photos)*

RIGHT: Fr. Edward "Monk" Malloy, CSC *(Photo courtesy of AP World Wide Photos)*

Nate Farley, Holy Cross seminarian *(Photo courtesy of Nate Farley)*

Tracy Hallahan (left) and Bob Wentroble (right), the Sheriff and the Mayor of the Neighborhood of Hope. *(Photo courtesy of Tracy Hallahan)*

Robert Vahalik, "Silo Man," with Tracy Hallahan *(Photo courtesy of Tracy Hallahan)*

Eddie Gadawski, proprietor of Gadawski's Tavern in Niagara Falls, New York *(Photo courtesy of Eddie Gadawski)*

Tudy Cummings has been called the greatest Notre Dame fan who ever lived, and such was her influence that, in 1976, she became the first woman—and the first fan—ever inducted into the Notre Dame Monogram Club, the exclusive alumni group made up of every athlete to earn a varsity letter, in any sport. Wearing her famous ND hat in this photo, she is shown here at a postgame meeting of her Trunk Club sometime in the 1970s, attended by Joe Montana, second to the right. *(Photos courtesy of Michael Cummings)*

After parking their cars and arriving on campus and before doing anything else, the pilgrims of Notre Dame will likely visit a man-made cave called the Grotto, situated behind Sacred Heart, down a flight of granite steps, and cut into a slope of steep pitch. Deep and dark in the permanent shade, it resembles, with its stonework, an exhumed catacomb. At a one-to-seven scale, the Grotto is a replica of Our Lady of Lourdes, the Marian shrine in southern France. Aside from the stadium, it is the most visited shrine on campus, and every year its cavern will receive a quarter of a million pilgrims. *(Photo courtesy of Chestertonlep)*

A small, little-known statue shielded by trees and underbrush sits not far from the Grotto, on the site of a long-gone seminary building. It is the only object left after the university razed the ancient structure. The statue is of Saint Therese (1873–1897), a French Carmelite nun, patroness of foreign missionaries. After a home-game weekend, her statue at Notre Dame will be surrounded by flowers, votive candles, pebbles, coins, rosaries, holy cards, and religious medals left by pilgrims who have prayed at her feet. *(Photo courtesy of Chestertonlep)*

Sgt. Edwin Colton, Jr., with his father, Edwin Colton, Sr., in the Notre Dame locker room *(Photo courtesy of Edwin Colton, Jr.)*

RIGHT: Athletic director Kevin White *(Photo courtesy of AP World Wide Photos)*

BELOW, LEFT: John Affleck-Graves, executive vice president of Notre Dame *(Photo courtesy of AP World Wide Photos)*

BELOW, RIGHT: Tyrone Willingham *(Photo courtesy of Corbis)*

The revolt had started gathering momentum after the Boston College loss, simmered through Tennessee, and blew into the streets after Notre Dame lost, 38–41, on another last-second field goal, at home to the University of Pittsburgh team with a record of 5-3. Before the alma mater played, chants of "Fire Ty" rose in the stands. *(Photo courtesy of James Leito)*

Charlie Weis at his introductory press conference *(Photo courtesy of AP World Wide Photos)*

but also a clearinghouse for Notre Dame football tickets. Through the Buffalo alumni club and other connections, Gadawski gets his supply, which he disburses over the counter of the bar. "Everybody in here's a Notre Dame fan," he has said before. "But they can't get tickets. And then I started getting 'em tickets. Tickets, tickets, tickets." He did a pantomime: dealing the cards off the top.

Gadawski raised his glass of wine. "Larry. *Salud!*"

"*Salud.*"

Larry DeLong, owner of the Portage House strip club, sipped off a shot glass of Crown Royal. Just before the bar closed for the afternoon, he was Gadawski's only customer, a frequent state of affairs, since the Portage House has done its business just around the corner from Gadawski's bar for the last thirty-odd years. He and Gadawski trade status as regulars at each other's establishment. Larry has dark hair that looks wet, and it spills down his neck and is slicked over his scalp in a kind of comb-over. He has a scruffy brown beard and droopy eyes, which make him resemble a hound dog. He wears a pinkie ring and a gold chain that depends into a snarl of chest hair. Drinking his shots of Crown Royal alongside a Coors Light draft, he went over his plan for the rest of the day and night. It involved the Seneca Casino and playing Let It Ride until the bus pulled up at Gadawski's at seven the next morning. Long ago Larry had become a Notre Dame fan where once he had been an agnostic. The passion of his neighbor had reformed him. "I might not meet you for the bus," he said to Gadawski. "If I miss it, you'll know I'm headed to Notre Dame in an armored truck."

Larry, despite his perpetual blank expression, seemed as excited about the trip as his friend. Though he had been to many Notre Dame games before, he asked about the itinerary once they had reached campus.

"Go down to the Grotto," Gadawski said. "Kneel. Pray." He looked at Larry for a second. "And then we'll drink!"

This constituted a capsule version of every Gadawski pilgrimage since the man had begun making them. As best he can remember, he first set foot on campus in 1946, after he was discharged from the army, the year that Frank Leahy began composing his four-year stretch of thirty-six wins, two ties, zero losses, and three national championships. "I'm goin' back a lotta years," Gadawski says. "A *lotta* years."

He cannot isolate any particular moments or experiences, but when asked about those Leahy games at Notre Dame Stadium, he enters a kind of private reverie. "I seen some good ones there. Yeah. *Oh*, boy, I seen some good ones. Those were good years. Ach, those were *tremendous* years." Once he had got himself settled into business in the 1950s, Gadawski began making pilgrimages more regularly. For a good two-decade stretch he didn't miss more than a game a season. A routine developed, a ritual developed, and Fish Fry Friday blended into the pilgrimage. Sometimes he brought his three sons along (more often once they reached adulthood), occasionally he brought his wife and two daughters, but mostly he went with his pals. They took the town like a boatful of Vikings. On Saturdays postgame, they stopped at their traditional drinking spots—Parisi's, Corby's, Joe's Tavern, even the Linebacker Inn—and staggered from one to the next. "I remember, we'd drink shots and beers, shots and beers," recalls Sweeney, the retired fire captain. "We don't drink shots and beers anymore. We're too old for that." One of their group would commandeer the piano at Parisi's, an Italian restaurant near campus, and pound out songs and take requests until the staff kicked them out. Old barman that he is, Gadawski, whenever he entered a place, would talk up the tender and grease his palm with a bill folded twice. The drinks would then flow until beyond last call. Mostly, Gadawski and his crew drank at Leahy's, the bar at the Morris Inn, which has over the years acquired a crowd of subway alum regulars who come in six times a year. Gadawski has known Murf, Leahy's head barman, since Murf's first season on the job in 1982. "When he got the bag, he toned it down," Murf says. "But he used to go wild, boy. He died and went to heaven every weekend. *Every weekend*." For housing, Gadawski had his connections as well. He and his group would stay at the home of a Notre Dame professor of biochemistry, Tom Nowak, originally of Niagara Falls. The Gadawskis had their own set of keys. Later, Gadawski befriended the manager of the Morris Inn, always booked solid by the whales for home-game weekends. But the manager was married to a Niagara Falls football star, and for Gadawski on Saturday nights she nearly always found a room vacated by a whale who had left early.

Every game day, the Gadawski entourage tailgated in the same spot next to the Joyce Center. Like the Neighborhood of Hope, they joined forces with groups from other cities—South Bend, Detroit, Dallas. Food from the Gadawski menu was spread across folding tables. The football-pool board came down off Gadawski's backbar and went up at Notre Dame on the tailgate of Gadawski's car. "Anybody was welcome. People would walk by, grab a beer, get their names on the board for the scores, and everything else. I'd say hundreds of people came. I'm talkin' from all over the country. We always met new people every game." Like many others, Gadawski's powerful draw to Notre Dame appears to be rooted in this very idea—the Notre Dame Family. "I got so many friends there now—as many friends at Notre Dame as back home. Friends! I'm not talkin' about a bunch of people. I'm talkin' about *friends*. And you know what happens? I love those people." Sweeney has noticed this as well, but he puts it in different terms. "It's like when you find a good seat at a good tavern. You always go back there, and you don't wanna leave. Eddie at Notre Dame, he found a good seat."

Forces have recently conspired to put an end to the Gadawski tailgate. First and foremost, since he no longer goes back to every game, the party lost much of its consistency. But then, this year, when a few of Gadawski's old regulars went to the Michigan home opener, attempting to keep up traditions, they pulled into the Joyce Center lot and received some bad news. The parking attendant barred their entrance. They now needed a special pass, which they had not needed in prior years. Unable to enter, they couldn't find their old mates, and the tailgate evaporated once and, perhaps, for all.

For all the intemperance of a Notre Dame weekend, Gadawski, like most other pilgrims, cut the profane with the sacred. After pulling off the interstate early on Saturday morning, before doing anything else, he made his first stop at the Grotto for a candle and a quick prayer. With the weekend festivities complete, his last stop before pulling onto the interstate on Sunday morning, no matter whether the hangovers churned, was 7 a.m. Mass in the Crypt Chapel in the basement of the Basilica. The priest who presided over this service called it a "no-frills Mass," and this and other elements appealed to Eddie Gadawski. "Lou Holtz went to that Mass," he says. "I used to beat him to Communion. Then I'd run outside and meet him out there and say hello. And then, me and the guys, we'd get in the car and have something to eat and then"—he whistles through his tooth—"*sayonara.*"

All through the hours leading up to kickoff on Saturday, October 23, Notre Dame vs. Boston College, the rain came down. The beer tents behind the Morris Inn grew packed with fans. Leahy's and the lobby of the Morris Inn became O'Hare on a day of mass cancellations. Out of the elements, Eddie Gadawski sat at a table inside Leahy's drinking Bud Light and awaiting kickoff. His camp surrounded him—Sweeney, David, Larry, Mary Beth, the Angels, and the rest. Gadawski had not been to campus since last season, and he had been missed. When he first walked into Leahy's on Friday, Murf said, "Gadawski! Holy cow. Where you been? I thought I saw you on *Most Wanted.*"

David was somewhat protective of his grandfather, and last night he had coerced him into quitting the Morris Inn bar perhaps a little earlier than the old man may have liked. They took a cab back. Pete McKee and the Buffalo alumni club had reserved for the pilgrims a block of rooms at St. Joseph's Hall, an old, creaky building on the other side of St. Joseph's Lake, adjacent to Moreau Seminary. St. Joseph's Hall had once served as the CSC seminary building, but, after Moreau was built in the late 1950s, had been converted into the Sacred Heart Parish Center. On home-game weekends, the parish in turn converted it, like Moreau, into a fan hostelry, $40 a night. The fans slept in rooms like monk's cells and waddled down the halls to communal bathrooms, a dose of dorm life.

On Friday night, Gadawski had wanted to hike from the Morris Inn back to the hall. On the way, he wanted to pay a visit to the Grotto, a ritual he had skipped when the bus had first arrived that afternoon, perhaps a little out of sorts following the beer shortage. David had convinced him to forgo the plan. "He shouldn't be walking all that way back," David said. "I don't want him to get hurt again. That wasn't fun having him in the hospital." Two years earlier, Gadawski on game day had descended the Grotto steps and said his prayers. Afterward, attempting to take a seat on one of the benches, he missed the bench. He landed hard, got up, soldiered on, feeling that a few drinks at Leahy's might resolve much of the problem and bring the blood back into his face. Instead, his friend the hotel manager called an ambulance. Not only had he cracked a rib, he had come down with pneumonia. He did not return to Niagara Falls on the bus and remained in the hospital for three days. "We were without our leader," said one of his crew.

Now, Gadawski was having reservations about hiking all the way over to the stadium, up the ramps and staircases into the upper decks, down an aisle stuffed with people, and into his seat on a wooden bench. Plus the rain. Plus the chill. Plus the lack of Bud Light inside Notre Dame Stadium. In the morning, when the rain had started, he had said, "Why would you come to the game and *not go* to the game?" But later in the day he told me, "I may be there; I don't know," and soon thereafter David was walking around the crowded beer tent holding two tickets aloft—his and his grandfather's—for sale to anyone for face. As it turned out, Gadawski would miss all the shrines on this year's pilgrimage.

This mirrored his whole approach to the 2004 season. In September he had wanted to travel to multiple games in addition to the bus trip, taking advantage of the warm weather. As each week passed, he postponed the idea until no warm-weather games remained. "I wish I felt better," he said around the time of the Stanford game, contemplating his missed opportunities. "I wish I felt *a lot* better. But you get to a point—not that you don't feel good—but you can't do too much." He therefore reset his goals. For many years, Gadawski and his wife had made use of Notre Dame's almost perennial appearances in New Year's Day bowls—Arizona, Florida, Texas, New Orleans—to take a vacation, their only vacation as a couple each year. At one point during the Holtz era, they made ten bowl games in a row. They had seen a national championship won, they had seen more than one national championship slip away. He wanted to take Irene to a bowl game this year. At eighty-four, with his legs weakening, with cancer likely still lurking somewhere in his body, he said, "Never know—this might be the last chance."

Speculation had it that if Notre Dame could just split the rest of the games on its schedule, with probable losses to Tennessee in Knoxville and to No. 1 Southern Cal in Los Angeles, Notre Dame would be bowl eligible at 7-4 and likely headed to the Gator Bowl in Jacksonville,

Florida, warm as South Bend in late September. And a win against Boston College this weekend would put them securely on the track.

For the Notre Dame fan base as a whole, the game against Boston College had become invested with meaning as well, ever since the Eagles had ended Notre Dame's chances for a national title in 1993 and had ended Notre Dame's 8-0 win streak in 2002. Over the last decade, Boston College had crept its way under the collective skins of Notre Dame people like an ugly case of ringworm. To most Irish fans, Boston College was little more than a chippy arriviste program filching nickels from the pockets of the Notre Dame Lazarus. Some Notre Dame fans, mostly students and alumni, had come to refer to BC as Fredo, a reference to the *Godfather*—Michael Corleone's idiot older brother. After their 2002 victory, BC players had ripped turf off the field of Notre Dame Stadium and rioted in the locker room like UK soccer thugs overserved by the pubs of Manchester. It did not help that BC was a Jesuit school, an order of priests with a reputation as arrogant and worldly, and therefore resented by other Catholics. Many fans wondered why Boston College was on the schedule at all. Defeat them and the win meant little, since BC was never a title contender. Lose to them and it would ruin the season. Knute Rockne, as brilliant a capitalist as he was a head coach would have agreed. He had a rule never to play other Catholic schools, for to do so might split the loyalties of Notre Dame's burgeoning Catholic fan base. But in 1992 BC went on the schedule, thus creating the "Catholic rivalry" that would have made Rockne cringe, and the Jesuits had now defeated the Notre Dame Holy Cross three years in a row. In the parlance of sports fandom, they "owned" the Irish. This year, however, BC had an even more underwhelming team than usual. Unranked, they had not won on the road except once, by eight points over Ball State University. Most people expected victory today and the extinguishment of the three-year Jesuit win streak.

At halftime Notre Dame led 20–7, thoroughly dominating the game; at the end of the third quarter Notre Dame led 20–14, no longer dominating the game, and at the beginning of the fourth quarter Eddie Gadawski said, "I don't know, Scottie. I don't know. They'll find a way to blow it." He was sitting in the same spot inside Leahy's. His family—his daughter, his granddaughters, his son Freddy, who had driven in for the game separately with a few friends—all sat inside the stadium. David and Sweeney and Suzanne, one of the Angels, and a few others watched the game with Gadawski. The TVs were going full blast and the place was mobbed. People were sprawled out on the floors. The rain had stopped just before kickoff, and now, in the fourth quarter, the clouds had parted in a corner of the sky and the sun shown through, an omen of something.

On BC's forty-yard line, Notre Dame had the ball on third and five, and Quinn the quarterback heaved a pass into the end zone, incomplete. "Goddamnit!" Gadawski said. "I can't understand why they go for a touchdown when they just need a *first* down. I can't understand it. I'm no coach or anything, but for Christ's sake."

"You make it sound awful easy," Sweeney said. "You oughta be down there callin' plays."

Notre Dame's punt sailed out of bounds and boos went up from the Leahy's natives.

Someone said, "What a shit punt!"

Gadawski addressed the Notre Dame sidelines and the men standing on it. "Think! Think! For Christ's sake, you punt at the other guy's forty-yard line?"

Back in Niagara Falls, Gadawski has prominently displayed behind the bar a publicity photograph of Tyrone Willingham, his arms folded, the Main Building in the background. The head coach's handwriting reads, "To Gadawski's Restaurant, Best Wishes, Ty Willingham." Before the season started, Gadawski held fast to optimism. "I think what's his name's gonna do pretty good."

"Who?"

"The head coach! He's got his team this year, he's got his draft choices in there, I think they'll do good. One thing I know, they're not gonna be lousy. But it's gonna take time! They gotta get the kids that *wanna* come down there and play for Notre Dame. They gotta get the good draft. It's gonna take *time*."

By about midseason, using evidence provided by the BYU defeat and the Purdue blowout, Gadawski seemed to have shifted his opinion. Enjoying a beer one evening while his son tended bar, Gadawski said in his singsong, out of nowhere and in a kind of lament, "Tyrone . . . *Ty*-rone . . . Oh, Ty-*rone!*" Billy Grace, an old friend and a

Gadawski's regular, sat at the bar and voiced his worry that Willingham might never attain high levels of success at Notre Dame.

Gadawski said, "I'm with you. It's the coaching—I don't give a shit,
it's all the coaching." Especially distasteful to Gadawski was Willingham's lack of demonstrable emotion on the sideline. "He doesn't have
any *demeanor* out there. Where's the demeanor? A kid could screw
up—and nothing. Game could be going to shit—nothing. What the hell
is this?" And he mimed a face, an imitation of Ty Willingham. An
index finger held to his cheek, his chin thrust out, his brow furrowed,
a hard, grave stare projecting from his eyes. "This don't mean shit."
And Gadawski used the index finger of his other hand, and he made
the identical expression. The Stare, The Look, the mesmeric counte-
nance that Willingham had famously perfected over the years—what
was once seen as an indication of the head coach's motivational skill
had become a source of high irritation.

With 3:42 left on the clock, Notre Dame kicked a field goal and held
the lead 23–17. With 1:33 left on the clock, Boston College went for it
on fourth down. The snap, the drop, a BC receiver wide open at the
sideline. He caught the ball across midfield, first down, and Leahy's
crowd erupted in on itself—an implosion. Groans from the chest like a
sucking wound.

Someone broke the silence. "If they lose this ball game, he'll be
fired. And there won't be any criticism."

With sixty seconds left on the clock, with Boston College on Notre
Dame's thirty-yard line, a receiver made a leaping catch in the end
zone to enduring disbelief in Leahy's Lounge. A lone woman's quiet
voice: "Oh no. Oh, no." And then a long, uncomfortable silence expanded inside the bar. Gadawski simply looked up at the television
screen. Then, someone laughed. The replay on TV demonstrated the
failed pass coverage and Gadawski said, "He got beat three times!" The
extra point made BC's lead an extra point, 24–23 (Notre Dame had earlier missed one of its), the enemy out front for the first time in the
game.

With thirteen seconds left on the clock, Notre Dame had the ball on
BC's forty-yard line. The ball zipped hard into double coverage and
bounced off shoulder pads. A fan beseeched the television, "Catch!
The! Ball!" Seven seconds left. A penalty flag, false start, Irish. Further

dismay inside Leahy's. The TV announcer said, "Notre Dame has been outplayed severely by BC in the second half. Severely." One second left, no time-outs remaining, and the field-goal unit scrambled out to the hashes, players tripping over other players as in the climactic scene of a screwball comedy. Amid the chaos, somehow the long-snapper snapped the ball to a player who caught it and jammed it into the ground, and somehow a kicker was there to take a swipe with his leg. The ball got airborne, but not for long, and worm-burned out of the TV frame. Zero seconds left on the clock.

Gadawski had switched to Budweiser for obscure reasons. As the Boston College players rushed the field, Gadawski said, "There goes my bowl game."

Outside, a vast depressive silence immediately descended over campus, interrupted only by the high, girlish shrieks of BC students celebrating inside the stadium and the murmured conversation of Notre Dame fans as they milled rather aimlessly about. Some fan's ten-year-old son was sobbing. A priest stood in the Morris Inn lobby. Someone said, "What did you think of that, Father?"

"Not much."

Nearby, a fan appeared to be on the verge of a nervous breakdown. He muttered to himself, "He's no coach! I'm tired of this shit. That's pure Arena League bullshit! Pooch-punting on the thirty-yard line? Jesus Chriminy! That's pure Arena League, pure fucking bullshit Arena League."

Gadawski said, "I wanted to take Irene to a bowl game. Now? No way. It's over." He shook his head like a man wincing after a missed putt. His jaw set. A wry half-smile.

"You still got more chances," someone said.

"No, I only got so much time left." Gadawski paused. He enlarged his smile. He winked. "I figure, fifteen years. Fifteen years and I'm bailin' out!"

Back from the game, his friends and family gathered around his table, arranging dinner plans. Gadawski canceled the idea of going to Parisi's, his old haunt. But then he said, "Whatever I wanna do, it don't make any difference. . . . I should go to the Grotto before I go home. It's easy. When we're done eating, I'll go down there, light a candle, go home, back to the hall."

Gadawski and his clan eventually ate in the Morris Inn dining room. Through dinner he said hardly a word, abdicating his position to Sweeney, who held court in his stead. When the check arrived and after Sweeney had performed his last toast, Gadawski said, "I'm goin' to the Grotto after dinner. On the way back to the hall."

The Judge said he'd be walking back with his sons. Eddie could walk along with them.

David and Mary Beth did not approve.

"Grandpa," David said.

"Dad," Mary Beth said.

"We'll take a cab, Eddie. It'll be safer," said Barbara, the lead Angel.

"Remember when you got hurt a few years ago. We don't want to have to leave you in the hospital again."

Gadawski, drinking a beer, looked tired. "I'll be fine! It's a short walk! I've done it a million times. I'll light a candle, say a prayer—I go every trip."

The Judge said, "Yeah, it's no problem. He can walk with us."

Definitively, motherly, Barbara declared, "We've already ordered a cab. So that's how we're getting back."

The conversation drifted to other places, other topics. All Grotto talk effectively shut down, Gadawski that night went to bed early. After a brief no-frills Mass the next morning in the chapel of St. Joseph's Hall, performed by the Notre Dame alumni priest who rode on the Buffalo holy bus, the convoy pulled out of the parking lot and reversed its pilgrimage. The ride back to Niagara Falls went off uneventfully, quietly and largely without alcohol. Barbara Antenson observed, "Eddie didn't have too much to say."

11

The Wailing Wall

After Notre Dame's fourth loss to Boston College in a row, the fans did not, this time, direct their anger at the Jesuits. In response to the desperate queries of a couple fans who had approached him after the game, a high-ranking CSC priest, long one of Monk Malloy's chief aides-de-camp, said, according to those fans, "Ty is a good man. He'll get his five years." He said his words definitively, then bottled the conversation. And yet, at around the same time, outside the Mendoza School of Business, where a postgame Mass had just ended, John Affleck-Graves, the new executive vice president, was heard to say, with a cryptic smile on his face, "We won't win another game. It's over." Graves, a native of South Africa, chair of the finance department, and the first lay EVP in the history of the university, had been elected to his office at the same time as Fr. John Jenkins, a close friend. Graves, then, was to Jenkins what Joyce was to Hesburgh—his right-hand man. In recent weeks, Graves had also addressed a number of alumni gatherings. Inevitably the subject of the football program arose. Paraphrased by an alumnus who had attended one of these meetings, Graves said, "Our coaches are well compensated. We expect them to win."

Here, then, were two high Notre Dame functionaries speaking a different language.

Notre Dame's "constituencies," as Monk Malloy likes to call them, are many and overlapping. On a normal day during the season, between six thousand and ten thousand people will direct their browsers to ND Nation—alumni, subway alumni, casual fans, though mostly die-hard fans, nobodies, and significant benefactors. Most of them are lurkers, but a lot of them are registered members and posters of varying prolificacy. (Membership, which costs nothing, is required to post, but anyone can read the threads.) After the Boston College loss, the number of average daily visitors doubled and tripled as fans who did not normally do so went to the Internet for coverage, discussion, guidance, rumormongering, and highly emotional vent. They signed up in such great numbers that ND Nation froze its membership rolls at around forty-five hundred.

It had long been the Internet's most prominent Notre Dame fan community, and as with all things Internet, its origins were humble. In the middle 1990s a group of Notre Dame undergraduates barnacled onto the university Listserv to create a forum called the Irish Recruiting Journal, or IRJ, dedicated, of course, to the discussion of Notre Dame recruiting. The site soon attracted an audience far beyond the campus dorm rooms. Among them was a subway alumnus living in Seattle named Scott Engler and a subway alumnus living in Omaha, Nebraska, named Mike Frank. A mortgage broker by day, Frank was a recruitnik of such fervor that over the years his hobby developed into his vocation. At the time, this subgenre of sportswriting—a cross between journalism and talent evaluation—was burgeoning into something more than a cottage industry. From like-minded individuals covering other college teams, Frank learned how to go about reporting on the university enrollment plans of star high-school footballers. He added his news and analysis to the IRJ site, and this began to draw an even larger audience. The IRJ received so many hits that the university kicked the forum off its overtaxed servers.

Scott Engler, a broadcast journalist by trade, a peripatetic news anchor for network affiliates, now with WB17 in Philadelphia, took over the site when the undergraduates received their degrees and left school. Engler was born on the South Side of Chicago and raised in northern New Jersey, perhaps two of the nation's most fervent subway alum hotbeds. After several predecessor sites went in and out of existence, Engler and a group of other IRJ regulars—including John Vannie and Mike Coffey—gave birth to ND Nation in 1999. Collectively they are known as BoardOps—the board operators. Soon after founding the site, they incorporated ND Nation. To cover the cost of the site's cyber-upkeep, they stage an annual fund-raising drive, like NPR. Except for one year in the early going, they've never had to pay out of their own pocket. Mike Frank, meanwhile, continued his vocation, hooked up with one of the two major college recruiting networks, the

Insiders.com, now called Scout.com, and began his own subscription Notre Dame site, which works as a kind of franchise.

Literally countless Notre Dame fan blogs and Web sites and forums exist on the Internet. In addition to ND Nation, there are perhaps a half dozen other free message boards. After ND Nation, the biggest is UHND.com—the "Unofficial Home of Notre Dame football." There are two major subscription pay sites, *Blue & Gold Illustrated* and Mike Frank's *Irish Eyes.* Feuds will sometimes erupt between members of the various boards for one reason or another, and this has given rise to a sub-subculture of cyber-fan communities. There are private, members-only chat rooms and ultrasecretive e-mail societies. There are covert message boards within message boards, accessible only to those in the know and requiring additional passwords—so covert, in fact, that I have been forbidden to reveal where these sites are located for fear that they will become overridden by the uninitiated and the unwanted. It's all a little Masonic and, to some degree, built on status.

On any of these sites, one acquires status by demonstrating insider knowledge. The most popular posters, no matter the Web site, are generally the ones who profess to have some kind of university connection, whether to the coaching staff, the athletic department, the administration, or even the development office. Enough psychological problems are manifest among the fans out there on the Internet that a lot of serious bullshit goes up on the boards. At ND Nation and elsewhere, however, enough well-connected people have memberships that a lot of truth goes up on the boards as well—a phenomenon demonstrated by the fact that every Notre Dame beat writer, bar none, lurks on the sites for tips, and also as a way to take the temperature of the masses, to get a feel for the sentiment of the fan base. So does the athletic department. Sometimes, when a reporter calls up and asks for confirmation on a bit of information, the athletic department will direct the reporter to a post on ND Nation and say that the post has it right. The administration lurks as well, but no one, of course, will readily own up to this. Posts are printed out on campus and placed onto desks inside corner suites, and the recipients of these printouts may sometimes wince. The record of the minutes at an administrative meeting once included a complaint that confidential information had leaked onto ND Nation, a factoid that itself leaked onto ND Nation.

Jeff Jeffers, of WNDU-TV, the dean of South Bend's television sports anchors, spends a lot of time lurking and freely admits it. "The fan boards, and ND Nation in particular, are more powerful than anyone gives them credit for. It's like trashy movies. No one admits to watching them, but everyone does. And it's somewhat unique to Notre Dame. It's a town meeting times a thousand. That's what it's come to. Not everything on there is true, but you'd be surprised at what is. And if it is true, you'd better have it, too. Or, at the very least, you'd better check it out. The guys who run it know their stuff."

Each site has its own posting rules that, if broken repeatedly, will get you banned and possibly blacklisted. Rule No. 18 at ND Nation reads, "Starting rumors in our forums is strictly prohibited. Spreading rumors in our forums (within tasteful boundaries) is heartily encouraged." The distinction between the two is subtle, yet one that is also taught in schools of journalism. Corollary rules warn that posters claiming connections to university insiders can expect a thoroughgoing evaluation by BoardOps, and messages regarding personal contact with "players, coaches, or administrators outside of the field/court—especially when those posts involve quoted or recounted conversations" will be "vetted" by BoardOps. "We reserve the right to prohibit publication." Sometimes protocol is followed, much of the time it is not, and BoardOps must keep a vigilant eye on what appears on Rock's House, ND Nation's football-centric forum. Engler feels a sense of responsibility and speaks like the broadcast journalist he is. "We want timely information, but not crazy speculation or, for that matter, information that might hurt people."

ND Nation also has a board of directors, for lack of a better term, a group of about fifteen men, all of them Notre Dame alumni save Scott Engler. Among others they include two cardiologists, the dean of a law school, the retired head of the international division of Citibank, a regional managing partner in a thousand-lawyer law firm, and the chief executive of a manufacturing company. They helped John Vannie draft the C4C letter, they donate to their alma mater in sums, they have friends in Dome offices, and they manage the scuttlebutt on the boards. If someone needs vetting, they have the ability to vet.

ND Nation has become a kind of news service with a thousand potential amateur correspondents and an audience approaching six figures. During times of high stress—and the loss to Boston College certainly qualified—the site will receive hundreds of thousands of hits. Fans incessantly click the refresh button. "We've blown out three servers already," Engler says. Their Web-hosting company will call up and complain that ND Nation has slowed every other site hosted by the company. Posts sometimes grow hysterical. Engler and the other BoardOps call it emotaposting, and at ND Nation it is strictly forbidden. See Rule No. 23: " 'I was angry/frustrated/[insert other euphemism for pissed off here]' is **never** validation for posting **anything**." See Rule No. 24: "DO NOT POST IN ALL CAPS." During the up-and-down 2004 season, fed up by all the emotaposting, BoardOps repeatedly spiked posts, killed threads, nuked the entire board, all in an effort to raise the intellectual level of the forum. They tacked warnings and admonitions to the top of the board—do not vent mindlessly, control yourselves. "Sometimes it's like talking to your kids," Engler said. BoardOps had always possessed a low tolerance for inarticulate posts—mindlessly rah-rah as well as mindlessly despairing. They banned and they blacklisted, and this made ND Nation by far the most articulate site in Notre Dame fandom and, possibly for this very reason, the most popular. But in the wider cyber-college-football-fan world, ND Nation had also acquired a reputation as totalitarian, draconian, fascistic. The handle *BoardOps,* in a fire-red font, appeared in the bylines of posts that meted out their punishments and harsh-toned reprimands. Behind the curtain projected by the BoardOps byline, they came across like Oz's wizard. In 2003, as the ten-year decline elongated into Willingham's regime, the anger/frustration/insert-pissed-off-euphemism increased to such an extent that John Vannie created a separate board for those who wished to vent. He called it The Wailing Wall.

It did not always work as a fail-safe. Much wailing still occurred away from the wall and out in the main forum. Despair had, indeed, infected Notre Dame Nation, the fan base as well as the synecdochic Web site, and morale after the BC game reached an all-time low. "I'm Starting to Crack," read one subject line. "A subway alum's lament," read another. "Anyone else stop putting their ND flag up at home?" read a third. Another fan said he no longer watched the games in real time. Instead, he taped them and checked the final score later in the day.

"That way, I'm pleasantly surprised when they win (Michigan) and don't waste my time and energy when they lose (Purdue)." Another fan said, "For the first time in memory I am not planning my Saturday around the ND game. . . . And I am resigned that there is no reason to hope."

On the boards, a longtime poster with the handle Beijing Irish related an anecdote. A 1968 graduate of Notre Dame, he is a partner high in the corporate tree of a management-consulting firm of wide influence. He currently lives in Prague, transferred there a few years ago from, of course, Beijing. For the BC game, he made the transatlantic pilgrimage back to his alma mater for the first time in eight years. He wrote a post that related his journey, but it was lost in a boardwide nuking. He recapitulated the gist in an e-mail to me. More than substandard football ("I traveled all the way from Europe only to sit in the rain and watch that pageant of incompetence and gutlessness"), he was taken aback by the "lack of spirit and enthusiasm" among the fans, particularly students and alumni. After the game, he visited a tailgate thrown by a few classmates. "The men were tight-lipped, shuffling and looking at the ground, not saying much. The place reeked of smoldering anger and resentment. I talked to one of the wives. She said she had come to hate football Saturdays. The drive back to Chicago had become torture, no conversation for miles; the kids were afraid to say anything. She was almost in tears. She said, 'This has got to change—it's destroying my family.' "

Because of its large audience, ND Nation, like the editorial page of a New York broadsheet, has the power to create opinion as well as reflect it. Maybe because of the site's rather imperial name, which through sheer taxonomy seemed to want to represent the whole of Notre Dame fandom, and doubtless because of the site's influence, the university required that ND Nation include a disclaimer on its home page—"ND Nation is not affiliated with, sponsored by, or endorsed by the University of Notre Dame"—the only fan site so required. "We're a little surprised they haven't tried to shut us down," Engler says. But the university has not attempted to do that, despite the overarching tenor of the Web site, which included bloglike editorial content written by the BoardOps boys. Beginning with the C4C letter, ND Nation had set out to forge a unified and coherent message, and that message, of course, was one of opposition.

John Vannie, chief drafter of the C4C letter, who composes all the pregame and postgame articles on ND Nation through the season, wrote in his Boston College "postmortem," "As the most storied program in college athletics drifts further into oblivion, Notre Dame alumni and fans can only hope those charged with its restoration will awaken soon from their decade-long slumber."

On October 26, three days after the BC game, Engler wrote a piece entitled "The Five-Year Myth and Forgotten Excellence" and published it on the site's home page. It took the "Call for Change" letter to its threatened conclusion—posthaste, Notre Dame ought to fire Ty Willingham. To continue with the status quo would risk the permanent marginalization of ND football. And it preemptively argued that Hesburgh's rule of the five-year contract had not only lost its validity, but did not represent true precedent. Only Bob Davie and the three failed coaches of Hesburgh's presidency—Faust, Kuharich (who resigned of his own volition after year four), and Brennan—had been extended that guaranteed privilege. But, like the C4C letter, Engler's argument went beyond technicalities. They wanted Willingham fired for a larger reason. " 'Play like a champion' is not a catch phrase," Engler wrote. "It's a legacy of excellence passed down through generations that has been forgotten by the very people empowered with preserving it."

The editorial content of the site was, in large part, designed to refute the mainstream notion that these particular Notre Dame fans had gone beyond the pale, that they were obsessed with wins and losses and were delusional about the success the Irish could expect in the twenty-first century—that they had lost all "perspective." This meant summoning data to destroy the widespread opinion in the sports media that the college game had passed the Irish by; that its high academic standards meant that it could not attract high-end talent; that it handcuffed its coaches with said standards; and, therefore, that it could no longer compete with programs free of said handcuffs. ND Nation believed that this was an excuse deployed by incompetent football coaches and the administrations that protected them—demonstrated by the fact that, according to any number of talent-scouting services, the Irish possessed far more prep all-Americans and players with similar high school accolades than all but two or three of the teams on its schedule. In other words, with competent coaching, Notre Dame should be doing better than records of 5-7 and 6-6.

More importantly, however, Engler said, "We wanted to get rid of the notion that this was a bunch of fanatics who wanted to win at all costs. That characterization is wrong." It was a characterization, a stigma—of the sports zealot, of the Internet fan mobocracy, of the lunatic fringe—that ND Nation and its members had come up against many times before. See Rule No. 22: " 'Perspective' posts are forbidden. Don't patronize the group with your personal moral about how there are more important matters in life than Notre Dame sporting events. It's insulting and unnecessary. Everyone here realizes the relative importance of sports." Michael Novak, an author and philosopher and former Holy Cross seminarian (he was never ordained) and former Notre Dame visiting professor, wrote about the stigma of the sports fan in his 1976 volume *The Joy of Sports.* He recounts the experience of James Wechsler, former editor of the *New York Post,* on New Year's Day in 1974. Wechsler was at a dinner party full of New York intellectuals of one stripe or another and "when he asked his hosts if he could slip into the study to watch the end of the Notre Dame–Alabama game, he felt a cold condescension circle out from the others. . . . His secret desire voiced, the others turned on him. A journalist snapped, 'It's the most *American* thing you can do!' Wechsler knew what he meant by that: 'How could an allegedly mature man squander time watching pros claw at each other for pay, or give a damn whether Notre Dame beats Alabama?' . . . The accusation made against Wechsler is a prejudice all believers live under: 'To love sports is to love the lowest common denominator, to be lower class, adolescent, patriotic in a corny way.' The *intellectual* thing, the *liberal* thing, the *mature* thing is to set sports aside."

To defeat this kind of stigma, Engler needed to explain why Notre Dame fans gave a damn. He says, "You want the team to win, of course, but it's not a selling-your-soul issue." In fact, it seemed just the opposite. To allow the team to wallow in inconsistent play, to not even compete on the same level as the best in the land—this invalidated all that

Notre Dame had come to represent to its fans. It invalidated the mythos proclaimed by Hesburgh—Notre Dame shall offer no apologies for striving for excellence in all pursuits. It invalidated the bootstrap ethos and myth of the American immigrant, grandparents and great-grandparents overcoming their second-class status while at the same time maintaining their Faith. To keep a coach on when all evidence pointed to his ineptitude amounted to both surrender and heresy, these fans seemed to believe, a cultural sin as well as a theological one. To lose on the field was also to lose some portion of your identity as a Notre Dame fan, as member of the Family, and therefore some portion of your soul.

With just this in mind, Engler started a thread in the summer of 2004, prior to the season—"The Broken Link: What has ND's football tradition meant to you?" The thread was a conscious tactic, a way to collect personal and disparate evidence, and marshal it into a kind of argument: should Notre Dame football become further marginalized, it would mean the destruction of a kind of culture, complete and fully realized, with its own mythology, rituals, language, economy, land-marks, shrines, documents, texts, songs, prayers, icons, and long his-tory of triumph and doubt and pain—its testings of the faith. If nothing else, that faith was now being tested. Engler's themelike question thus began another outpouring of sentiment. The posts were vignettes and short essays and pieces of memoir. They read like *Grotto Stories.* In-deed, about 90 percent of the resulting essays contained a Catholic spiritual element, not uncommon on the ND Internet forums, where posts go up seemingly every day asking for prayers for an ill relative or a recently deceased Notre Dame man or woman, alumni and subway. They request candles to be lit at the Grotto. Mike Coffey has said, "To a Notre Dame alumnus, or fan, helping someone spiritually is a very real thing. Other schools' fans don't tie that in to how they root for their team. . . . It's natural that it carries over to the electronic community. And here's another thing—people don't laugh at those posts."

And so the "Broken Link" essays also read like the fan biographies of Eddie Colton and Eddie Gadawski, Tracy Hallahan and Tudy Cummings—spiritual moments, familial moments, in the stadium and at the Grotto, watching games and taking the sacraments, origins of Notre Dame enthusiasm in downtrodden places, passing the enthusiasm down through the bloodline like an heirloom. In presenting its editorial message, it's almost as if ND Nation felt a kind of responsibility toward its constituency and its psychological pain. Swayed by the Web site's message and emboldened by it, the constituency responded. Posts went up that praised in gaudy terms the ND Nation community and its overall mission, most importantly the C4C movement: "Only the worldwide passion for Notre Dame's tradition of excellence could create such a place. And now, in my opinion, it's NDN that might best ensure that ND continues that tradition into a new century." It was as if the board had a single voice.

By the middle of the fourth quarter of the BC game, that voice had summarily ruled on the question of Willingham's fitness as a football coach. More than enough evidence had been presented, these fans felt. The board, and the fan base in general, became one giant rhetorical question: How could you beat the likes of Michigan and lose to the likes of Boston College?

On the boards criticism of Willingham's coaching quickly shifted to criticism of the coach himself. "Not once in his past one and a half years of mired mediocrity has he placed the blame on himself or his inept staff. It's always jive about 'failure to execute' or 'failure to make plays.' In other words, it's the players' fault." Up until BC, almost every message-board scribe prefaced his censure of Willingham's abilities with some such phrase as "Ty is a good man, an honorable man, but . . . " or "Ty is a great representative of Notre Dame; however . . . " No longer. He came to be seen as another element in Malloy's disastrous oversight of the Notre Dame football program. "Ty represents everything that has been wrong with ND football since 1997, the acceptance of mediocrity," wrote one scribe. "I used to believe he handled himself with dignity and grace," wrote another. "Then I read his most recent press conference and quotes from the *Tribune*. He is an excuse-making, finger-pointing loser."

Indeed, Willingham and his assistants had begun, perhaps naturally, to offer reasons for each defeat—talent parity across Division I, bad breaks, bad bounces, young team, failed execution. After Purdue, Willingham said, "Purdue beat us by a lot of points supposedly, but we had as many offensive yards as it did. If we turn those into scores, it's a different ball game. But you can't say that. That's not a competitive thing to say. But we believe that if we had executed and done some things, that's the team we have." And the voice of ND Nation replied, "This is the underlying goal of any poor coaching staff, or any under-performer in general: to convince others that winning and losing, suc-ceeding and failing, overcoming and succumbing, are all based on random chance." Parallels were drawn between Willingham and Bob Davie (and, indeed, every failed Notre Dame head coach in its history) until a term was coined to refer to the final eight years of Monk Malloy's reign—Davieham.

No matter how much heat Willingham took from the fans, they still directed most of their venom at the university leadership, and Malloy in particular. Long threads on ND Nation intensely dissected the poli-tics of the situation. As the board's preferred subject matter, the X's and O's of football had long ago given way to the X's and O's of Notre Dame politics. Odds were being laid as to whether the university would fire Willingham at season's end. The scenario was complicated by the fact that no one seemed to know how much sway Malloy held in this am-biguous time between two presidents. The whole matter could have been boiled down to a single question: How lame was this duck? It was generally agreed that Malloy would not stand for Willingham's ouster. The media backlash alone would likely be enough to scare the admin-istration from action. There would almost certainly be charges of racism—the school's previous two failed coaches, Davie and Faust, had received their five years. That Malloy, in his last significant act as president, would dismiss the first African-American head coach in Notre Dame history, one of only four in Division I, two years shy of the half-decade guarantee that Hesburgh had proclaimed, almost ex cathe-dra, as sacred—this was unthinkable.

But following Monk's own ouster the previous April, other forces had, of course, arisen behind the scenes. President-elect John Jenkins and his right-hand man, John Affleck-Graves, were, as yet, unknown quantities. Kevin White, athletic director, stood firmly in the Malloy camp, or so most of ND Nation's tipsters believed, especially after White, never known for his prose style, had defended the direction of the program under Willingham by calling the season "discernible progress." It seemed that any move to dismiss Willingham would need to rise out of the same body to which Hesburgh had signed over the university forty years earlier, the same group to which the alumni group of 412 had addressed their "Call for Change" letter—the board of trustees.

"Stewards of the University and its glorious football history," one poster wrote, "where the hell have you been?"

"One thing we have learned in the last ten years is that as bad as it seems, it only gets worse," wrote another.

The consensus seemed to be that only a disastrous 2004 season would move the trustees to action. Disastrous, however, was a relative term. To many Notre Dame fans disaster had been an applicable concept since the Brigham Young loss in September, notwithstanding the Michigan victory. But, they worried, people who did not follow the team as closely as the diehards might determine that Willingham and his team had simply suffered a few bad breaks, that he "needed more time," as his defenders liked to say. Therefore, the fans began to deliberate a calculus of win-loss ratios that would succeed in convincing the key Notre Dame decision makers of Willingham's ineffectiveness and the necessity of his removal. After the BC defeat, Notre Dame had a record of 5-3, with three games remaining—at Tennessee, home against Pittsburgh, at Southern Cal. If judged on sheer athletic talent and home-field advantages, Notre Dame would lose the first and last games and win the middle, producing a record of 6-5. But Willingham had always shown an exasperating knack for upsetting stronger teams every once in a while, and losing to weaker teams not so once in a while. Which pretty much meant you could throw your predictions to the wind.

"I will confess . . . I hope UT wins tomorrow, I hope Pitt and USC win as well. I want this nightmare over with. This has to end now."

"For the first time in my life, I will be cheering against Notre Dame."

An enormous debate ensued as to the ethics of rooting for the enemy in order to achieve a greater good. One group of sophists, heading down to the game in Knoxville, purported to solve the problem by wearing bags over their heads for the duration of the contest. The whole issue marked an inflection point of much Sturm und Drang. The terms *bandwagon fan* and *fair-weather fan* were derisively applied.

Opinions dissenting from the party line did occur, though in diminishing number—the old Pollyanna vs. Cassandra schism.

Hoping for losses struck the Pollyannas, as it had Billy Powers and Tudy Cummings, as treasonous, whatever their thoughts on the merits of Willingham as a football coach. On the day of the Tennessee game, one of those Pollyannas, Jim Maloney, sat in his house in Chesterton, Indiana, halfway between South Bend and Chicago, surrounded by his family. On a big-screen television that took up a quarter of the wall in the family room, Ty Willingham jogged out of the tunnel at Neyland Stadium with his boys in their white away-game jerseys.

Peggy Maloney said, "Too bad, Ty. I think you're probably outta here."

Her father, Jim Maloney, thought this a bit premature. "I hope not! But if he doesn't win games like this, he's gonna have a hard time."

On the Notre Dame fan message boards, Jim Maloney is known as Chesterlep, and in his guise as Chesterlep, Jim Maloney is famous. As far as message board personalities go, his fame is rather unorthodox. At first it is not at all clear what his posts are meant to communicate. About three times a day a post will go up on ND Nation, UHND.com, ESPN's Notre Dame message board, NotreDameFans.com, and the open forums of *Blue & Gold Illustrated* and Mike Frank's *Irish Eyes*. The posts carry subject lines that say things like "Lep's Player of the Game 10/25" or "New Unique Stadium 11/16" or "2 Million Thanks 11/19," in which Chesterlep expressed gratitude toward his audience for helping him pass the "2 million mark for individual picture views since Jan. 03." Every one of his posts contains a link to Chesterton-lep.com, and each new post indicates that Maloney has uploaded a fresh digital photo album. Omnibus, archive, gallery, treasury, the Web site consists of a hundred thousand images of Notre Dame campus sites and game-day scenes and player photos and fan homages—all of the pictures shot by Maloney or Darlene, his wife, or one of their children or grandchildren or some Irish fan with a camera whom they've met through the Internet and induced into going on assignment. Their subjects range from the typical—Domes, spires, Grotto caves, stadium facades, in all seasons, in all weathers, and at every time of day—to the strange and the surprising—graves in Cedar Grove cemetery, obscure statuary, ancient trees on wooded pathways, gargoyles, doorways, lampposts, architectural details. For Jim Maloney and Darlene, taking these pictures and uploading them onto their Web site has grown into an all-consuming hobby. "Everyone we know says we're nuts, but that's okay," Maloney says. Their site has created a community of its own, especially among those subway alumni who have never made the trip to campus, and their site has become a massive virtual pilgrimage tour. The fans send Maloney grateful e-mails by the hundreds.

He has not seen a game in Notre Dame Stadium since 1984. In that year, he was in a car accident and suffered nerve damage from the neck down. Arthritis has since crept into his limbs, he can't move around too well, and the crowds at the games have become too much for him to handle. He does, however, try to make it to every pep rally, which he photographs profusely, and he assigns his corps of stringers to record game-day scenes. Whenever weather permits, he and Darlene hop in the car and drive the hour to South Bend for another round of shooting, always looking to improve their craft. Imperfect older pictures come down and aesthetically superior ones go up. He also likes to observe pre-season training camp, snapping pictures of the players in their pads. This year, in August, he stood near the fields with a camera around his neck. A small plump man with a thick orange-brown beard going gray at the tips, aged sixty-one, he wore a tweed driving cap. Hair spilled out of the cap and nearly to his shoulders. He held in his hand a resplendently gnarled and lacquered blackthorn walking stick. Give him a pipe and he could have been a crofter on a kame surrounded in all directions by emerald isle. His parents were born in County Sligo, and Maloney grew up in Gary, Indiana, son of a steelworker and ardent subway alumnus. His alma mater is the University of Indiana, Bloomington, the sports teams of which might as well not exist, including the basketball. For thirty-seven years he has taught high school, mostly social studies and geography, and a ceramic jar on a table next to his La-Z-Boy says ASHES OF PROBLEM STUDENTS.

Watching the Tennessee game, he sat in his La-Z-Boy like a pasha on his pillows. Unquestionably he was the lord of his domain, and he struck an imposing figure. He wore a flannel nightgown of blue-and-green plaid, and it draped around him like a muumuu stitched from the material of a dozen kilts. Whenever at home, because of the pain in his joints, he prefers his nightgowns, custom-tailored by Darlene, a professional seamstress. He has a closetful of them in a selection of designs and color schemes. "Don't worry," he said. "At school, I wear clothes."

Almost the full Maloney clan had gathered for the game, as they do eleven times a year. Darlene sat in a second La-Z-Boy. Scattered about on couches and the shag-carpet floor were three daughters, a son, their spouses, and three grandchildren of college age. All of them were devout Notre Dame fans. A Celtic cross rested atop a stand-up piano. A PLAY LIKE A CHAMPION TODAY sign hung above the door. Against the side of the television leaned a framed lithograph of St. Patrick—halo, scepter, miter, beard long as a wizard's, snakes slithering around his ankles and through his legs and into the sea and out of Ireland. The lithograph usually hangs on a wall, but Maloney takes it down and puts it next to the television for the duration of football season. It serves as a kind of charm as well as an homage to his father, who did the same thing, though against a radio, fifty and sixty years ago while Frank Leahy coached on the Irish sidelines. When the team struggled, his father would fix his gaze on old St. Pat and mutter oaths to the icon.

As the broadcast began, Maloney focused his attention on the screen. "Don't write it down if I curse. Because that only comes when they lose."

I asked him if he thought Notre Dame would lose.

"I'm always pessimistic," he said. "I'm Irish."

A blimp view of Neyland Stadium, awash in Volunteer orange, appeared on the TV screen. Maloney said, "All this orange is going to kill me. It's like the British Army under Cromwell."

Already he looked exhausted. "By the time the game starts, I'm just worn-out, because I get too excited. And the boards, the message boards—they're driving me crazy. They're traitors. These people, they want to *lose* to get rid of Willingham."

Inside a pocket sown into the belly of his makeshift, Maloney kept a pack of extra-long Pall Mall Light Menthols. As the game wore on— 7–3 Notre Dame, 7–10 Tennessee, 14–10 Notre Dame, 14–13 Notre Dame—he drew the cigarettes out of his pocket, one after the other, and he drew their effluvia through his beard and into his lungs. His whiskers seemed to act as a kind of second filter. Inside his ashtray grew a heaping litter of butts. During particularly tense games in the past he has gone through three packs. As plays developed, he chewed his nails. He put his hands to his cheeks like the figure in *The Scream* painting. He moaned and he guffawed. He closed his eyes for long periods. He put his palm to his brow as if suffering from a migraine. He pulled the visor of his driving cap down over his eyes, then cocked it to the side like a street urchin's. In the aftermath, after the tackle, he lit another cigarette—visible relief—and the stress sighed from his body with a long jet of menthol.

Earlier in the season, Tennessee's first-string quarterback had gone down with injury, and now, on the last play of the first half, its backup quarterback, Erik Ainge, dropped back to pass. A Notre Dame linebacker came off the edge and pile-drove Ainge to the turf, shoulder first. The backup did not immediately rise.

Maloney's son, Sean, registered his pleasure. "Yes! He's down!"

His father said, "Hey! That's not nice."

"That's not nice? What did you teach us when we were kids?"

Maloney looked at his son. He looked at me. "Blood makes the grass grow," he said. "What can I say?"

At about this moment, as Ainge walked off the field and into the locker room, the fan message boards nearly blew apart with doomsday speculation. Because of the quarterback injury, Tennessee, ranked No. 9 in the nation, would likely fall to the Willingham-led Irish, saving the coach's job and ensuring the continuation of mediocrity for who knew how long.

As expected, Tennessee's third-string quarterback could mount no effective passing game. The Tennessee running backs, also depleted by injury, ran into the teeth of Notre Dame's high-quality defensive line. The Volunteers had no ability to exploit the weak Irish secondary, and the fourth quarter developed into a scoreless struggle. As the minutes wound down, with Notre Dame holding the lead 17–13, Maloney said, "No one thought we could beat 'em but me!"

One of his daughters said, "Don't say that. We still have one more down."

Maloney covered his eyes with his hands. On Tennessee's final play of the game, fourth and eighteen yards, the third-string quarterback stood under center. In the Maloney family room, there was a curious before-the-storm quietude. The quarterback threw an incomplete pass, and Notre Dame took over on downs and knelt its way to victory.

Maloney has a throaty helium squeak of a voice. It is, indeed, as one would imagine a leprechaun's. Now, with the game clock at zero, his voice went up half an octave more. *"It's over!"* Maloney said. "It's! Over!" From his La-Z-Boy, the Irish pasha punched his fists like pistons, like body blows. "Yes! Yes! Take that, people! Attaway! Take that, you dirty old orange *people!"*

He paused to consider the moment. "I wonder how they'll react to this on the boards. They'll still want Willingham fired, I'm sure. It doesn't matter what he does." A little while later, still basking in victory, he said, "I'm gonna get on the boards and say, 'See, you traitors, you!' Ha! People were actually suggesting rooting against 'em. They oughta be ashamed.

"Disloyalty pisses me off. When I read those posts, I count to ten and cool off. It takes all I can *not* to say something." Perhaps because the previous Tuesday George W. Bush had defeated John Kerry, a political metaphor suggested itself to Maloney. "I'm in the Polly group because the Pollys are like liberals. They hide. Because if they come out—the other side will kill you. Pollys don't post because they know they'll get torn apart. It's like a constant wake on these boards, even after we win. It's like hiring the wailing ladies to go to a funeral parlor and mourn and wail. I mean, c'mon, guys. We won.

"When the season is over, then you can work on stuff. Then you can think about making a coaching change. But during the season, he's your *captain.* It's like spitting on the captain of the *Titanic* while it's going down. You should be saying, 'Keep bailing! Let's go!' "

Darlene said, "I mean, giving up on Notre Dame is like giving up on one of your kids."

"That's why I don't post. They always say, 'Oh, you Pollyannas, you don't care if we lose.' Yeah, right. *I* don't care. *Me. I* don't care. I don't think so."

Maloney had not always been in the Pollyanna camp. His father raged at the head coach as much as he did at the solemn figure of St. Patrick, and young Jim followed in these footsteps. "I was even worse than my father. All the way into grade school and high school, I couldn't talk after a loss for a week."

"Whaddaya mean into grade school and high school?" Darlene said. "When I met you, you wouldn't talk until Tuesday."

"Yeah, well. It's just so hard. I get tired. To be mad till Wednesday, it's too hard. So it doesn't take me as long to recover anymore. Part of that comes with age. You know another game is coming next week, you know there will be a next season. You just gotta keep going. And those guys on the Internet, they're younger. I was the same way once. It's a good thing they didn't have a message board when I was younger, because I'd be on there railing away. Every win is precious, though."

Darlene reflected on the cyclical nature of history. "Notre Dame is like the phoenix. They'll rise from the ashes again."

"They just gotta hurry," Jim said. "When you get older, they gotta hurry up a little. One more national championship. Just one more— before I go."

In Tennessee, in Neyland Stadium, Kevin White was observed immediately after the conclusion of play gleefully hugging Ty Willingham and grinning madly, as if the candidate to whom he had committed a six-figure donation had just won office in a runoff election. He essentially said to reporters that Ty Willingham was here to stay—the vote of confidence. ND Nation howled. The revolt had begun. It had started gathering momentum after Boston College, it simmered through Tennessee, and it blew into the metaphorical streets after Notre Dame lost its very next game, 38–41, on another last-second field goal, at home to a University of Pittsburgh team with a record of 5-3, which had earlier in the year beat Furman, a Division I-AA football program, by the same exact score. After the game, anarchy truly seemed to reign. Whereas the Boston College defeat was mostly depressive, Pittsburgh was expressive. Before the alma mater played, chants of "Fire Ty" rose in the stands, bellowed by Cassandras. They received looks of tisk-tisk derision from groups of Pollyannas. In the student section, the seniors had witnessed their final home game as Notre Dame undergraduates. A day later I overheard an undergrad say to his friend, "The entire senior section had to be put on suicide watch. Bill started crying."

"He was crying? Because we lost?"

"Yeah. I've never seen anything like it."

People seemed to have lost their minds. In one of the stadium rest-rooms, a man had forgone use of the trough. He was observed urinating onto his cell phone and muttering the phrase, "Can you hear me now?" Pittsburgh's receiving corps racked up 334 yards and five touchdowns on the day (the latter statistic never before accomplished by an Irish opponent at Notre Dame Stadium), and sometime after the game, Notre Dame's defensive coordinator received a phone call from a fan who had got hold of his office phone number from an earlier e-mail ex-change with the coach. Pleasantries were not exchanged. Their phras-ing was indelicate. The fan made some suggestions regarding the strategic inabilities of the coach, and the coach suggested a mano a mano with the fan somewhere in a dark place in South Bend.

Out at the Neighborhood of Hope, hope seemed to have left the premises. Bob Wentroble, the Mayor, and George May, one of his friends, had broken with tradition. Along with flying the Notre Dame flags, they raised the standard of an alien school. Its colors were red and white and its insignia was a giant *U*—the Utes of the University of Utah, the head coach of which was Urban Meyer. He was a former as-sistant at Notre Dame under both Lou Holtz and Bob Davie. He was in fact, something of a Holtz protégé, and he shared many traits with Notre Dame's most recent messiah. An offensive wizard just like his mentor, he had taken a few of Holtz's schematic ideas, based to some degree on the option, and advanced them into the twenty-first century. Hugely ambitious, he came from Ashtabula, Ohio, and grew up a fer-vid Notre Dame buff, a Catholic whose parents had named him after a pope. Just like Holtz, Urban Meyer was another football-coach subway alum. After his understudy gig at Notre Dame, he took the head job at Bowling Green and turned that middling program into a giant-killer with a two-year record of 17-6. A shouter, an intimidator, a jarheaded disciplinarian with unorthodox motivational ideas and practice meth-ods designed to emphasize "unity" and "team," he was, like Holtz, a turnaround artist. He moved on to Utah, where he again revitalized a moribund second-tier Division 1 team, going 10-2 his first year there. No one could figure out his offenses, and now, in 2004, he was, week by week, heightening his national profile and assembling an unde-feated record. Through his brief head-coaching career he had Notre Dame out-clauses written into his contracts, just like Holtz. Should the

Irish offer Meyer his "dream job," as he repeatedly called it in the press, the Irish could get him for cheap. No one seemed to care that Meyer's idea of a dream job seemed to entail leading any team with a large fan base, since his contracts included identical out-clauses for both Michigan and Ohio State. Still, he seemed at times to be publicly lobbying for a Notre Dame position that might or might not open up in the near future. The *Chicago Tribune* ran a long profile of Meyer in early November. A sidebar story carried the headline "Irish hold place in Meyer's heart" and quoted the coach as saying, "It's the purest form of college athletics and it always will be." To many Notre Dame fans, Urban Meyer "got it," and as the season wore on, they began to covet him as the next messiah. Not every Notre Dame fan was convinced, however. They wondered about his "gadget" offense, the weakness of the competition faced by both Utah and Bowling Green, the fact that he used junior-college transfers to reinforce the talent on his rosters, the fact that he'd stayed only two years apiece at each of his head-coaching stops, and, by far the most damning of all, that he claimed Bob Davie as "one of my best friends." But these concerns did not matter to the Neighborhood of Hope or thousands of other Notre Dame fans. More than hope for Urban Meyer, the Utah flag represented the hope that Willingham would be gone.

Meanwhile, the Pittsburgh defeat seemed to have broken the Neighborhood's spirit. A fistfight almost broke out after the game. The Mayor's nephew, big as a noseguard, his head shaved bald as a cue, a prison guard at the Pennsylvania State Penitentiary, walked out of the stadium and back to the Neighborhood stricken with fury. All along the way he shouted to the heavens, "I'm not coming back until this fucking coach is gone!" He began violently chucking tailgate gear into the Wentroble pickup bed until he had to be nearly restrained. Without further words, he walked off toward his car, parked three miles away. No one saw him again that night. He drove immediately back to Pittsburgh. Bobby Wentroble, the Mayor's son, said later on, "Our lives are Notre Dame football, and when they lose, we don't deal with it so well." He himself sat cringing through the Pittsburgh defeat with his father in the stadium, and he arrived back at the Neighborhood amid the internecine chaos. "Everybody was pissed at everybody. Everybody was pissed at *me!* It was not a pretty sight. This is what Notre Dame has done to people."

It did not take long for the people to respond. The letter-writing campaign probably began, with a trickle, during the week after the loss to BC. On ND Nation, people started posting rough drafts, and the board turned into a literary workshop. It also emboldened other fans to take similar action. The snowball rolled, the groundswell rippled. The works read in similar fashion to the C4C letter, except that these were sprinkled with personal detail. "Mailing Address of Kevin White, please," read a subject line. "I'm going to send him my two cents. . . . If some of us are going to storm the castle, it would be nice to know where the keep is. I need it for my missive over the wall, wrapped around a brick, so to speak."

It was determined that another petition, a "Call for Change" redux, would not be effective. After the BYU loss in September, BoardOps opened up the C4C letter—better described now as the C4C movement—to anyone who wanted to sign. They collected names as well as e-mail addresses to verify that they were dealing with individuals. By the week leading up to the Southern Cal game, 4,615 people had signed, and BoardOps launched a mass e-mail to everyone on the list. What was needed now was a grassroots effort to bury Notre Dame in an avalanche of correspondence expressing supreme dismay. E-mail, fax, USPS—by any means possible, make your individual voices heard. At the top of Rock's House, BoardOps posted the names and business addresses of key Notre Dame figures. The Reverend Edward Malloy, President. The Reverend John Jenkins, President-elect. John Affleck-Graves, Executive Vice President. Kevin White, Ph.D., Athletic Director. Scott Malpass, Chief Investment Officer. Philip Purcell, Chairman of the Athletics Committee of the Board of Trustees. Patrick McCartan, Chairman of the Board of Trustees.

The letters and e-mails and faxes deployed all the argumentative appeals—emotional, ethical, and logical.

"The Faust-Davie five-year 'precedent' might be convincing if they had done something dramatically better in their last two years. Coach Faust, however, averaged six wins per season his first three years and then six wins per season his last two. Coach Davie averaged seven wins per season his first three years and then seven per season his last two. . . . Even if the team somehow wins another game this year, that will give [Coach Willingham] an average of 7.3 wins per year. As a further illustration of the relevance of the first three years, consider that Coach Willingham averaged 6.33 wins per year his first three years at Stanford and ended his tenure there averaging 6.28 wins. I am sure we agree that averaging seven wins or so per year is not satisfactory at Notre Dame."

The letters sometimes contained other information.

"I'm writing on behalf of my family, which endows a scholarship."

And the letters at other times brought such information to bear.

"So it is with those thoughts in mind, and with a heavy heart, that I have decided to withhold my donation this year."

"While I make this decision amid personal conflict and reluctance, I do so out of duty and respect to my father, grandfather and their countless counterparts who now observe Our Lady's football program from the 50-yard line seats of above. I cannot, in good conscience, contribute monetarily to an administration and athletic leadership at Notre Dame that perpetuates mediocrity."

"Although we have committed to funding this $100,000 endeavor, the timing of the money transfer is at our discretion. Since we are agreeing to endow excellence, we cannot in good faith, nor without disrespecting our father, begin to fund the endowment until the University has decided that it will commit to returning football to excellence."

In nearly all of the letters, "mediocrity" and "excellence" were the catchwords. The last excerpt comes from a letter composed by David and Tim Angelotti, twin brothers and Notre Dame alumni. Their gift was to finance undergraduate research pursuits in the chemistry department. Class of 1985, David Angelotti is a construction manager at a commercial building company and Tim is a professor of medicine at Stanford. Their father, Nicholas, a chemical engineer, grew up in Cleveland, the son of Italian immigrants. He was a 1950 Notre Dame graduate. "That's the class, during the Leahy years, that never lost a game their entire four years," David Angelotti said later. "If you want to learn about what sports mean to Notre Dame, stop by the reunion, class of 1950. Their whole being is wrapped up in it. Not because they're rabid football fans, but because of Notre Dame's underdog role. The underdog immigrant role." The endowment was named in honor of their father, who died early in 2004, "after watching one of the worst seasons in the history of Notre Dame football," the brothers wrote in their letter. They also wrote, expressing an opinion in concord with many, "Notre Dame was founded on its Catholic identity, but it was football that made it a household name. We should not be ashamed of the role sports have played in building the University."

Many of the letters were genuinely difficult to write. One family of alumni—a father and his two sons—endows a Notre Dame scholarship, and they suffered something close to a generational conflict. Their letter did not threaten to terminate the family's endowment, but it did express alarm and disappointment with the Notre Dame administration. One of the sons wrote to me in an e-mail, "I think it took a great amount of courage for my dad, a scholarship donor, to sign that letter, and I know many others similarly situated with the university who did the same." His father was in the Tudy Cummings category, a fan (and in this case alumnus) who implicitly trusted, and defended, Notre Dame and its leaders against all criticism, including the employment status of Willingham. On this point, the father and his sons disagreed. "I attribute Malloy's intransigence on the matter to stubbornness and malfeasance. My father cites Malloy's well-intentioned 'pastoral concern' for Willingham's feelings." But by the end of the Pittsburgh game, the ten-year decline had accumulated to the point that Willingham's third year on the job seemed to encapsulate and embody the entire stretch of bad football and even worse decision-making at Notre Dame. Through those years, "It was pretty tough being a Notre Dame fan," the son said, and the family at last came together. "ND football got so bad that even folks like my father, who have never had one bad thing to say about ND in their lives, felt compelled to sign their name on a letter to ND that basically said, 'I can't take this any longer. You have royally screwed this up for far too long. Enough. End it.' "

Brainstorming on ND Nation produced other methods of delivering the point to Notre Dame's leadership. Someone proposed redirecting the yearly donations they would have contributed to Notre Dame to a charity foundation started by Ara Parseghian. Books arrived by FedEx at the office of Kevin White—copies of the 2003 tome *Return to*

Glory: Inside Tyrone Willingham's Amazing First Season at Notre Dame by Alan Grant. Across the cover, one person scrawled the word *Bullshit.* Someone on ND Nation had T-shirts made up that said on the front FIRE TY! and on the back PLAY LIKE A CHAMPION AGAIN! "Proceeds go to the Armed Services Relief Fund," said a post on ND Nation advertising the shirts.

(It should be noted that all previous Notre Dame head coaches had received similar treatment at one point or another. FIRE DAVIE shirts were ubiquitous starting in 1999, his first losing season. On the lawn in front of Davie's house, which sat on a cul-de-sac in a secluded, upscale neighborhood in Granger, FOR SALE signs began to appear by the dozens. The lawns of Devine and Faust were similarly decorated. When Devine went 7-4 one year, during a game the fans unfurled an enormous sheet painted with the words DUMP DEVINE. Two years earlier, he had led Notre Dame to a national championship. Even Ara Parseghian got hate mail, after playing for a tie against Michigan State in 1966, the so-called Game of the Century. Notre Dame that year won the title, and yet Parseghian would never entirely live down his decision. After Terry Brennan posted his first losing record in 1956, he began receiving shipments of women's pink underwear in the mail from irate fans.)

The C4C message appeared to be gaining traction. When Engler put up his "Forgotten Excellence" piece on the site's home page, sympathetic e-mails arrived in the ND Nation in-box by the hundreds. The piece also struck a few nerves the other way. For every hundred supportive notes, one or two angrily dissented. But they formed a clear minority. Around this time, the *South Bend Tribune* conducted an online poll: Should Notre Dame fire Ty Willingham? By November 17, fourteen thousand people had voted, and 90 percent of them had voted yes.

On the Friday before the Southern Cal game, the last of the season, the Notre Dame Alumni Club of Los Angeles arranged a Mass for late afternoon, part of a slate of events surrounding the annual rivalry. A hundred or so people showed up, many of them dressed in Notre Dame garb. The service ended with the choir of Notre Dame High School, a Holy Cross prep academy in the San Fernando Valley, singing "Notre

Dame, Our Mother" and then the "Victory March." The parishioners swayed to the first and clapped to the second as if sitting in the stands at the stadium. After the Mass had ended, a contingent of eight CSC priests stood outside the doors of the cathedral, a giant postmodern amalgam of beige adobe blocks. The priests greeted the people, some of whom gathered in a receiving line before the tall, robed figure of Monk Malloy. He rose above just about everyone else. His white vestments draped to his ankles. A headset microphone thin as a filament hung in front of his mouth; Malloy had earlier delivered the homily. Here on the cusp of Advent, the reading had been from the book of Revelation. "All the dead were judged according to their deeds." "I also saw the holy city, a new Jerusalem, coming down out of heaven from God." And in the homily Malloy offered his commentary. "And then in the last, the most telling of all images, we hear about great and eternal Jerusalem. That victory, that place, that experience that can be ours if we're faithful to the call of the Lord. In the end we have nothing to fear."

Malloy, as president of Notre Dame, was the most prominent priest on display, perhaps even more so than red-capped Cardinal Mahoney, archbishop of Los Angeles, who had celebrated the Mass. As Monk glad-handed with alumni, another priest hovered at the periphery, arms behind his back, largely ignored by the churchgoers. No one seemed to recognize him. Of middle height and weight, he blended into the crowd. He wore his simple priestly blacks, his Roman collar, and his rounded shoulders bespoke his career as an academic—professor of medieval philosophy and theology, an Aquinas scholar. He had a boyish face and light brown hair combed to the side like a prep schooler. He was fifty years old but looked fifteen years younger. When he did have occasion to greet an alumnus or an Irish fan, his obscurity forced him to offer his name. Then the spark of recognition would light in the interlocutor's eyes. They were talking to Notre Dame's next president.

A fan presented him with a question. "Who do you like tomorrow, Father?"

"Notre Dame of course," he said affably. "Who else? Southern Cal is in for a fall. They're too pumped up. They're overconfident."

When it came to the politics of the football program, a relatively new train of thought had arisen among the tipsters on the message boards and in certain quarters on campus. In this fresh theory, Jenkins, though still something of an enigma to most people, had become the linchpin. His public statements to that point had been so obvious that they might have gone unsaid. In an interview with the *South Bend Tribune* the previous spring, he had said that his plan for the university involved "maintaining its traditional excellence in undergraduate teaching, improving it as a key research and graduate institution, and maintaining the university's Catholic identity." Identical, in all respects, to Monk Malloy's vision for the school as well as Hesburgh's.

But, in this fresh theory, all hope that the university might reinvigorate its traditional identity (read: fix football posthaste) fell to the desk of the president-elect and his vice president, Affleck-Graves. There were reasons for this hope, based on an assortment of facts. Jenkins was a protégé of Fr. Timothy Scully, CSC, the former executive vice president. Scully was viewed in some quarters as a power-hungry egomaniac, and in other quarters as a man of vision and genius. Around campus he was feared. A tenured professor of political science, he was also known as an exceptional teacher. He had founded the ACE Program, a highly successful service project in which freshly minted university graduates spend a year teaching in underprivileged schools around the country. He was a favorite among several important trustees, none more so than the most important trustee, Chairman Patrick McCartan, the former managing partner, now semiretired, of Jones Day, a Cleveland-based firm specializing in corporate law.

It was well-known that Scully was not on the best of terms with Monk Malloy. At one point the presidential heir apparent, Scully had resigned his executive vice president's post following an unsavory episode in February 2003 in which the priest, allegedly with alcohol on his breath, had exchanged some hostile words with a local television reporter attempting to cover a Mass being celebrated for a missing Notre Dame undergraduate. Scully didn't want the press at this private family event, and he was angry. The reporter, a woman, filed a police report, claiming that Scully "grabbed my arm." She did not press charges, but the episode led to a painfully uncomfortable public outing—L'Affair Scully as it has become known—that exposed a schism at the highest levels of the university's leadership. "There's never been any rupture like there is now," an anonymous administrator told the *South Bend Tribune.* A special committee of the board of trustees, headed by McCartan, conducted an internal investigation of Scully's merits. It found nothing untoward about the priest's behavior and recommended that Scully remain at his post. By that point, however, Scully had already quit, though he might not have done so of his own accord. Wielding the vow of obedience, the Congregation of Holy Cross might have reassigned him. No one in Corby Hall, at any rate, was willing to talk about it.

Even more tellingly, the *Tribune* reported that Malloy and a slew of his allies had threatened to resign if Scully were permitted to stay on as EVP. "Monk had a letter ready to go," one Notre Dame insider told me. "And other officers were ready to walk." But that proved unnecessary, and Malloy and everyone else stayed on instead of Scully. Malloy had evidently won this early battle with McCartan, but he did not win the war. The schism seemed to split the university into Monk loyalists and Scullyites, and McCartan was believed to be in the latter camp. It has been said, for instance, that McCartan had given Malloy a number of negative performance reviews. When asked about the process that led to his retirement, Malloy told me, "You'll have to ask the board of trustees." And with that he shut down that particular line of conversation.

Scully, meanwhile, retrenched, went back to teaching full-time, and remained firmly in the chairman's camp—or, possibly, vice versa. It was believed that he still had his eyes on the presidency, but since Malloy had stacked the board with his own nominees, such an ambition would have to wait for more favorable conditions. When Jenkins was announced as the next president, therefore, many people on campus viewed him as "a Scully puppet," as one faculty member told me. Whatever the validity of this charge, Scully and McCartan, at the very least, quite likely had the ear of the president-elect, and McCartan, in particular, was thought to sympathize with the sentiment expressed in the "Call for Change" letter. He wanted football fixed.

The situation, as ND Nation's most in-the-know posters claimed, was fluid. Or, as one of them wrote, referring to the behind-the-scenes wranglings perhaps even then occurring, "Expect this to get fugly. If it isn't already."

Outside the Coliseum on the day of the Southern Cal game, much of the talk at the many Notre Dame tailgates involved the only and obvious question of the day—the employment of Ty Willingham and the attitude of his bosses. Los Angeles and environs has a strong alumni presence and—the immigrants of the East having followed the Golden Dream—a strong presence of subway alumni. Irish Joe Sweeney, as he's sometimes called, Notre Dame class of 1974, founding and managing partner of a South Bay law firm, wore a hat that said NOTRE DAME/ 1973 NATIONAL CHAMPIONS, a team for which he was head student manager. He wore shorts and boat shoes, though the sky was brown and threatening rain, and the temperatures were growing colder, into the fifties. His son, Steve, had traveled from South Bend for the occasion. A junior at Notre Dame, he had made it to every game of the season except the first, against Brigham Young. He held a beer and excitedly explained his T-shirt idea, based on his travels: 2004: LAST VOYAGE OF THE TY-TANIC. Elsewhere among the Notre Dame tailgates a placard had been raised. It said FIRE TY.

Some fans, however, were predicting an upset, given the proclivity of Willingham's teams for bewildering inconsistency. Southern Cal, at this point, was the undisputed No. 1 team in the nation. With Louisiana State, they had shared in a national championship the year before, their first since 1979. In 2002, they had gone 10-2, and the year before that, 6-6, slowing awakening from a dead period of nearly twenty years during which they had burned through four head coaches and achieved a winning percentage of .590. From 1983 through 1995, Southern Cal did not beat Notre Dame. In many ways, Notre Dame's era of decline made Southern Cal's look medieval. But with the hiring of Pete Carroll in 2001, the Trojans had rapidly pulled off their renaissance. Now, near the end of the 2004 regular season, SC looked unbeatable, an appearance that would become fact after the January bowl games.

The rain began to fall just before kickoff and did not end until the rout was well under way, in the middle of the fourth quarter. The first half of play defied the spread. Notre Dame played ball control and "dominated the trenches," as the sportswriters say. A Southern Cal defensive player later said that Notre Dame's offensive line was the most physical he had seen all year. At the end of the first quarter, the Irish led 10–3. The Irish defense forced the Trojans to punt again and again, and the Irish offense moved at will. Nearly a quarter of the Coliseum wore blue or gold or green, and these fans were filled with a brief and unexpected euphoria. Any thought of losing to SC in a blowout to force the departure of a head coach lost any and all relevance. That if Notre Dame could potentially take down the best team in the land in enemy territory, a team Notre Dame had played every year since 1926—the Glamour Game, arguably the greatest rivalry in college sport—that a winning outcome had even become a possibility, seemed to produce in these fans in Los Angeles such a ravenous hunger for victory that it blotted out the external world.

The external world, however, reappeared in the middle of the second quarter, when Southern Cal's coaches had made their adjustments. The Trojans scored fourteen fast, unanswered points, and the SC quarterback, who would go on to win the Heisman Trophy based in no small part on his performance this night, found the weaknesses in the Notre Dame secondary. He later said, "It was like taking candy from a baby."

The Notre Dame fans all sat in a horseshoe around the west end zone. A middle-aged woman sat hunched and soaking in her Fighting Irish parka, looking miserable. She addressed the dissipating crowd. "Embarrassing! Embarrassing! UCLA will put up a better effort next week than ND did! Embarrassing!"

There was talk about whether Notre Dame would accept a bowl bid, since despite this loss, they had ended their season 6-5, bowl eligible. The options were limited. No one wanted Notre Dame to accept.

"The Insight.com Bowl? What is that, a porn site?"

An elderly man stood up to leave. The rain had began to fall once again.

"You had enough?"

"I've had enough of this coach!"

Steve Sweeney alone bellowed rhythmically into the night, "Fire Ty! Fire Ty!"

The middle-aged lady responded to Sweeney as if he had begun a conversation. "Ty sucks. Bill Diedrick sucks. And the defense sucks. And the whole team sucks! They gave us false hope for three years!"

Leading 34–10, Pete Carroll called a fake punt. Caught off-guard, Notre Dame was flagged for pass interference—first down, and on the very next play, touchdown.

The final score was 41–10, the third year in a row that Willingham and Notre Dame had lost to Southern Cal by thirty-one points.

Outside the Coliseum, the Notre Dame tailgaters packed up and immediately left. It was cold and a stiff wind had kicked up—the Santa Ana. Everyone's clothes were soaked through. It was as if the weather of northern Indiana had descended with the Notre Dame plane into Los Angeles airspace.

Malloy, Jenkins, and the CSC entourage, who had all watched the game ensconced somewhere high and dry in the press box, entered a waiting limousine. They were escorted from the Coliseum to a hotel in Anaheim, where the next day they would preside over another Mass, this one organized by the Notre Dame alumni club of Orange County. In the back of the limo, as Malloy discussed the arrangements for the next day's events, which included no small amount of benefactor schmoozing, everyone else kept silent. Jenkins yawned again and again. He leaned against the door and fell asleep.

12

Just Like Everyone Else

On Sunday, November 28, the morning after the blowout loss to Southern Cal, Monk Malloy said in his homily, "I demand excellence in everything." His words were firm. He did not mention any kind of sporting endeavor, but everyone in attendance understood to what he was referring. His words inspired energetic chatter in the lobby of the Anaheim Hilton, where the Mass had taken place. Disneyland was next door. Two nights before, a lethargic pep rally had occurred in the same ballroom, complete with canned remarks from former Irish greats and from Chuck Lennon, Alumni Association director, who marched around the dais in his letterman's sweater. Willingham, not in attendance, had delivered a videotaped message to the faithful, his visage projected onto an enormous screen. He signed off by saying, "So tomorrow let it be a great game."

Malloy's homily inspired far more excitement than Willingham's words two nights earlier. In the lobby after the service, someone said, "Wow, he means business."

That evening, Kevin White, on behalf of Notre Dame, accepted an invitation to the Insight Bowl, formerly known as the Insight.com Bowl, formerly known as the Copper Bowl. A rather dreary assignment, the game would take place three days after Christmas in Phoenix, Arizona, atop the converted baseball diamond of the Arizona Diamondbacks. Almost no one among the fan base wanted to see Notre Dame participate. And, yet, the Insight people knew that to invite Notre Dame would mean a large draw at the gate. Indeed, they sold out their tickets within days.

Nonetheless, a train of thought among certain Irish fans holds that the university should decline invitations to any game not taking place on New Year's Day or immediately thereafter. To not achieve a record permissible for clearance into a first- or second-tier bowl meant the team had played lousily all season. Take your medicine and stay home. This notion, of course, was attacked by the outside world as the height of arrogance. Consequently, press reports covering the Insight acceptance were somewhat snide: how far the once-mighty Irish have fallen. "USC wins national championships," wrote Jay Mariotti of the *Chicago Sun-Times*. "Notre Dame flirts with Tire bowls." It was true, however, that Notre Dame had not won a bowl game in eleven years. Maybe they could break the streak out there in the desert among the wintering geriatrics. The coach, meanwhile, found other ways to spin the Insight circumstances.

"We're excited and I think our young men are excited," Willingham said on Sunday. "There are a lot of places in this country where you could spend the holidays, and Phoenix will be a delightful spot for our team and our fans."

But any talk of bowl games served as a mild diversion to the big topic. The conventional wisdom had recanted any hope of a coaching change. The tipsters were receiving ominous signals—it appeared that Malloy and his allies held a strong grip, despite any perceived lameness on the part of the duck. The absolutely uninformed may have viewed Malloy's homily as an indication of a shift in policy on the part of the outgoing president, that Willingham was sure to be fired. But they were wrong, and Notre Dame's public acceptance of a bowl bid was a clear enough indication.

Sometime on Saturday, after the game, Scott Engler proposed an idea on ND Nation. The site had begun as a student distraction, and now it would get back to its roots. To jog Notre Dame's leaders with a more immediate show of dismay over the evident maintaining of the status quo, Engler proposed a protest rally, a sit-in, a happening. The student members of the Web site immediately took to the notion. Brainstorming on ND Nation to the point that Engler and company created a separate board so the kids could concentrate on their machinations away from the general post–Southern Cal emotaposting, they became the organizers of a movement they called the Student C4C. They ran off fliers and distributed them around campus. Many priests live among the students in the dorms, and Father Jenkins's residence was on the first floor of a dormitory called Keenan. Under the door of the president-elect, one enterprising fellow slid a flier. They contacted the local media—the *Tribune,* the Associated Press, the television stations. They e-mailed ESPN. Two years earlier, in Willingham's first season, the motif of The Shirt had been, of course, RETURN TO GLORY. The organizers decided to congregate on the steps of the Main Building on Tuesday evening. There, in the shadow of the Dome, one by one, they planned to ceremoniously drape their outmoded The Shirts on the steps in solemn protest. A student with a bullhorn would then read from a lawyerly document signed by every sympathizer present. In part, it read:

Whereas the current leadership of the Notre Dame Football Program took over the following:

- *11 National Championships*
- *7 Heisman Trophy Winners*
- *115 All Americans*
- *The best name in football recruiting*
- *And a lucrative national TV contract.*

Whereas Notre Dame Football has failed to meet all standards set by Athletic Director Dr. Kevin White three years ago.
Whereas Dr. White affirmed the University's commitment to a National Champion–ship caliber football team upon the arrival of Tyrone Willingham as coach.
Whereas Notre Dame has more players in the NFL than any other school, demonstrating the tremendous potential of athletes coming to the University.
Whereas the aforementioned players deserve the best leadership and coaching for their unwavering commitment and sacrifice for the University.
And Whereas Tyrone Willingham has led the team to the following:

- *The same winning percentage as fired Head Coach Bob Davie.*
- *As many 20 point or more losses in three years as in the previous 40 years of Notre Dame football.*
- *A 13-15 record since the 8-0 start in 2002.*
- *The third worst passing defense in the nation in 2004.*

- *The 107th, 90th, and 79th ranked offenses in 2002, 2003, and 2004 respectively.*
- *3 consecutive 31-point losses to USC.*
- *3 consecutive losses to Boston College.*
- *3 consecutive seasons in which the team lost its final regular season game.*

Therefore, be it resolved, that we the undersigned, do hereby declare our Call for Change in the administration and leadership of the University of Notre Dame's football program.

It was not at all clear how many students would actually show up at the rally. There appeared to be about thirty or so behind its organization, and what support existed in the wider student body was unknown. Fliers had gone up on the walls of a dorm on Sunday night. When the organizers woke up the next morning, the fliers had vanished from the walls. They scheduled the demonstration for 5:30 p.m. on Tuesday. It turned out, of course, to be unnecessary.

At around noon eastern time on Tuesday, a cryptic post by a Notre Dame undergraduate with the handle Arsenal went up on ND Nation. It advised the student protesters that by one o'clock in the afternoon, a protest rally might seem a little redundant. It contained no further information. Eating his lunch at the dining hall, Arsenal had overheard a group of players talking. Evidently a surprise team meeting was to take place later in the day, and as one of the players put it, "The shit is going down."

Sometime before 10 a.m., Mike Frank, of Mike Frank's *Irish Eyes,* original IRJ recruiting man, received an e-mail from one of his subscribers. Frank was sitting at home in South Bend, several miles from campus, drinking his coffee and contemplating his day, which would entail getting a start on the college football recruiting season that heats up after the conclusion of the regular one. He had a list of star high school prospects that he would call for updates. He and his wife had also recently been contemplating their status as South Benders. Angel Frank, a redheaded Brit from the southwest of England, had given up her professorship at Chichester College to make a life with her husband in the States, following Notre Dame football as a livelihood. Business was okay but stagnant. The money the Franks earned from their Web site did not seem to justify their presence in South Bend. Mike Frank could just as easily perform his work in his hometown in Nebraska, be closer to family and friends, and perhaps, as a side job to supplement his income, go back to brokering mortgages. He and his wife had decided before the season to give it one more autumn. If business did not pick up, they would pack up and head back to Nebraska.

With this e-mail, however, they would put all that aside. The subscriber, an alumnus, had a connection to the athletic department. "Something is happening," the subscriber said—Willingham had been fired. Frank then made a call to Mike Coffey, to ask if he or anyone else had heard similar rumblings. They had not. Sometime thereafter a second e-mail arrived, this one from an anonymous person using an anonymous Yahoo! account. To this day Mike Frank has not determined the identity of the correspondent. The e-mail urged Frank to call John Heisler, the head flak in the Notre Dame Sports Information Department, SID, and pose a question: Is Willingham resigning or is he being fired? "And I guarantee you he'll say, 'No comment.' " Eerily, uncannily, the anonymous e-mailer further commented that he or she knew that Mike Frank had discussed rumors of a firing with others. "I'd appreciate it if you kept that quiet, and let things play out," the e-mail said.

It then dawned on Frank that the e-mail had perhaps come from someone on the inside. He turned to his wife and said, "Holy shit. They fired Ty."

At around 12:30 p.m. eastern time, a notice appeared on the home page of the official Web site of Notre Dame athletics, UND.com.

> *The University of Notre Dame announced today that Tyrone Willingham will not be retained as its head football coach.*
>
> *Willingham finished 21-15 overall in three seasons (2002–04) as Irish head coach.*

At that moment, ND Nation no longer existed. The rush of traffic wiped it off the face of the cyberworld. Typing the Web address into your browser led to a blank white page. Error message: *Timed out.*

The news zippered across Times Square. It scrolled with the head-

lines under CNN, CNBC, Fox News, MSNBC. ESPN broke from its programming. Sportswriters and sports pundits the nation over scrambled to the story. Sports radio channels dedicated nearly every minute
of their broadcasts to the developing situation. Among other themes,
they explored the question of whether Notre Dame had become "irrel-
evant." Bob Davie's gruff baritone droned on ESPN radio about how
three years was "not enough time." He went on to use this fresh media
platform (he was contacted by just about every major sports scribe in
the nation following the firing) to argue that five years, in his case, was
not enough time, either. In firing Davie, "the administration bowed to
alumni pressure," a bit of information he delivered as if it were some
kind of scoop, and not the process by which head coaches have been
fired since the dawn of collegiate sport. He claimed that it was impossible to win consistently at Notre Dame—too much pressure, too much
scrutiny. He was on the air for perhaps twenty minutes dissecting the
news. ESPN did not stop doing the same for another two weeks.

At 3:30 p.m. Tuesday, Nate Farley, the seminarian, walked oblivi-
ously into his Pastoral Ethics class. "I hadn't heard anything. Not even
murmurs." All day he had been at his prayers and amid his books, getting a head start on approaching finals week. The room was abuzz. The
students were all in the master's of divinity program—M.Div.—and the
topic of conversation had nothing to do with theology. After absorbing
the first jolt of the news, Farley's initial thought was "It's sad to see a
coach like that not succeed. Willingham is a wonderful man." His second thought was a little less pastoral: "Even if Notre Dame has that
five-year thing, after three years it's time to evaluate your coach." And
they had evaluated.

Tracy Hallahan, in Cincinnati, heard the news from a friend over
his Motorola two-way radio. Hallahan was driving his van on the way
to a job site. His first thought was, shots of Jameson all around! He
worked till eight that night, then headed to the bar to celebrate.

"How many sins of an Irishman?"

The phone in Bobby Wentroble's classroom rang at around 1:30
p.m. The son of the Mayor of the Neighborhood of Hope was at the
chalkboard teaching math to seventh-graders. He actually said, "Hold
on, boys and girls." And the secretary on the other end said, "You have
an urgent phone call from California. From a JJ?" JJ was his cousin, the

brother of the guard from the state pen who had erupted after the Pitt loss a few weeks before. When Wentroble heard the news, he didn't believe it. He put the phone back on the receiver and went back to the board. The phone rang a second time. This time the secretary mentioned the name of a friend, another Notre Dame fan from Pittsburgh. "He says he has an important message."

The Mayor, meanwhile, was on the phone nonstop throughout the day. He answered his calls each time with the same phrase: "Bye-bye, Ty!"

Eddie Colton was on duty behind the wheel of his prowler, down near Wall Street and Broadway. The news came across his radio via the voices of Mike and the Mad Dog, on WFAN, the New York sports-talk logorrhea. Eddie Colton was, like most everyone else, "shocked." Loyal to his good friend Father Malloy, he knew the president had not pulled the trigger. He summed up his thoughts later on: "I guess the trustees are really powerful over there."

Eddie Gadawski, in Niagara Falls, was pouring a customer a drink. Working his lunch shift, he stood behind the bar of his shrine, his signed photograph of Tyrone Willingham staring over his shoulder. He saw the news on the TV, tuned to ESPN. He later said he was not surprised by the turn of events. He reacted instead with submerged pleasure—"He had to go!" His autographed Willingham remained, nonetheless, in position.

Bishop Jenky was in New York City, attending a convention of bishops. There to commemorate the twenty-fifth anniversary of the death of Fr. Fulton Sheen, they also wished to sponsor his beatification. Among a group of other high prelates, Jenky stood inside the sacristy of St. Patrick's Cathedral. Many of the bishops and priests in attendance were also Notre Dame fans, some had received degrees from the university, and the discussion did not involve the evangelical deeds of Sheen. Their opinions on the firing "ran the gamut," Jenky said later. "They certainly recognized that it wasn't among Notre Dame's best public relations moments." Walking down Fifth Avenue in his bishop's attire ("I was in my full battle regalia"), Notre Dame fans stopped him on the sidewalk in the hopes of getting the scoop. Some recognized him, others simply figured that a Catholic bishop ought to have the Notre Dame scoop. Jenky also sits on the university's board of trustees, and he knew only as much as anyone else in front of a television.

The phone behind the bar at Leahy's in the Morris Inn began ringing not long after the announcement and would not stop until the place closed down. Leahy's attracts a group of regulars each home game during the season, subway alum from all over the country—California, Arizona, West Virginia, New York City, Maine—of the type who come in for the entire home slate. Over the years, Murf, the barman, has become their off-season, on-campus connection to the dish. Murf documented each long-distance call, not including repeat callers. He was trying to break the record for phone calls placed to him at the bar after a coaching change. There were twenty-eight after Holtz. By 5 p.m. he reached twenty-four and by the close of business thirty-seven.

At his home in South Bend, Mike Frank continued to stare at the news on his TV. He sat there a couple hours. An announcement came that Kevin White would be delivering a press conference at 4 p.m., eastern time. "I never wanted to be a sportswriter," Frank has admitted before. Mostly this feeling arises out of personal reasons, for his job obliterates his status as fan. "I hate it, actually. I miss the game. I don't get to tailgate. I can't chat with my buddies after the game because I'm interviewing players and coaches. The whole reason for why I got into this is ruined. My subscribers say, 'Oh, man, what a life you have.' But I kind of envy *them*." At other moments, he simply doubts his abilities as a reporter, and one of those moments was now, in the aftermath of the Willingham dismissal. At some point it occurred to him that it might be a good idea to drive the three miles to campus, maybe get some reactions. The rest of the Notre Dame press corps was likely there already, roving around the Joyce Center, lingering outside SID, outside the football offices, finding players and assistant coaches and sub–athletic directors for comment and reaction. Angel, in fact, had to suggest to her husband that he should, maybe, follow suit.

"If there's one thing I've learned," he said later on, reflecting, "it's that I'm a terrible journalist."

Kevin White at the press conference looked as if his prize golden retriever had just been hit by a box truck. He said he had not begun the search for a new coach. He suggested that he had had no influence in the decision to fire.

"I think it's fair to say I report to the president, and at the end of the day, I serve at the will of the president of the University of Notre Dame."

A reporter asked, "I talked to you about three weeks ago, and you basically told me that Tyrone Willingham—you were behind him a hundred percent. What specifically changed in the last three weeks?"

And White replied, "I anticipated that question," and the press corps laughed. "Let me just say that—and it's a sobering moment—but let me just say this: That I'm going to be behind every one of our coaches until they are no longer our coaches. And that's the way I think it needs to be done. And I think that's what our coaches expect and deserve."

Most famously, however, in tones that conveyed both exhaustion and gloom, he said, "I was thinking about it this morning—from Sunday through Friday, our football program has exceeded all expectations in every way." And with that line, as well as with his sullen, defeated demeanor, White succeeded in dropping an ounce of gasoline onto a public-relations firestorm that was already blazing away.

Among the first items ESPN ran on its Web site was a reader poll. The headline said, "Vote: Is Notre Dame Facing Extinction?" This question might have come as a shock to those eighty-three hundred Notre Dame undergraduates who, having delivered their tuition checks to the registrar, would have seen on their bank statements that the checks had cleared. Any university facing extinction would, I'm sure, have the decency to refund the money.

No one has ever accused ESPN's headline writers of being the framers of the intellectual context of the nation, but the title of that reader poll provided an indication of just how vehement the opposition was to Willingham's dismissal. In the days that followed, the hysteria and criticism went on unrelentingly. And this, in turn, produced a defensive, paranoid hysteria in the fans.

"Brace yourselves," read a post on ND Nation. "They are out in force and on a mission to tarnish the dome—permanently if they can. Many of them will never let ND live this down."

From the second the news hit, everyone knew it was coming. Combine the issue of race with a historical antipathy to Notre Dame among many in the sporting press and the population at large, and what emerged was likely the most intense media coverage of a coaching change in the history of sport.

Like all good literature, the coverage of Willingham's dismissal both echoed tradition as well as advanced it. Whenever the team suffers a down period, of course, Notre Dame football is dead for all time. Whenever it makes changes to end the down period—or, indeed, whenever it achieves success—it is a "football factory." (See *Tarnished Dome,* Looney, Yaeger, 1993.) Among the traditional literary devices deployed by sportswriters sports-writing about Notre Dame is a tone full of spleen. It's almost as if, in the distant past, Notre Dame had somehow hurt their feelings. Some Notre Dame partisans have conjectured that more than a few sportswriters grew up fans of the Irish, but when it came time for them to apply to their dream school, they were rejected, forcing them to attend a backup college and hold a grudge that lives on in their articles.

But this critique suffers from pettiness. More likely the vitriolic tone rises from several other factors. It has long been said that Notre Dame does not tend to produce neutral feelings in the observer of college football—the old love-'em, hate-'em dichotomy. Any team that achieves success over a long period invites resentment, and because success attracts a large fan base, the sportswriters can easily increase their audiences by baiting said fan base.

The tactic is evergreen, and it can move between positive and negative commentary. All one need do is look at Notre Dame's season-ending record. If the record is lousy: Dead, proclaimed in mocking tones. If it includes three or fewer losses, the sports columnist has two choices of theme: Football Factory or Return to Glory, depending on when in the upcycle he publishes. If a win streak presents evidence of the start of an upcycle (See Willingham's first year), he works the Return angle. If an upcycle has already lasted a bunch of years, he should feel free to work the Factory angle (See, once again, *Tarnished Dome.*) And if, boon of boons, the university makes a move to end a downcycle by canning a coach, he can simultaneously call Notre Dame both Dead *and* a Factory. This produces consistency in the sports scribe.

"Notre Dame, football factory, fired its coach Tuesday," wrote sportswriter Pat Forde of ESPN.

"We're talking about Football U, folks," wrote sports columnist Christine Brennan, no relation to Terry, of *USA Today.*

"Is Notre Dame Facing Extinction?" wrote ESPN's sports-headline writers.

But the amount of hate for Notre Dame that exists does make one wonder whether purely cynical motives alone can explain the spleen of the sporting media. Instead, their intellects appear to be insulted by what they deem Notre Dame's "hypocrisy." Because the university believes it can win championships without sullying itself by bending the rules, it is therefore "holier-than-thou." This, of course, flows directly out of the Holy Cross charism and Fortress Notre Dame and Hesburgh's amendments to it, as he articulated in his response to the *Sports Illustrated* Dead-Factory critique after the Terry Brennan firing, 1958: "There is no academic virtue in playing mediocre football and no academic vice in winning a game that by all odds one should lose. . . . There has been a surrender at Notre Dame, but it is a surrender to excellence on all fronts, and in this we hope to rise above ourselves with the help of God." "Hypocrisy" comes into play when Notre Dame "proudly" and "arrogantly" flaunts its "integrity," then goes out and does something akin to sacking a head coach who, as White put it, "from Sunday through Friday . . . has exceeded all expectations."

In the minds of the sports scribes, these ostensible contradictions always seem to make Notre Dame "just like everyone else." Across the decades, the university has been revealed to be "just like everyone else" at least seven times (a list that excludes the Rockne era, when these tropes were just beginning to form)—the Frank Leahy era of dominance, the Brennan firing, the Faust firing, the Holtz "tarnished dome" era of dominance, the NCAA wrist slap of 1999, the Davie firing, and now, of course, the Willingham firing. This, in turn, causes the observer to wonder just how the university has been able to rise from the mass of "everyone else" so often that the sports scribes can, yet again, reveal Notre Dame to be "just like everyone else."

"This is a story about arrogance," wrote sports columnist Michael Wilbon, of the *Washington Post.*

"With this one craven move, the Fighting Irish officially changed a famous saying on a campus building from 'God, Country, Notre Dame' to 'Notre Dame: Just Like Everyone Else,' " wrote sports wit Jim Caple, of ESPN, thus chronicling another surprising development at the school in the wake of Willingham's ouster: to redo the carving over the entrance to the Basilica, the chiselers must have performed their university-sanctioned vandalism under cover of night.

It is, perhaps, a little like dropping an anvil on a pea to bring the principles of logic to bear on the genre of the sports columnist, but many confused arguments went to print the day after Willingham was fired. Sports columnist Jay Mariotti of the *Chicago Sun-Times* appeared to argue simultaneously that Willingham deserved to be fired, but that it was a mistake to fire him. The headline atop his column summed up his position: "Firing continues string of ND blunders, but Ty had to go."

ESPN's Pat Forde, a member of the Football Factory School, sounded a little hurt. He wrote, "This might come as a shocking revelation to the deluded Subway Alumni and others who believe that a decently trained mule can go 10-1 at Notre Dame, but it's not a sure thing in South Bend anymore." Acute Notre Dame observers and fans had long understood the soaring demands of the job and, therefore, had long understood the necessity of hiring a coach with demonstrable skill and record of success at the highest levels, an attitude that might have come as a "shocking revelation" to Forde, since it meant that he agreed with them. Forde's brother is a Notre Dame graduate, and Forde himself has stated that he is a lifelong Notre Dame fan, which perhaps makes him, to borrow his own phrase, a delusional Subway Alumnus.

Forde went on, "This is a challenging job, and the more distance Notre Dame gets from its last national championship, in 1988, the harder it gets. The talent disparity between the Irish and Trojans on Saturday night was shocking (and, yes, much of that falls on Willingham's shoulders). That won't change overnight. . . . It's true that Willingham had given the school dramatically diminishing returns. After starting 10-1, to the astonishment of everyone, he went 11-14. His teams were blown out with alarming regularity, including three straight 31-point losses to the Trojans. And every big win (two against Top 10 Michigan teams, at Florida State, at Tennessee) was undercut by a galling loss (three straight to Boston College, Syracuse, BYU). But what, exactly, were the rational expectations for this Notre Dame team? Did anyone in August look at the roster and see the pieces of an elite-level team? Did anyone predict this to be a Top 25 team? Did anyone think in August that 6-5 would be an outrage?"

If one were to analyze the argument here articulated by Forde—which seemed to represent the conventional wisdom on the matter—it would produce the following pieces of deductive reasoning:

> *It's hard to win at Notre Dame.*
>
> *Notre Dame's football team sucks.*
>
> *Willingham's performance as head coach of that team has sucked. (In Forde's own words, Willingham is largely responsible for the "talent disparity" between Notre Dame and Southern Cal, as well as those "dramatically diminishing returns" and "blowouts" of "alarming regularity.")*
>
> *Therefore, Willingham's suckiness is a good fit for Notre Dame's suckiness.*
>
> *Therefore, Willingham should not have been fired.*

No one, at any rate, analyzed Forde's logic. His column went safely into oblivion, living only long enough to bait a few Notre Dame fans, and Forde went on to other pursuits, likely biding his time for a column in which he could extol Notre Dame's Return, and, later still, as the team began racking up wins, bemoan its Return to the Factory.

Alan Grant, meanwhile, author of *Return to Glory,* took a few moments out of his schedule to deliver his thoughts both on the air and in written form, again on the ESPN Web site. (It is worth remembering that Grant played under Willingham at Stanford.) To start his ESPN column, Grant patiently went through all the tropes. He derided the Notre Dame Hypocrisy ("They want to win by any means necessary. They just won't admit it.") as well as the Notre Dame Arrogance ("The Board of Trustees, the boosters and the wealthy, self-important alums—better known as Domers—apparently don't have that kind of time. They want it all, and they want it right now."). *Self-important* was a phrase that popped up here and in many other Dead-Factory sports columns, as was the pejorative appellation *Domers,* used by

Grant with such dexterity in the above sentence that you can almost here his voice contemptuously emphasizing it. Grant's primary line of reasoning entailed the following, an excellently complete anthology of every form of Notre Dame complaint: "Back in the late '80s and early '90s, Notre Dame was the dominant program in the land and the Irish were living off their sterling, holier-than-thou reputation. But the truth is they were just like everyone else." He cited an anonymous Notre Dame player from those times, who mentioned the University of Miami–Notre Dame games of the period, which "spawned the infamous 'Catholics vs. Convicts' T-shirts." The player said to Grant, "Who were they fooling with that? We were every bit as bad as they were." One can argue the merits of this comment—it sounds like playful braggadocio—but Grant treats it as fact. Grant then went on to write, "But, see, Willingham doesn't recruit that type of player. That type of player—the renegade who believes he can act without consequence—just isn't Willingham's type of guy. That type supposedly isn't Notre Dame's type of guy, either." More deductive reasoning à la the sporting press: The only time in the last thirty years that Notre Dame has been any good is when Holtz recruited thugs. Willingham doesn't recruit thugs, and Notre Dame claims it doesn't want them, either. Therefore, Notre Dame should be happy with a team that performs at a level below its teams from the past that had a lot of thugs.

It would seem then, according to Grant at least, that only the morally depraved and intellectually indifferent are capable of playing superior football—"that type"—an assumption that the athletes on some portion of the NFL's rosters would likely take issue with.

With his "that type" thug theory of championship football, Grant was not the first former football player turned wordsmith to diagnose Notre Dame's post-Holtz mediocrity by deploying a stereotype. The Golden Boy, Paul Hornung, Notre Dame class of 1957, proclaimed in a radio interview after the 2003 season that the university needed to loosen its academic requirements "because we must get the black athlete if we're going to compete." After dropping that choice remark, Hornung, then a Notre Dame football commentator for Westwood One radio, lost his job and garnered immediate censure from the university and its image makers.

Both Grant and Hornung were playing into the old "academic standards" canard, a variation on the Dead theme: without "that type" or "the black athlete," Notre Dame could not win at football. (Notre Dame's roster in 2004 had fifty-one African-American players and forty-five white players.) No one seemed to believe Notre Dame's director of admissions, Dan Saracino, who said again and again that academic requirements for athletes had not changed at Notre Dame in more than forty years. "We get beat and have gotten beat over recent years by young men who we clearly wanted to come here," Saracino said to the *Observer* in April 2004. In other words, superstar high school players who academically qualified for Notre Dame—whether or not these players could be described as "that type" or "the black athlete," I'll leave to Grant and Hornung to determine—chose to enroll at other schools on Notre Dame's schedule and, in playing for those teams, came back onto the field to score touchdowns against the Irish. "I'm frustrated that we seem to be having less success in recruiting compared to the past," Saracino said in the same interview, and with that comment he seemed to lay the fault at the feet of Notre Dame's previous two head coaches.

ESPN's first headline, just after Notre Dame released the news, said, "Two black head coaches in I-A." New Mexico State had fired its black head coach Tony Samuel not long before, but this had garnered far less press than even Notre Dame's acceptance of an invitation to the Insight Bowl. Notre Dame, thanks to the size and geographic breadth of its fan base, was on a different scale entirely. One writer for the *Sporting News* called Notre Dame's head-football position "the preeminent coaching job in any sport at any level." When Willingham was hired, the plaudits went up. Almost everyone said Notre Dame had sent a message to college football, which had lagged in sickening fashion the progress made in college and professional basketball, in the NFL, in the major leagues. Four black head coaches out of 117 programs whose black athletes make up 44 percent of their combined rosters—and now, three years later, Notre Dame had fired by far the most famous among them.

The Black Coaches Association, an organization of collegiate-level African-American coaches in all sports, immediately decried the firing. "We respected the visionary appointment of Coach Willingham in 2001 by Father Edward Malloy and Kevin White. However, we have a grave concern about the premature termination of Tyrone's five-year contract. It is disappointing to see the University of Notre Dame refuse to honor its professional commitment to an individual of the high character and stature of Coach Willingham." Willingham and Notre Dame actually had a six-year contract, under which, after a period of time, the university could review his performance and dissolve the contract with a per-annum buyout of a very large number—probably close to his annual salary, which media speculation pinned at between $1.5 million and $2 million a year. Willingham and his agent had agreed to this. And, quid pro quo, Willingham and his agent had written into the contract provisions that would allow him to walk away from Notre Dame before the end of the six-year term. No contract, therefore, was broken. What Notre Dame did break was the five-year precedent set in the 1950s by Hesburgh.

The association stopped short of charging racism. Many other sports-page scribes did as well, but the subject clearly influenced their outraged tones. Alan Grant did not stop short. He wrote, "I've already heard people say that Willingham's color had nothing to do with the decision to fire him. Thanks in advance, all of you who will try to drive this point home over the next few days. But in the meantime, check this out: Faust and Bob Davie got their full five years before they were let go. Willingham didn't."

Others dismissed racism out of hand, including Jay Mariotti. Skip Bayless, another omnipresent ESPN shouter as well as professed contrarian, chose to defend Notre Dame this time around. "I spoke with John Wooten, who heads the NFL's minority hiring program," Bayless wrote in an ESPN piece, "More myth than coach," which also argued that Willingham as a football tactician was overrated. "Wooten believes the NFL is making progress with five black head coaches and two candidates—New England assistant Romeo Crennel and Pittsburgh assistant Tim Lewis—who could land jobs by next season. Wooten said: 'All you can ask for is interviews, and we're getting those. Once you get a job, you're on your own. You have to perform.' "

John Walters, Notre Dame class of 1988 and now a reporter for *Sports Illustrated,* wrote, "Here's what I know: Two of Notre Dame's previous five coaches before Willingham, Gerry Faust and Bob Davie, did struggle in their third seasons. Davie went 5-7 and Faust 7-5. Neither improved significantly in the two more seasons they were allotted and, in retrospect, perhaps the university should have pulled the trigger on their tenures earlier." Indeed, an epigram had been on the lips of Notre Dame fans since the blowout loss to Purdue in early October: what you must do eventually, you should do immediately.

No one in the press seemed to care that Notre Dame's 2004 graduation rate for African-American football players was 76 percent. (Calculated by the NCAA, the percentages included four classes worth of students and allowed them six years to achieve their degrees.) Michigan, for comparison's sake, graduated 47 percent of its black football players. Tennessee graduated 30 percent. Interestingly, these figures and what they might indicate merited no coverage or mention or investigation or casual inquiry by anyone in the media.

On the day after the news, Michael Wilbon's entire column in the *Washington Post* attacked what he believed to be the racist institution of Notre Dame. "The powers-that-be at Notre Dame, way too many of them anyway, never wanted Tyrone Willingham in the first place. The alums and the club boosters who donate tens of thousands of dollars and who influence opinion in South Bend never coveted Ty Willingham in the first place. They tolerated him. They made their peace with him being there. They hoped he would win. But they didn't want him. The whole three years Willingham was there, the power brokers stood with arms folded and feet tapping, staring at the clock trying to determine when his time would be up. For the most part, they were never emotionally committed to him. They never loved him or treated him like 'The Coach.' The thinking was that if he went 10-1 every year, he could stay, and at that point they might even grow to like him."

The charges grew more serious. "Notre Dame, the school that never before fired a coach before his initial contract expired, fired the first black head coach the school had ever hired in any sport. I'm sure everybody ever associated with Notre Dame will tell you color had nothing to do with letting Willingham go, that it's totally a coincidence, which is like spitting in somebody's face and telling him it's a rain drop. . . . They want to live in Pleasantville as long as possible, and Pleasantville, in case you didn't notice, doesn't include black coaches telling white boys how to block or tackle, which is why there are only two black head coaches in Division I-A. People at institutions such as Notre Dame don't sit around anymore, even off the record, talking about getting rid of a person because he's a certain color. Such a conversation, if proven, would be illegal in this country, and most folks aren't that dumb. Intolerance has increasing subtlety. But the passionate distaste for Willingham in some quarters, including on campus after a loss, had an unmistakable stink to it."

No matter how rhetorically bankrupt these arguments might have been (Wilbon, for instance, after admitting he had no proof, essentially reasoned, I say Notre Dame is racist, therefore it's racist), the incontrovertible facts remained. White Catholic men had fired a black head coach, even though, in the past, white Catholic men had granted more time to white head coaches. It made for some pretty damning sound-bite logic. But to dip below the surface of those facts and the headlines they produced was to see other issues at play, which had little to do with race and much to do with a historically unpeered football program mired in a decade-long decline.

13

Messiahs and Pariahs

When ND Nation came back online, the banner headline reprised the message that had gone up after Malloy had announced his retirement:

HERE COME THE IRISH

This expression of unity among the C4C set, however, by no means extended to campus or other portions of the Notre Dame Family. On the steps of the Main Building, where the Student C4C rally had been scheduled to take place, a different kind of gathering formed, an impromptu protest put together quickly by the leaders of the campus African-American club. There are only 308 black undergraduates at Notre Dame, of which between 30 and 40 came out to show "solidarity to Ty because we feel that this termination was unjust," one of those undergrads told Maddie Hanna, a student-reporter from the *Observer*. A few of the demonstrators carried placards. NEVER BEFORE, NEVER AGAIN. WE WANT TY BACK. $ COST ND ITS INTEGRITY. As it happened, about twenty of the organizers of the original rally showed up as well, there to celebrate the news. With a student body that is roughly 80 percent Catholic, Notre Dame has never been known as a diverse place, and the racial divide on the steps was clear. Debates developed between the two groups, and though they were not shouting, their voices grew tense with emotion. Other people milled around, not so sure what to do with themselves. The local media, which had received word of the original Fire Ty demonstration, was on hand to take stock. Cameras and reporters with notepads surrounded the spokespeople and took down their solemn comments for or against the firing. The following quotations were made to the *Observer*, the *South Bend Tribune*, the local TV news crews.

"There are a lot of issues here that make his termination questionable."

"This is bigger than a race issue. This is about a man with a family."

"This is a step in the right direction. At the same time, we have to make sure that we get a topflight coach to get back to championship football."

"The issue is losing a good friend, and that he didn't get a fair chance. It's about members of this community feeling like they don't belong, and that it's our job to make them feel like they belong."

"To fire him like they did—that's just cold. So cold. I'm shocked."

"People were in tears outside the library because of Ty's firing."

"Something needed to be done with the football team. There were some issues. There were some awful losses."

"With all the pressure on them, I don't see how they could do anything else. Last year was terrible, and this year wasn't much better."

In subsequent days the African-American club met off campus to discuss the firing. They said they did not feel comfortable convening on campus. David Moss, their faculty adviser, an assistant vice president for Student Affairs, said, "To them, Notre Dame no longer had the same sense of security as it once did." He likened the feeling to having your house broken into—what had once felt safe somehow no longer did. Several students consulted him privately about transferring out of Notre Dame, though in the end everyone decided to stay. Of the firing, Moss says, "It only perpetuated the stereotype that black people aren't welcome here. Maybe the firing wasn't racially motivated, but it still had the impact to take us back a few steps." Notre Dame, he said, had been "making progress dispelling the popular idea that the university was, historically, not as hospitable to blacks as other places. Somehow that idea got into the unofficial network of the African-American community. And once that stereotype is in there, it's hard to get rid of."

Several football players were at the rally as well, including the freshman tailback Darius Walker. To Maddie Hanna of the *Observer* he declined comment, telling her that Willingham had instructed his team to say nothing on the matter. Rumors, however, quickly spread about some of their reactions. There was talk of a "player revolt." When Willingham and Kevin White met with the team on Tuesday afternoon to deliver the news, many of the players were stunned, bewildered, belligerent. Willingham, molder of men, had been to these boys, as quarterback Brady Quinn later said, a "father figure." An e-mail had gone out to the roster at 11 a.m. calling the athletes to the meeting. Quinn believed that it had something to do with Insight Bowl preparation. "I was speechless," he said. "I didn't quite know how to react." Others already knew what to expect, including Ryan Harris, a starting offensive lineman. He was sitting in his midday Economics lecture, when a student with a laptop and Internet access—wired campus that it now is—leaned over to him and whispered, "Ty's been fired."

At the team meeting, according to Harris, emotions ranged from anger to sadness to joy—the latter response from those who had ridden the bench and perhaps felt they weren't getting their due. As with any head-coaching regime, Willingham reportedly had his favorites. "A few people were happy," Harris said, but most were not. Rumor had it that Justin Tuck, the team's star defensive end, exploded with rage, shouting his displeasure at Kevin White. Later he was heard to say, in the heat of the moment, "I hate Notre Dame." He would eventually decide to turn pro with a year of eligibility remaining.

On Wednesday, the athletic department gave the press corps access to four players, the team's de facto leadership—Quinn, Harris, linebacker Brandon Hoyte, and tight end Anthony Fasano. They sat at folding tables surrounded by cameras and reporters. Quinn said, "I think we lost a tremendous leader."

"Is three years enough time?" a reporter asked.

"Personally? No. Think about it. That's not even allowing him to get one recruiting class through."

"So why did they do it?"

"I don't know. You're asking the wrong guy."

"The fans and the alumni seemed to want Ty gone."

"They don't know what goes on inside the program," Quinn said, with an edge to his voice. "They're on the outside. They have no idea. If they have any love for this university and us as players, they should trust us."

But then he said, "Everything happens for a reason. Faith and God will allow something good to come of all this. Not only for us, but for Coach Willingham and his family."

Famous former Notre Dame football players echoed the remarks of Quinn and the criticism leveled by the sporting press. Chris Zorich, a beloved nosetackle of the Holtz era, told the *Chicago Tribune,* "At the end of the day, it's how many wins and losses you have, which I understand. But we have now become a Miami, a Florida State, an Oklahoma. We have become a football factory. We used to be the ones who did it differently. I will always support Notre Dame football, but I have a really, really bad taste in my mouth." Zorich seemed adept with the traditional metaphors. Elsewhere, he said, "It really tarnishes what Notre Dame is all about." On television, Aaron Taylor, an offensive lineman of the Holtz and Davie years, and now a college football commentator for ABC, criticized the firing in similar terms, as did Raghib "Rocket" Ismail, beloved by the fans like no other, now a commentator for ESPN's *College GameDay.* Mike Golic, a linebacker of the Faust years, also an ESPN pundit, did as well. Not surprisingly, these remarks did not go over well among the fan base. Certain posters on ND Nation and other Internet message boards responded as if these men had snitched to the Feds and sold out the Family.

It seemed as if any Notre Dame alum with a public venue near at hand availed himself of the opportunity to offer his opinions on the firing. Ralph McInerny, the murder-mystery paperback writer and Notre Dame philosophy professor, known for his traditionalist views on Catholic higher education, wrote an op-ed piece for the *New York Times.* Given his conservatism, one might think he would have sympathized with the firing as a move to return Notre Dame to its O'Haran conventions. He did not. "The original idea of college sports was that games are a moral crucible that prepares one for life. The sad thing about the Willingham firing is that winning at all costs now seems paramount. Fans are by definition fanatic, but a university administration should take a longer view."

On Wednesday, December 1, Willingham faced the press for the first time since the Southern Cal game. He appeared in the briefing room inside the Joyce Center looking fit, rested, fresh—in good humor and at fighting weight. His hair, though, was a little gray at the temples. He wore a black T-shirt under an olive-drab blazer, and he looked Hollywood—he could have just flown in from the coast, cutting deals. He pulled verbal gags on reporters.

"Tyrone, over here. What do you feel your three-year legacy was here at Notre Dame?"

Willingham stared at the reporter for a moment and, after a beat, he said, "I'll let you write that up."

"Mr. Willingham."

"Yes."

"Given the tremendous stress that you have been under, how will you—"

"Does it show?"

Laughter rose from the gallery. The reporter stuttered. "Well, I just. Yes, um . . ."

"I'm joking, Joe. Don't take me seriously."

The reporter started again. "How will—how will you look back years from now on your three years here at the university?"

"I think you asked the same question that was kind of asked over there. So I'll let you two collaborate on the answer."

Further laughter from the press corps, and this news conference meant to address the end of Willingham's Notre Dame employment had, momentarily, the atmosphere of an awards ceremony immediately following the annual golf scramble of the South Bend Rotary Club.

His opening remarks, however, had been serious and seemingly well rehearsed. He said the right things so well that the term *class act* would be applied to him even on the fan message boards, in their new-found generosity. He reinforced his Molder of Men approach.

"I have to say I'm disappointed—I think that very much hits the mark. But at the same time I understand that *I* did not meet the expectations or standards that I set for myself and this program. And when you don't meet your own expectations, you make yourself vulnerable to the will of others. So, today, I'm no longer the head football coach at Notre Dame.

"And that does not mean that life ends. You go forward, as I expect this program to, and I expect our young men to. My goals have always been to help our young people be absolutely the best that they can be in all areas, both on and off the field, and I believe I have been true to that in my time here at Notre Dame. I am appreciative of the opportunity. I'm appreciative of what our administration has done, of what Dr.

Kevin White has done—and the Notre Dame family. And I'm just disappointed with what *I* didn't do, more than anything else."

There was no irony evident in his voice. But when the press corps put to him their weightier questions, he gave hints, pulled back, clammed up. The most interesting questions, what everyone wanted to know, received no answers.

Terrance Harris of the *South Bend Tribune* tentatively began, "Coach, what do you think it says about this business when a coach is only given three—"

"Terrance, let me stop you." The coach shook his head. He spoke slowly and almost in a whisper. "Not going there."

"All right. Well." And Harris broke off—he sounded so crestfallen that the coach unleashed a guffaw, and the press corps exploded with him in a tension-bursting laughter.

Another reporter took a stab. "Ultimately, who do you think made this decision?"

"That's not for a realist to be concerned about—only that there *was* a decision."

A reporter made a reference to the censorious response to the firing from the Black Coaches Association—two African-American coaches left in Division I. "Do you have any feelings or thoughts about that?"

"Plenty," Willingham said, and he stared at the reporter for a pregnant second. "But none of them will be expressed now."

"You talked about Sunday afternoon—you started getting wind that there was some sort of process going on. Can you tell us what was said to you, or . . . ?"

"No. Those are private conversations."

"Okay. Well, perhaps, um, Sunday, you accepted a bowl bid. This team accepted a bowl bid. I assume you—"

"I was very excited they accepted the bid."

"—I assume you thought you were going to coach the Insight Bowl. What changed between Sunday and Tuesday?"

"I cannot respond to that. I think there are parties you should talk to—if you desire to. They have an answer."

At one point Willingham quoted Martin Luther King, though without seeming to deliver any ulterior implication. A reporter had asked if he had given the team any parting advice. "I think when I arrived in

2002, I told them these words by Dr. Martin Luther King, who said that if a man is called on to be a street sweeper, he should sweep streets as Beethoven composed, as Shakespeare wrote poetry. He should sweep streets—and I think I misquoted the line—but he should sweep streets so well that all the hosts of heaven and earth say, 'There lived a great street sweeper.' It is with that attitude that I approached them in 2002, and it's the same attitude I approached them with yesterday—that they should strive always to be the best they can be."

It was no wonder he had charmed large portions of campus and inspired rallies on his behalf. In the days that followed, a group of students printed up T-shirts that said on the front INTREGRITY. When she heard the news, on Tuesday, Erica Genise, Willingham's administrative assistant since his Stanford days (though she bore the rather mandarinic title Director of Football Operations) reacted to his firing with explosive rage and had to be physically restrained by campus security. An administrator named Chandra Johnson, age fifty, who served as the assistant director of Campus Ministry, shaved her head in protest. She drew press coverage and told the *South Bend Tribune* that her pate would remain bald until Notre Dame won another football national title. "Because when we do, that will be justification for some people. Not for me, but for some people."

"Has Notre Dame changed for you in the last couple days?" Willingham was asked at his farewell presser.

"No, it hasn't. It is still Notre Dame. It is still—*I* think—a great place to be."

"Is there any sense of relief at all?"

"No."

"What advice would you give your successor?"

Willingham looked at the reporter quizzically. "What advice would I give my successor?" He stared at the microphones and the voice recorders sitting on the table in front of him. He paused for a long time. "You have to excuse me. My Rolodex is working, because there are a lot of things I could tell him. But I'm trying to figure out what would be the one thing. That's probably what you're looking for, right?"

"Well, if there's a few that you wanna share . . ."

"That would take too long."

And again the media laughed. When he came up with his piece of advice, it was sort of a letdown, a little banal, a little insipid. "Be yourself. Be yourself. That's always what's important."

The instant the university went public with Willingham's dismissal, many people believed it would take eleven hours for Notre Dame to announce a successor. As it turned out, it would take twelve days—perhaps the longest twelve days in the history of Notre Dame football. Rumors were afoot all through Tuesday from decently placed campus informants. Urban Meyer to Notre Dame. Ty Willingham to the University of Washington, which had recently fired its head coach after three years and a 2004 record of 1-10. Immediately after the firing, the talk at Leahy's in the Morris Inn centered on Willingham's flirtation with Washington. Like ND Nation, Leahy's has a reputation for rumormongering, but given the bar's proximity to the premises of power, it also shares with ND Nation a reputation for having the correct rumors—and on Tuesday night a Leahy's regular added his rumor to the mongering: Willingham had already met with people from Seattle and had already accepted a job.

"Of course, as you know, today there is, I think, a lot of rumors about what is taking place and what has already taken place," Willingham said at his farewell press conference, addressing the scuttlebutt, which he went on to deny. "And I was somewhat surprised by one I saw. I think it was that, two weeks ago, I was contacted by the University of Washington. There was no *official* contact with the University of Washington. In any contact with anyone, my position would have been very simple and straightforward. I'm the Notre Dame football coach. I came to do this job and only this job."

Later, Terrance Harris asked for clarification, and Willingham admitted that, yes, there had been "informal contact" with the parties. But, he said, "The answer I gave you was exactly what I told them."

Next question.

As it turned out, on the same day that incoming Notre Dame head coach Charlie Weis would give his introductory press conference in the Joyce Center briefing room, Willingham would give his at the University of Washington.

But on Thursday, December 2, the day after Willingham's farewell presser, Kevin White and Fr. John Jenkins boarded the Notre Dame private jet and flew to Salt Lake City. The Internet fan chat rooms reached capacity. Separate from the message boards, chat rooms are venues upon which conversations happen in real time. Each major Notre Dame fan Web site has a chat room, where members invariably congregate during times of high stress, good news and bad. The yearning for Urban Meyer had grown into a kind of lust. What had been simply a wish before Willingham's firing had become a one-man coaching search. He was The One—the subway alum with the Holtzian outclause. He already "got it," no on-the-job training required. Furthermore, to get Meyer in place so quickly after the firing would go a long way to staunch the flow of bad publicity. Indeed, it appeared increasingly obvious that perhaps the chief reason Notre Dame had fired Willingham was the ready availability of a coach so blatantly on the market. But the fan base had grown agitated. Not until the University officially announced its next head coach would Bobby Wentroble, for instance, son of the Mayor of the Neighborhood of Hope, ease his anxieties. Neither a message-board nor a chat-room denizen, Wentroble said, "I'm nervous. I can't keep doing this every couple years. Who do we get? I can't keep living like this. Obviously my first choice is Urban Meyer. He loves Notre Dame, he's been here before. But I'm nervous. I don't know."

There was reason for concern, and it existed in the looming presence of a palm-tree campus close to the beaches of the most talent-rich football state on earth, where 4.4 track stars and three-hundred-pound linemen are plucked from the local high schools like citrus from a grove. Midseason, the University of Florida had fired its head man, Ron Zook. Like Gerry Faust, Zook had been an excellent recruiter but a lousy coach, and though his teams lost at a slightly slower clip than Willingham's (Zook went 23-14 at Florida), Zook enjoyed a roster with more talent by any measure. Zook had been Florida's head coach for two and a half years, a circumstance that drew a few mildly critical comments from the sporting press; the University of Florida, evidently, was already a factory of football, though one that, like the state, was a little nouveau riche. The university had already passed on Steve Spurrier—the Old Ball Coach, the Gator legend, the *New Yorker* profile

subject, recently let go by the NFL Washington Redskins—who had almost single-handedly created Florida football as a national power in
the 1990s. Other than Spurrier and Oklahoma head coach Bob Stoops,
only one name had seriously entered the mix for Florida since it had
fired Zook in October. A rumor had circulated on a Florida fan site in
November: Florida had struck a deal with Urban Meyer. Both the
coach and the school, at the time, vigorously denied it, but certain conditions seemed to reinforce the gossip. Just one year earlier, Bernie
Machen, the University of Florida's new president, had come from the
same position at the University of Utah, where he had overseen the
hiring of Meyer from Bowling Green. And yet for ND fans, everyone
knew that Meyer had only one "dream job," and, a little ironically,
most Irish partisans dismissed the Florida business as the gossip of
overeager fans.

The pursuit of Meyer was possibly the most publicly scrutinized
coaching search of all time. On Tuesday night, Avani Patel of the *Chicago Tribune* somehow got through to Meyer on the telephone. He was
upset that he could be reached so easily. "Reading between the lines,"
she said later, she determined from his tone that no deal had yet been
struck between him and Notre Dame. Many fans could not imagine
this. Why fire Willingham without another coach inked and ready to
go? This, everyone knew, was how Notre Dame had gone about hiring
Lou Holtz. Once the university went public with Faust's firing, ND had
Holtz ready for the podium—no downtime, no scrutiny—a search conducted "under the radar," as they like to say. With the advent of the Internet and the twenty-four-hour news cycle, however, such a search
today was nearly impossible. Reporters from around the country descended on Utah. They swarmed Meyer after practices. The undefeated Utes were preparing for their BCS bowl game, and their coach
had no substantive comments.

A jet with the Notre Dame seal on its body had arrived in Utah on
Thursday evening. From the airport to downtown Salt Lake City, Jenkins and White and an unidentified Third Man rode in a black Chevy
Suburban with tinted windows. (A rumor spread that the Third Man
was, in fact, Lou Holtz, a false rumor. The Third Man's identity has
never been discovered, and most likely he was some athletic department assistant carrying binders.) A news helicopter followed from the

air and broadcast the long, slow drive like O.J.'s escape. Three television news vans, a car containing reporters from the *Salt Lake Tribune,* and another car containing a zealous "unidentified fan" (as the *Tribune* reported the next day), all pursued Notre Dame from the ground. The Suburban signaled left but hung a right. It went down a dead-end street; it doubled back. It went under highway overpasses, disappearing from the chopper's view. It lost the chopper. It accelerated through yellow lights and lost everyone but the *Salt Lake Tribune.* It pulled into the parking garage of the Grand American Hotel. "The three men stopped for a moment at the front desk, then headed to the elevators and, presumably, their rooms," the *Tribune* intrepidly reported. "The stakeout was on, right? Well, not exactly. It was realized a few minutes later that those elevators didn't go to the rooms; they go to the parking garage. The Fighting Irish had thrown the slip."

So, evidently, had Urban Meyer. Patel's bird-dogging paid off on Thursday morning, when she did a telephone interview with Meyer, before Meyer's meeting that night with Jenkins, White, et al. She posed the question: Are Notre Dame fans "correct in assuming an offer would be made Thursday night"?

Meyer replied, "There's absolutely no truth to that. I don't anticipate what you said is going to happen. As a matter of fact, I know that's not going to happen."

He knew because he had already cut a deal with Florida—in principle, but not signed—something that he had possibly neglected to tell Kevin White and John Jenkins before they'd got on their airplane in South Bend. He had also neglected to tell this to Bob Chmiel, an old colleague of Meyer's, an assistant during Holtz's last years and Davie's first and a subway alum born in Chicago who lived out a portion of his boyhood dream on the sidelines of Notre Dame Stadium. The two had a telephone conversation on the day of the Willingham firing. After the phone call, Chmiel says, "I was under the impression he would take the Notre Dame job. He said something like, 'You know how I feel about Notre Dame.' I said, 'You *better* take this job.' He didn't. We haven't spoken since." Chmiel goes on, "I was nothing short of shocked that he didn't accept. I thought it'd be a call-and-accept situation."

On Thursday night inside the chat rooms, the fans also assumed Meyer "would be Irish," as they like to phrase it, whether it's a high school prospect accepting a Notre Dame scholarship offer or, now, a messiah coming home. On Mike Frank's *Irish Eyes,* over three hundred people out of several thousand subscribers were chatting in the chat room. Three hundred was all the software could handle—a capacity crowd. Mike Frank was the moderator, and he relayed what information he could from his sources, which largely overlapped with those same Notre Dame staff and trustees known to ND Nation's alumni BoardOps.

The *Irish Eyes* chat room was, at this point, wavering between confidence that a contract awaited only Meyer's signature, and fear that Florida would sweep in (or had already swept in) with a highly sweetened counteroffer—10:30 p.m. eastern time on Thursday, 8:30 p.m. mountain. At this moment, Meyer allegedly was talking to White and Jenkins. It seemed as though officials from the Gators of Florida had scheduled a meeting with Meyer immediately before or after Notre Dame—the timing wasn't clear.

"Does Notre Dame realize that not a lot of work is getting done elsewhere because of this? Inconsiderate if you ask me."

"This is a must get. With everything that's happened the last eight years it can't turn into a public 'Notre Dame turned down again' type situation."

Frank's name appeared on the chat-room scroll in a red font, and his subscribers assaulted him with questions. Many sent their queries via instant messenger.

"Guys, I can't answer all these private messages. I need to chat here. I can't answer them. Sorry."

"Mike, can you prove the existence of God? NOW!!"

"Turn to booze."

"Mike, are you confident?"

"Confident, Mike?"

"Mike, please tell us you're confident?"

"I am confident. I've been confident, but I must admit, Florida sneaking in the backdoor is cause for alarm. But I do know how much Urban has said his dream is to coach at ND. When your dream is in front of you, you take it."

"That's right, he's Catholic. We throw in 5,000 years of plenary indulgence . . . for everyone in his family."

The best-informed posters and message-board administrators had assumed the status of informational pastorate to the masses, calming them with soothing words and divinations of success—fear not, for all will be swallowed up by victory. Mike Coffey on ND Nation posted a prayer, "Trust," by St. Francis de Sales, patron saint of the press.

Do not look forward to the changes and chances of this life in fear;
Rather look to them with full hope that, as they arise,
God will deliver you out of them . . .
Be at peace then, and put aside all anxious thoughts and
   imaginations.

But at this point, a strange thing happened. Coffey and Frank and all other tipsters found themselves cut off from the central scoop. No one knew what was going on—not the message-board ministry, not the mainstream media, and not even anyone's sources inside the athletic department or the Main Building. Only the men in Utah really knew what was happening. Bits of information came down, but only sporadically and through a cipher. Beat writers with years of source cultivation saw the flow of cross-checkable information dry up. "There's truth on every level," Jeff Jeffers, dean of the South Bend sports anchors, told me sometime after the brouhaha had subsided. "During the coaching search, for instance, two very good sources were giving me diametrically opposite things."

Mike Frank's chat continued across midnight and into Friday.

"Mike, if Urban stuns us, who should we look at next?"

"You should look at me closing this lemonade stand. I'm out of the freaking business if he spurns the Irish."

"What is Notre Dame's backup plan?"

"Mike—bottom line, before sleep. Are you still very very confident?"

"Everything that's been said has indicated he's signing. I've heard Friday, Monday, who knows. At this point, who the hell knows. I'm as confused as anyone."

This lack of comprehension occurred largely because of uncertainty at the very top. Notre Dame's leaders appeared to have assumed exactly what the fans had—if offered, Meyer would be Irish. As said many times on the night of the Salt Lake tête-à-tête, the president of a university does not get on an airplane to fly to a meeting without an offer in hand and more than a little assurance that the offer will be accepted. Back in South Bend, the *Observer,* the *Tribune,* the TV stations sent reporters and photographers and cameramen out to the airport west of town. Although they ended up not going through with it, the *Observer* editors wanted to assign a photographer to every landing strip in a forty-mile radius, just in case. If the prevailing attitude was correct, if Meyer had indeed agreed to a deal, then the twenty-eighth head coach in Notre Dame history would stride across the tarmac in the wee hours of the South Bend morning along with Jenkins and White. Sometime around 2 a.m., the plane came down out of the sky and taxied to a stop. The tarmac might as well have been water, but from the plane's hatchway Urban Meyer did not emerge to walk atop it.

The next day, December 3, brought a seeming end to Notre Dame football as Notre Dame fans knew it. There was something eschatological about it. Across the morning and afternoon as the details trickled out, it became impossible to separate news from rumor, scoop from speculation, but the outcome by 5 p.m. was indisputable: the University of Florida would announce Meyer as its new head coach the next day, while Notre Dame would continue its search like Diogenes with his lantern. The *Times-Union* of Jacksonville, Florida, carried a story in its morning editions—Florida and Meyer had a deal in principle. The source was Urban Meyer's father. But denials of the scoop quickly circulated from South Bend news organs. WNDU, with Jeff Jeffers at the helm, reported that "two sources close to the negotiations deny" the news out of Florida. In the chat room on Mike Frank's *Irish Eyes,* hope retrenched, quickly evaporated, made its return, and blew up again.

"About two hundred people have their nooses ready."

"Someone call the Pope and get him to threaten excommunication."

"This is crazy," Mike Frank posted in the chat. "Seems like every ten minutes it's all ND, then it's all Florida, then it's all ND."

The information came from people on the phone with people in Notre Dame SID, with subadministrators in the Main Building, with people who knew people who sat on the board of trustees. Voices into cans vibrating strings connected to other cans, the fans played telephone.

Some of the items that vibrated the string: Out in Salt Lake the night before, Meyer had expressed his desire for what came to be called "waivers" or "concessions"—six footballers per year who would not meet Notre Dame's already diminished academic requirements for scholarship athletes—an SAT in the 800 range but, more important, a set of required "core" college-prep classes. Meyer allegedly wanted Notre Dame to overlook some of these requirements. Six waivers per year would equal roughly 25 percent of the team. There were other rumors as well: That Notre Dame came back to Meyer with a compromise—three waivers, with Jenkins getting final say on the admittees. That Meyer on Tuesday or Wednesday went on to demand, in addition, the acceptance of junior-college players, whom Notre Dame had never before admitted because the university believed they would be less likely to succeed in a rigorous academic environment. That junior-college players equaled deal breaker. That Meyer had requested that Notre Dame send him the team's recruiting notebook so he could get a jump start on that task. That Notre Dame had shipped said notebook to Utah overnight via Federal Express. That Notre Dame "lowballed" Meyer at first with a salary rumored to be as low as a comical $300,000 a year. That this infuriated Meyer. That Notre Dame quickly matched what Florida had already offered—around $2 million per annum. That Meyer broke away from his meeting with Jenkins and White to make a phone call to Florida. That Meyer broke away to make a phone call to his good friend Bob Davie. That Bob Davie had given Meyer this rather loaded but obvious advice: *It's tough to win at Notre Dame.* That Meyer's wife refused to live ever again in the Midwest, least of all South Bend, Indiana. That Meyer had had a deal with Florida in principle since the moment Zook had got sacked. That Meyer had had a deal with Notre Dame in principle since the moment Willingham had got sacked. That by Friday afternoon Notre Dame was furious with Meyer. That Notre Dame felt "misled" by Meyer. That if Meyer still harbored any dreams of coaching at Notre Dame, Notre Dame would make sure that those dreams forever remained inside Meyer's head, which along with his body was now persona non grata at the thin places of South Bend.

If nothing else is ever truly confirmed, one fact remains: Meyer had a deal by the end of December 3 with Florida. This is when things got eschatological—The End—and chat rooms and message boards across Notre Dame fandom lost their collective minds.

"This officially ends our Saturdays."

"Good going ND Admin. New president. Same crap."

"ND football may have just died."

"Yes ND football is in BIG trouble . . . this could be the nail in the coffin."

"Arrogant ND."

"Be a football school for once."

"Let some thugs in."

"Ty is the perfect man for ND."

"Admissions or winning NCs, what do you want?"

"Notre Dame football is dead."

"Can we get Ty back?"

While the chat raged on, ND Nation on Friday evening shut down its message board and locked it to the masses. The Wailing Wall had subsumed Rock's House. BoardOps intoned its displeasure and attached a message to the top of the board. "Okay that's it. We don't have the time or inclination to hover over this board all night policing the wild rantings. Losing Meyer is a bad situation, to be sure. But there's plenty of blame from both sides in this and plenty of searching yet to do for a coach." So powerful had the notion of Notre Dame Head Coach Urban Meyer become that the first gut reactions from the fans seemed mostly to impugn Notre Dame along the lines of its most virulent critics. After the ten-year decline, after all the off-field embarrassments and mistakes, after so much middling football, after the frenzy and outrage surrounding Willingham's dismissal, Urban Meyer had come to represent the most immediate remedy and savior, no matter his résumé, which was both highly impressive and somewhat lacking. Without him, it seemed as though all Notre Dame's critics were right—as though Bob Davie had hit the mark: *It's tough to win at Notre Dame.*

"I wonder if anyone will finally believe me when I say that ND is not that attractive of a job for a lot of coaches because of the pressure. If they can't even get Meyer, that says something."

"Why did we fire Willingham again?"

"ND's actions suggest they have finally decided to go public with the fundamental process of de-emphasizing football. If that is the case, then . . . whaddayagonnado?"

"I am embarrassed to be an ND fan."

"We should never have revamped the stadium."

"NBC is going to put ND on the Bravo Channel."

"We're the biggest joke in sports."

"It's Notre Dame—it's part of our new tradition."

The headlines for the most part agreed. The outrage quickly turned to highly satisfied ridicule. Jay Mariotti, *Chicago Sun-Times,* pulled off the difficult task of actually sneering in his column headline. "Notre Dame no dream job after all/ When a man lusts after a fantasy for years, only to thumb his nose when it's offered, something must be wrong and dysfunctional about it." Several days later, ESPN's nightly highlight show *SportsCenter* dedicated thirty minutes of programming to the post-Meyer Notre Dame coaching search (Notre Dame had evidently faced down extinction if ESPN was willing to chronicle the place so intently), which included sports columnists and interview subjects with limited affiliations to the school proclaiming that no coach had any interest. "It used to be the best job in sports. Now, it doesn't even make the list," said the *SportsCenter* anchorperson. Chris Connelly, who last anyone saw had been reciting the latest pop-music news on MTV, said in a report on the search process, "The ND job is less sought after than a tax audit."

The chat room on Wednesday included gallows-humor coaching-search speculation.

"Bring back Holtz."

"Faust."

Gerry Faust probably wasn't on the list. Neither was Holtz. Approaching seventy years of age, he had just resigned as the head coach of the University of South Carolina to make way for former Gator and Redskin Steve Spurrier. Holtz left behind in South Carolina a rather ugly situation—a fight breaking out with Clemson after his farewell game, players arrested, players kicked off the team, and a five-year record of 33-37. More than anything, it appeared as if Holtz needed a little rest. According to an informed trustee, however, immediately after Meyer signed with Florida, Holtz made a bid to come out of his

two-week retirement. For around forty-eight hours the lobbying occurred on Holtz's behalf from a few highly placed Friends of the University. The old messiah apparently wanted a second chance—this
time as a kind of interim coach, maintaining the program for a year or
two until a long-term candidate could be located, just as Hugh Devore
had done in 1963 between Kuharich's resignation and Parseghian's
hiring. "He gave it forty-eight hours and then he gave up. He quit the
effort," the trustee told me. "As they say, 'You can't go home again.' "

Once the fans had time to live with the turn of events for an hour or
so, sentiment largely came back the other way. As Urban Meyer's father told the Florida newspaper, his son felt he could win more
quickly at Gainesville, where the roster ran deeper with talent than the
one at Notre Dame, and many Notre Dame fans came to view this as
yellow, gutless, spineless, weak.

"ND should not change the admissions standards for any coach."

"Refusing to compromise your standards is not arrogance."

"Rule #1: go after a coach who doesn't talk to Bob Davie."

"Screw him. He's the enemy now. We need to look at other possibilities."

"ND football is dead."

"We are not dead."

"We are dead."

"If we're dead, then leave."

"UM = false idol."

14

A House Divided

No one could have believed it on Friday, but things would get even worse. The dark night of the Notre Dame soul lasted for a little over a week.

On December 8, 2004, Fr. Edward Malloy, CSC, flew to New York City for a conference sponsored by a Street & Smith's trade magazine called the *Sports Business Journal.* The conference was called the Intercollegiate Athletics Forum, and Malloy sat on a panel entitled "The Business of Intercollegiate Athletics: The Chancellor/President Perspective." Among his copanelists were Gordon Gee, chancellor of Vanderbilt University; Steadman Upham, president of the University of Tulsa; Jon Wefald, president of Kansas State University; Scott Cowen, president of Tulane; and Karen Holbrook, president of Ohio State University, an institution then being investigated for football booster and recruiting violations by the NCAA, whose president, Myles Brand, was the seventh panelist. Malloy had committed to appear at the conference long before the Willingham ejection. He knew that a question regarding the affair would arise, and perhaps he had sketched out an answer in his mind beforehand. His remarks were not otherwise prepared. He later told the *Observer* that he wanted to "clarify the record." The media and other outraged parties had blamed Willingham's firing on the leadership at Notre Dame in general—administration, board, athletic department, wealthy benefactors—and Malloy, as sitting president, received much, if not most, of the criticism. Over the next few days and weeks his remarks would grow in infamy until, today, they are viewed in some alumni and fan circles as treasonous, perfidious, selfish, and emblematic of Malloy the administrator, the last words of a "milquetoast" president, as one alumnus has described him—Notre Dame's version of U. S. Grant.

His remarks lasted about a minute and a half. ESPN and the Street
& Smith scribes were on hand to record it. Most famously Father Malloy said, "In my eighteen years, there have been only two days that I
have been embarrassed to be president of Notre Dame: Tuesday and
Wednesday of last week, because I felt we had not abided by our precedent . . . which was a five-year window for a coach to display the capacity to be successful within our system and to fit. Both Kevin White
and I have a very high regard for Tyrone. Having lost to Southern Cal,
we had a meeting called by my successor with a strong presence of the
board of trustees, which led to a result.

"There was also the phenomenon of the messiah coach. Everybody
wants to be on the A-list. This year, I think there are fourteen college
football positions that have changed or are changing. There are probably three people that are on the messiah list, which means eleven programs have no messiah.

"Notre Dame will get a coach. I hope that that person does well.
But I think the philosophical shift [reported elsewhere as "hit"] we
have taken is a significant one. . . . I'm not happy about it, and I do not
assume responsibility for it. I think it was the wrong move, and the fact
that other schools have made similar choices after three years suggests
that they are feeling the same pressures that we are.

"I'm a good soldier, and in times of transition, people can disagree.
I don't think there is a lack of goodwill or that anybody is to be blamed
for a racist decision or anything else. I just think there was a lot of pressure in the works.

"All the good coaches who get fired will get another job, in college
or pro. Their future is not at risk, but what happens in the transition is
that the institutions get tarnished in ways that I think, in the long run,
we pay a huge price for."

The predictable headlines ensued—Notre Dame, once again, derisively in the public eye. The story line now: Notre Dame was a House
Divided, and divided, evidently, by trustees with an inordinate interest in Notre Dame football. "Malloy rips Irish decision," said the
Chicago Tribune. "Notre Dame President Blasts Firing," said the *Washington Post.* "Notre Dame's President Says He Opposed Firing Willingham," said the *New York Times.* Matt Storin, public relations man for
the university as a whole, former editor of the *Boston Globe,* Notre

Dame class of 1964, immediately sent up the flak. "There was debate and disagreement as there often is with any major decision at an academic institution."

Large portions of Malloy's constituencies and the Notre Dame Family were not pleased. The term *betrayal* was used. He had aired the university's "dirty laundry," and what was embarrassing were Malloy's public comments, not the firing of a football coach. Others felt that Malloy should have put up a fight at the time of the decision or resigned outright then and there.

One Notre Dame alumnus, class of 1991, a professor of philosophy at a small college in the midwest, composed a short essay and posted it on ND Nation—"How Not to Be a Notre Dame Man." He seemed familiar with the O'Haran concepts, and his sentiments summed up the reaction of certain fans and alumni to Malloy's words.

There are ancillary things about being a Notre Dame man . . . but the most important are found in the motto above the door of the Basilica: "God, Country, Notre Dame." Ed Malloy fails in at least two of these areas:

God: A NDM needs to realize that the glory of God comes before everything else. This means that Notre Dame men are called to excel at everything they do, for God's glory, including academics, family, business and football. We know that God has blessed us greatly, and we dare great things for His sake, in all our endeavors. Malloy has been willing to sacrifice the excellence of the university in football not for the glory of God, but for the cheap glory of the admiration of aspirational peers.

Notre Dame: A Notre Dame man loves the University that formed him with a love usually reserved for family. He sees it as his alma mater, the mother who nourished him. Since Notre Dame is named for the Mother of God, this is more than metaphor. A NDM would never promote himself at her expense. Malloy has, through his words to the media about the Willingham firing, attempted to inflate his own reputation at the cost of Notre Dame, the mother that nourished him. . . .

Let's recall: he wasn't embarrassed by Kim Dunbar . . . by the age discrimination case, by the George O'Leary hiring, or by the

airing of the Vagina Monologues *on campus on Ash Wednesday,
but he's embarrassed at the firing of an ineffective football coach.*

*Finally, a genuine son of Notre Dame knows that he is part of
a family, and that family disputes are best settled within the
family. . . .*

University presidents everywhere, perhaps some of them "aspirational peers," seemed to have a different opinion. They too spoke of
"values," but the term's meaning diverged from that used by the Notre
Dame faithful. Scott Cowen of Tulane later wrote an essay published in
the *Chronicles of Higher Education,* "The visibility of athletics, combined with its psychological impact on fans, can make it almost impossible to have intelligent, balanced discussions about it. Otherwise
thoughtful people can become irrational, making it difficult . . . for the
university to apply the same scrutiny to athletics that it applies to academics." Vanderbilt's Gee said to the *Times,* "I think what Father Malloy said was one of the most courageous things I've heard in my
twenty-four years as a university president. What he basically said is
that the value system of the university and the value system of the athletic department have been totally disrupted." Gee went on, "If this
were done at University X, people would say that's just the way they
do things. This was done at a premier academic institution with a solid
record of winning and a values system that it failed to stick to in this
case." The view of this university president seemed to be that excellence in football is not a value. It is, on the contrary, a vice. An academically serious university cannot do both. There are no shades of
gray. What these university presidents had to say about the NCAA investigation into possible booster violations at Ohio State—and the
value-system disruption that this may have caused—has not been
recorded.

I spoke with Father Malloy over the phone a couple of months later
and asked if, given the powerful reaction to his words, he regretted
having said them. He responded immediately and emphatically.

"No."

And then there was a long pause. He would proceed no further
with that subject. "I've said what I've said about the decision and the
process." But he did seem a little apologetic about refusing to expand

on his feelings. "Let me say that I've been invited by multiple radio and television and print media people to elaborate on what I said, and I refused all of those interviews. So my not talking about the topic is not peculiar to you."

Malloy told me that his comments at the forum were part of the American collegiate zeitgeist at large—"messiah coaches" and "Internet mobocracies" and "the thin boundary between professional and amateur athletics" and "the temptations of boards of trustees relative to athletics, and so on." He said, "The context of the discussion among the presidents and chancellors would suggest that all of these were issues that everyone recognized. So if I were to give a talk about the challenges of intercollegiate athletics, those topics would all be on it. It wouldn't necessarily have anything to do with Notre Dame. It would have to do with everything that's going on in the world that we inhabit."

Malloy has spoken and written at length on one in particular of the above "challenges." In his volume *Monk's Reflections: A View from the Dome*, he wrote:

> *The role of alumni with regard to intercollegiate athletics can be controversial. Often an institution's fans include more than alumni—at Notre Dame we have our subway alumni, fans who have not gone to Notre Dame but have developed a high degree of identification with us. Some of these fans are "fanatics" in the pejorative sense of the term, with a distorted sense of the priorities of the institution. They allow the success or failure of athletic teams to be the source of their institutional loyalty. Almost all studies, including some we've conducted, show no direct correlation between the success of athletic teams and the overall health and well-being of the institution, and that goes for success in fundraising and student recruiting.*
>
> *Occasions may arise when athletic administrators need help from the central administration in curtailing inappropriate lobbying or pressure from alumni and fans—and sometimes even from trustees or regents. The board, as the final institutional authority, must ensure that the intercollegiate program is not allowed to take on a life of its own or to distort institutional priorities. It is tragic*

that on a few campuses board members with a particular interest in athletics have failed to support the president or chancellor in relationships with the athletic program. One of the great strengths of Notre Dame is that that has never been true here.

"A skull-and-bones society," "a kind of cabal," "the power divisions of the university," "shadowy, sinister figures," "the group"—in media reports and in campus gossip, the seven men who'd converged to discuss the fate of Ty Willingham seemed to reside in a world of secret handshakes and hermetic insignia. It was as if the Opus Dei of an infamous best seller had had its hand, as well, in the sacking of a football coach. By university policy, all personnel matters are held in confidence, and Notre Dame's trustees have an unofficial mandate never to discuss school business with the media. There is, within Notre Dame's leadership, a certain culture of secrecy—at least according to popular reputation. Some have likened it to the Vatican, and it rises, in part, from the notions of Brotherhood and Family held dear by the Congregation of Holy Cross and, therefore, by the university as a whole. Thus, when Malloy went public with his feelings, he broke a kind of unwritten code, thereby upsetting even those people in the Family who might otherwise have agreed with him. Meanwhile, Fr. John Jenkins and his right-hand man, Executive Vice President John Affleck-Graves, refused media interviews almost daily following the Willingham firing. Anyone expecting "transparency" then, as if this were a congressional hearing, might as well have gone to the rock for water.

Into this vacuum, conspiracy theories began to pour—a football-mad faction of the board of trustees had hijacked the university and fired its coach, a faction led by Board Chairman Patrick McCartan and backed by Fr. Timothy Scully, Malloy's old nemesis. Malloy's comments in New York gave ammunition to this thesis. The meeting of the Group of Seven, called by Jenkins, had contained a "strong presence of the board of trustees, which led to a result," Malloy had stated. And: "I just think there was a lot of pressure in the works." Malloy seemed to be hinting at inappropriate trustee involvement in Willingham's firing, and given his writings on the subject, the theorists began to connect a few dots. Notre Dame's Faculty Board on Athletics, which reports to the NCAA, issued its censure of the firing, which also contained oblique references to this same anxiety about the role of trustees in the situation: the faculty board was not included in the conversation, and the swiftness of the decision to fire caused the faculty board "concern."

More fuel came from David Duerson, former Notre Dame defensive back, class of 1983, former Chicago Bear, and now a sausage magnate in suburban Chicago. He was also a Malloy-appointed trustee. During his tenure, he had talked up such things as JumboTrons and sided with Malloy on so many issues that he had fallen out of favor with the C4C set of Notre Dame alumni and fans. On December 10, on a radio talk show in Chicago, he gave his feelings vent, echoing Malloy in New York. Like others, he left open the question of race. He also said, "Was I completely surprised Ty was released? No, not given the win-loss record, particularly the last two years. But it was the way in which it was handled. . . . It should have involved the entire board. We should have at least been involved in the discussion instead of the blindsided nature in which it was handled."

When I asked Malloy this question directly—was Willingham's firing the result of overzealous trustees overstepping their bounds—Malloy understandably dodged and pursued generalities. Again he talked about the zeitgeist rather than the incident. He tried to erase the lines between the dots. "I don't want to connect any concerns I have about boards and how they function with that particular event. I think I indicated when I spoke at the forum in New York City that I thought one of the great temptations of a board had to do with athletics. I think that's descriptively true around the country." Myles Brand, chief of the NCAA, seemed to agree with Malloy. He told the *New York Times*, "I think what's happening is that we're bringing to the surface these issues. Particularly the role of trustees in decision-making. We've talked about it quietly in the past. It's time now that we talked about it publicly."

Partly to dispel these mounting allegations of trustee involvement, Fr. John Jenkins on December 15 convened a meeting with the faculty board to explain "the process" that led to the firing. He made a statement, and he took questions from the floor. No reporters were present, but the university later released Jenkin's speech. It was also, in part, a rejoinder to Malloy's comments a week earlier. He essentially denied being a puppet. He took issue with the term *pressure*.

"First, it has been said that there was inappropriate Trustee involvement in this decision. As to me personally, I was not pressured into any action I took by any member of the Board of Trustees. As I said, senior university administrators did contact me to express concern (though not to pressure me), but neither the Chairman of the Board nor the Chair of the Athletic Affairs took the initiative to contact me about this situation. I took the initiative to ask their respective opinions."

Jenkins also laid out in his statement a cursory time line of events.

Sometime on the morning of November 29, the Monday following Notre Dame's thirty-one-point defeat to Southern Cal, Jenkins walked past the full-length portrait of Father Hesburgh hanging outside Room No. 400, Main Building, and entered the Office of the President. He had some things on his mind, and he suggested to Malloy that they schedule an immediate meeting with "other leaders of the university" to discuss Willingham's performance. "Fr. Malloy made it clear that he did not favor making a change, but expressed a willingness to have a discussion." This must not have been the first time that Jenkin's thoughts on Willingham's performance were discussed; Willingham in his press conference said that he'd first heard on Sunday that his job might be in jeopardy. But the real hashing out of the arguments for and against dismissal did not occur until Monday's conclave. Into the meeting Jenkins brought Kevin White, University Provost Nathan Hatch, and Executive Vice President John Affleck-Graves. He also telephoned two trustees—Patrick McCartan, chairman of the board of trustees, and Philip Purcell, chairman of the board's athletic affairs committee—and conferenced them in "because this was a decision about such a high-profile issue." The summit lasted through Monday morning and afternoon and into the night. "All parties in that meeting expressed their views."

What views each party had on the Willingham matter came out through process of elimination and a little deductive reasoning.

Patrick McCartan. Notre Dame class of 1954. Former managing partner of Jones Day, with two thousand attorneys worldwide and $1 billion in annual revenue. Chairman of the board trustees for the previous five years. Age, seventy. Lives in Cleveland. Trial lawyer who made his name defending corporations against hostile takeovers.

Member of Augusta National. Formidable mind, passionate football fan. Believed to sympathize with the C4C movement. Vote: dismiss.

Philip Purcell. Notre Dame class of 1969. Embattled chairman and CEO of Morgan Stanley; would later resign from those posts under stockholder pressure. Shares of the firm rose on the news. Winnetka, Illinois. Age, 61. C4C sympathizer. Chair of the trustees' athletics committee. Vote: dismiss.

Nathan Hatch, provost since 1996. Appointed by Malloy. Second-in-command and in charge of academe. Age, fifty-eight. Religion historian. Native of South Carolina. Protestant. Educated at Wheaton College, Illinois, and Washington University in St. Louis. Several months later, in early 2005, he would announce his resignation to become president of Wake Forest University. Vote: unknown.

Kevin White, athletic director. Hired by Monk in the wake of the NCAA sanctions, etc. Putative hirer of Willingham, of whom Willingham said in his farewell press conference, "For those of you that are close to our program, you will know that Kevin White and I have been very close. We've had conversations weekly, daily. So Kevin and I have always been very close and Kevin has always kept me informed of everything about our program as I have kept *him* informed about everything about our program." Grew reclusive after the firing. Seen wandering the streets of Phoenix sometime during Notre Dame's stay in Arizona for the Insight Bowl, an invitation the players had chosen to accept. Vote: support.

Monk Malloy, sitting president. Set to step down from his post on July 1, 2005. Rumored to have issued a directive to the athletic department around the time of the Stanford game, mid-October, to the effect of: Willingham will remain in his job no matter what. Evidently the grumbling had grown strong enough even by mid-October to convince Malloy such a directive was necessary. Did not want his legacy to contain both the hiring and firing of Notre Dame's first African-American head coach. Vote: support.

Malloy's vote, however, had one very large condition, a condition repeatedly stressed by Jenkins in his statement to the faculty board. "The decision to retain or dismiss a coach lies with the athletic director and ultimately with the president of the university. We are in an unusual position this year, because we have both a president and a president-elect. It has been and remains my understanding that, although Fr. Malloy is president and holds authority for decisions, it is appropriate for me to be involved in decisions which will influence future years when I will be president. Although no formal agreement between Fr. Malloy and myself has been articulated about specifically which decisions I will be involved in, we have been operating with an informal, good faith understanding that my voice will be brought in and influence decisions on matters relating to the period when I will be president." In the end, it is somewhat clear that Malloy abdicated, and Jenkins, for the space of a day, at a meeting having to do with football, took office seven months early.

John Jenkins, president-elect. It has been speculated in private by one Notre Dame staff member that Jenkins "doesn't give a shit about football." The staffer was, of course, being hyperbolic. What this person meant was that Jenkins, if given his druthers, would, in this staffer's opinion (an opinion shared by others as well), be content enough with the football status quo under Willingham and extremely hesitant to incite controversy by firing him. Jenkins, the scholar of ancient and medieval philosophy, would likely not have had the firmest understanding of the problems developing on the football field and in the football offices under Willingham. In other words, he might have needed a little help to gain that understanding.

"In recent weeks," Jenkins said in his speech, "a number of high-level administrators at the university came to me expressing concern about the football program. We had had mixed success on the field during the past two seasons, and the concern was about the trajectory of what is clearly the most visible athletic program in the university." Jenkins did not name any of these "high-level administrators." Those with some knowledge of the people involved in the decision have conjectured who those "administrators" could be. The name most often uttered is John Affleck-Graves.

John Affleck-Graves, executive vice president. No. 3 in command at the university. First lay EVP in school history. Duties include overseeing $800 million operating budget, $3 billion endowment. Age, fifty-three. Chair of the finance department. Professor of high finance, revered by his students. Seemingly without enemy on campus, respected and well liked. Tall and trim and athletic, a long-distance runner. Has completed ninety-five marathons, one in less than three hours, and two superendurance fifty-six-milers. Native of South Africa. Catholic. Educated at the University of Cape Town.

Some have called Affleck-Graves "the prime mover." As the season unraveled through October and November, Graves had made comments, both in public and in private, indicating that he did care about football in its purest sense. He was in accord with the C4C letter drafters—to let Notre Dame football continue to slide in performance would be to wreck a sine qua non American cultural institution. Though from South Africa, Graves had been a professor and then an administrator at Notre Dame for the last eighteen years, and over that time he was said to have acquired a love for the sport of football as played by Our Lady's University. He wanted Notre Dame to be excellent at it once again, and sooner rather than later. There was a sense of urgency. "Because December through February is so critical to recruiting for a football program," Jenkins said to the faculty board, "and because clarity about the future is so critical to recruiting, it was clear a decision had to be made quickly either to retain and support the head coach, or dismiss him." As measured by the talent scouts and recruiting "analysts" who follow high school football, Notre Dame's recruiting class in 2003 had been the worst in thirty years. It is well-known that the best high school prospects want to play in a winning program and play for coaches who will adequately prepare them for possible inclusion on NFL rosters. When a program goes 5-7 and 6-5 in consecutive seasons, the best prospects will make the obvious conclusions. To continue with the status quo, Graves and others might have argued to Jenkins, would mean a further decline in talent, and therefore further discouraging win-loss records, and therefore a further decline in talent—a kind of negative snowball to permanent mediocrity, an implosion. "What you must do eventually, you should do immediately," the saying goes, and it's possible that these very words went into Jenkin's ear.

Graves: dismiss. Jenkins: dismiss.

Other high-level administrators advising Jenkins might well have come from university development and finance. This is a contentious area. As Malloy wrote in *Monk's Reflections,* as Father Hesburgh wrote in his memoir *God, Country, Notre Dame,* as professional higher-ed fund-raisers will say over and over, as internal Notre Dame studies and independent long-haul, thirty-year sociological surveys have shown— the performance of university sports teams does not affect, one way or the other, the performance of university fund-raising.

But ten years of decline and yet another season of crushing losses appeared to induce a kind of boiling point within Notre Dame fandom. According to campus gossip, several benefactors in the six-figure range, in the eight-figure range, expressed their displeasure with the direction of the football program. To whom they may have expressed their attitudes, and what they may have said, exactly, Campus Gossip could not say. There was, as well, the C4C-induced groundswell, the letter-writing campaign that had begun after the Boston College game, all the expressions of dismay, the withholdings of donations, the anecdotal scuttlebutt coming from student solicitors indicating that some people were displeased enough to forgo contribution or pledges to the 2004 Annual Fund. How many people and how much money is anyone's guess.

One official in university development later told me that only a small number of people threatened to withhold financial gifts at the end of the 2004 season. "With every coach we get those kinds of letters. That's gone on for years. In Faust's final years we got them—even with Holtz. But, then, you look at the names on the letters, you look at the record, and you see that most of these people have never been supporting the place. They're part of a fringe element."

The officer did admit, however, that the "emotional climate" on campus and within the Notre Dame Family at the end of the season certainly did not constitute a fund-raising-friendly situation. "Notre Dame is an emotional place. I mean *top to bottom,* it's an emotional place. That can be very very good, but it can also be very very challenging." The official said, "Make no mistake, many of our donors are concerned and are fans and want to see the team do well. I know we've picked up a significant number of donors over the years because they were first interested in football. And sometimes we have to hold people's hands when the football program is not going well. It plays on their emotions as much as it does on the students or the general alumni. But overall most of our donors are loyal; they'll certainly say things and be critical, but they'll be loyal through it all. There is a correlation between the overall climate of the university and financial support—but it all balances out. I think we were still going to have a solid year of support no matter what happened, if Ty was retained or let go." Though Notre Dame's alumni and benefactor base may not have refused to donate in massive numbers, they did, indeed, emotions running high, express their C4C-like dismay.

I asked Malloy if he'd noticed an increase in the number of such communiqués he'd received toward the end of the season. "Not particularly," he said. "But how does one ever know? We have a hundred and ten thousand graduates. So if twenty wrote you, does that represent the hundred and ten thousand? People don't tend to write you if they're happy. I don't get that much mail during football season—despite what people may think. I get positive mail about the program and coaches, and negative mail. It just goes along with the territory." After Willingham was fired, "we tended to hear from another constituency who didn't write before," Malloy added.

"Another constituency?"

"Yes. Many of the people who wrote, or commented publicly, were unhappy with what took place, and they expressed their unhappiness. Some *were* happy with what had happened. But it's always a question of making a judgment on how representative any expression of opinion is at any given moment—and whether that makes a difference in what's the right thing to do."

I spoke with a lower-tier trustee about what role the seeming fan and alumni groundswell might have played in the firing. "I think it played a part," the trustee said. "How big a part, I don't know." He said he had received at least fifty letters in all, most of them CC'd to Kevin White, Father Malloy, and Patrick McCartan. They began arriving the Monday after the Southern Cal game. "It certainly looked like an organized effort. It almost seemed like a lawyer group got together. All of them seemed to be lawyers. All were alum. It was like a big chat room got together and wrote them. I'd never got letters like that before, ever."

He added, "And then there's the fact that we're launching a big fund-raising drive."

Capital campaign number three in the university's history. Goal: some amount above a billion dollars, but the final target not yet made

public. As yet unnamed. Nicknamed, in the meantime, the worst-kept
secret on campus. Age, less than a year. Received university approval
from the board in the summer of 2004. Now awaiting enough seed capital to go public with momentum. Chaired by J. W. Jordan, Chicago financier, Notre Dame trustee, class of 1969, who, with the university,
would announce in February 2005 a $40 million donation, the second-
largest single gift in Notre Dame history. The university in the past has
always excelled at inducing its alumni to contribute—Notre Dame
ranks usually No. 1 or 2 in the nation with regard to alumni giving in
any given year, trading places with Dartmouth. Some people have
speculated that the fan groundswell—emotional, filled with nostalgia,
worried about the lasting and, in their eyes, essential identity of their
university—might have affected the "climate" of the capital campaign's early stages. In this way, Notre Dame fandom may have added
its own voice to the discussion. Vote: dismiss.

Jenkins, however, has denied that money received a vote. The development official, who has intimate dealings with the still-secretive
capital campaign, agreed. "I'm more immersed in this thing than almost anybody else. Believe me, Ty's firing did not happen because of
that." In late January 2005, Jenkins conducted an interview with *USA
Today*—his one and only after the firing. The reporter asked him point-
blank if fund-raising played a role in the decision to dismiss, and Jenkins replied, "I can say categorically that financial considerations
weren't even mentioned in our discussion, at least any discussion I
had with anybody."

If he didn't discuss this with anybody, other issues likely came
into play, including the seeming availability of a subway-alumnus
head coach doing good work in Utah. Another theory exists on campus: if it weren't for Urban Meyer and his out-clause, Willingham
would have been granted a year of reprieve. Of perhaps even greater
concern may have been Willingham's contact with the University of
Washington, which some Notre Dame people believed constituted
more than a simple one-off rejection of interest on the part of the then-
Irish head coach. In the same *USA Today* interview, Jenkins also denied flat out that this was a factor. The gossip said otherwise, and
because the meetings were closed, "and no one is talking," as one insider put it, all of these factors exist merely as plausible explanations

in the chatter of the gossipers, in the minds of the fans. All of these potential reasons, then, both those admitted by Jenkins—the repeated
and obvious on-the-field failures, the deterioration in recruiting talent,
the need to act quickly, the emotional turmoil among fans and alumni,
the continuation through 2004 of the ten-year decline—as well as
those factors that were theoretical—the money, the messiah, the alleged Seattle "flirtation"—all of it conspired to create the Case against
Willingham.

"After sleeping on the issue for one night," Jenkins said to the faculty, "the university administrators decided, with the concurrence of
the trustees, to make a change." It seemed as if the entire, great motivating tension of Notre Dame—its curse and its blessing—had coalesced around a single event, a moment in time, a synod, a choice. Both
sides of the argument believed that their views represented the True
Notre Dame. To fire was to break precedent and favor winning above
all else and was, therefore, morally corrupt and un-Catholic and
un–Notre Dame. "Especially at an institution like Notre Dame where
ethical behavior is so important, to not honor Tyrone Willingham's five
years I think is a mistake," one former trustee told me, summing up the
case of the Willingham supporters. It would send a message to the rest
of the world at odds with what Notre Dame supposedly stood for, that
honor must come before victory. Untrue, said the other side. To fire
was to acknowledge that excellence is achievable in all facets of the
game—a coach doesn't need to cheat to win; he can oversee a team
with integrity and scruples, he can make sure his players are actual
students, and he can, at the same time, as the song says, "win over all."
He can, to borrow Kevin White's phrase, do as well on Saturdays as the
rest of the week. This was the central truth and myth of Notre Dame.
The school had a duty, inherent in the Holy Cross charism, to prove to
the world that such things were possible. The school had a duty, inherent in the charism, "not to be like everyone else," but "better." Cyn-
ics described this notion as, at best, hopelessly naive and, at worst,
hollow arrogant palaver, little more than a sales pitch. Believers called
it the necessary path in the life of a human being in the world, a world
that happened to include football. Win it all, and win with dignity—
maybe such a thing was naive, but someone at least needed to make the
attempt. If it wasn't going to be attempted, drop football. To fire a coach

who was failing to do it all, and to find one who could—this was pro–Notre Dame.

Of the groundswell from the fans, the trustee who had received all the alumni letters told me, "That was impressive, that people care that much. I think we want our alumni to be good men and good women. Good spouses, good children, good parents. I think we stress that with how we educate our students. And maybe they thought we weren't doing the same thing in this area, in football. If you're always striving for excellence, why settle for mediocrity? I think a lot of them saw it as a public embarrassment."

If it was one thing both sides agreed on, it was that Notre Dame and its football meant more to great numbers of people—whether they called themselves fans or not—than a sport involving boys and a field and a score at the end of the day.

One does not know if the seven men involved called on the Holy Spirit for assistance, but it seems likely they would have.

The votes were tallied. Jenkins, Affleck-Graves, McCartan, and Purcell—yea. Malloy and White–nay. Hatch, no one knows. He has not and will not comment on the matter publicly. Reports in the press have said the group voted 5–2 to fire. But the five might have included Malloy's abstention. In the end, however, it didn't matter. By 10 a.m. on Tuesday, White delivered the decision to Willingham, and the dark night began.

"In closing," Jenkins said, "I want to say something about the relationship between Fr. Malloy and myself. As is obvious to all, he and I disagreed about the dismissal of Coach Willingham, although he deferred to me on this decision. Although I did not fully appreciate it at the time, this put Fr. Malloy in the very difficult position of being blamed for and having to defend a decision he strongly opposed. It was for this reason, I believe, that Fr. Malloy made some widely reported comments, which put me and the university in a difficult position. Fr. Malloy and I have spoken about this matter, and we each regret and have apologized for any difficulty each of us has caused the other."

The firing and Malloy's subsequent criticism of it caused considerable tension and anger within the CSC community, as it did within Notre Dame fandom as a whole. About a week after the firing, and a few days after Malloy's sojourn to New York, Jenkins and Malloy called an "extraordinary meeting" of the Holy Cross priesthood at Notre Dame to discuss the purported rift between the two. Every CSC who could be there, was there. They gathered inside Corby Hall. The meeting lasted forty minutes. "The purpose was to say, 'No bad blood. No ill will,' " one CSC priest told me. It seemed largely to have worked, according to those in Corby Hall:

"The problem is, with the group of men in this house—they're well educated, and they have strong personalities. And there's something about Notre Dame athletics, every graduate of this school, religious included, feels empowered, feels entitled to make decisions for the athletic department. Every single one, and it's like their birthright to do it. It's the same thing with John and Monk. Everyone feels they could have handled it better than John or Monk did, but they weren't in the middle of it."

"The Willingham firing was disappointing to a lot of us. I'm not sure it was worth it. I don't know if it'll go away quickly or not, because it involved our reputation, our integrity. The feeling was he should have gotten his five years, or at least another year. But, still, after the last couple seasons, most felt he was not the guy for the job, at any rate."

"It's possible that good and prayerful people look at a situation and come to two different conclusions. Then it becomes a judgment call. And I think that John has good judgment."

"I think Monk was just expressing his feelings. I know his remarks were absolutely from the heart. When you think of the sewer of intercollegiate athletics, I think he's with the angels on this one. He did not intend to sound critical of John. He did not intend to take it outside the family. But you knew that's how it would play—and that's what it became in the media, with all this 'house divided' stuff. And I hasten to say—I don't think Father Jenkins's role was inappropriate. He's a man of great learning. He's very pious. And there's no bad blood between them that I know of. I've since been standing between both of them with a drink in hand, so I know there's no bad blood. People forget that universities are places where people have opinions and take stands. It's the coin of the realm. By next August or September, it'll all be over. On to the next season. It'll be wiped clean from people's memories."

"I don't think we handled the firing so well. But, I'm not sorry to see him go. To me, Ty was kind of a continuation of Bob Davie. He's too nice. He didn't excite the team. Regarding the actual firing, I felt bad for Monk and how he handled it. His office blessed the decision, but he was against it. In any event, I wish he'd have said that the day of the firing. Maybe he should have said, 'Even though I'm not in favor of it, I'm not going to be around, so it's Father Jenkins's decision, and we'll go with it.' Just about everyone didn't like how it was handled. Some people were for it, some against it—people had varying opinions—but they were more concerned about how it was spilling over into the public forum. In the end, though, I think maybe we've come out much better. There was some suffering, pain, and concern. But at Notre Dame, there's enough goodness. It'll bounce back from something like this. And if Charlie Weis does well, believe me, this will be forgotten."

15

"But There's Also an Easter"

News that Notre Dame had hired Charlie Weis leaked out on December 11, 2004, twelve days after Willingham's firing. The post-Meyer coaching search was so scrutinized by the media and so peppered with fictional candidates "turning down" Notre Dame that it seemed like forty days. Weis, apparently, had been Notre Dame's second choice, behind Meyer, although four other coaches were formally interviewed as well. Back-channel flirtations had also allegedly occurred with Mike Shanahan, head coach of the Denver Broncos, who, if hired, would have become an instant messiah. According to a frenzy of rumor that blew into the chatrooms around December 9 there was mutual interest, as there had been three years earlier, after Davie and before Willingham, when Shanahan had approached Notre Dame about the job opening. He'd won his Super Bowls, he'd grown up Irish-Catholic in Chicago—formula for a subway. Evidently he wanted to end his career by returning his boyhood dream school to the proverbial glory. He'd do it for something like $3 million a year, a sum that turned off the Notre Dame administration. They deemed it unseemly, and too much money. No deal. Now, in December 2004, rumor had it that negotiations went no further than talks between so-called third parties, and ended for reasons of timing and NFL postseasons and complicated coaching contracts and other hassles. Shanahan later denied on Denver radio that anyone affiliated with Notre Dame had ever approached him.

As with the arrivals of both Bob Davie and Ty Willingham, the initial reaction to Weis among the fans was lukewarm, mostly because of the Meyer disappointment. But other concerns nettled the fan base.

Weis had never before been a head coach beyond a season at a New Jersey high school in the same year, 1989, that Lou Holtz came close to winning back-to-back national titles. With his own team, Weis won a state championship. It was believed that only a "home run" coach could undo the damage of Willingham and Meyer and Davie and Malloy and ten years of failure. To further mix the sporting metaphors, Weis was not perceived as beyond a ground-rule double.

But as the fans did their research, they began to discover his charms. Possibly the most creative and strategically gifted offensive mind in the NFL, Weis was offensive coordinator for the New England Patriots and the chief aide-de-camp in the regime of Head Coach Bill Belichick. In this position he had, of course, helped the Patriots achieve, after the 2004–05 season, three Super Bowl victories in four years. Coaching pedigree always seems of high importance to football fans, and Weis had it. He had learned under two very different stylists, first from the great bruising manipulator Bill Parcells, and second from intellectual strategy wonk Bill Belichick. In line with that pedigree, Weis had a reputation as a masterful teacher of football technique, and he had a work ethic beyond what normal people would think of as healthy, as he would go on to prove. From December through early February, he famously conducted two jobs. As Notre Dame's head coach, he assembled his staff and attempted to salvage a recruiting class damaged by enormously bad publicity. As the Patriots' offensive coordinator, he helped game-plan the club undefeated through the NFL postseason. He slept something like four hours a night.

Most important, though, the likelihood of him "getting it" was enhanced by his having attended Notre Dame, class of 1978—the first head coach alumnus since the failed Joe Kuharich. Indeed, Ara Parseghian was the first non-alum to coach the Irish since Jesse Harper, Rockne's predecessor. Alumnus coaches were formerly Notre Dame tradition as staunch as the five-year contract, and with the firing of Willingham and the hiring of Weis, Notre Dame was simultaneously breaking tradition and returning to it. The oddity was that Weis had never played football above the high school level. He had simply been a student. He had simply been a fan. He had grown up German-Catholic in Bergen County, New Jersey, and like many of his generation, he had become a Notre Dame enthusiast during the Era of Ara by

watching the famous Fighting Irish highlight show on Sunday mornings, hosted by Lindsay Nelson. He was such a fervid fan of football
that he had, by all accounts, essentially willed himself to the highest
levels of the sport.

He grew on the fans after his initial press conference, and grew on
them even more when he hired a coaching staff considered among the
best in college football. A rumor spread around the fan message
boards. When an NFL talent scout was asked to compare the staffs of
Willingham and Weis, he said something to the effect of "That's like replacing mall cops with a SEAL team." Weis's public appearances revealed him to be a confident wiseacre—cocky, honest to perhaps a
fault, whip-smart. When he spoke in public, he stumbled for the right
words like an English professor in front of a classroom. During his time
in the high schools of New Jersey, he'd taught English literature. He
also dropped the *G*'s in his gerunds and displayed a wit and ease that
won over the press corps despite a rocky start to their relationship.
Early on, Weis had warned that all access to players and assistant
coaches must first pass through him. If he read any anonymous quota-
tions in a story or column—welcome to the blacklist. The media complained, but the complaints soon gave way to glowing reports.

His appearance also drew commentary in the press. He weighed in
the middle two hundreds, a big, imposing man, six foot three. He
walked with a slight limp caused by a botched gastric-bypass operation that had nearly killed him. At one point he weighed over three
hundred pounds. A wiry brush cut of gunmetal gray stood up straight
from his head. He often wore black suits, black shirts, black neckties,
allowing the fans and sports columnists access to metaphors having to
do with the Five Families of the tristate area. As football coaches will,
he had a sideline demeanor and a practice-field demeanor that did not
exclude the profane, which might have scared off a coaching-search
committee more concerned about superficial image than effectiveness
in a job. He had actually paid a visit to the Notre Dame team during
spring drills, 2004, during which he got along nicely with Willingham,
but also reamed the team in colorful language for what he considered
their lackluster effort. Weis's effort seemed beyond impugning. He
pledged to recruit like a madman. He spoke of Notre Dame in terms
one would expect of an alumnus. He said things like "I love the cul-

ture. I think there's an aura here. And as I've told the kids, if you can't feel this place—if you can't feel it—then it probably isn't right for you." This quote, which appeared in *Notre Dame Magazine,* put to bed any question of his getting it.

Again it seemed as though the fans were preparing to assemble the details of the coming legend—as many of them had when Willingham arrived. Again, immediately upon first hiring, a Notre Dame head coach had begun to create his own cult. Hope returns, as it always does, in times that are new.

A poster composed a statement on the matter for ND Nation. Subject line: "Paradigm Shift."

> *I sense here and elsewhere a disorientation with our new circumstances . . . our habit is to worry, obsess and think about how our coaches may be missing something or screwing it up. All of that has changed. Now we have a coach who knows what needs to be done, who cares about ND and wants to win with a dangerous and fanatical passion that none of us can know, who will work his ass off every hour of the day and who has the competence to get it done. As a result, I am officially setting aside my worrying cap. We are now where we need to be, with a coach who knows more than me, cares more than me and will get it done. I can now resume my proper role of observing, following and enjoying.*

Ten years of failure and public embarrassment will produce circumspection like a psychological tic. Euphoria among some fans over New England's Super Bowl victory in February, and Weis's role in it, caused other fans to raise their concerns, their appeals for "cautious optimism." On campus, CSC priests, faculty, and staff echoed the sentiments of the fan base, on a range between cautious and optimistic.

"I don't think we handled the firing well, but I feel extremely excited about Charlie Weis. I think it's gonna take off. With Charlie Weis, I'll tell ya, there's a charisma. Whoa. When he talks—he has something to say. He talks like a coach, he walks like a coach. You just know he'll say something worth hearing."

"I'm hoping that the corner gets turned with Weis. But who knows.

The program hasn't really been anything but an embarrassment the last ten years."

"Oh God, we didn't deserve anything this good. Charlie, he's just remarkable. I think he's going to do an incredible job. My impression is that he was definitely the right choice."

"I'm a Notre Dame man, but even I didn't like the way some things happened. But everyone wants to put that behind us. We've got a new coach. Hopefully he won't go one and ten next year."

"Charlie has his work cut out for him. If three out of the four last recruiting classes are mediocre, things are gonna be difficult. Now, he might be able, with good coaching, to do one hell of a job. And he showed a lot at New England, that's for sure. But, on the other hand, like it or lump it, Belichick was the head coach."

"Institutionally speaking, a change in leadership at the top is typically a good thing for an organization. It brings in new ideas. It's a good way to revisit best practices. It creates an unusual opportunity for growth and improvement. It's the same thing with the football program and Charlie Weis. You get a kind of charge. There's a new energy that you wouldn't have had if the same people had stayed."

Spring practice came and went, more highly scrutinized by fans and media than any spring practice since, of course, Ty Willingham's first year. Excitement rose with the day, and the caution crept out of the optimism. Around the country, people had already begun preparing for the coming season. The pilgrimages were in planning stage. The alumni filled out their ticket-lottery applications in numbers that might reduce the odds of winning the most sought-after games. A window on the official Notre Dame athletics site counted down the days—110, 109, 108—until the season opener. Plans were laid on ND Nation for gathering in Pittsburgh, September 3, 2005, for Notre Dame's first game of the season. Posts went up on the Internet: "Where's the nearest Catholic church to Heinz Field?"

From his prowler somewhere near Battery Park, putting in another double shift, Eddie Colton mused on the prospects of Weis. "We shall see. We shall see." He believed that Willingham perhaps got a raw deal and supported his friend Malloy through the whole ugly brouhaha. Colton's temper had been lost on certain Saturdays during the Willingham era, but, he said, "Am I gonna beat up on the guy? No. To me, I met the guy once, he's a gentleman, he's a nice guy. Don't forget two years ago he won coach of the year." Calls squawked on his police radio as he spoke through his cell phone. During Malloy's infamous trip to New York in December, Sergeant Colton escorted the dignitary on a ride-along. "I've got the utmost respect for that man," Colton said. "It's tough. I don't wanna see a friend down in the dumps, getting hurt, you know? Or be embarrassed. He's a friend, I respect him, I put him on a pedestal." He had spoken to Monk a few times since the firing and the resulting firestorm. "I don't wanna get into the politics. Do I know the people involved? Yes. Kevin White is a friend. I think probably they say the toughest jobs in the world are president of United States, head football coach of Notre Dame, and being a New York City cop—or the mayor of New York. Well, you can add also one of the toughest jobs is being athletic director of Notre Dame. That's no bargain either."

All through the winter and spring Colton and his fianceé planned their wedding. It would take place in June at the Basilica. Reception up in VIP level of the press box, hovering over the field, Touchdown Jesus visible on the left through the wall of windows, wedding photographs on the fifty-yard line. The couple spent a few days at Notre Dame in the winter arranging their arrangements. Florists. Caterers. Hotel rooms for guests flying in from back East. Set to retire in the summer as well, Colton contemplated his plans for the future. He would perhaps look into a job with the Notre Dame Police Department—NDPD. He did not yet know if he could convince his new wife to move from Brooklyn to northern Indiana. At the very least he would have his pilgrimages, he would have his Grotto therapy. In 2004, he had gone to just one game, against Pittsburgh. This year, he thought, he might go to three, he might go to four. "You know, it's a shame what Kevin and Father went through, but it's all gonna work out in the long run. Trust me." He did not quote Father Malloy, but he might as well have: "There's a Good Friday, but there's also an Easter."

Tracy Hallahan and his wife, Diane, were in a car accident in February, not long after Weis was calling plays in the Super Bowl. Hallahan broke some ribs, suffered bone contusions. Diane broke her shoulder in four places and required two surgeries. When he told me the news, I said, "After hearing that, it's hard to talk about something as silly as a football team." And he said, "No—no way. That's the thing that keeps me going!" Two months later, on April 23, he set up shop in his traditional tailgating slot for the annual spring intrasquad scrimmage, the Blue & Gold Game. For the first time, the university sold "VIP" tickets to the game. When they went on sale, they were gone within two hours. For the first time, the university sought a "sponsor" for the game—the Notre Dame Blue-Gold Spring Football Festival presented by Chick-Fil-A. On the weekend of the scrimmage, temperatures plummeted into the thirties—colder than at any game during the 2004 season except, perhaps, the home finale against Pittsburgh. Flurries came out of the sky. Before the weather forecast, predictions for attendance went as high as forty-five thousand, fifty thousand, which would have broken a Blue & Gold record, set in the spring of Gerry Faust's first season. There were rumors that tickets had sold out. As it happened, weather and all, twenty-three thousand fans showed up, including Hallahan, still recovering from his injuries, and the entire Neighborhood of Hope. They clutched their beers and went into the game and came back out afterward and clutched further beers—scrimmaging for another season of pilgrimage come fall. Hallahan's level of excitement seemed to rise all through the day of the Blue & Gold Game. "I do believe we got the right guy," he said. "You better believe we're back."

Billy Powers, the mailman who moved to South Bend from Yonkers, returned to Yonkers and got a job working the lines for Consolidated Edison. He sees his son every weekend. As soon as the season ended, his loyalty to Willingham did as well. The losses to Boston College and Pittsburgh, the routing at the hands of Southern Cal, all had convinced Powers to shift parties, Pollyanna to Cassandra. Now, with a new coach installed, he could reclaim the Pollyanna and go back to his natural position. "There's a new energy with Weis there," he said. "I just thank God he was available." He's planning to make two trips this fall, and he's planning to take his son.

Across the state, in Niagara Falls, Eddie Gadawski tended bar and made his runs. He was waiting for another chance at a bowl season—perhaps this one a BCS—and he was waiting for the mail to arrive with his publicity photograph of Charlie Weis, signed by the man with good tidings to the subways of Gadawski's. He planned to hang it above the cash register. No decision had yet been made on the autographed picture of Tyrone Willingham.

Mike Coffey, aka El Kabong, one of ND Nation's BoardOps, had begun a new book project. Already he had published a volume on Notre Dame basketball, *Echoes on the Hardwood,* and now he was in the research stage of a book on the rise of Internet fan sites and their effect on college athletics. On that topic he had some insider knowledge.

Mike Frank and his wife, Angel, bought a house in Granger. They moved out of their rental and into the suburbs and were planning on upgrades to the *Irish Eye* Web site. Nebraska would remain in Nebraska. Frank had plans to expand his staff: hire a beat writer, hire an editor, and make *Irish Eyes* the Notre Dame football Web site of record, with Frank as a kind of Arthur Sulzberger of Irish fanzines. After Willingham's firing, amid the heat of the coaching search and then the building enthusiasm of Weis's early recruiting efforts, his subscriber numbers had nearly doubled. He seemed to have found his boon. "I do think it's sad—really sad—that someone gets fired and my business takes off," he said. He and Angel had moved to South Bend just after Willingham had completed his "return to glory" first season. "Things were exciting when we came here," he has said of those times. "Things were really looking up." And so they were again.

Nate Farley, professed seminarian, was making arrangements for the coming academic year, the whole of which he would spend in Goodyear, Arizona, outside Phoenix, at the Holy Cross–owned St. John Vianney Parish. It's called the "pastoral internship year," and a seminarian is meant to spend those two semesters learning the work of a parish priest. During the fall, Farley would not have much time to spare as he settled into life at St. John Vianney, and he somewhat rued that he would, in all likelihood, miss Notre Dame's first season under Charlie Weis.

Jim Maloney, aka Chesterlep, slipped at school and injured his hip and took himself out of commission in his last semester as a high school teacher after a thirty-eight-year career. He hoped that physical therapy would put him in shape to take full advantage of two converging developments—the era of Weis, and his own retirement from the classroom. In addition to his hip, the major concern in the Maloney household surrounded Coach Weis's plans for fall practice—would he keep it open to the public and, therefore, the cameras of Chesterton-Iep? Retirement offered unmapped territories of leisure time in which the Maloneys planned to pursue their photographic mapping of Notre Dame, the pilgrimage site. This, along with their excitement at the prospect of chronicling the new era, would, they hoped, speed Maloney to recovery. Depending on his mobility this fall, for the first time in many years, since the days of Gerry Faust, they were considering attending a game at Notre Dame Stadium.

Back in September, at the Michigan game, on that day of unexpected victory, I had met a woman named Amelia Barcza. Hours before kickoff, at around nine in the morning, I ran into her inside the Basilica. Every home-game weekend, she worked at Sacred Heart as a volunteer tour guide. She looked to have reached her ninth decade, and she hobbled along and pointed out to the pilgrims the Gregori murals, the stained-glass windows and presentation pieces and cameo studies, the Gothic and baroque altars, the monstrances, the frescoes, the portrait of St. Bernadette of Lourdes. At the moment only a few people were in the church, silently gazing up at the blue-and-gold ceilings. For a home-game weekend it was peculiarly quiet. Amelia Barcza leaned against a pew in the nave, not far from the baptismal font near the front entrance, resting before the rush. She was small and wizened and so frail she seemed to need the pew to remain upright. A globe of white hair surrounded her head. In a wavering voice like Katharine Hepburn's, she told me about a banner she'd seen hanging from a dorm window just after Willingham had been hired in January 2002. It was a bedsheet spray painted with the words BACK TO GLORY. The phrase did not impress her. "What do you mean 'back to glory'?" she said, as if addressing the sign-makers at this very moment, here in the nave of Sacred Heart. "We were never *out* of glory."

Acknowledgments

My gratitude to the following, without whose guidance and encouragement this book would not have come off. Kevin DiCamillo, the prime mover, the former instructor, who suggested the whole idea in the first place. Phil Eden and Carleen Eden and Aimee Eden and Ryan Morris, the nuclear family, plus in-law. P. J. Mark and Jack Sallay, the agent and the editor. Charles Newman, the nonpareil. Jere Odell and Jody Odell, my innkeepers in South Bend. Herb Down, the original subway alumnus (in my experience), of Erie, Pennsylvania. Justin Becker, Paul Winner, Tim Hickey, Chris Weideman, Michael Geertson, and Marc Doussard, who listened to raw manuscript words and whose advice was, at times, taken under consideration. And, of course, Leyla Yerlikaya, who listened to the largest volume of such words, and whose ear for discovering and routing the boring and pedantic is without flaw. And, finally, my thanks to all those people who appear in this book and all the others who do not, but who generously offered their time and insight and answered many questions over and over—all the alumni and subway alumni and Notre Dame faculty and staff—what is called the Notre Dame Family.

This page constitutes an extension of the copyright page.

About the Author

Scott Eden was graduated from the University of Notre Dame in 1997. A former staff reporter for the Dow Jones News Service in New York, he received a master's degree from the Writing Program at Washington University in St. Louis in 2002.